ST HUGH'S: ONE HUNDRED YEARS OF WOMEN'S EDUCATION IN OXFORD

St Hugh's: One Hundred Years of Women's Education in Oxford

Edited by
Penny Griffin

FIDELITAS

MACMILLAN

REGENT'S
UNIVERSITY LONDON

First published 1986

Published by
THE MACMILLAN PRESS LTD
Houndmills, Basingstoke, Hampshire RG21 2XS
and London
Companies and representatives
throughout the world

Typeset by Latimer Trend & Company Ltd, Plymouth
Printed in Great Britain by
Anchor Brendon Ltd,
Tiptree, Essex

British Library Cataloguing in Publication Data
St Hugh's: one hundred years of women's
education in Oxford.
1. St Hugh's College—History
I. Griffin, Penny
328.325'74   LF797.0853
ISBN 0-333-38486-5

*Dedicated
to
the memory
of
Miss Wordsworth
who founded St Hugh's
and
Miss Moberly, and Miss Jourdain,
who created it*

Ye Somervillian students, Ye ladies of St Hugh's
Whose rashness and imprudence Provokes my warning Muse,
Receive not with Impatience, But calmly, as you should,
These simple observations – I make them for your good.

Why seek for mere diplomas, And commonplace degrees,
When now – unfettered roamers – You study what you please,
While man in like conditions Is forced to stick like gum
Unto the requisitions of a *curriculum*.

(A. D. Godley, *Oxford Magazine*, 19 February 1896)

Written just before the rejection in March of a proposed resolution to admit 'qualified women' to the degree of BA.

Contents

viii   *Contents*

List of Illustrations

Preface

In preparing a book about St Hugh's, it has been a matter of some pride to discover the number of first-time achievements for women in Oxford which lie to the credit of 'ladies of St Hugh's': amongst others, the first woman to read Botany, the first women to obtain First Class degrees in: English, History, Jurisprudence and Physics; the first woman professor; the first woman Senior Proctor; the first woman President of the Oxford Union; the first woman President of the Experimental Theatre Club; the first woman student from West Africa; and even the first twelve-year-old, female undergraduate.

Starting with four students, who were offered 'a less luxurious way of living than at Lady Margaret Hall', and who occupied a smallish rented house in Norham Road, St Hugh's now has approximately 300 undergraduates, and over 60 postgraduates, and owns an entire block of residential North Oxford – the 'Island Site', as it is called.

The College was convulsed and nearly destroyed by a vicious internal row in 1924, dramatically terminated by the death of the Principal, Miss Jourdain. It was moved from its buildings during the Second World War, and scattered in houses and hostels all over Oxford. It survived these major upheavals. At the time of writing, it is still fighting for the ideal for which Annie Rogers, who sat on St Hugh's Council for 42 years, a redoubtable warrior in the cause of women's education, fought hard and long – to give women the same chances in the University as the men. St Hugh's is still single-sex, and has not gone co-residential, knowing that to do so would be immediately to depress, not only the overall number of women undergraduates, but also the already diminishing career structure for women dons in Oxford.*

The pages that follow trace the College's chequered history: they tell of the early years; of 'the Row'; of the building up again, in the late 1920s and 1930s, of morale and strength; of the gradual acquisition of property, and the loving nurture of the garden; of the lives, careers and hopes of many of those who were educated at St Hugh's. In the 'Reminiscences', voices speak from the past, each one describing different people, different pursuits – and a different Oxford.

Oxford itself figures prominently in these pages, as an integral part

*Since the time this book was written, St Hugh's Governing Body has voted for the College to relinquish its single-sex status, and 'go mixed'.

xi

of the life of St Hugh's undergraduates, an essential 'back-drop'; so does the battle for the education and the status of women to be equal to those of men. Women's education today, and women's education in the future, form a major part of the book's theme.

Through all the following pages, St Hugh's must be viewed as an exemplar of women at Oxford, one college out of five, to whom many struggles, in a male-dominated university, were common. It may, as such, throw light on how women view their university education, and how they utilise it.

After 100 years of enabling women to be educated at Oxford, St Hugh's faces uncertainty about its future rôle and identity. May the shades of Miss Moberly, first Principal of St Hugh's, who fought tenaciously for the identity of the College, and Annie Rogers, untiring champion of women's education in Oxford, direct the College's future path.

The views expressed in this volume are individual to each author. No attempt has been made to reach a consensus on events, or attain uniformity of opinion.

Penny Griffin
Highgate, 1985

Acknowledgements

I would like to thank: Miss Trickett, Principal of St Hugh's, for her unfailing help and encouragement over this project; Ian Honeyman, the Senior Bursar of St Hugh's, for much practical help received, especially in the printing and distribution of the questionnaire and call for reminiscences; Deborah Quare, Librarian and Archivist of St Hugh's, for her enthusiasm and unstinting help, which has been too great to be quantified; Miss Betty Kemp, for her infinite patience, in helping me check and re-check minute details of St Hugh's history; and the Fellows of St Hugh's, for their hospitality and tolerance.

Special thanks are proffered to those Senior Members, too many to be named, who returned their questionnaires, which were completed with wit and candour.

We are greatly indebted to Senior Member, Dorothy Sefton-Green, Senior Lecturer at the Polytechnic of North London, who advised on the computer program for the questionnaire, and extracted the information; to the Polytechnic of North London, for the use of their equipment; to Senior Member, Hope Roper, for further work on extracting information from the questionnaire; to the Management and Personnel Office of the Civil Service, the Equal Opportunities Commission, the Department of Education and Science, and the National Union of Teachers, for information.

I would like to express my gratitude to those Senior Members who sent in reminiscences. Alas! The number of them is so great, that it has been impossible to print more than a selection of extracts in this volume; but in their entirety, they will provide an invaluable addition to the College archive.

I am, also, most grateful to those Senior Members who answered my frantic call for photographs, many of them violating precious albums to help me. I would like to thank Mr Thomas, of Thomas-Photos, Headington, for his careful and loving restoration of old and faded prints, and for his permission to use his work; I would also like to thank the *Oxford Mail* for their permission to use their photographs of events at St Hugh's; and Senior Member, Julia Davey, for undertaking the task of making prints from the many snapshots submitted, and, herself, taking other necessary photographs.

Mr Bryan Harrison (Corpus Christi), Mr Roger Highfield (Merton), Mrs Janet Howarth (St Hilda's), Mrs Jean Robinson, Librarian of Keble College, and Senior Member, June Lancelyn Green are also thanked for help received.

Finally, I should like to express my gratitude to the husbands and sons of Senior Members, many of them Oxford men, who have, some way or other, had a hand in the writing of this book. Of these last, I would offer my particular gratitude to my own husband, Jack Waterman, himself from Jesus College, who, at an extremely late date, took over the compilation of the chapter of reminiscences, on the withdrawal, for domestic reasons, of Priscilla West. Without his help, the publication of this book in time for the Centenary would not have been possible.

                                                    Penny Griffin

Notes on the Contributors

Sarah Curtis is Editor of *Adoption & Fostering*, a professional journal for social workers, lawyers and doctors, concerned with children and families. She read Greats at St Hugh's College, from 1954 to 1958. On leaving Oxford, she became a journalist, and was one of the first women to work as a reporter on *The Times*. She is the author (with Gillian Crampton Smith) of two series of educational material for teenagers: *It's Your Life* and *Thinkstrips*. She is a juvenile court magistrate, and has stood for Parliament twice as a Liberal.

Penny Griffin was an undergraduate at St Hugh's College from 1944 to 1947, reading English. She married soon after leaving College, and spent a number of years bringing up a small son and daughter. In 1956, she became a school-teacher, teaching English, and eventually English and Drama. In 1966, she became Lecturer in Dramatic History at the New College of Speech and Drama, a training college for specialist teachers of Speech and Drama. In 1971, working as a part-time student at Birkbeck College, London, she obtained a PhD and became a Senior Lecturer in 1972. In 1974, the New College was absorbed into Middlesex Polytechnic. She edited the Polytechnic's *Learning Resources Bulletin*, and several other Middlesex Polytechnic publications. She left Middlesex in 1982. She edited the *Newsletter* of the British Theatre Institute from 1981 to 1982. Her publications include an edition of *Ibsen's Ghost: or Toole-up-to-Date*, by J. M. Barrie and a number of articles on varied subjects.

Phyllis Hartnoll went up to St Hugh's as a Scholar in 1926, and in 1929 was awarded the Newdigate Prize for English Verse, gaining also, in 1947 and 1964, prizes for a Poem on a Sacred Subject. She is believed to be the only member of the University to have attained this triple distinction. As a Gold Medallist of the Poetry Society, she gave a number of poetry readings, and lectured on poetry and drama at RADA and extensively in the USA. After leaving St Hugh's, she worked for a time in Blackwell's Foreign Department, and in 1934 joined the staff of Macmillan, London, where she remained until her retirement. It was her work for Macmillan on the Fourth Edition of Grove's *Dictionary of Music and Musicians* that led to her appointment as editor of *The Oxford Companion to the Theatre*, whose fourth edition has recently appeared.

Betty Kemp was appointed Fellow and Tutor in Modern History at St Hugh's College, Oxford, in 1946, a post she held until her early retirement in 1978. On her retirement, she became an Emeritus Fellow of the College. From 1940 to 1945, she was at the Treasury, and from 1945 to 1946, was Lecturer in Modern History at the University of Manchester, where, from 1970 to 1971, she was Hallsworth Research Fellow. From 1982 to 1983, she was a Leverhulme Research Fellow. Amongst her publications are: *King and Commons, 1660–1832*; *Sir Francis Dashwood, an Eighteenth-century Independent*; *Votes and Standing Orders of the House of Commons*; and *Sir Robert Walpole*.

Rachel Trickett is Principal of St Hugh's College, Oxford. She was an undergraduate at Lady Margaret Hall, Oxford, from 1942 to 1945, and obtained a First Class BA Hons in English. She became an MA in 1947, and an Honorary Fellow of Lady Margaret Hall in 1978. On going down from Oxford, she became Assistant to the Curator of Manchester City Art Gallery, a post she held for a year. From 1946 to 1949, she was Assistant Lecturer in English at the University of Hull. From 1949 to 1950, she was Commonwealth Fund Fellow at Yale University. She returned to the University of Hull as a Lecturer in English in 1950, leaving in 1954 to take up the position of Fellow and Tutor in English at St Hugh's College. She continued in this post, until her appointment as Principal in 1973. Her publications include *The Honest Muse: a Study in Augustan Verse*, and six novels: *The Return Home, The Course of Love, Point of Honour, A Changing Place, The Elders* and *A Visit to Timon*.

Baroness Warnock is Mistress of Girton College, Cambridge. She was educated at St Swithun's, Winchester, and at Lady Margaret Hall, Oxford. She was a Fellow and Tutor in Philosophy at St Hugh's College from 1949 to 1966 and she left St Hugh's to become headmistress of Oxford High School, GPDST, a post she held until 1972. She then became Talbot Research Fellow at Lady Margaret Hall, from 1972 to 1976. However, in 1976 she returned to St Hugh's as Senior Research Fellow, a post she held until 1984, when she left St Hugh's to become Mistress of Girton College, Cambridge. She has sat on a number of Royal Commissions, advisory committees and committees of inquiry, frequently as chairman, including: Committee of Inquiry into Special Education (Chm), 1974–8; Advisory Committee on Animal Experiments, 1979– (Chm); Royal Commission on

Environmental Pollution, 1979– ; UK National Commission for UNESCO 1981– ; Committee of Enquiry into Human Fertilisation, 1982–4 (Chm); and has been a Member of the IBA, 1973–1; SSRC, 1981; FCP, 1979; DUniv Open,1980. Her publications include *Ethics Since 1900*; *J. P. Sartre*; *Existential Ethics*; *Existentialism*; *Imagination*; *Schools of Thought*; *What must I Teach?* (with T. Devlin); *Education, a Way Forward*. She was awarded the DBE in 1984, and was made a life peeress in 1985.

Priscilla West is the daughter of the author and well-known writer of children's books, Roger Lancelyn Green. She was educated at Cheltenham Ladies' College, and at St Hugh's College, where she was the Jubilee Scholar from 1970 to 1973. She is currently engaged on writing a novel.

Introduction

Phyllis Hartnoll

In the eyes of a university which has endured for over 800 years, a century may not seem very long; but in the history of women's education it bulks large; for that is the time it has taken for St Hugh's College to progress from four students in a small rented house to 334 undergraduates in four purpose-built halls of residence and six or more commodious houses. The chapters collected in this volume show how this transformation was accomplished, and how nearly it did not come to pass. They show also what can be achieved by dogged perseverance in the face of unexpected difficulties and a clash of personalities. From each such buffeting by fate the fledgling enterprise emerged stronger than before. If the future holds for the College more troubles of a like nature, let us hope the result will be the same!

St Hugh's Hall, as it was originally called, was founded for 'girls from modest homes' who could not afford the fees demanded at Somerville and Lady Margaret Hall, but nevertheless felt they too could profit by the education available at Oxford. As the economies envisaged were to be made entirely on the housekeeping and not on the academic side, it is evident that from the beginning our founder, Miss Elizabeth Wordsworth, had in mind the dictum of her namesake – 'Plain living and high thinking are no more', and was resolved to restore the status quo. This, with the assistance of Miss Moberly, to whom we owe the survival of the Hall in its very early days, she did most successfully, particularly, in the opinion of many generations of students, with regard to food. Forty years after the foundation of the College, meals were very similar to the one described by Virginia Woolf after dining in a women's college in about 1927 – gravy soup, beef and greens, prunes and custard, biscuits and cheese, all washed down with cold water. She contrasted this spartan fare with the Lucullian banquet recently offered her by one of the men's colleges; but she forgot that some hundreds of years after *their* foundation Sir Thomas Moore could write: 'Then may we yet like poor scholars of Oxford go a-begging with our bags and wallets and sing Salve Regina at rich men's doors.' Luckily for us there was always the College tuck-shop, with a variety of thick glutinous chocolate bars at 2d each – a luxury which inspired a new gloss on the old tag 'De gustibus non est

1

disputandum' – 'Everybody does not like the same tuppeny.' Does College still have, or even need, a tuck-shop? Judging by the sumptuous (and vinous) repasts enjoyed there recently – and not only at Gaudy dinners – one would say not.

It is interesting to see, in the following pages, how strongly it was impressed on women students – they did not become undergraduates until 1920 – that their acceptance by the University depended to a large extent on their own behaviour. Frivolity was forbidden; punctuality, hard work, neatness and order reigned supreme; flirting and dancing had no place in their lives. As late as 1908 the House Rules of St Hugh's Hall enacted that 'students are not permitted to go out to dances, and to this there is absolutely no exception'. To avoid all occasion of scandal, chaperons were *de rigueur* everywhere, not only at lectures, but at tea parties, picnics and even when watching cricket. It would be some time before St Hugh's had its own cricket club, and arranged dances on its own premises. And even longer before chaperonage died out, even though it was scaled down to 'another woman', usually a fellow-member of the College. In 1928 I was seen coming alone out of a man's lodgings in the Iffley Road. The Principal sent for me. 'Who' she asked frostily, 'was your other woman?' I explained that our host, a famous rugger man, had gone down with mumps, which I had had, but my 'other woman' had not. So I took the risk of going alone to pour out, and butter buns, while the team gave its captain a blow-by-blow account of the match. 'Most unwise', said the Principal, and gated me for a fortnight.

One of the problems not raised in the present volume, though it figured in the correspondence columns of *The Times* a couple of years ago, in connection with women's rowing, is dress; a frivolous subject, but one which must have been important to the lives of 'girls of slender means'. To judge from old photographs, a long dark skirt and a cover-up blouse were deemed sufficiently innocuous. But as high fashion caused skirts to become shorter and tighter, things came to such a pitch even inside College that one Principal was heard to remark, as she followed the progress of a miniscule skirt down the corridor: 'If Miss J. must wear trouser-legs, I wish she would wear two.' Her wish was fulfilled not many years later, when women took to trousers for all occasions, even for dinner, for which, in earlier days, everyone changed, some into *demi-toilette*, others into modest afternoon frocks of an indeterminate shade. It was obvious that those in charge of 'undergraduettes' (as they were sometimes unfortunately called), in addition to their other onerous duties, kept a weather-eye open for changes in fashion. Shortly before one summer term every student of St Hugh's received a card headed 'Simplex munditiis', pointing out that bare arms were not permissible with academic dress, so for occasions on which gowns had to be worn, as at lectures and tutorials, the current fashion for sleeveless dresses should be ignored, and 'a sufficiency of washing frocks with sleeves should be provided'.

The question of what to wear with academic dress must often have been a fruitful source of discussion and experimentation, except of course to those dedicated women to whom all dresses are alike. One of my tutors solved the problem neatly by buying a dress length of the silk used to line MA hoods, and having it made up in a simple, long-sleeved, high-necked style. This she wore to official functions under her gown, and very handsome she looked in it! At one moment in my own college career the same problem momentarily arose. I was called upon to read the Newdigate at Encaenia in company with an otherwise male list of prizemen. What should I wear under my gown? Trousers were not even thought of; the one dark suit which had seen me up to and including Schools was far too shabby. Finally the Principal and the Dean of Degrees arrived at a solution – a new dark clerical-grey suit, with a white tucked blouse, and a college tie (in those days one could buy ties and scarves in St Hugh's beautiful mixture of colours, now, alas, unobtainable). This one touch of colour was vetoed at the dress rehearsal, as being too garish, and I dwindled into a black tie bought for the occasion.

The changes in the academic position of women are well recorded in these pages; but woman is after all a sociable animal, and a look at her relationships with others helps us to judge the gulf fixed between the different generations. The distance between 'Then' and 'Now' is as great as that envisaged by Kipling when he wrote: 'The wildest dreams of Kew are the facts of Khatmandhu, And the crimes of Clapham chaste in Martaban.' Certainly the wildest dreams of those who, when they eventually filled two houses in Norham Road, were not allowed to go from one to the other without a hat could hardly have envisaged the modest concessions granted us in the 1920s; and undergraduates then, chafing under their 'other woman' and a 10 p.m. curfew, could hardly have foreseen the almost total freedom allowed to young women in the 1980s.

Yet through all the changes, the ultimate end has always been the same – to maintain, and to prove, that young women are as well able to receive, and profit by, an Oxford education as young men. That women have managed, in a bare 100 years, to shed so many of the restrictions originally imposed on them without endangering their status as responsible adults shows how well the foundations were laid, and how much self-discipline must have been practised by successive generations. Given another 100 years, what may we not attain to? – perhaps that unbiased, sex-free equality of which our pioneer women dreamed. But while rejoicing in a freedom hitherto unknown, it is to be hoped that the new socially, politically, economically and professionally emancipated women of the future will not forget or deride the struggles, amply documented here, by which their freedom was obtained.

1 Women's Education

Rachel Trickett

The idea of 'women's education' grew up in the second half of the nineteenth century, but that does not mean that before then there was no education of women or that there were no educated women. Queen Elizabeth I, by the standards of any period was exceptionally educated and educable, the delight of Grindal and Ascham, her distinguished tutors, who grounded her in Classical and Modern Languages, in Theology, History, Music, Mathematics and the sciences. She remained throughout her life a scholar as well as a politician. The learned ladies or blue stockings of the eighteenth century were as well instructed in the scholarship of their time as any graduate today, and Fanny Burney in her *Diary* gives a not unenvious account of Sophie Streatfield, famous for her Greek learning and her beauty, whose other more extraordinary accomplishment was that she could cry at will. Some girls' schools had already been founded in the early eighteenth century through the charity of livery companies and city merchants, though for the most part they concentrated on teaching reading and needlework. The Abbey School at Reading had the distinction of boarding and teaching Jane and Cassandra Austen for a while, and Jane Austen's own view of education for girls comes across very pointedly in her description of Mrs Goddard's establishment in *Emma*:

> Mrs. Goddard was the mistress of a School – not of a seminary, or an establishment, or anything which professed, in long sentences of refined nonsense, to combine liberal acquirements with elegant morality upon new principles and new systems – and where young ladies for enormous pay might be screwed out of health and into vanity – but a real, honest, old-fashioned Boarding-school, where a reasonable quantity of accomplishments were sold at a reasonable price, and where girls might be sent to be out of the way and scramble themselves into a little education without any danger of coming back prodigies.

Elizabeth Barrett describes her sickly adolescence at Hope End as:

.. a retirement scarcely broken except by books and my own
thoughts ... There I had my fits of Pope – & Byron – & Coleridge – and read Greek as hard under the trees as some of your
Oxonians in the Bodleian – gathered visions from Plato and the
dramatists – and ate & drank Greek & made my head ache with it.

At seventeen she published *An Essay on Mind with Other Poems*, and
received a fan letter from the blind Greek scholar, Hugh Stuart Boyd,
who lived near by. She promptly fell in love with him, and acquired
in the process a great deal of his erudition. George Eliot's powerful
intellect could scarcely have benefited more from a university education than it did from her own researches, though one thinks of her
as a natural Somervillian. All these examples should remind us that
brilliant women in any age, as long as their circumstances were
fortunate enough, had the capacity to devote themselves to scholarship and distinguish themselves for learning. Sometimes, too, as in
the case of Elizabeth Elstob, 'the Saxon Nymph', the eighteenth-
century pioneer Old English scholar, the circumstances were not
financially fortunate; she had little money, but came from a learned
home. Nor did any of these women feel that there was something
specifically feminine in the studies they chose, or that women should
not attempt the same subjects as men. Jane Austen even hints at the
absurdity of having 'new principles and new systems' especially
devised for girls.

    Nevertheless, by the middle of the nineteenth century the question
of formal higher education for women had already been raised. Lack
of professional qualifications which were increasingly required for
responsible posts meant that many intelligent and learned women
could hope for nothing better than the position of governess, unless
they were fortunate enough to make their way by some other talent
such as writing, or unless they were rich. Tennyson's *The Princess*,
published in 1847, was said to have been written in response to
rumours of a project for founding a college for women. His son
Hallam reports Tennyson as saying that the two great social questions
impending in England were 'the housing and education of the poor
man before making him our master, and the higher education of
women'. The intention of the poem was to warn woman, before the
great movement for education began, that she 'is not undevelopt man
but diverse'. Tennyson, as so often, was remarkably prescient about

his own times in predicting this movement for higher education. Whether his attitude in *The Princess* was in any sense influential is harder to say. The opponents of degrees for women in Oxford and Cambridge certainly maintained that any kind of academic course for women must be different from those for men; the spectre of 'unisex' rose well before its time under their horrified gaze. The most extreme opponents, like Lady Bracknell, were against anything that tampered with the natural bloom of ignorance in girls; the less fanatical worried about the effect of overworking on female health, for women's natural conscientiousness was at once acknowledged. One of the alternatives proposed by opponents of admitting women to degrees at existing universities was the foundation of a women's university, to be called the Queen's University, into which the various societies that had grown up in Oxford and Cambridge and London could be amalgamated. This idea found favour particularly at Cambridge, though no proposals were made as to how it should be endowed and staffed, but the women tutors quietly maintained their opposition to it, or to anything that might weaken their claim to be treated equally with the men as far as academic opportunities were concerned.

The history of the movement for full membership of the University for women in Oxford has been written by one of its most formidable protagonists, Annie Rogers, closely associated with the Society of Home Students (now St Anne's College), and with St Hugh's, where she was a member of the College Council and *Custos Hortulorum*. Her book *Degrees by Degrees*, published by the OUP in 1938, is a fascinating and often wryly funny account of the forty-two years' fight which in Oxford was won in 1920, to admit women as full members of the University with the right to supplicate for its degrees. The right to take its examinations had been acquired much sooner, and it is interesting to see that the position of women today in Oxford and Cambridge was achieved not through any complete amalgamation of their societies into the collegiate system (this did not happen until after the Second World War), but through their determination to attend lectures, take examinations and make use of all the facilities for learning that the universities could offer them. In fact it was an academic enterprise from the start, based on the conviction that in matters of scholarship no distinction should be made between men and women. Questions of residence, discipline, outside activities or integration into the full social life of a university were always secondary to the overriding academic argument, as they still should be. There is room for argument about the best way in which men and women can work or live together in any academic society but none about women's right to the same educational opportunities as are open to men.

Annie Rogers dates the start of the campaign from the foundation of the Delegacy of Local Examinations in Oxford in 1857, and its application ten years later to Hebdomadal Council for power to examine girls as well as boys. Her own success in the Senior Locals as they were called in 1873, when she was top of the list of senior candidates, entitled her to Exhibitions at Balliol and Worcester Colleges, which, being a girl, she could not take up. In response to quiet pressure from women to be allowed to proceed to take university examinations, the Delegates of the Local Examinations persuaded Council to pass a statute instituting separate examinations for women corresponding to Responsions, Moderations and the Final Schools. This statute was passed in 1875 (almost thirty years after the publication of *The Princess*). The old obsession with a syllabus suitable for women was implicit in its provisions – no obligatory Latin or Greek, and a strong bias towards modern subjects. But modern subjects were already infiltrating the university syllabus, and women who wanted to take these examinations needed to be able to attend university lectures and classes. Again, it is interesting to see that the gradual increase in the influence of faculties as opposed to colleges helped the women's movement. Lectures had already been organised in various university centres in England and Scotland for interested women to attend; and it was from these beginnings that Bedford and Queen's Colleges in London, and Newnham and Girton in Cambridge had sprung. In Oxford, in spite of opposition, enough Professors and dons were prepared to admit women to their lectures – held most often in individual colleges – to enable them to reach the necessary standard for the new examinations. The foundations of Lady Margaret Hall and Somerville in 1879 were the first step in providing a base for women coming to Oxford to study. Those already living in lodgings were to be the responsibility of the Association for the Higher Education of Women in Oxford, which, until its dissolution in 1920 was the body almost exclusively involved in working for the women's cause. Annie Rogers was a permanent member of this Association. The various stages of the campaign, the set-backs, the advances are entertainingly traced in her book. She herself was a most accomplished tactician, urging her supporters on at the right time, and holding them back (more often the latter), with a sure sense of the advantages of masterly inactivity. Her brother records a brilliant piece of her advice: 'Never argue with your opponents; it only helps them to clear their minds', and it was by such strategies, and her intransigent determination not to compromise on the essentials, that Annie Rogers and her supporters finally won. The First World War, as she herself contended, was the real occasion of the victory (as it was in the fight for women's suffrage), but the academic successes of women students, and the dedication of their supporters, were the real cause.

No such dramatic change was occasioned by the Second World War. Life for women undergraduates in the 1930s was not very different from life for women undergraduates in the 1950s. Chaperonage had been dropped, girls were not confined to their own colleges either socially or academically. But the colleges themselves were still not entirely independent; they were governed by Councils with outside members sitting on them; their own gate rules were often stricter than those of the men's colleges, their atmosphere was inevitably more protective, sometimes more defensive. To someone like myself, who came up as an undergraduate during the Second World War, there was, however, no sense of academic restriction and certainly no feeling of discrimination against women. It was remarkable, too, how various were the backgrounds of my contemporaries. In the early days of women's education there was little chance that a girl whose parents could not pay the fees would find her way to Oxford or Cambridge. Collegiate life was inevitably more expensive than attending a provincial university and living at home. Similarly, the women's colleges were too poor to pay good salaries to their tutors, and it was almost axiomatic that anyone who could afford to earn so little was likely to have some private means. This is not to underestimate the sacrifices many women dons made, for few of them came from rich backgrounds. An atmosphere of plain living and high thinking – the atmosphere that prevailed in women's colleges up to and beyond the Second World War, has its academic advantages. It fosters ambition, determination and an ideal of service and devotion to the college which characterised women's societies from the start. Nevertheless, it was important that the colleges should become broader in their outlook and in their intake, and the gradually increasing opportunities for girls from poorer homes to come up on more generous scholarships than individual colleges could afford to offer – the state, county and borough scholarships which were then awarded on Higher School Certificate results – were important factors in achieving this. It is too often assumed nowadays that before

the Butler Education Act there were only a sprinkling of undergraduates from state schools in Oxford or Cambridge. When I was up,
though we were in a minority in the University, those of us who were
on state scholarships were a large and unoppressed minority. In
wartime, with food and clothes rationing and general austerity,
distinctions of background and wealth seemed irrelevant, and the
experience of university life was peculiarly unhidebound and free. Of
the small intake of my year at Lady Margaret Hall (1942), three are
now heads of Oxford or Cambridge colleges; one a head of a Durham
college and Pro-Vice Chancellor of that university and another
headmistress of a distinguished direct-grant school in the North.
Only one of these five came from a privileged or academic home. The
rest came to Oxford on state scholarships.

When I came back to Oxford as a don in 1954 there were some
vestigial traces to be discerned of an inward-looking and defensive
attitude among women, but they very soon faded. At first women
tutors in various faculties tended to meet together to discuss the
lecture list and consult about their own contributions; we jealously
guarded our separate women's college entrance examination; we were
aware, too, of some more general neglect. Though women tutors were
respected for their scholarship before the war, they had seldom been
asked to examine, to supervise or to take part in university administration. The war had broken down some of that discrimination if
only because there were too few men available for these duties. But
this was already changing rapidly. The first woman Professor in
Oxford, Agnes Headlam-Morley, had been elected; scholars of the
distinction of Helen Gardner and Dorothy Hodgkin were as well
known outside Oxford as in it; women began to be appointed as
chairmen of Faculty Boards; a particular office, that of Assessor, was
created to enable women to share in proctorial duties. Most important
of all to their sense of equality, the women's colleges became full
collegiate societies with their own charters and statutes and a Governing Body composed solely of their own Principal and Fellows.
Complete parity had been achieved – the shade of Annie Rogers
satisfied. The one inequity that existed was the proportion of women
undergraduates to men in the University as a whole – lower than the
national average. How to remedy this became a matter first of private
discussion, eventually of public policy.

The great change in Oxford education since the last war has, of
course, been the opening of the men's colleges to women. There is no
doubt of the success of this policy in increasing the number of women

studying in Oxford without any lowering of standards. The whole process, which seemed so revolutionary when it was first proposed, has quietly become a *fait accompli* and we are left with the sort of equality that surpasses even the hopes and expectations of the first supporters of women at university. Annie Rogers could have taken up her Balliol or her Worcester Exhibition without creating any stir, and I have little doubt that she would feel considerable satisfaction with this turn of events. Only three single-sex societies now remain, all of them women's colleges. To many this seems anomalous and even retrograde. To others there is still a case for their survival. At first it might seem that any such case must strengthen the old fallacy our original supporters fought so strongly against, that there must be some distinction between education for men and education for women. But academically speaking there is no such distinction, and has not been since 1920. How women can best make use of these academic opportunities is the real issue, and there are some women who still feel that they can work better and feel freer in a single-sex institution. The high proportion of women in Oxford owes a great deal too to the existence of three single-sex women's colleges; to change would be to depress the numbers at once. But the most worrying aspect of the advent of mixed colleges is the very low proportion of women tutors in those which were originally male. Inevitably the greatest number of women academics is concentrated in the women's colleges, and those mixed colleges which were originally female. We must hope that this imbalance will gradually change. It would be ironic and tragic if a move which was started to increase the numbers of women undergraduates should end by decreasing their chances of entering the academic profession.

Another anxiety arose in the summer of 1984 with the publication of the Norrington Table. This graded list of college results is a sufficiently blunt instrument – its statistical range being too narrow for any real significance – to be dismissed by the colleges themselves. But its impact on schools and intending candidates is none the less important. In 1984, with the exception of Somerville which remained in twenty-first place, all the women's colleges, including those which had recently gone mixed, were clustered at the bottom of the table. Is this a serious sign that the brightest girls as well as the brightest men have decided to apply for the better-known and older colleges? If this is so, there is little to be done about it. The women's colleges can compete in comfort, and in the teaching of many subjects, with the older men's colleges, but they can never compete in glamour. Age and

ancient reputation breathe the last enchantments of the Middle Ages
which Matthew Arnold saw as Oxford's prime attraction. The *Oxford
Times*'s curt advice to the remaining single-sex colleges to go mixed as
soon as possible so that they can become known among boys' schools
was pessimistic nevertheless. Are even the present two women's
colleges which have gone mixed – Lady Margaret Hall and St
Anne's – so associated in the minds of male candidates with petticoat
government that, though they have appointed at a reckless rate many
men Fellows, they will fail to attract first-class men candidates? If
that is the case, any further change to mixed societies will increase the
number of competent but mediocre men and women. It would
certainly decrease the number of women in comparison with that of
men. The advantages, or the justice of such a shift in numbers have
yet to be argued and proved.

There is no evidence yet of a move to equal the number of women
and men in Oxford – indeed, the Equality of the Sexes legislation
might work against any such deliberate intention. This is, in itself, an
argument for the retention of some single-sex women's colleges, but
it is not an argument likely to raise the spirits of women tutors who
have been used to teaching the best, not the second-best pupils in
their subject.

Another concern that is generally discussed with regard to co-education is the stereotypes that are already revealing themselves in
mixed comprehensive schools. The equation is commonly seen as
arts – women; sciences – men. There is much evidence now that this
shift has taken place with the decay of single-sex grammar schools,
and indeed it has often been the reason for the sympathy of many
Maths and Physics tutors in women's colleges with the idea of going
mixed. If there is no pool of talented girls in their subjects, the desire
to be able to select competent men is completely understandable. Yet
it would seem unfortunate if in the women's mixed colleges the
science entry were dominated by men, as the arts entry is, for the
most part, by women in the men's mixed colleges. This unhappy
polarisation that has already been established in mixed schools should
not, if it can be avoided, be prolonged.

There are not yet enough reliable statistics to provide answers to
these questions, and we are left to make decisions of enormous
importance often without sufficient evidence. There is no way of
predicting what will happen in the future but it is impossible to
imagine that the remarkable success of the movement for women's
education over the last 100 years should now be reversed. Women

themselves will determine the pattern of the future in their education. Their colleges are free to make their own decisions; they themselves are at liberty to choose how to further their careers, and in what sort of environment.

I have written only of Oxford women's education here, because it is that aspect of the subject I know best, and from my own experience. But no history of women's education could ever be written without some mention of the remarkable range of opportunities in other universities which gradually opened to women in the course of the last 100 years. The movement for women's education in America in the nineteenth century showed that instinct for experiment which has given American institutions so much vitality and variety. Colleges for women like the Seven Sisters were founded earlier than the Oxford or Cambridge colleges; others were co-educational from the start, like Oberlin College. Again, some have remained single-sex; others have adopted co-education, and the peculiarly strong feminist movement in America seems, paradoxically, to have grown stronger since so many institutions went mixed.

In England, London University was earlier more hospitable to women than the older universities; Royal Holloway College was founded in 1886 on the model of the American colleges for women, and its founder had intended it to give its own degrees as they did. Bedford and Queen's College were founded earlier than the Oxford societies and women were admitted to degrees in London, and at Trinity College, Dublin long before they were at Oxford. (This last fact caused some consternation in Oxford and Cambridge, as Dublin was a university whose degrees they recognised as entitled to be incorporated with their own. A number of women before 1920 had in fact accepted Trinity's offer to acknowledge their performance in the Oxford and Cambridge examinations and to confer degrees on them, though the fees for this were high.) The older provincial universities have a more liberal history with regard to accepting women than Oxford or Cambridge, and have always been generous in appointing them. The eight years during which I taught at the then University College of Hull revealed no trace of prejudice against women as students or as lecturers. Indeed the arts subjects were almost entirely subscribed to by women students, though the proportion was reversed in the sciences. Throughout the country, women have taken full advantage of the opportunities universities have offered, and it is now extraordinary to find a girl who does not assume that she will proceed to some career or profession after her degree. What the

Victorians would have made of the results of their campaign – whether they would have been appalled at the problems equality necessarily brings with it, or delighted at the fulfilment of their ideals – is hard to guess. Certainly women's higher education has given society the great benefit of more trained minds, more devoted and conscientious members willing to take over the most responsible and exacting work. Whether this situation will last, or whether new circumstances will produce fewer jobs for women, the possession of knowledge, a disciplined intelligence, and a habit of reason, can never be a disadvantage. We should not confuse education with salvation, as there is always a tendency to do, but though women's education has hardly solved the problems of society, it has made innumerable women happier, more useful, more self-reliant and more interesting. Not everyone can reach what the brilliant few achieved even in the past, but it can be no bad thing that the majority of women now have something more to think about than the week's menus or the next love affair.

2 The Early History of St Hugh's College

Betty Kemp

Nothing could have seemed less likely to develop into a college than the rented house in Norham Road where four young women students assembled in October 1886 to form St Hugh's. 'Foundation' is indeed rather too solemn a word for its opening, which was the result of a decision by Elizabeth Wordsworth, then principal of Lady Margaret Hall[1] to use an unexpected windfall to rent and equip a house for the reception of 'a very few . . . really poor students', and to put them in the care of a 'head' capable both of running the house, and of giving the students the sort of religious and moral guidance that she herself gave to students at Lady Margaret Hall. So right from the beginning, St Hugh's was different. It was a 'house' rather than a hall of residence, not because of its aim, which St Hugh's can well be proud of, but because it was, as Elizabeth Wordsworth said, 'a private venture'. It was not founded by a committee of well-wishers to women's education, as were Lady Margaret Hall and Somerville Hall, the two halls of residence for women students opened in 1879, nor was it governed by one. Instead, it had a single founder, whose interest lay in the purpose it was to serve, not in the kind of institution it was to be. St Hugh's was an experiment; its purpose was to make it possible for women of modest means to live and study in Oxford. In 1886, Elizabeth Wordsworth had been Principal of Lady Margaret Hall for seven years. Her experience there was very relevant to her aim in founding St Hugh's and to her dealings with it.

She explained her aim in a letter, dated 14 May 1886, to the high church newspaper *The Guardian*. Seven years' experience at Lady Margaret Hall had convinced her that

> while there is a sufficient number of lady students willing to pay for the luxury of a room to themselves, and other things to correspond, there is a still larger, and we fear a growing, number who find the charges of the present Halls at Oxford and Cambridge (even the most moderate) beyond their means. It may be added that many of the clergy especially[2] are forced reluctantly to send their daughters

15

to 'unsectarian' places of instruction[3] because the Church has done
so little for their needs. We are going to try to meet this difficulty
by opening next October a small home-like house (under a lady in
whom we have the fullest confidence) as the nucleus of what we
hope may eventually prove a more important undertaking ...
Students will attend the same lectures and go through the same
academic course as at the Halls already in existence ... The
religious teaching will be on the same lines as at Lady Margaret
Hall. An extrance examination, on the lines of the First Public
Examination for Women, will be a *sine qua non.*

Students at St Hugh's were to pay £45 a year for board and lodging;
this was £15 less than Somerville and £30 less than Lady Margaret
Hall. That is, the economy imposed by the lower fees was to be
economy in living expenses, not in education.

The need for economy of this kind was far from being simply a
problem for women students, and it is this that links Elizabeth
Wordsworth's scheme, and indeed her phraseology, with contemporary plans for university reform, and in particular with plans for
meeting what Benjamin Jowett called 'the claims of poor students'.[4]
Reformers of very different views agreed that expense was at least one
reason for the narrow field from which Oxford drew its students, and
that what made an Oxford career expensive was not the cost of
education (which was moderate), but the cost of living: high college
fees. The first Royal Commission had emphasised this in 1852, and
insisted that economies were possible. A few colleges had made
economies; St Edmund Hall – the only one of the medieval Halls that
was to survive – had made a sustained and successful effort to keep its
fees low; the University tackled an intractable problem by making
provision (1868) for non-collegiate students, of whom there were
some 300 by the 1880s; Keble College, founded in 1870, set out to
give its students 'the same educational advantages as members of
other Colleges' combined with 'economy and simplicity of living'.
For Elizabeth Wordsworth the example of Keble, with its emphasis
on 'economy and simplicity of living' as a Christian virtue, was
particularly relevant. She hoped that, as Keble produced parsons and
schoolmasters, St Hugh's would produce church workers and
schoolmistresses.

The house that Elizabeth Wordsworth chose for her experiment
reflected her ideas and her own not particularly affluent circumstances. 25 Norham Road was, and is, a modest family house, semi-

detached, with eight rooms. It is on the left-hand side of Norham Road, at the far end from Banbury Road, and looks over the gardens of Fyfield Road. She named it after St Hugh of Avalon as a tribute to her father who, like St Hugh, had been Bishop of Lincoln, a diocese which until 1542 included Oxford. She rented the house on an annual lease of £50, and chose for its head a woman whose background seemed much like her own, and who was certainly capable of giving 'religious teaching . . . on the same lines as at Lady Margaret Hall', This was Anne Moberly,[5] whose father, George Moberly, died in 1885 and was succeeded as Bishop of Salisbury by Elizabeth Wordsworth's brother John. 'All I hope', Elizabeth Wordsworth wrote, 'is that she will be an economical housekeeper.'

For the four students who assembled in 25 Norham Road in October 1886, 'a more economical standard of living', or as Elizabeth Wordsworth put it, 'a less luxurious way of living than at Lady Margaret Hall' meant plain fare, small or shared rooms, scanty furniture, and a dining room that served also as a common study. This room, as one of the four students wrote, had 'little tables in the corners at which we wrote and into the drawers of which we put the notebooks and paper, the result of our labours . . . There was no library and no chapel, hardly any garden, no tennis, and no boat.' For Anne Moberly, economy meant a salary of £40 a year, compared with Elizabeth Wordsworth's £100, and no secretarial help. There were two maids, and with their help, Anne Moberly ran the house.

There is, however, a limit to what economy can do, and at first sight it is puzzling that Elizabeth Wordsworth did nothing to lessen the difficulties that were bound to arise from the unpromising combination of low fees, with lack of any other resources. After all, the example of Keble was before her eyes, with its national appeal and its eminent trustees and members of Council; its warden, Edward Talbot, was Chairman of the LMH Governing Committee and, she said, 'approved' her St Hugh's experiment. Yet she made no appeal, national or local, for friends or financial help, and her letter to *The Guardian* clearly provided a very limited publicity. Above all, she did not strengthen St Hugh's with the moral support – which she herself had at LMH – of a Governing Body, Committee or Council, composed of friends of women's education. She informed the LMH Committee of what she intended to do at the same time as she wrote to *The Guardian*, and apparently after she had taken the house in Norham Road, and approached Anne Moberly. The information was received, perhaps naturally, without enthusiasm.

One explanation of the puzzle must be that Elizabeth Wordsworth thought of St Hugh's as a means to an end, not as an institution to be fostered for its own sake. Of course she hoped that it would succeed, and grow in numbers, because it embodied her aim, but her aim was to help girls of moderate means, not to found a new hall of residence. There is another explanation: St Hugh's was 'hers' in a way that LMH was not, and she wanted to keep it so. It was to be 'quite independent' of LMH and its Committees, and it was to have no Committee or Governing Body of its own – or, rather, Elizabeth Wordsworth was to be its Committee. She seems to have regarded the LMH Governing Committee not as a support but as a somewhat unwelcome bridle; she had, she said, been glad of the experience of working with a Committee at LMH, but it 'will be an immense saving of time and trouble' to dispense with one at St Hugh's. The statement is revealing. She wanted a free hand, and St Hugh's was to be a sort of compensation for her lack of one at LMH. This may have saved 'time and trouble' for her. It could not, however, save them for Anne Moberly. As Elizabeth Wordsworth remarked with satisfaction in 1887, Anne Moberly 'is coming out to be a capital housekeeper'. But she was much more than that. She had probably, and not unnaturally, expected her position at St Hugh's to be the same as Elizabeth Wordsworth's at LMH; certainly she behaved, from the beginning, as if St Hugh's was a third hall of residence, and, even beyond that, a college in embryo. If she had not done so, St Hugh's would not have survived. She valued her election to the Committee of the Association for the Higher Education of Women in 1888, at the same time as the heads of Somerville and LMH, as a sign of St Hugh's 'equality of status', and she spoke of the establishment of a St Hugh's Committee[6] in 1891 as 'an achievement': it seemed to be the first step away from the 'private venture'.

It proved to be a deceptive step. The Committee was not a governing body, like the LMH Committee. It had no definite powers and no fixed meetings. It in no way replaced Elizabeth Wordsworth's sole responsibility for St Hugh's, and she was not bound to ask, let alone to take, its advice. She had, of course, put herself in an unusual and potentially uncomfortable position: to be Principal of a hall of residence and founder of a separate 'house' for women students was not an easy combination. Perhaps it called for qualities of tact she did not possess; perhaps – though this is little more than a guess – she regretted the establishment of the St Hugh's Committee, powerless though it was. None of this is enough to explain why, in 1893, she decided to turn St Hugh's into St Hugh's Hostel – a hostel for LMH students – but it must have been a factor in her decision. It certainly explains why she did not consult or even inform the St Hugh's Committee about her plan.[7] She was, of course, bound to submit it to the LMH Committee, for it was, after all, a plan for LMH, and she did so in 1893. She saw a number of advantages for LMH. The first was financial. St Hugh's – surprisingly – was more than paying its way. It had grown in numbers, and moved. In 1887, Elizabeth Wordsworth had rented 24 Norham Road (adjoining 25); the two houses together took ten students. In the following year – a few days before the start of Michaelmas Term – she bought the leasehold of 17 Norham Gardens, next door but one to LMH, and let it to St Hugh's.[8] It took twelve or thirteen students, and had many of the amenities lacking in Norham Road, including a garden next to the University Parks, where nightingales still sang, and it was near to the river. A new wing, built in 1892, added twelve students' rooms, a dining room and a separate room for a chapel.

In 1893 there were twenty-five students, and, in spite of low fees, there was 'a margin of something like £200 a year'. If Elizabeth Wordsworth's plan were accepted, this margin could be used for common purposes: for example, the new LMH chapel (not yet built) could be used by St Hugh's students when they became LMH students. There was no proposal to raise fees; students living in St Hugh's Hostel would pay lower fees than other LMH students. There was another advantage. Elizabeth Wordsworth liked hostels: her ideal women's hall was not one large building, but a 'federation' of small groups living in detached houses. The absorption of St Hugh's would let LMH grow in numbers without losing the form she liked.

Luckily for St Hugh's, the LMH Committee saved it. On 7 June 1894, after investigation and report by a sub-committee, the Committee rejected Elizabeth Wordsworth's proposal 'that St. Hugh's Hall be amalgamated with L.M.H. under the title of St. Hugh's Hostel'. The sub-committee admitted that amalgamation would bring 'a moderate financial gain', but set this aside. It emphasised 'the very great importance' that all its members attached 'to the desirability of making some provision in Oxford for the education of women students of small means'; for this reason they would 'be very sorry to destroy an institution which is, as at present conducted, successful in making such provision'. It was suggested that, 'in the near future', consideration might be given to some sort of federation, leaving 'the two Halls . . . as independent bodies'; nothing was ever done about this. The defeat of amalgamation was an unsolicited, and perhaps unexpected, tribute to the achievement of the first seven years of St Hugh's. This achievement was Anne Moberly's. Nevertheless, neither the defeat nor the achievement could secure St Hugh's against the possibility that its founder might, in the future, again try to change its nature – and perhaps in a way that avoided reference even to the LMH Committee. At the same time, although Elizabeth Wordsworth's plan had been defeated, the reasons for its rejection could well have given her satisfaction, and perhaps they did; for they were a vindication of her aim in founding St Hugh's, and a recognition that it had not proved impracticable. Her plan would have killed St Hugh's but it did not sacrifice her aim;[9] a final proof, surely, that this, and not the kind of institution St Hugh's was to be, was what she really cared about.

There can be no doubt that her aim was well-founded. There was a potential demand for more, less expensive, residential accommodation for women students in Oxford, and it came largely, though not entirely, from the sort of middle-class professional groups that she envisaged: daughters of parsons, certainly, but also of doctors, solicitors, schoolmasters. This class was not unlike the class of young men whose exclusion from Oxford was deplored by university reformers. But, for women, the demand was sharpened by the urgent and growing need for qualified headmistresses and women teachers to staff the new girls' high schools – some boarding, but predominantly day schools – formed first by the Girls' Public Day School Trust, and, in growing numbers in and after the 1870s, by local trusts, companies, churchmen and church societies. St Hugh's played a large part in meeting this need. It soon became known as the College which produced headmistresses and by 1899, already had six to its credit.

Potential demand was not the only reason why 1886 was a good time to increase the number of women students in Oxford; if Elizabeth Wordsworth's prime concern had been the admission of women to Oxford degrees, she might well have chosen the same year. For there had recently been two important reforms in the position of women students in Oxford. In 1875, the University had authorised 'Special' women's examinations, corresponding to University First and Second Public Examinations, for women over eighteen. They were set by the Delegacy for Local Examinations (which in 1867 had opened its own school examination to girls) and were not restricted to women living or studying in Oxford. The organised teaching of women students in Oxford who wished to take these examinations began three years later, with the formation of the Association for the Higher Education of Women. The AEW, as it was always called, made arrangements for the teaching (by lectures, tutorials, classes) of all women students in Oxford, whether they lived at home, in lodgings, or in the two residential Halls (Somerville and LMH) opened in 1879. It had its own tutors and kept a list of others willing and suitable to teach women. Some of these were Professors (many of whom were well-disposed[10] to the education of women and gladly taught or lectured to them), some were 'free' tutors,[11] rather fewer were College tutors. The teaching of women was, in fact, one aspect of university extension teaching and those who taught women often also taught for the Extra-Mural Delegacy, which was established in 1878. By 1886, the first two inroads had been made on this system. In 1883, the first College lectures[12] were opened to women, so beginning the process of reducing the number of lectures the AEW had to provide. In the next year, after petition by the AEW, the Delegacy for Local Examinations was empowered to use certain University examinations[13] for women students, instead of the Special women's examinations. Women students, therefore, began to take some of the same examinations as men undergraduates. Over the next ten years, other University examinations were substituted for the Special women's examinations, and when two new Honour Schools were established (English in 1895 and Modern Languages in 1904), women were from the first allowed to take their examinations. The supersession of the Special women's examinations was important outside as well as inside Oxford, for it increased the value – to the outside world – of the qualifications women students could gain in Oxford, in comparison with other universities. The particular comparison here was Cambridge, where, though women could not take degrees, they had taken the Tripos examination since 1872, at first unofficially and from 1881 officially.

These advances in the position of women students in Oxford, added to potential demand, promised well for Elizabeth Wordsworth's experiment. But the institution she founded to carry it out was weak. The amalgamation project of 1893–4 showed that this weakness could only be remedied at its founder's expense; it also showed that St Hugh's had no power to escape from its founder's unfettered control. Fortunately, defeat seems to have lessened her interest in St Hugh's, or at least disposed her to share her financial responsibility. This provided the escape, for shared financial respon-

sibility meant shared control. The Trust Deed which effected this was drawn up at the end of 1894: it was the first St Hugh's constitution. The property of the Hall – the leasehold of 17 Norham Gardens – was transferred to four Trustees, of whom Elizabeth Wordsworth was one.[14] they were ex-officio members of the Committee, which, renamed the Council, became the governing body of the Hall. The Council co-opted four new members. One of them, Cosmo Gordon Lang,[15] became Chairman; the other three were tutors, not simply friends of women's education. This made them particularly valuable recruits. Walter Lock,[16] then Sub-Warden of Keble, had been the first tutor to sit on its Council; he was co-opted in 1885. Annie Rogers[17] and Edith Wardale were both AEW tutors, taught St Hugh's students,[18] and were soon to be St Hugh's tutors. They were, therefore, a link between the teaching of students and the government of the Hall. Looking back, one is suprised to see such a link at the very beginning of St Hugh's independence: it is one of the most important differences between a hall of residence and a college, and St Hugh's was barely secure even as a hall of residence. Annie Rogers was already known as a redoubtable fighter in the campaign for the opening of degrees to women, and came to symbolise it. She was a stalwart Liberal, a lover of constitutions and statutes, with an expert knowledge of University ones, and an indefatigable pamphlet and newspaper controversialist, dry, sometimes caustic, but herself good-tempered and imperturbable. As a member of the AEW Committee since 1879, and Secretary since 1894, she was in the forefront of the first move to open the BA degree to women in 1895. This move, as she said, the St Hugh's Council supported 'in spite of the not very friendly attitude of its Chairman'. Somerville Council also supported the move, but not LMH. Edith Wardale, as an Old Student, was the first representative of an element in the government of St Hugh's which was later formalised and it was to last until the 1950s. She added to her First Class in English (1889) a doctorate from Zürich, and became a distinguished and well-known philologist.[19] Her father and her uncle, Edward Gay,[20] were two of the four Trustees of the Hall.

The 1895 Trust was the first landmark in the development of St Hugh's. Indeed, it 'made' St Hugh's as an independent institution by solving the problem of the relations between the Hall and its founder: Elizabeth Wordsworth became a member of the Council which replaced her as the Hall's governing body.[21] The generation that followed was a period of initiative and expansion in many directions:

in numbers and ownership of property,[22] in the acquisition of friends and supporters, in the organisation of Old Students, in the first appointments of tutors, and in the beginning of participation by Old Students and tutors in the government of the College. The second landmark came in 1910–11, when St Hugh's ceased to be a private trust and became a public corporate body. This landmark coincided in time, as the first had done, with a battle over the position of women in Oxford: the move for the recognition by the University of the five Societies of Women Students.[23] As in 1895, this was a battle for women – or, now, for the societies they belonged to – not for halls of residence, and again the AEW was the prime mover. This time the move succeeded. The battle was not a fierce one, partly at least because 'recognition' was seen to be an issue separate from the issue of the opening of degrees. Indeed, recognition was supported by some who opposed the opening of degrees, but thought it desirable that women students should live in approved and controlled places. Recognition created, for the first time, a monopoly: only 'registered students' – students belonging to one of the five women's societies – were entitled to enter for University examinations. The establishment of the Delegacy for Women Students, which entered registered students for examinations, set the seal on this monopoly.

At the beginning of the 'recognition' period St Hugh's became a public corporate body, with a constitution that gave it, as Catharine Thompson wrote in 1912, 'a more stable financial basis and a much wider and more democratic constituency'. The Trust was wound up in 1910 and in 1911, St Hugh's was registered as a company under the Companies (Consolidation) Act of 1908, taking the name of College in place of Hall. The Articles of Association defined the composition of the corporate body, 'the College': members of the Council, students who had resided for not less than two years and taken a final examination, and tutors who were not Old Students. The Council was composed of certain ex-officio members (for example, Principal, Treasurer, Vice-Principal, and one tutor and one lecturer if paid by the College), together with eighteen elected members. The elected members were to serve for three years; each year three were to be elected by the College at a General Meeting, and three by the Council. There was one casualty: the office of Visitor, established in 1895 and since then held by two distinguished Bishops of Oxford – William Stubbs and Francis Paget – disappeared, presumably because it was unknown to company law.

The innovations lay in the introduction of the principle of election for the majority of Council members and in the definition of the electoral body. This gave former students, as one of them said, 'an indirect share in the government of the College'. It was not an entirely new share: Edith Wardale had been on the Council since 1895, and since 1908 the Council had included one member elected by the Old Students' representative – but it was certainly a larger one. As Catharine Thompson wrote in the *Club Paper* for 1912, in four years, members of the College would elect half the Council, 'a very real possibility of influence'. There was good reason to welcome this. From the beginning, the Hall had valued and greatly benefited from a close relationship with its former students, and, in 1895, had created a category of former students – Members of St Hugh's Hall – who were entitled to receive its Annual Reports. The formalisation of this relationship in the definition of 'the College' was natural enough. In any case, what other definition of 'the College', in 1910, could there have been?

It seems that, if the existing Council had had a free hand, it would have modified the definition, not of the College but of the Council, so as to include tutors among its provision; without it, tutors were in danger of having less say in the government of the College after, than before, 1911. There were seven tutors by 1910,[24] and five sat on the Council. All seven were AEW tutors as well as Hall tutors: that is, their 'salary' consisted of fees from the AEW and, from the Hall, board and lodging and payment for extra duties (e.g. taking charge of a house). The Board of Trade lawyers ruled that tutors could not be regarded as 'salaried officers of the College' if they received fees from the AEW; none of them, therefore, could take the one ex-officio seat on the Council. They were not, of course, precluded from being elected to it, but if they were elected their membership would be personal, not official (just as it had been before 1911), and, moreover, for a limited period (as it had not been before 1911). Sooner or later, the question of ex-officio membership was bound to be raised again. In fact, for a few years after 1911 the number of tutors on the Council remained much the same, but as time went on, the number began to fall. By the end of the war, it was smaller than it had been in 1910.

It is perhaps surprising, and certainly evidence of a progressive Council, that the question of ex-officio membership of tutors was raised as early as 1910. For until 1908 there had been no formal recognition that St Hugh's had tutors, nor decision that it ought to have them – only, it seems, Anne Moberly's determination that it should. Tutors were indeed not an essential element in an Oxford hall of residence for women students, for it was AEW tutors who made arrangements for students to attend lectures, work in laboratories, and be taught in pairs or groups. Hall tutors, defined as women who themselves taught or generally advised Hall students, were a luxury. They were, however, a luxury that Anne Moberly intended St Hugh's to have. She began, soon after the 1895 constitution ensured St Hugh's survival, by appointing as tutors, women who held the post of Vice-Principal.[25] The first she appointed in this way, and the first woman to be designated 'tutor', was Dora Wylie, described in 1898 as 'vice-Principal and resident History tutor'; another, Eleanor Jourdain, Vice-Principal in 1902, was made French tutor in 1905. Again, women who were already AEW tutors were appointed as St Hugh's tutors. Combining posts in this way made it financially possible for Anne Moberly to appoint as many as five tutors by 1907; it also enabled her to secure able and experienced ones. In the following year, the first vital step was taken towards defining and regulating their position. Largely as a result of pressure by two tutors who were on the Council, Annie Rogers and Mrs Lettice Fisher,[26] Council recognised that the Hall had tutors and decided that in future they should be formal Council appointments, made on the recommendation of the Principal. Terms of appointment were laid down (including tenure for one year, renewable for periods of five years) and the existing seven tutors were deemed to have been appointed, on those terms, for a five-year period from 1908. The Principal was to 'assign pupils' to tutors; it would hardly have been possible, at that date, to define their duties more precisely. In 1909, two new tutors were appointed under these regulations: Cecilia Ady[27] (History), and Helena Deneke[28] (English Literature), who had been Librarian and in charge of 28 Norham Gardens since 1904. Both were resident and both were Old Students. In 1915, when Miss Moberly retired, the Council made the first definition of the duties and authority of the office of Principal. At the time, it altered the way tutors were appointed and made a further approach to a definition of their duties. In future, tutors were to be appointed by the Council on the recommendation not of the Principal, but of a Council committee of which the Principal was a member. They were 'to report each term to the Principal on the students under their charge' and to obtain reports from 'teachers outside the College with whom they have arranged for their pupils to work'. These 1908 and 1915 definitions of the office of tutor were of the utmost importance, for they, more than anything else, began to take St Hugh's irreversibly out of the hall of residence stage. Moreover, the reforms of 1908 and 1915 erected a structure on which, after the war, the committee on the constitution could build when it set about the next stage – making tutors ex-officio members of the Council. In 1910, however, when tutors had only just become Council appointments, it would have been unrealistic to expect any tightening of the relation between teaching students and governing the College. The Board of Trade, after all, was not concerned with promoting St Hugh's development into a college. But it was to prove unfortunate that, in the years after 1915, just as tutors and the tutorial system were becoming more organised, the number of tutors on the Council began to fall.

The position of Old Students held no problems like this. Anne Moberly regarded 'the co-operation of its students', past and present, as vital for the well-being of the Hall, and welcomed former students' share in its government. Informal contacts between the Hall and its Old Students were strong from the beginning. Old Students visited and stayed in the Hall, made gifts for the Chapel, for the Library and for general amenities; in 1899, past and present students presented Miss Moberly with her portrait, by W. Llewellyn, which now hangs in the Mordan Hall (the Mordan Library until 1936). Small size, family style of living, economy itself, and a very real sense of being pioneers and building up customs and traditions, all contributed both to the interest which Old Students had in the Hall and its doings, and to a strong feeling of community between former and present students. By 1893, an informal association of Old Students was meeting, from time to time, in London; in 1898, it reorganised itself as St Hugh's Club, with present as well as former students as members. Eligible for membership, on payment of a subscription, were Old Students, and present students who had completed one year's residence; the committee included, ex officio, the Senior Student of the Hall.[29] In 1898, when the 100th student entered St Hugh's, the club had sixty-seven members. It met twice a year and published, once or twice a year, a *Club Paper*, a booklet containing names and news of Old Students, a letter from the Senior Student to Old Students, miscellaneous notices and items of news, and notes and comments on happenings in Oxford and, sometimes, in the world outside. The letters from the Senior Students are informal, family letters about 'Oxford in general and St Hugh's in particular': the surprisingly numerous Hall societies, lectures, concerts and social events, Miss Moberly's Sunday evening talks and Dante readings, accounts of visits from Old Students and friends of the Hall, as well as

general Oxford news. The *Papers* lapsed in 1920, but revived briefly
in 1926 and 1927, when there was a thin *Club Paper* as well as a
Chronicle, the organ of the new Association of Senior Members
created by the 1926 College statutes. The Club, however, lived on
into the 1930s, and was open to present[30] as well as former students: a
reminder that both Club and *Paper* were different from their successors.

The *Club Papers* are a mine of information about the life and
activities of Old Students and, even more, present students, in the
days before students became undergraduates and particularly in the
very early days when records are scanty and the Hall consisted of
Miss Moberly and a handful of students. In 1899 and 1900, Miss
Moberly herself contributed two articles on the early history of the
College, and in 1901 one of the first four students, Grace Parsons,
contributed her reminiscences.

The first four students deserve to be remembered. They were the
only ones to experience the year in the rented, semi-detached house at
the far end of Norham Road, looking out over the gardens of the
Fyfield Road houses. Only one of the four was a parson's daughter:
Charlotte Jourdain, younger sister of Eleanor Jourdain, one of the
LMH students Miss Moberly had met and talked with when staying
with Miss Wordsworth in the spring of 1886. (Eleanor Jourdain's first
service to St Hugh's was helping Miss Moberly to fit carpets and
curtains at 25 Norham Road in October 1886.) Charlotte Jourdain took
the Pass degree examinations, taught for a time in private families,
and in 1908 entered an Anglican religious community. She spent four
years in Japan, returned to England in 1924 and died in 1928.
Constance Ashburner, whose father was a farmer in America, also
took the Pass degree examinations, taught in two GPDST schools,
and, in 1900, became headmistress of Lincoln High School. She died
in 1909. The other two were scientists, both from Aske's School,
Hatcham. Only two women had taken Natural Science before them.
Grace Parsons was the daughter of a Writer at Lloyd's. She was the
first woman student to take Botany, and the only candidate in 1889,
'the misguided female', as the *Oxford Magazine* put it, 'who seeks to
be examined in Botany'. She was successful, just, for after a debate in
Convocation it was decided – by three votes in a thin house – that
papers should be set even though no undergraduate would take them.
This was an interesting precedent, even though the situation was not
likely to arise often. Grace Parsons was placed in the Second Class.
She took a Dublin MA in 1906 and taught in several high schools.

Jessie Emmerson, daughter of a board school inspector, took Chemistry and was placed in the Third Class. After teaching in high schools, she became in 1902 a lecturer at Yorkshire College, Leeds, and taught there in the years of its conversion into Leeds University. She kept her post until she married in 1910.

In 1951, when she wrote a short note of reminiscences for the College *Chronicle*, she recalled the set of library steps which Dr Watts supplied for her use in the chemistry laboratory, 'for in those days we were not supposed to show our legs' – and afterwards labelled by him 'sacred to the memory of Miss Emmerson. Never to be used again.' She and Grace Parsons, who wrote her reminiscences fifty years earlier, in 1901, both note the kindness and hospitality shown to them by the Professors and others who taught them, and by other residents in North Oxford. It is clear from other reminiscences that this was a prominent and valuable part of student life before 1914.

By any standard, the 1886 year was a good beginning. Although it would be absurd to draw conclusions from the pattern made by four students, it is not uninstructive to look at it in relation to the general pre-1914 pattern. The general pattern shows the same preponderance of middle-class background, mainly middle/professional – parsons, doctors, schoolmasters, solicitors, some civil servants, university teachers, army and navy officers. But there is also, from the beginning, a 'non-professional' middle-class element – daughters of manufacturers, industrialists, merchants of various kinds, farmers, auctioneers, estate agents – some certainly richer than the 'professional' group, some poorer. A few students were clearly very well off, but they were, as clearly, the exceptions. There is hardly a trace of aristocracy – which, anyhow, rarely sent its daughters to universities – and not much of landed gentry; in the years immediately before 1914, there was a tiny handful of students whose background was working class rather than middle class. The proportion of parsons' daughters is at first higher in the general pattern than in 1886: 43 out of the first 100 students (to 1898) were daughters of clergymen, nearly all holding country livings, but after this the proportion declined as numbers grew. Very few students – none in 1886 – do not go on to a career, ended by marriage and quite often broken or ended by a period of looking after parents. Teaching of some kind is dominant, including university and training college teaching, and a high proportion of heads of schools and colleges. There is a small, but decreasing, amount of teaching in private families. There is also a small and fairly steady entry into Anglican communities, often teaching or missionary orders. The subjects taken in 1886 are quite different from the general pattern. Even in the early years, the proportion of students taking Pass examinations was very much lower than the 50 per cent in 1886, and it decreases sharply towards the end of the 1890s. The handful of students – including a number of foreigners – who stayed for less than three years, taking no examination or only one or two papers, also dwindled away at the end of the 1890s. The 50 per cent of scientists in 1886 is striking and must have as much to do with the school from which the two girls came as with St Hugh's. Nevertheless, the number of students taking Natural Science in the years before 1914, compared with those taking other subjects, is larger than one would expect. The most popular subject was English, both before and after the Honour School was established in 1895. It had twelve First Classes by 1914, compared with three in Natural Science, two each in History and Modern Languages, and one each in Jurisprudence and Literae Humaniores. A total of twenty-one First Classes for students entering the Hall before 1911 is not a bad record: it is about one in ten students.

It is 'true', but peculiarly distorting, to say that teaching was almost the only career open to women students before 1914. Secondary or high school teaching was a new and exciting career. Most of the schools were young – even by 1914, few were as much as thirty or forty years old. The need for qualified and capable staff and headmistresses was great. Headmistresses were often young; a number of St Hugh's headmistresses were appointed immediately or only a year or two after leaving Oxford. By 1910, St Hugh's had produced 19 headmistresses and 106 schoolmistresses. In the 1920s and 1930s, several headmistresses were elected to the College Council, and in 1929, one of them (Beatrice Sparks, whose third headship was Cheltenham Ladies' College) was made an Honorary Fellow.

Teaching did not mean only high school or boarding school teaching. Some taught abroad: for example, two of the 1898 students (both suffragettes) became heads of schools in India, and a 1909 student, having established a school for miners' children in British Guiana, went on to teach in a school for Siamese princesses in Bangkok. Some founded their own schools; among the well-known ones were Miss Batty's school, which became Wychwood, in Oxford, and St George's in Switzerland. Some became lecturers or heads of training colleges and some became university teachers. One of the earliest of these was Margaret Lucy Lee, (1890), co-founder of Wychwood who combined teaching there with being Vice-Principal

of St Hugh's (1895), AEW lecturer, English tutor at St Hilda's, tutor
to the Society for Home Students, and lecturer at King's College,
London (1902). In the 1890s and early twentieth century, several
became lecturers at the London women's colleges – Bedford and
Royal Holloway College – and in colleges in the United States, and,
rather later, in the newer universities and university colleges in
England and Wales.

After the turn of the century, a few students found administrative
or other non-teaching posts. Edith May, who gained a First in
German in 1897 and in English in 1899, became secretary to
Manchester University Women's Appointments Board and, in 1917,
Supervisor of Women Staff for a large business company. Dorothy
Hammonds (1904) was the first woman Divisional Inspector of
Schools, then Chief Inspector, and after retirement a member and
Vice-President of the GPDST. Miriam Homersham (1909) trained
as an accountant and founded her own firm of accountants. Dora
Ibberson (1910) became a Ministry of Labour Inspector, a member of
the Central Assistance Board and finally Welfare Officer in Trinidad.
She helped Margaret Bondfield, the first woman Cabinet Minister, to
write the book *Our Towns*. Others were employed in social work
under the Charity Organisation Society and, later, under local
authorities.

There was no sense of deprivation about being students and not
undergraduates. Lack of degrees and gowns were marks of pioneering, not marks of inferiority. Dorothy Hammonds in later life
confessed to being proud of not having a degree because 'they did not
then award them to women'. Decorum – symbolised by chaperonage
and 'the College hat' – imposed rules which, before 1914[31] were not
perhaps very different from those of ordinary life, and other rules, for
example those for attending lectures in men's colleges, were thought
of, and laughed at, as quaint customs rather than unjustified restrictions. Women attending lectures in men's colleges sat together and,
for some years, they sat not in the body of the hall but at High Table.
A woman who was rash enough, or unfortunate enough, to be the
only woman attender, sat there with a chaperon. This certainly made
her conspicuous; after one such experience in Balliol, in 1898, a
student was so shaken that for the rest of the term she sent three
postcards a week to her chaperon, explaining that she was unable to
attend each subsequent lecture of the course.[32] 1909 seems to have
been 'the first time' that a woman student could, by herself, attend
lectures 'unaccompanied by a (knitting) chaperon'. 'We were the

largest year ever . . . *sixteen*', one of them wrote. 'It was made plain by Miss Moberly and Miss Jourdain that on us had descended the honourable and perilous destiny of doing nothing to hinder the eventual acceptance of women as members of the University.' This is the 'Annie Rogers argument' for good behaviour: that it would actually help the movement to open degrees to women by removing a potential objection to the presence of women students in Oxford. Perhaps it did: at any rate apprehensions about the behaviour of women in Oxford, which had been voiced in the past, were not voiced when degrees were opened in 1920.[33] Miss Moberly had certainly used the Rogers argument before 1909; probably Miss Jourdain had too. One is reminded of the 'constitutional' suffragists, and – given the date – the militant suffragettes, who pointed out that forty years of 'good behaviour' had not brought 'votes for women' any nearer. 'Degrees for women', however, produced no militants, no counterparts of the suffragettes in Oxford. Moreover, many supporters of 'degrees for women' were as uninterested in 'votes for women' as they were in other aspects of the women's movement. It is often thought that lack of militancy, and single-mindedness, helped their cause.

Some members of St Hugh's did show an interest in the suffrage question. Their interest may have been aroused, and must surely have been stimulated, by acquaintance and friendship with St Hugh's' first great benefactor, Clara Evelyn Mordan. She was born in 1844, the daughter of a prosperous manufacturer of propelling pencils, who took her in 1866 to hear John Stuart Mill advocating women's franchise, on the eve of his amendment to the second Reform Bill. In the 1880s and 1890s, she was a member of the executive committees of the London Women's Suffrage Society, the Central Society for Women's Suffrage and other women's societies, and contributed generously to their funds. In 1906, she 'joined Mrs Pankhurst' – that is the Women's Social and Political Union – and was, as *Votes for Women* recorded in 1915, 'one of the first women of the older generation to recognise the meaning of the new movement . . . the militant Suffragists'. She was the first subscriber to the WSPU campaign fund; she gave practical help at by-elections and she spoke 'with wit and humour' at suffragette meetings. In June 1908, she helped to finance and spoke at the great Hyde Park rally and procession organised by the WSPU.

Clara Mordan first visited St Hugh's in 1897, after hearing Miss Rogers lecture, in London, on women's education. This was the year after the defeat of the proposal to open the BA to women. On the day after Miss Mordan's visit, she sent Miss Moberly £1000 to endow a scholarship, and she then began to pay regular visits to St Hugh's. She formed a firm and lasting friendship with Miss Moberly, was co-opted on to the Council in 1902 and became a Trustee in 1907. The students 'really got to know Miss Mordan', as one of them wrote in the *Club Paper*: she took a great interest in their activities, 'especially Sharp Practice',[34] and invited holders of the Mordan Scholarship to stay with her in London. After she became ill, Miss Moberly wrote to her regularly about St Hugh's affairs. Clara Mordan's replies left no doubt of her deep affection for the College. 'My connection with St Hugh's and with yourself', she wrote in 1912, 'has been one of the joys of my life', and in November 1914, two months before she died, 'My connection with St Hugh's and with yourself will always remain one of the wholly satisfactory episodes of my life.' In all this, there is no reference to Miss Wordsworth: another sign that, by the late 1890s, Miss Moberly and the new Council were firmly in the saddle.

The first Mordan Scholar, whom Miss Mordan got to know well and with whom she remained friendly, was Margaret Crick.[35] She and her rather younger contemporary Theodora Bazeley,[36] wearing their Dublin MA robes, marched with the 'St Hugh's contingent' in the 1908 WSPU procession. The procession had been advertised on the Hall notice-board. The St Hugh's contingent was led by Eleanor Jourdain and Edith Wardale, wearing their doctoral robes: some of the crowd hailed 'the two French doctors'[37] good-humouredly as Archbishops of Canterbury and York, others as Proctors sent by the University of Oxford to keep order. Eleanor Jourdain's description of the procession was printed in the 1908 *Club Paper*. The 1910 procession was also described in the *Club Paper* – this time by Margaret Crick and Theodora Bazeley – and in the same year the then Senior Student, Leslie Beckmore, successfully urged the formation of a separate St Hugh's Old Students Suffrage Society, open to present students after their first year. In 1911, it was decided that this society should be affiliated to the National Union of Suffrage Societies: some stated their preference for the WSPU, and it was explained that only individuals, not societies, could belong to the WSPU. Eleanor Jourdain described the suffrage procession of June 1911 with its 'large contingent of St Hugh's old students' and their handsome green and white banner, in the *Club Paper*.

Clara Mordan was prevented by illness from taking part in both the later processions: in 1911, she became incurably ill with consumption. She was, therefore, unable to attend the St Hugh's Council

meeting of 9 November 1912. This was the meeting at which the
Treasurer, the Reverend George B. Cronshaw[38] proposed that the
College should buy the leasehold of 'The Mount' (the large house at
the south corner of the junction of St Margaret's Road with Banbury
Road, set in four acres of grounds) for the purpose of demolishing the
house and building on the site. 'Years before' this Clare Mordan and
Anne Moberly had determined that the next step for St Hugh's must
be a new, purpose-built, collegiate building. Anne Moberly drew
plans for college buildings and gardens; Clara Mordan said that 'she
meant to endow them', calculated the cost, and asked about suitable
'large houses within grounds'. 'The Mount' was just such a house.
Nevertheless, the Council's decision to borrow in order to buy the
leasehold, demolish the house, and erect a building for seventy-one
students, with Chapel, Library, Hall and Senior and Junior Common
Rooms, was an act of faith and extraordinary courage. Although Clara
Mordan wrote to Miss Moberly in December, and to Mr Cronshaw
in January 1913, explaining that 'several thousands of pounds' would
come to St Hugh's on her death, and more than twice as much again
on the death of her residuary legatee, Mary Gray Allen, both the
bequests were, after all, in the indefinite future, and their size
uncertain. Moreover, soon after the decision was taken, Miss Mordan
became too ill to attend to business or to respond, as no doubt she
would have done, to Miss Moberly's request for an advance from her
promised legacy. The whole operation – purchase of freehold, demolition and building – therefore took place against a stream of bank
loans and hand-to-mouth borrowings, notably from generous friends
and relatives of Miss Moberly.[39] Demolition began in the summer of
1914; the building was planned to be finished in September 1915.
War, and difficulties and delays in obtaining materials and men, made
this impossible. It also reduced the value of Miss Mordan's legacy.
January 1915, when she died, leaving not money but investments,
was the worst possible time for selling securities. Nevertheless, the
legacy was undoubtedly a turning point. Without it, and the stead-
fastness of four members of the Council – Miss Moberly, Miss
Jourdain, Miss Wardale and Mr Cronshaw – there seems no doubt
that either building would have been abandoned altogether or the
plans severely 'simplified'. As it was, nothing was sacrificed except
the College wall, planned to surround the grounds but left 'for the
present', flanking only the St Margaret's Road boundary. The wall
remains today as it was left then: a much stronger boundary wall than
any the College has built since. Its unfinished state symbolises, for

those who like symbols, that the College has never stood still: the four acres the wall was planned to enclose are now only about a quarter of the College grounds.

The building was occupied, though not completed, in January 1916. For the next two terms, students and tutors watched the last stages of 'the stone-paved terrace spread out in front of the South windows, and the Chapel, Library, Hall and Common Rooms emerge with a distinctive character and taste of their own' and the early stages of 'what we hope will be a very beautiful collegiate garden'. All work on the building was finished by October 1916. The Chapel was dedicated by the Bishop of Oxford on Ascension Day, 1916; the Library above the dining hall was named the Mordan Library; the garden was the special care of Miss Rogers, until she died in 1937. She became one of Oxford's great gardeners, and St Hugh's' one of Oxford's finest college gardens.

In November 1914, 'now that the new buildings for the College are in course of erection', Anne Moberly resigned, leaving the date for her actual retirement to the Council, which chose March 1915. Without her there would have been no College building and, as certainly, no College. Miss Rogers, who knew something of her early struggles, and indeed, unhappiness, described her achievement as 'the most remarkable in the history of women's education'; Miss Wardale spoke of her 'creation' of the College; and the then Secretary of Council, Alice Greenwood, (who can only have known by hearsay of the years when the survival of St Hugh's was in doubt) wrote that 'to say that the College *is owed* to you is only to say, what is common knowledge to us all'.

It seems to have been a foregone conclusion that Eleanor Jourdain should succeed her, and 'after some words of warm appreciation from Miss Rogers and Mr Cronshaw' the Council elected her in January 1915. This was the last Council meeting that Elizabeth Wordsworth attended; she had not attended regularly for some years. She had retired from LMH in 1909 and lived in Rawlinson Road, a stone's throw from the new St Hugh's building. She endorsed the Council's official tribute to Miss Moberly and seconded the Chairman's proposal to elect Miss Jourdain – a fitting curtain to her thirty years' relationship with St Hugh's. Eleanor Jourdain was the eldest of the talented and individualistic children of Francis Jourdain, vicar of Ashbourne in Derbyshire. She was an academic head – she had been a History Scholar at LMH and had taken a Paris Doctorate in 1904 – and she had academic connections in Oxford. She had, before becoming Vice-Principal in 1902, founded a successful private school at Watford and a finishing school in Paris. She was, in fact a professional woman – competent and socially gifted – a contrast but a complement to Anne Moberly. She had been Vice-Principal for thirteen years and French tutor for ten and had been, as Miss Moberly said, a 'very great support' to her. Her first task as Principal was to find the temporary accommodation for students that building delays had made necessary.

Miss Moberly and Miss Jourdain had both agreed – against members of Council who had wished to stop building in wartime – that the war would increase the number of parents who wished their daughters to have a university education, if only because more of them would want or need careers. They were right: the war, which depleted the men's colleges both of undergraduates and of dons, increased the number of applicants for places at all the women's colleges. St Hugh's had 45 students in 1915, 64 in 1916, 81 in 1917 and 107 in 1919. The increase continued after the war and by 1923 St Hugh's was the largest women's college, with 151 undergraduates. Until it should be possible to extend the College building (that is, until the remainder of Clara Mordan's estate became available),[40] undergraduates who could not live in College were housed with near-by 'hostesses' in north Oxford. But in 1919, Eleanor Jourdain bought the leasehold of 4 St Margaret's Road and let it to the College. This was the first 'College house': like its successors, it ranked as part of College because it housed a tutor as well as undergraduates. It also pointed the way to a policy which the College has pursued ever since: the gradual acquisition of the leaseholds (and in time the freeholds) of the houses on the fringe of the College garden – along St Margaret's Road, down Woodstock Road and Banbury Road, and later along Canterbury Road – enclosing the area which came to be known as the 'island site'. Most of the houses were used to accommodate students. In the next year, the College leased 89 Banbury Road ('The Lawn') from Lincoln College and, in 1924, Joan Evans[41] bought the leasehold of 82 Woodstock Road for College use: this was the largest of the houses to be acquired, and took sixteen or more undergraduates.

War work formed a regular part of students' lives: digging in allotments and in the part of the College garden set aside for vegetables, work at the Army Supplies Depot at Didcot and in canteens in the town. Social life was concentrated in the College, chaperon rules lapsed, lecture audiences were largely composed of women. Students leaving College joined the Women's Services, worked in new and old government departments, in factories (usually as welfare officers), and on the land, took the place of men in boys' schools and in the newer universities. Many were employed in posts not previously held by or open to women, and some of these kept their posts after the war.

One of the earliest supporters of women's education remarked, after the failure of the attempt to open the BA degree to women in 1896, that degrees for women would probably have to wait for votes for women. And so they did. Discussions about opening the BA degree began before the war, but the final proposals were not made until 1920. This was fortunate, for the general postwar climate of opinion, as well as the Franchise Act (1918) and the Sex Disqualification Removal Act (1919), no doubt explain not only why these 1920 proposals went much further than those of 1895, but also why they were accepted without opposition. The main difference was the opening of the MA as well as the BA – so conferring membership of Convocation – and radical changes in the position of women tutors. Women students became members of the University: they lost the honourable fifty-year-old label of 'student' and became undergraduates, wearing gowns and, instead of a mortar-board, a specially designed cap, embodying 'a judicious compromise between Portia and Nerissa', which was, as Annie Rogers said after experimenting with St Hugh's students, 'becoming, and can be adjusted to varieties of coiffure . . . does not catch the wind and does not get shabby'. In November 1921, St Hugh's students presented 'an antique chair for use at High Table in commemoration of degrees for women'. Most old students who were qualified for the BA took it and the MA at once; those not qualified were allowed until 1926 to complete their qualifications – this often meant simply taking Responsions. Women tutors who received MAs by decree, as did Principals, became not only members of the University, but University teachers, eligible by Special Statute passed in 1921, for membership of Faculties, Faculty Boards, examining Boards and University Committees. The existing thirty women tutors expected opposition to these changes, if not to the opening of degrees. They therefore prepared a paper 'Relation of women students and teachers to the University', appealing for 'a share in the general life and work of the University'. As it turned out, this paper was not needed, for, as Annie Rogers remarked, 'nothing was heard of any organised opposition'.[42] These changes, which made women students members of the University and transformed the relation of women tutors to the University, were a triumph for 'women', not for women's colleges. Two consequential changes did affect the women's colleges: the abolition of the AEW, in 1920, made college tutors solely responsible for arranging their pupils' work, and the abolition of the Delegacy for Women Students, in 1921, transferred to colleges the duty of entering students for University examinations. But these changes affected the five women's societies, not only the four women's colleges. So once more two causes – on the one hand women's degrees and membership of the University, and on the other hand women's colleges – are seen to be distinct.

This is again clear in the postwar movement for reform of the St Hugh's constitution, which was the outcome not of the enhanced position of women tutors in the University but of the much older 'College' wish that tutors should share in the government of the College. The seed was sown, perhaps, with the first link between teaching and college government in 1895. The lack of secure tutorial representation on the Council, which the Council had failed to obtain from the Board of Trade in 1911, grew more conspicuous as, after 1915, the number of tutors on the Council declined. It was the immediate and direct cause of the Council's establishment, in June 1921, of a committee on the constitution. Eleanor Jourdain and Annie Rogers were two of its six members. Its first interim report, in October 1921, recommended 'changes in the constitution of the College with a view to . . . a larger representation of the teaching and administrative staff'. After considering ways of effecting this, including a final application to the Board of Trade,[43] the committee recommended, in November 1923, that Council should end the College's life as a company and apply for incorporation either by Royal Charter or by an Act of Parliament covering all four women's colleges. After consultation with the other three, Council decided to apply for a Royal Charter. The first College statutes were drawn up, and the Charter applied for, by the end of 1925, and in 1926, the Charter was granted and the statutes approved.

The Council's wish that its membership should include tutors was thus the spur to constitutional reform. The spur was, however, sharpened by a strengthening of the position of tutors within the College. By the end of the war, the College's connection with the AEW was felt to be outgrown. The AEW had been vital for the position of women in the University, and remained so until 1920. It had also been vital for St Hugh's, because it had made possible the appointment of its first tutors. But the AEW spoke for women, not for women's colleges. It was not helpful, and it began to be seen as an

obstacle to the development of an independent college tutorial
system. In the last two years of the war, and in the immediate postwar
years, St Hugh's appointed tutors who were not AEW tutors; they
received a guaranteed, minimum salary from the College and could,
therefore, even on the Board of Trade definition, be called 'salaried
officers of the College'. Council also further defined tutors' duties and
terms of appointment, and in 1919, ruled that fees payable by the
College for tuition by its tutors should be paid direct to them and not
through the AEW. The tutorial work of the College, and tutors
themselves, were becoming more organised. A tutorial fund was
established. Staff meetings – tutors and administrative staff – were
held regularly from October 1918, and tutors' meetings from April
1920. Tutors' meetings dealt primarily with assignments of students
to tutors. Staff meetings had much wider scope: they discussed
general College problems. These included discipline, chaperon
rules,[44] College plays, fees and retaining fees, pensions and, in 1922,
the constitution. These were steps towards the establishment of a
purely College tutorial system. Nevertheless, it should be emphasised
that tutors who were also AEW tutors did not regard themselves as
any less College tutors; indeed, it was they who had first pressed, in
1908, for the definition of the office of College tutor as a Council
appointment.

The move for ex-officio representation of tutors on the Council was
also a move, though not a deliberate one, for an adjustment of the
balance of power between Old Students and tutors. Under the 1911
constitution, Old Students had more power and tutors less, than in
the days of the Trust. Before 1911, tutors had been co-opted on to the
Council; after 1911, they became members only if elected by 'the
College' – that is, in the main, by former students. Most tutors so
elected were themselves former students, and this created a blurring
of functions and of power. The tutor/Old Students members of
Council wore two hats and had, in addition, a constituency to nurse;
they needed the support of Old Students for their election, and they
were in a position to enlist the support of Old Students in so-called
'tutors' causes'. There was everything to be said for separating the
two: that is, for having on the Council Old Students' representatives
who were that only, and did not feel or need to feel that they
represented tutors as well. This was an automatic consequence of the
ex-officio representation of tutors achieved in 1926.

The constitution then established lasted, in essentials, for twenty-
five years. It was a 'mixed' constitution. The Council lost the

predominantly elective character it had had since 1911. Tutors became, by virtue of their office, Fellows and members of the Council. The Principal remained, by virtue of her office, a member of the Council, not its Chairman. The Old Students elected three representatives, one each year, by postal vote, to serve for three years. They were the only elected members. The Council itself co-opted six 'outside' members and had the power to co-opt, if it wished, three extraordinary members. At first the number of official members – Principal and Fellows – was about half of the total. Although, looking back, this constitution may seem a half-way house, a stage in an inevitable drive towards self-government, this is not how it looked at the time. The 'inevitability' of self-government may have become apparent at some time after 1926, but it had by no means been apparent in the previous forty years. Moreover, there was much to be said in general, and everything to be said in 1926, for the idea of government by a mixed Council, and this was, after all, what the Council would have liked even in 1911. There was also much to be said for the particular mixture that was devised in 1926. Annie Rogers,[45] who played a prominent part throughout the discussions, liked the mixture; it defined, she said, 'a new category' of Oxford constitutions, unlike any other, yet having some features in common with some of 'the five categories' of existing (men's) colleges and halls. This is a useful reminder that mixed constitutions and Councils were not only found in women's colleges; some men's colleges had them too, or had done in the past.[46] The fact that St Hugh's students and tutors were women made less difference to its constitutional development than might perhaps be expected; if the first forty years are to be regarded as the time it took to reach incorporation by Royal Charter, then progress was quick rather than slow.

1926 marks another achievement more specifically related to women: the completion of forty years of successful pioneering in a field that was itself new – the extension of university education to women. This achievement cannot be measured in terms of constitutions, and did not wait for them. It began when St Hugh's opened in 1886, before the difficulties arising from what Anne Moberly called 'the unique circumstances' of its foundation were fully understood, let alone surmounted, and it seemed stimulated rather than diminished by them. The part St Hugh's played in the first half of these forty years, when 'men dons taught us, for we had no dons of our own', as an 1890s student remarked, was different but no less valuable than its part in the second half, when St Hugh's had tutors and was building a college tutorial system. In one sense, the earlier part must be judged more valuable, for what St Hugh's did then, in the houses in Norham Road and Norham Gardens, was to enable women students to be taught and examined in Oxford by University teachers and examiners. This could not have been done in any other way. It was in these years, too, that the lower fees charged by St Hugh's were of the greatest value to parents of would-be students. These were very great services, by women, to women's education, and they were based primarily on the conviction that the movement to open Oxford University education to women was of the utmost importance, and that St Hugh's was a part of that movement.

(This chapter is based mainly on material in the College archive. I have also been much helped by four chapters on the history of the College, written by Miss Procter.   B.K.)

Notes

1.   1840–1932. Daughter of Christopher Wordsworth, Bishop of Lincoln (1868–85) and great-niece of William Wordsworth; Principal of Lady Margaret Hall (1879–1909) and a member of its Council until 1922. She was not interested (as both heads of the Cambridge women's colleges were) in the 'women's movement' and 'women's rights', and she shared the not uncommon Oxford view that the opening of degrees to women was not in their best interests. Her uncomplicated Anglican faith, her love of talk (with her avowed preference for the talk of 'liberals', with whom she did not agree) and her spontaneity and inconsequentiality in conversation, were attractive, and she fitted in well to post-Tractarian (or second-generation Tractarian) Oxford – all the better for her being in no sense a feminist. Some of her characteristics – initiative, self-confidence, and a liking for her own way, and a certain naïvete – may be seen in her founding of St Hugh's.

2.   She was particularly worried about the effect of the agricultural depression of 1884–5 on the clergy.

3.   She did not name these. They must have included London University (which opened degrees to women in 1878) and perhaps Manchester (which did so in 1883). But what else? No doubt she sympathised with *The Guardian*'s alarm at the 'lack of Church influence' and 'undenominational character' of Somerville and the two Cambridge women's halls. But her concern in 1886 was wider than *The Guardian*'s and not confined to those who could not afford the fees at the one 'sectarian' hall, Lady Margaret Hall. I do not think this was simply tact on her part.

4.   'Poor students' must be taken, in its context, to mean primarily sons of those middle and professional classes who might be expected to benefit from a university career, but could not afford to come to Oxford. Elizabeth Wordsworth's wish to help the daughters of the clergy and

other professional men may be compared, for example, with Professor James Mozley's 'great hankering to know why bankers, industrialists, barristers and other professional men' did not send their sons to Oxford – though Mozley suggests that expense was not the only deterrent.

5. Charlotte Anne Elizabeth Moberly (1846–1937), tenth of her parents' fifteen children. Her father was the son of a merchant established at St Petersburg; her mother Mary Anne Crokat, 'the beauty of Naples', the daughter of a Scottish merchant at Leghorn. The happiest period of George Moberly's life – and perhaps of his daughter's – was his long and successful headmastership of Winchester (1835–66), where all the children were born. The family was on terms of intimate friendship with the families of Charlotte Yonge (1823–1901) and John Keble (1792–1866), who were neighbours at the farmhouse where the Moberlys – known as 'the Daisy Chain family' – spent their summer holidays. They were Anne's godparents and she was influenced by both. George Moberly was a High Churchman with some liberal views: he did not take part in the Tractarian controversy. He called himself 'an inconsistent Liberal' and did not forget his 'Balliol past' – he had been (1826–34) one of the 'brilliant Balliol tutors' who worked with Jenkyns, the anti-Tractarian Master, 'to make Balliol the foremost College in Oxford'. Moberly had a great affection for Keble but often disagreed with his views. Anne Moberly was familiar with the standards of scholarship through her father (and also her brothers and brothers-in-law, many of whom had distinguished academic careers in Oxford). She clearly found those standards, and that kind of society, congenial. She herself read French, Italian, Latin, New Testament Greek and a little Hebrew. In her father's later years, she acted as his secretary: she describes him as 'a liberal churchman' and this probably describes her own position. Her delightful biography of her father, *Dulce Domum* – in fact it is the biography of his family – shows her relaxed and with wide sympathies. It was published in 1911 and rapidly went into a second edition (and later a third and fourth). It has notes and comments by Charlotte Yonge, whose picture of the family describes Anne as 'deep in books, playing the piano, and unconsciously preparing for her future work'.

6. Its chairman was Sir John Caesar Hawkins (1837–1929), 4th Bt, of Kelston, Somerset, who lived at Kelston, Banbury Road. He was an authority on the synoptic gospels and received an honorary DD at Encaenia, 1923. His second cousin, Edward Hawkins, was Provost of Oriel from 1828–82 (and critical of the Tractarians and Newman's idea of 'pastoral' tutors); he and his wife were friendly with Anne Moberly's parents at the time of George Moberly's appointment as headmaster of Winchester. Other members were Mrs Catharine Thompson (see Note 15, p. 43); Edith Pearson, Vice-Principal of St Hugh's (1889) and of LMH from 1890, Secretary of St Hugh's Council (1895–1900); and Mrs Alethea Mackarness, widow of John Fielden Mackarness, Bishop of Oxford (1870–88), and a Liberal in politics. She was the daughter of Judge Coleridge and connected with the family of Charlotte Yonge.

7. The Committee had previously met three times a year, but it met only once while the LMH Committee was considering Elizabeth Wordsworth's plan. At this one meeting, in January 1894, there was no formal notification or discussion of the plan. I have found no evidence of any informal consultation with Committee members, who must have known about the plan.

8. At a rent of £150 a year, which covered interest at 4 per cent on the mortgage, and on her own loan to St Hugh's, and left her with a margin of some £30 a year.

9. The ideal of low fees did not wholly die for many years, even though the difference between those of St Hugh's and those of the other women's halls was much reduced by 1914. It could, of course, be argued that the need for it declined with the increase in state and county scholarships. Anne Moberly, perhaps naturally, was less sympathetic to the ideal than Elizabeth Wordsworth was.

10. They perhaps thereby derived some compensation for sparse undergraduate audiences. It is well known, for example, that Balliol History tutors – and presumably other college tutors – advised their pupils not to attend the University lectures given by Professor (Bishop) Stubbs; he was, however, a valued 'women's lecturer'.

11. For example, James Edwin Thorold Rogers (1832–90) whose comments on 'hack College tutors' suggest that women students were sometimes luckier in their teaching than men undergraduates. He was Tooke Professor at King's College, London from 1859; Drummond Professor of Political Economy in Oxford in 1862; not re-elected in 1867 because of his liberal opinion, but elected again in 1888; lecturer in Political Economy at Worcester 1883; MP 1880–6. His major work, *A History of Agriculture and Prices in England, 1259–1793* (8 vols), is a perfect example of the original research which, as he said, college tutors did not do. He was active in University administration and examined both for Classics and for Political Economy. He supported the admission of women to University examinations and degrees and the revival of non-collegiate membership of the University. When his daughter Annie qualified, by her performance in the 1873 Oxford Senior Local Examinations, for an Exhibition at Balliol or Worcester (and Worcester offered one) he wrote to the Vice-Chancellor saying that he saw nothing in the University statutes which barred women from being matriculated and taking degrees; but he refused to let her be a test case.

12. This was progressive as well as valuable. Professors' lectures were open to the public but college lectures were private occasions and not – without special arrangements – open to undergraduates from other colleges, let alone women. Keble College benefited from such arrangements, which became more common after the 1880s. For women, the AEW made the arrangements and paid the fees for attendance. By 1906, all colleges had opened their lectures to women, thus greatly reducing the need for additional AEW lectures. Individual lecturers were of course entitled, if they wished, to exclude women. It

was not until much later (well into the twentieth century) that most college lectures were open to undergraduates from any college.

13. The First and Final examinations for the Honour School of Mathematics, Modern History and Natural Science, and the examination for Classical Honour Moderations.

14. The others were Rev. J. Wardale, Edward Gay and Mrs Ethel Romanes. She was the widow of J. G. Romanes, eminent scientist, and founder of the annual Romanes Lecture, who, when he retired to Oxford in 1890, became a member of Christ Church. She wrote a life of Charlotte Yonge, who was Anne Moberly's godmother.

15. Fellow of All Souls (1888) and vicar of St Mary's (1894–6), lecturer for the Extra-Mural Delegacy, Archbishop of York (1909–28) and of Canterbury (1928–42). He was Chairman of St Hugh's Council 1895–8. He was succeeded by Henry Lewis Thompson, the next vicar of St Mary's, who was Chairman from 1898–1904: he died in 1905. His wife Catharine (neé Paget) was on the 1891 Committee, and the 1895 Council, Secretary of Council (1901–13) when she left Oxford, an honorary member of St Hugh's Club (1912), and a friend of St Hugh's until she died in 1936. James Matthew Thompson, Fellow of Magdalen from 1904, historian of the French Revolution, was their son. Her brother Francis was, as Bishop of Oxford, Visitor of St Hugh's (1901–10).

16. Tutor of Keble from 1870, sub-Warden (1881–97), Warden (1897–1920); member of St Hugh's Council (1895–1923); died in 1933.

17. Annie Mary Anne Henley Rogers (1856–1937) was the eldest child and only daughter of Thorold Rogers and his second wife, Anne Suzanna, daughter of H. V. Reynolds, Treasury Solicitor. She was educated at home, largely by her father. In 1873, she won first place in the Oxford Senior Local Examinations, but was unable to benefit from this. From 1877 to 1879 she worked for and passed the Women's Examination in Classics. In 1878, she became a tutor for the AEW, and from 1894–1920, she was secretary of this body. In 1894, she became a member of St Hugh's Council, and served in that capacity until 1937, with the exception of the year 1924–5. In 1908, she became a tutor at St Hugh's, a formal Council appointment, and continued as such until 1921. From 1910–20, she was a member of the Delegacy for Women Students, and in 1920 she was secretary of the Delegacy of the Society of Home Students. In 1936, she was made an Honorary (Jubilee) fellow of St Hugh's. After 1921, when she resigned her St Hugh's tutorship, she happily divided her time between St Hugh's committee on the constitution, established in 1921, and St Hugh's garden. There are two garden memorials to her: the small garden on the north side of the university Church, and the sundial on the terrace of St Hugh's.

18. I do not know whether any one hoped that this combination of Council membership and teaching 'would not form a precedent' – a hope expressed in 1880, when a member of Keble College Council, H. O. Wakeman, historian and Fellow of All Souls, taught Keble undergraduates.

19. Vice-Principal of St Hugh's (1889–94); resident lecturer, Royal Holloway College (1894–5); treasurer, St Hugh's (1895–9); AEW lecturer; in charge of 28 Norham Gardens (1900–4); St Hugh's tutor (1903(?)–23); member of Council (1895–1941); Honorary Fellow (1929).

20. One of the Hall's earliest friends; his gifts included a Hall boat ('The Ugly Duckling'), 1891; a much-used dance floor in the dining room at 17 Norham Gardens, 1892; shelving for the Library, 1900; and, from time to time, money for Hall scholarships. He entertained and sometimes housed students at his home, 'Invermore', now 82 Woodstock Road, so beginning its long association with St Hugh's: it has been a College house since 1924; its library has served as overflow for books, both before and after the building of the Moberly Library in 1936, and as lecture room; it is now renovated as the College Law Library.

21. She was Domestic or House Treasurer until 1900 (alongside a Joint Treasurer who had overall financial control). As Trustee, she was an ex-officio member of the Council until 1911 and a member of the new Council until 1915 but did not play a prominent part after 1900. In 1915, she and Anne Moberly were made Honorary Vice-Presidents. She had resigned as Principal of LMH in 1909.

22. By 1910 there were forty-two students; the leasehold of 28 Norham Gardens (opposite 17) was acquired in 1900, and that of Fyfield Lodge in 1909.

23. The Home Students became a Society, with a Principal, in 1893: it was governed by the AEW until 1910 and then by the University Delegacy for Women Students; St Hilda's Hall was opened in 1893, and for the first three years, its students were members of the Society for Home Students.

24. Non-resident: Annie Rogers (Classics), Edith Wardale (English), Mrs Lettice Fisher (History), Jane Willis Kirkaldy (Natural Science); resident: Eleanor Jourdain (French), Helena Deneke (English, then German), Cecilia Ady (History). In 1910, all except Miss Kirkaldy and Miss Ady were members of the Council.

25. A mainly secretarial office, which in 1895 became a Council appointment; council then defined its duties as 'to assist the Principal in such ways as she may require', and particularly with correspondence with the AEW. The salary in 1895 was £30 a year; Miss Moberly's salary was raised to £50 in 1894 and £70 in 1895.

26. Wife of H. A. L. Fisher, then teaching in Oxford; she was History tutor and a member of Council 1901–12, resigning from both, when her husband became Vice-Chancellor of Sheffield University.

27. Cecilia Mary Ady (1881–1958) was the daughter of the Reverend Henry Ady and Julia neé Cartwright (author of Italian Renaissance biographies). She was at St Hugh's from 1900–3. She obtained a First in Modern History. In 1909, she came to St Hugh's as a tutor, a post which she held until 1923. She was elected to the Council for the first time in 1913, and in 1915, became Vice-Principal, a position she held for three years. In 1919, she was in charge of a College house, 4 St Margaret's Road. In 1924, she left St Hugh's, and became a tutor at

the Society of Home Students. She remained in this position until she returned to St Hugh's in 1929 as a Research Fellow. She obtained a DLitt in 1938, and in 1950, became an Honorary Fellow of St Hugh's. She was Secretary of the Association of Senior Members of St Hugh's from 1932–55. From 1920–50 she was one of the representatives of Oxford Diocese on the Church Assembly. She was the author of books, articles and reviews on the Renaissance period (including: *Bentivoglio of Bologna*, 1937 and *Lorenzo dei Medici*, 1955). She taught St Hugh's historians the Renaissance Special Subject until the mid 1950s. Her legacy to the College was used to refurnish and decorate the Chapel.

28. Helena Clara Deneke (1878–1973) was the daughter of a wealthy London merchant of German origins. She was a student at St Hugh's from 1900–3, and in 1903 obtained a First in English. She was Librarian of St Hugh's from 1904–13 and was in charge of 28 Norham Gardens. In 1907, she became an MA of Dublin University. From 1909–13, she was a tutor at St Hugh's. She was the first Old Students' representative on the Council (1908). She left St Hugh's in 1913 to go to Lady Margaret Hall. She was tutor and Bursar there from 1913–38. Her home, at 'Gunfield', Norham Gardens, between St Hugh's and Lady Margaret Hall, was a centre of musical activity.

29. An officer, corresponding to the later President of the Junior Common Room, who presided over meetings of all students, then called Hall meetings. She was elected from among third- and fourth-year students, and held office for a year.

30. After two years' residence, instead of one. The 1932–5 *Chronicle*, which describes a club dinner in 1932, states that life membership then cost 15 shillings.

31. This was less true of the 1920s – an unfortunate aftermath of the Proctors' assumption of authority over women students, when they became undergraduates. The Proctors' rules for women undergraduates and mixed societies and occasions, which were first issued in 1923, and after 1925 were drawn up without consultation with the women's colleges, seem sadly out of step with ordinary post-war life and conventions.

32. She confessed this at the 1966 College Gaudy, and calculated she owed the College 'about thirty shillings for those chaperon fees'. The fee was 1s 6d an hour. Her debt was to the College, because the Hall had, presumably, paid the AEW for providing a chaperon.

33. They were, however, voiced in 1927, in the debates which ended in the limitation of the size of the four women's colleges: 160 for St Hugh's and LMH, 150 for Somerville and St Hilda's. But the main question then was, as the *Oxford Magazine* put it 'whether Oxford should be a man's University, with a certain amount of women admitted, or . . . a mixed University'. The decision, by 229 votes to 164, was for 'a man's University'. (The quotas were raised in 1948, 1952 and 1953; in 1957 they were abolished.)

34. A method of debating and the name of a popular Hall society: speakers were chosen, by lot, at the beginning of each debate. The many references to Sharp Practice in the *Club Papers* (e.g. 'the terrors of

Sharp Practice', 'the changing fashions of Sharp Practice') leave no doubt that it was an important part of Hall life.

35. Daughter of the vicar of Leafield. She began to read Mathematics (1898) and, after a year at home to nurse her mother, returned in 1901, took Maths Mods, and then read History. She taught at Whitelands Training College until 1914, when she became Principal of Queen Mary's College, Lahore. She married Sir Miles Irving (Indian Civil Service); they retired to Oxford in the 1930s. She died in 1946.

36. Born 1882, daughter of an estate agent. She read Zoology (1902), taught at various training colleges (including Whitelands) and from 1832, was Principal of three in succession. She died in 1936 and is a College benefactor.

37. The second 'French doctor' may have been Mildred Pope, French tutor at Somerville, rather than Edith Wardale; the context does not settle this.

38. Fellow of The Queen's College, Treasurer of St Hugh's (1906–21). He had already been responsible for the building (1909) of the St Hugh's Chapel in the garden of 'Gunfield', the house between 17 Norham Gardens (St Hugh's) and what is now LMH Old Hall. He gave outstanding benefits to St Hugh's by his financial expertise, knowledge of University administration, and unstinted time. When he resigned in 1921, the Council paid tribute to 'the enormous debt the College owes to him for his wise guidance, hard work, and cheery optimism all through the great financial difficulties of the early days of the College'. He died in 1928, shortly after his marriage, and election as Principal of St Edmund Hall.

39. Clara Mordan had praised Miss Moberly's 'gift of inducing people to make loans' in 1900, when it was already clear that the Hall could not have expanded as it had without constant loans, on advantageous terms, from a small group of friends – most of them 'friends of Miss Moberly'. Her gift was equally valuable now.

40. Her residuary legatee, Mary Gray Allen, died in 1925. £36 000 (less death duties) came to the College, and the Mary Gray Allen wing was built in 1936.

41. Joan Evans (1893–1977) DBE, DLitt, DLit(London), Hon. LittD (Cambridge), Fellow of University College, London, Chevalier de la Légion d'Honneur, was the daughter of (Sir) John Evans (1823–1908), antiquarian and numismatist, and younger half-sister of (Sir) Arthur Evans (1851–1941), excavator of Knossos. She was Miss Jourdain's goddaughter and also her executor. She was a student at St Hugh's from 1914–17, obtaining both a BLitt and a Diploma in Archaeology. From 1917–22, she was the College Librarian. She was a member of Council from 1922–58. In 1936, she was made an Honorary (Jubilee) Fellow. From 1951–8 she was a Supernumerary Fellow. She was a distinguished antiquarian and scholar in the fields of History of Art, Architecture and Jewellery; President of the Royal Archaeological Institution (1948–51); first woman Director and (1959–64) President of the Society of Antiquaries, and its Gold Medallist in 1973. She was an honorary member of many French learned societies. She was a

valuable member of St Hugh's Council – independent and decisive – and a constant and generous benefactor to the Library, and to College amenities and funds. Her gifts were practical and imaginative (e.g. the creation of the Endowment Fund), and nearly always anonymous, as were her gifts to needy students, scholars, and museums and learned institutions in Britain, France and Crete. Among her many publications were: *English Jewellery* (1921), *Monastic Life at Cluny* (1931), *Romanesque Architecture of the Order of Cluny* (1938), *Time and Chance* (1943), *Cluniac Art* (1950), *A History of the Society of Antiquaries* (1956), *A History of Jewellery* (1964), *Monastic Architecture in France* (1964), *Prelude and Fugue* (1965).

42. She suspected that the reason for this was not so much change of heart as preoccupation with the controversy about the abolition of compulsory Greek as an entrance requirement. It was abolished just before the women's reforms were finally passed; women were certainly amongst those who benefited. A.D.K. Peters (1919) recounts how she managed to take up a place at St Hugh's without Greek. She had taken the Cambridge Previous exam intending to go to Cambridge, but changed her mind, and studying the Regulations found that she could offer Cambridge Previous, which did not contain Greek, rather than Responsions.

43. The Board of Trade agreed to alter the Articles of Association to allow 'any member of the staff', to a maximum of seven, to sit on the Council, but this left the principle untouched.

44. In 1922, in response to a petition from the students, the staff meeting decided that third- and fourth-year students, and students aged twenty-five or more, might act as 'chaperons for the river'. This is perhaps an example of an attitude which was rather more liberal than the Proctors' in their first dealings with women students.

45. She resigned her tutorship in 1921, but remained a member of Council until her death in 1937.

46. Amongst them Keble and St Edmund Hall (though the mixture was different) which, like St Hugh's, became self-governing in the 1950s.

3 The Row

Rachel Trickett

The history of the St Hugh's College 'Row' has been written up at length in Lucille Iremonger's *The Ghosts of Versailles*, and briefly in the second volume of Hilary Spurling's biography of Ivy Compton Burnett, *The Secrets of a Woman's Heart*. A recent television play, *Miss Morrison's Ghosts*, gave a distorted and inaccurate version of it. There is no formal, detailed and disinterested record of the event.

When I came to St Hugh's as English tutor in 1954, one of the protagonists, Cecilia Ady, still lived in St Margaret's Road and was a Senior Research Fellow of the College. Joan Evans, Miss Jourdain's goddaughter and a member of the Council involved in the original incident, was still a member of the College Council. Elizabeth Francis, one of the tutors appointed by Miss Jourdain in the course of the 'Row' was a senior and widely respected Fellow and tutor in French at St Hugh's. Understandably, the matter was then thought much too delicate and painful to be discussed in public, even thirty years after the event, and very few Fellows of the College had any idea of the facts of the case. Rumours circulated and anecdotes were repeated, but for the most part all that was known was that Miss Ady had not been reappointed to her tutorship, that the College had been split into warring factions, that the Chancellor of the University had eventually adjudicated – and it is a measure of the diplomacy of his pronouncement or of their failure to read it carefully that supporters of both sides felt able to claim he had justified their position – and that Miss Jourdain had died of a heart attack a few days later.

The effect of such secrecy was to provoke uneasy suspicions and propagate legendary stories, half-true, half-false, but above all to neglect the academic context of the episode and to see it rather in terms of a personal vendetta and a personal tragedy. St Hugh's had survived and flourished, and its reputation in the University, damaged at the time of the Row, now stood high. But the occasional lack of confidence the College manifested came, no doubt, from the recollection of this event, the desire to forget about it and to sweep the facts out of sight. As we approach the College's Centenary it seems to me that we now have the confidence, the understanding and the detachment to record the whole episode as part of our history. It is, at

48

one and the same time, a tragic story of the clash between two able and ambitious women, and an important stage in the acquiring of an independent College constitution. It deserves to be related dispassionately.

In 1903 Miss Moberly decided that she must have help with the administration of the College and appointed as Vice-Principal, with the approval of the Council, Eleanor Jourdain, headmistress of a small private school for girls in Watford, and a talented teacher and French scholar. The Jourdains were an unusually gifted family. Eleanor's sister Margaret was a connoisseur and art historian, her brother Philip a brilliant Cambridge mathematician: her younger sister Milly (like Philip an invalid), showed a slight but genuine talent for poetry. Eleanor herself had wide and lively interests in History, Philosophy, general literature and in the supernatural. Enough has been written about her claims to telepathy and precognition, and the part she played in the celebrated 'Adventure' – the story of her and Miss Moberly's extraordinary experience at Versailles. They are important here only in so far as they cast light on her character and her influence over other people. It was this strain in her make-up, as well as her efficiency, which established her friendship with Miss Moberly, and which helps to account for the fascination she exercised over students and fellow tutors. In some it was the fascination of admiration, in others of repulsion. She was a woman who roused strong responses.

Among those who disliked her was Helene Deneke who taught German for the College and was especially devoted to Miss Moberly. In 1913, two years before Miss Jourdain became Principal she left St Hugh's to teach at Lady Margaret Hall, and much later wrote a confidential account of her reasons for the move which is now in the College archive. In this she accuses Miss Jourdain of untrustworthiness, and cites the case of her submitting two different authorities – Donald Tovey and Henry Hadow – an instance of what Miss Deneke felt to be intellectual dishonesty which shook her faith in the evidence collected in support of *An Adventure*. Miss Deneke's memoir is openly biased against Miss Jourdain, but even the Principal's supporters (Eveleen Stopford, for example, whose account of the Row is written in sympathy with Miss Jourdain) admit that she was not much concerned with scrupulous accuracy. Intellectually she was alert and capable; she possessed remarkable powers of administration and organisation; her great personal characteristic was vivacity – an excellent foil to Miss Moberly's more introverted temperament. That she had a gift for friendship and intimacy is evident, though her enemies considered it both contrived and potentially dangerous. Those who responded to her charm with few exceptions remained devoted to her.

The tutor who was closest to Miss Jourdain between the years 1910 and 1915 when she became Principal was Cecilia Ady, who herself had been an undergraduate of the College and was invited to come back as History tutor. In the College archive there are letters from Miss Jourdain to Miss Ady written in the most affectionate tone to her 'Baby Don', or, in playful reference to Miss Ady's Italian studies, 'Cara Mia Cecilia', which are openly revealing in what they tell of the state of the College as Miss Jourdain then saw it. Miss Moberly appears to have lost much of her interest in administration, to have withdrawn more and more into her family circle, and to have became capricious in her treatment of Miss Jourdain. Helene Deneke is singled out as a troublesome member of the Senior Common Room and her move to Lady Margaret Hall remarked with relief and approval. These are good letters (apart from their local interest): stylish, light in touch and, though critical, stopping short of self-pity. They are affectionate, candid and confidential in the vein of letters to a close friend.

When in 1915, Miss Moberly decided to retire early from the Principalship, Miss Jourdain was chosen as her successor. Almost her first act was to persuade the Council to appoint Miss Ady Vice-Principal, an office she held from 1915 to 1918. From the vigorous development of the College through the difficult war years, the new team appeared to be a success. In 1916 the main College building was erected largely through Miss Jourdain's skill and determination, and the number of students continued to rise. Miss Ady was a brilliant tutor with the gift of exciting her pupils intellectually; she was also acquiring a reputation for scholarship in the University which helped to establish the College's academic name. Yet in the document Miss Jourdain presented to the Council meeting of 24 November 1923 at which Miss Ady's reappointment as History tutor was disputed, the Principal wrote:

> . . . she carried out certain official duties (such as those connected with the Scholarship Examinations) but never supported my authority in the College either in matters of policy or discipline, and I was obliged therefore on the expiration of her appointment as Vice-Principal to tell her that I could not recommend her for reappointment.

Behind this generalised attack can be sensed the paradoxical situation that developed with Miss Ady's rise to power. She, who had been Miss Jourdain's close friend and confidante, was now gradually perceived as a rival. Cecilia Ady, known to her friends and colleagues in the College as 'The Child', was certainly the star pupil, some might have said the spoiled darling of St Hugh's. She was the only child of a beauty, Julia Cartwright, and was bred in a cultivated, devout and scholarly home. Her own personal plainness and shyness were compensated for by intellectual brilliance, gradually disclosed powers of leadership and organisation, and, not unnaturally, strong ambition. Her position as Vice-Principal to a similarly ambitious, less scholarly but equally gifted Principal was entirely different from Miss Jourdain's in relation to Miss Moberly. Miss Jourdain had none of Miss Moberly's diffidence and social nervousness; she did not need support or guidance; she was looking for an obedient lieutenant who would help her carry out her plans and policies for the College. Miss Ady's independence, which had once seemed delightful waywardness in a young protégé, now began to look like opposition. Her established position in the College and the University gave the Principal no scope to further her career. There was nothing Miss Jourdain could offer her beyond the Vice-Principalship to bind Miss Ady in gratitude as she, for thirteen years, had been bound to Miss Moberly. Miss Ady on her part must have pondered from time to time, however innocently, the pattern of Miss Jourdain's career so far, and the likelihood that hers would run on the same lines. Many who knew her thought of her as Miss Jourdain's natural successor; some believed that she thought so of herself and was working to that end.

The clash of two such strong, ambitious and capable personalities in this situation might have been foreseen. But as far as we can judge neither of them envisaged it, especially since their affection for each other had been deep and genuine. The rift was gradual and at first went unnoticed by colleagues. It might have remained so for longer had it not been for those changes in the academic status of women for which all the women's colleges were working and planning. The Principal was as dedicated to the aim of full membership of the University for women, and their admission to its degrees, as any of her colleagues. She used this aim as an argument to her undergraduates for strict propriety and obedience to the rules: they were in the van of an important movement and they must show themselves disciplined and serious-minded for the sake of the cause. In 1920, two years after Miss Ady ceased to be Vice-Principal, the University took the step of admitting women to degrees and that particular battle was won. Miss Jourdain was less sure, however, of the growing movement among women tutors to take more part in the administration of their own colleges, and to promote for each a constitution which would establish their rights and privileges, similar to those of men Fellows in the older societies. In principle she was in favour of such a development. In practice she was cautious and somewhat suspicious of the effect it might have on her own position.

By 1922 and 1923 the College had grown and acquired new tutors in main subjects. Miss Ady and Miss Wardale (who had long been English tutor and was a staunch supporter of college constitutions) were joined by Miss Shaw (French), Miss Everett (English) and Miss Toynbee (Classics), young women all active in the new movement. These three tutors resided in College, and Miss Jourdain, fearful of Miss Ady's influence over them, asked her to leave residence and live at home – her mother's house being opposite the College lodge in St Margaret's Road. But this home was too near to prevent Miss Ady becoming a natural leader of the new tutors in their conversations and discussions in the Senior Common Room, where they openly talked about their views on a constitution, their ideas on how to acquire it, and their frustration over what they saw as the Principal's antagonism. They were supported by non-resident tutors and lecturers, and a split developed between these eager academics and the administrative members of the SCR – not an uncommon situation, even today. They were often citing the progress of other colleges – Somerville in particular. A letter survives from Miss Jourdain to Miss Annie Rogers (a member of St Hugh's College Council) protesting that colleges must go their different ways, and that her particular problem at St Hugh's was the shortage of understanding resident tutors to help in administrative work and to support her authority. In 1923, two separate issues had brought the friction between the administrative staff and the tutors to a head – both mentioned by Miss Jourdain in her submission to the Chancellor at the subsequent enquiry. One was the matter of a pension fund for tutorial staff, the other the question of the constitutional status of tutors' meetings.

The tutors had made their own proposals with regard to a pension fund, but recognising that the College's finances were in no state to meet them, they agreed to leave them aside for the moment. Miss Jourdain's annoyance over this matter was purely on the technical point of whether the issue should have been discussed (as it was) without her. Her statement on this does suggest an element of paranoia: she was not in disagreement with the tutors, merely angry that they had not taken what she considered the constitutional means of putting their views forward. More disputable was the matter of the new post of Vice-Principal. She had informed Miss Ady and the other tutors that she felt the need for this sort of assistance. The office had lapsed in 1918. In her submission to the Chancellor Miss Ady was to say this about her own experience of it: 'I soon realised that the Principal's aim was to centralize the work of the College as completely as possible, even to the smallest detail of administration. I accepted this solution, and while undertaking a certain amount of secretarial work, I gave myself chiefly to my Tutorship.' But, though Miss Jourdain had run the College single-handed as far as discipline, day-to-day administration and admissions were concerned since 1918, her increasing sense of isolation and her fear of Miss Ady's influence on the tutorial staff prompted her to propose that the office of Vice-Principal should be revived. In Trinity Term 1923 a committee was set up, which included Miss Ady, 'to define the duties and fix the salary of the Vice-Principal'.

Miss Jourdain's patience snapped when Miss Ady reported informally to tutors that the duties of the Vice-Principal as discussed at the committee turned out to be more properly those of a Dean, and used the occasion to press them to ask for the office of a Senior Tutor. This seemed to Miss Jourdain an attack on her own position and on that of the new Vice-Principal. She reiterated that it should not have been discussed at a meeting of no constitutional status, and took it as evidence of deliberate hostility to her position in the College. The tutors, on their part, were especially anxious to have the status of tutorial meetings properly defined, and resented the fact that at that time non-tutorial members like the Principal's secretary had an equal right with them to vote at such meetings. They were strongly supported in this by some of the men Fellows who were members of the Council. In June, A. J. Jenkinson, an Economics Fellow of Brasenose, a member of the Council, wrote to the Principal saying that he intended to propose a motion with the object of defining the relations between staff and tutors' meetings and the Council. Miss Jourdain again took this as a personal attack, but maintained that she held her hand and did not bring up the matter of the tutors' disloyalty and Miss Ady's insubordination (as she saw it) until after the arrival of a new Vice-Principal, and until she had given Miss Ady the chance, as she was now non-resident, to change her ways.

In none of the documents I have seen is it made clear when Miss Jourdain realised that Miss Ady had forgotten to request the Council to consider her re-appointment as History tutor which had, in fact, technically expired in the spring of 1923. Miss Ady herself evidently forgot this technicality; she cannot, we must assume, have been reminded of it. Whether the Principal noticed it or not at the time it is now impossible to know. But the bitterness and hostility of both parties in Michaelmas Term 1923 was clearly about to lead to a crisis of some sort. The new Vice-Principal, Miss Firth, in a misguided exhibition of loyalty to Miss Jourdain, tried to draw Miss Ady into an admission of hostility and intrigue against the Principal, and sent Miss Jourdain a damaging written account of how she thought things stood, of her observations and of her conversation with Miss Ady. It is hardly surprising that conflict was unavoidable at this stage. There were faults on both sides. The Principal, while maintaining the legalities of the present constitution, was engaged in a personal defence against what she took to be a personal intrigue to undermine her authority. The tutors, while working for a new constitution which would define their status more exactly and guard their independence, talked openly to students and colleagues outside the College about the Principal's intransigence. What is astonishing is the sequence of events that followed.

On 8 November a special meeting discussed the suggestion that the Senior Tutor should preside at tutorial meetings if the Principal were absent. Miss Jourdain called a further special meeting for 21 November after protesting that the original proposal was an undermining of the position of the Vice-Principal, who must act in place of the Principal on official occasions. At this second meeting the tutors offered a modest compromise – that the Senior Tutor present should act as secretary to any such meeting. But between these two meetings the whole issue had been superseded by a much more drastic occurrence. On Sunday 18 November, Miss Ady received a brief note from the Principal asking to see her on College business between 10 and 10.30 the following morning. No mention was made of the nature of the business, and the message as Miss Ady transcribed it, has the curtness and the casualness at once of intimacy and hostility. Miss Ady presented herself in the Principal's room at 11 a.m. on Monday 19 November and found she was in the presence of the Chairman of the Council (J. Munro, the Rector of Lincoln College), the Secretary of the Council and the Principal. The Principal then read out to her a statement accusing her of disloyalty and asked her to withdraw from her post. It was revealed to her for the first time that her appointment had technically expired, and she was once more pressed to resign.

Miss Ady responded with characteristic spirit, denied the charges, and announced that she would appeal to the Council which was to meet in five days' time. Miss Jourdain in her submission to the Chancellor says that after this extraordinary scene she wrote to the Chairman saying she 'anticipated three possible lines of action. 1. The non-reappointment of Miss Ady. 2. The giving to her of a Term's notice which I hoped would be represented by a Term's fees. 3. Her re-appointment, in which case I should resign.'

The astonishing thing about this incident is that the Chairman of Council, the Head of an Oxford college, should not have warned Miss Jourdain of the dangers of her action and of its impropriety. The accusations made against Miss Ady were hardly short of libel, as Professor Brierly, the Chichele Professor of International Law and one of her supporters on the Council who eventually directed her response to the enquiry, pointed out. The Council itself shortly recognised this when it went out of its way to say that there were no imputations made against Miss Ady, save the one that she was unable to co-operate with the Principal. The Rector of Lincoln, as President of the Council, maintained to other members that he was not convinced by the Principal's accusations of disloyalty, but that he supported her because it seemed to him that if the Principal and a tutor failed to agree, and one would have to withdraw, it must be the tutor. Such an attitude would scarcely have gone uncontested in a man's college, and it is a remarkable example of the anomalous position of the women's colleges that so many members of the Council took his view as axiomatic. Miss Ady's Council supporters, especially A. J. Jenkinson of Brasenose, saw this as characteristic of the disabilities under which women tutors suffered. St Hugh's was said to be commonly called 'The School', and 'the Headmistress contingent' (Jenkinson's phrase) on the Council – powerful Old Students who had become heads of prestigious girls' schools – were, for obvious reasons, on the Principal's side. She was herself an ex-headmistress, and like the rest of them, based her views of authority on institutions very different from the self-governing oligarchies of the Oxford and Cambridge colleges. The Rector in his capacity as Chairman of St Hugh's Council acceded to a procedure which would not have been possible in his own society. To the women tutors and their supporters this was grist to their mill; their whole contention was that until women academics were given the same status as male colleagues, their colleges would never be genuinely equal to the ancient societies of the University. And in fact this was so, in spite of all advances, until after the Second World War.

The Council met on 24 November and discussed the question of Miss Ady's re-appointment under 'Principal's Business'. Miss Jourdain read out her complaint; Miss Ady answered, then both withdrew.

The minutes give little impression of that dramatic meeting; the correspondence in the Ady and Rogers files flesh them out for us. Unfortunately there is no Jourdain file in the College archive, and we have no first-hand account of the event from any of her supporters. Discussion was evidently heated, but a move to defer the matter for further consideration (which would have been wise in the extraordinary circumstances), was precluded by Mr Jenkinson's intervention. He impulsively moved that Miss Ady be re-appointed History tutor, and the proposal, duly seconded, was moved and lost by one vote. The unfortunate Archdeacon Archer Houblon, previously President of the Council, and to be re-elected to that office when the Rector prudently resigned after Christmas, fled before the vote was taken on the excuse of having to get back to London. Six members of Council resigned at once, together with five tutors, who had intimated their intention of doing so if Miss Ady were not re-appointed. The formidable Annie Rogers, with her unerring political instinct, thought it wiser to remain on the Council and fight, as it were, from within the enemy's gates. She was the Council's Trojan Horse for the rest of the crisis, and it is from her voluminous files of correspondence that we learn most of the conflicting opinions thrown up by the occasion and the subsequent campaign.

Miss Ady and her supporters – Miss Wardale, Miss Everett, Miss Shaw, Miss Toynbee, Miss Scott Holland and other lecturers – lost no time in publicising what had happened. The Principal's submission to the Chancellor indicates that she had not foreseen the furore this would occasion. She stands firm on her rather dubious constitutional ground, but, again astonishingly, seems to have been confident, in spite of the undergraduates' almost unanimous support for the tutors, that her position was unassailable. The staggering loss of all her most distinguished staff, the vote of no confidence in her and the Council passed by a majority of Old Students at a General Meeting of the College on 15 December, seem not to have moved her to reconsider her attitude. Eveleen Stopford is right to point out that this does not support any view of her Machiavellian skill in winning round opinion or in political manoeuvring. It is impossible not to feel bewilderment and pity for her blindness to the implications of what had happened. She was entirely persuaded of the rightness and justice of her cause, and she held to this with such conviction that none of her supporters seems to have had the sense or the wisdom to appeal to her better judgement. They were apparently mesmerised by her complete confidence. The Council indeed backtracked on her original accusations regarding Miss Ady, but gave her the immediate power to appoint tutors replacing those who had resigned. Especially alarming was the general boycott of St Hugh's students which spread through the University in support of Miss Ady and the tutors with almost immediate effect. To some extent this gave the Council and Miss Jourdain a moral justification they seized on at once. The innocent sufferers, the undergraduates, in spite of their support for Miss Ady, were the victims of an irresponsible act on the part of thoughtless partisans. The harsh decision of these contrasted with the care and courageous consideration of a persecuted and misunderstood Principal.

Miss Jourdain made every effort to replace the resigning tutors with suitable successors, but it was not possible in so short a time – between December 1923 and Hilary Term 1924 – to do this successfully. Eveleen Stopford was one of those who accepted a post; her account of her experience in the following term, though sympathetic to Miss Jourdain, indicates the appalling difficulties these women encountered. The only entirely successful and lasting replacement was Elizabeth Francis, who had no connections with the College and had applied in the normal course of looking for a post, and who was always grateful for that opportunity, however dubious it seemed to those who knew the internal situation. Miss Ady and her supporters tried to defeat the Principal's efforts to replace them by setting out the circumstances of their resignation to headmistresses and principals whose pupils might be moved to apply, and to Old Students of the college. There is even evidence from potential candidates of threats of jeopardy to their future careers. On the other hand, it is commonly known that some third-year students were taught informally by some of the tutors who had resigned, so that the students they felt responsible for, and the Schools results, would not be affected. But those undergraduates who came up in 1923 and were not personally committed to either side remember the period as painfully uneasy, until Miss Gwyer took up her appointment in Michaelmas Term 1924 and a new phase began for the College.

The Council, having attempted to minimise the charges brought against Miss Ady by the Principal, were so embattled in face of the boycott and the indication of lack of confidence from Old Students,

that they foolishly rejected a suggestion from the current undergraduates' parents among others (made on 29 December 1923) that a
Judge of the High Court should be asked to intervene in the matter on
the grounds that this was a case of personal antagonism rather than of
principle. Such a response was at once seized on by the tutors' party,
and reasonably so, as an indication of inconsistency and disarray. It is
still extraordinary to anyone reading the documents that the Council
behaved with such lack of common sense. To have allowed Miss
Jourdain to arraign Miss Ady on personal grounds in the first place
was a mistake; to have accepted the resignations of the five tutors in
the second place was folly; and to have rejected an appeal for impartial
arbitration from parents and Old Students now compounded these
imprudencies. But personal feeling had run so high that to have
compromised would have looked like deserting the Principal, who
was seen by her supporters as a much maligned woman, bravely
maintaining her position in the face of a cleverly concerted attempt to
unseat her. No wonder the Rector of Lincoln thought it best to resign
from the Presidency at this juncture. The previous President, Archdeacon Archer Houblon, was voted into the hot seat in his place – he
who had avoided voting in the first instance. His letters to Miss
Rogers can only arouse a bemused sympathy for his predicament. He,
like his predecessor, was outmatched by the force and the justice of
the tutors' case as presented by their supporters; he, like the Rector,
was repelled by the antagonism, sometimes the vindictiveness, of the
allies on both sides.

On 1 March 1924 the Council, presented with a further request by
Old Students and parents of current undergraduates to ask the
Chancellor to act as Visitor, acceded to the proposal, but invited Lord
Curzon to take into special account the action of tutors of other
colleges in boycotting the teaching of undergraduates from St
Hugh's. Curzon replied briefly to the Chairman that he would only
act without constraint or conditions and if it was assumed that his
adjudication would be entirely disinterested. His offer was accepted
and the date for the enquiry set for 22 March 1924. The Chancellor
appointed Mr Clausen KC, Counsel for the University, to receive the
evidence of witnesses. There is a file of their depositions in the
College archive. The tutors had the advantage of Professor Brierly's
assistance and support. His letters to Miss Ady and Miss Rogers after
the event and before the judgement, show that he was impressed by
Clausen, and a little alarmed by Jenkinson's impetuous defence of
Miss Ady and her allies. Neither side was depressed by the exper-

ience, or unhopeful of the outcome. On 1 April Lord Curzon communicated his decision to the Vice-Chancellor, the Chairman of St Hugh's Council and on the same day to the editor of the *University Gazette* in which it was published on 2 April. He found that no imputation rested upon Miss Ady. He also found that the 'so-called boycott' by other women tutors was not Miss Ady's responsibility, and that 'those ladies, in intimating their intention of witholding their co-operation, should it be invited, with the new Tutors of the College, did not exceed their rights'. He found that 'The unfortunate occurrences which have formed the subject of this enquiry demonstrate a want of understanding between the Administrative and Tutorial Staffs which has been detrimental to the interests of the College.' He was of the opinion that 'in order to prevent the recurrence of similar troubles the Council should take steps to secure a more defined and harmonious co-ordination among the College authorities. It will be for the Council to consider what constitutional reforms are desirable for this purpose, and whether such reforms should be accompanied by changes in personnel.'

However far short of the triumphant vindication some of Miss Ady's supporters had anticipated, the Chancellor's judgement was entirely in their favour. The need for a constitutional definition of tutors' status is implicit in his findings; the reference to changes in personnel could not refer to Miss Ady, who did not seek re-instatement, but only to administrative staff, and evidently the Principal herself. It was in this sense that the College Treasurer, G. R. G. Radcliffe, the Bursar of New College, who had always been a strong supporter of Miss Jourdain, interpreted the findings. In a letter dated 10 April 1924 to Miss Rogers, written to try to persuade her to refuse support for the re-appointment of the resigned tutors of St Hugh's after the Principal's sudden death, he says:

> I myself undertook the task of telling the Principal that an early resignation was necessary, and I understand that the Chairman will tell the Council that Miss Firth does not seek re-appointment. I need not dwell on the pain it caused me to make such a communication to the Principal or on my present feelings in realising that I had unwittingly embittered her last hours . . .

Ideas of seeking Miss Jourdain's early retirement had been current even before the 'Row' and even among her sympathisers on the Council. There is evidence of these in the College archive. But she had clearly not expected the outcome, and there is good reason to suppose that the Treasurer's communication was the occasion of the heart attack from which she died on 6 April 1924.

Her death, as much as the last year of her life, was a disaster for the College. Feelings that might have been allayed became inflamed again; her supporters accused her opponents of having hounded her to death. Rumours that she had committed suicide were spread by her opponents. The assiduous Miss Rogers was said to have gone round Oxford on the day of her death canvassing for Miss Ady to be appointed her successor. The resigned tutors were not reinstated and the College lost the services of two such distinguished women as Dorothy Everett (who was bold enough, in face of all advice to the contrary, to re-apply) and Jocelyn Toynbee. Deep divisions between Miss Ady's and Miss Jourdain's supporters and previous pupils were intensified. The whole matter was more easily forgotten in the University at large than in the College. The newly appointed Principal (after a temporary interval), Miss Barbara Gwyer, was presented with a situation that the boldest might have refused. Her skill, reconciling spirit and diplomatic instincts saved St Hugh's from what could have been a gradual decline compounded by indifference and hostility from the University, and division and strife from within. The College owes to Barbara Gwyer more than can be fully conveyed.

Miss Jourdain's story evokes pity and, nowadays, bewilderment, that she should have been so unaware of the danger into which she had put herself and her college. She gave much to St Hugh's. Its original expansion, its Main Building, airy, dignified and pleasant still to live in, bear the marks of her skill and influence. She took great care over every detail of its design and construction. Under her guidance, the numbers of students at St Hugh's rose from about 50 to over 150, thus making it the largest women's college in Oxford. She was genuinely concerned with the future of her pupils, and her autocratic instinct for discipline and obedience was tempered with charm and personal consideration. But by the 1920s she had become convinced that her position was secure and her mind was closed to any disagreement. She could not conceive that the world would not take her part. Miss Ady, on the other hand, knew well enough that success meant planning, perseverance and perspicacity. I believe that each of them was honest in her view of what was best for the College, and, especially in Cecilia Ady's case, for the future of women's education. Miss Ady's loss of her future at St Hugh's (where she would almost certainly have become Principal after Miss Jourdain if the quarrel had not occurred) and the resignation of the tutors, assured the future of women tutors and Fellows and their independence in the women's colleges. We can be saddened equally by Miss Jourdain's death, Miss Ady's disappointment, the divisions these two powerful women caused; but we have every reason to be grateful for the academic outcome of this complicated dispute. Looked at from outside, the struggle seemed to many, one of constitutional importance that eclipsed the personal issue. A. J. Jenkinson wrote to Miss Rogers on 25 November 1923: 'the action of the Tutors has very much raised women in my estimate from the constitutional point of view. Indeed I think the action of the Tutors of St Hugh's will go down in the History of Women's Education like that of the Fellows of Magdalen in the History of the University.'

In spite of the tragic outcome at a personal level, I think we may now look at the whole episode in this larger dimension.

4 Reminiscences of Seven Decades

Priscilla West

INTRODUCTION

The following chapter is compiled from reminiscences sent by Senior Members, in answer to an appeal for written memories of life at St Hugh's. Each person on the College mailing list was sent a sheet of questions concerning their time at St Hugh's, and Oxford, to jog their memories, and help them formulate their ideas. 358 Senior Members replied. Some wrote at great length, making use of diaries and their letters home, as well as their own memories. Others wrote a few comments on the 'prompt sheet'. All have been used though not necessarily quoted. It would have been simpler to 'distil' each decade, using reported speech and only occasionally quoting; but it was decided to let as many contributors as possible speak for themselves, as it seemed more important to give the flavour of individual reminiscences. This policy is reflected in the lack of balance between decades; for some, notably the 1920s, 1930s and 1940s, produced more contributors.

Each decade forms a self-contained unit. As well as being part of a chronological sequence, each one can be read for itself alone. Obviously, from decade to decade, there is repetition in certain areas; but, it was felt that as much interest lies in what had been unchanging in a woman's life at Oxford, as in what has been individual to each decade.

There are considerable gaps in the picture presented in each decade. Each person who sent in her reminiscences, told of a different St Hugh's – a different Oxford. In compiling this chapter, it has been necessary to present majority views, offset by individual exceptions. The views expressed, and the events remembered by the self-selecting sample of people who wrote in, the majority of whom are still in touch with St Hugh's, will, probably, in no way present a satisfactory picture of life at St Hugh's for others.

To give some idea of what it was like to be a student before 1908, the date at which our oldest contributor, Miss Ethel Wallace, matriculated, material has been used from reminiscences of old students, published in the St Hugh's *Chronicle*, and from the journal of Dorothy Hammonds, written in 1905 and 1906, now held in the College archive. The years 1916 to 1917 are supplemented by letters written by Molly McNeill, to her mother, and given to St Hugh's by her sister.

Material for the framework of College and University events has been extracted from the St Hugh's *Chronicle*, referred to as the *Chronicle*, or attributed as *Principal's Report* or *JCR Report* from the same source. Occasionally, this material has been augmented by information from newspapers, periodicals or books.

For the sake of consistency, contributors have been referred to by their maiden name. A list of all contributors to each decade, whether they have been directly quoted or not, will be found at the end of the chapter.

THE EARLY DAYS, AND THE 1920s

The earliest reminiscences date from the days when the college was still housed in 17 and 28 Norham Gardens and Fyfield Lodge, and called St Hugh's Hall, before its recognition as one of the five Societies of Registered Women, and before its incorporation. Under the new principalship of Miss Jourdain (from 31 March 1915), the college sold 17 Norham Gardens and gave up other rented accommodation, in readiness for the move in the autumn. However, by September it was clear that the new building would not be ready, and Wycliffe Hall was rented for the Michaelmas Term. Although the Chapel, Library, entrance hall, staircase and adjoining rooms were still unfinished by the end of the term, the college moved into its new premises. Dorothy Parr remembers seeing the masons still at work, putting finishing touches. In Hilary Term, the work was finally completed and the building dedicated on Ascension Day, 1916. The Council expressed their gratitude for the efforts of the architect and contractor and recorded their appreciation of the beauty and collegiate character of the building.

With each addition to the building there was a commensurate increase in the facilities available, including the gradual establishment of a college Library. Miss Rogers in her 'Historical Reminiscences' of 1928, mentions that there were under 300 volumes in 1890; the *Chronicle* says that there were 1000 in 1898, 2629 in 1908 and 5000 in

1918–19. It is reported by Katharine Dawson that Joan Evans, Librarian from 1917 to 1922, 'spent much of her own money building up the Library'. Perhaps the greatest new asset was the garden which under the care of Miss Rogers, Mr Ball, and Mr Harris in particular, developed into one of the most beautiful of the Oxford gardens, a constant source of delight to each generation of undergraduates. 'I remember being taken up to Oxford to see the new building in the autumn of 1916 soon after it had been opened . . . the original garden was very beautiful and much appreciated' (Felicia Stallman). Eduarda Fowler refers to 'the beauty of the garden, particularly the terrace, running the whole length of the beautiful original building at the back'.

The students of this period are witness to some of the greatest changes in the history of both the College and the University. They saw the establishment of women's right to higher education, which in theory was equal to men's, although it has taken many generations to achieve any real parity. They were not unconscious of their position as pioneers and, in consequence, are among the most serious to have offered reminiscences. The earliest belong to Ethel Wallace, who went up to St Hugh's in 1908, who was not only unusual for her time in considering further education at all, but the more so in that she wished to read a science subject: she recalls that 'When some of my Evangelical friends . . . heard that I was going to read science at Oxford, they were horrified and predicted that I should become an atheist.' St Hugh's Hall was a possibility for her, because it charged the most reasonable fees. She says 'By sharing a room with another student for the first two years, St Hugh's Hall would take a student for only £70 a year.' She shared a room with a school-friend and relates that in 17 Norham Gardens 'there was the dining room and a chapel, and both Principal and Vice-Principal lived there. There were also bed-sitters for third and fourth year students. At 28 there were only bed-sitters for first and second year students with Miss Deneke in charge.'

At this time, there were only four resident dons and under thirty students. In consequence, the atmosphere was closer and more intimate: students and dons knew each other better perforce, and while the rules of chaperonage were still extremely strict, there was necessarily far more participation in each other's lives, so the early reminiscences centre on the characters of the dons. Miss Moberly, the Principal 'was very shy with a deep voice, kind-hearted, reserved, sensitive but with a keen sense of humour' and deeply religious. 'On

Sunday evenings she gave lecture-talks to which we were practically obliged to go. They were held in her own sitting room and were informal ... I shall never forget her course on the Five Visions of the Apocalypse' (Ethel Wallace); Miss Wardale (one of St Hugh's first ten students), in her 'Early Reminiscences', published in the *Chronicle* (1930) writes 'While etiquette ruled the other Halls with some severity, under Miss Moberly's influence the members of St Hugh's lived on the easiest and most friendly terms amongst themselves.' Muriel Holland writes of '... dear old Miss Moberly soon retiring. I still remember going to tell her my brother had been killed in action – we didn't see much of her as a rule'; but by 1923, Hilary Gent says 'I knew Miss Moberly in the manner in which well-brought-up undergraduates "called upon" such venerable figures – complete with visiting cards – at the beginning of each term.'

Miss Wardale says of her: 'I must stop to say something of what St Hugh's owes to its first Principal. No-one could have been found better suited for that post than Miss C. A. E. Moberly. Her early experience had given her insight into what collegiate life should be, and into the aims and nature of true scholarship, while her interest in girls and sympathy with them made every student look upon her as a personal friend, and her own personality and charm gave just that touch wanted for the social life of busy students.' Miss Jourdain, the Vice-Principal, 'was a very different sort of person, though equally brilliant in her own way. She was very vivacious and far more approachable than the Princ., though she had a very piercing eye which, we said, looked you through to the very holes in your stockings' (Ethel Wallace). Dorothy Hammonds' journal for 7 December 1905 humorously relates having unexpectedly to sit next to Miss Jourdain at breakfast: 'MKM [M. K. Mowell] sits in the seat of the mighty, the VP [Vice-Principal] being at the High. It is gratuitous to say that she filled her place with grace and majesty.' We are also given a glimpse of her acting as chaperon at a St John's smoking concert, 'as pleased as Punch', and roaring with laughter at a 'comic, not to say Music Hall song illustrated by a fandango and accompanied by some excellent whistling ... DMH fancies she hasn't caught the words.'

It was while Ethel Wallace was up that 'Miss Moberly and Miss Jourdain on a visit to France had their controversial ghostly experience at Versailles'. 'I am certain', she says, 'that they were perfectly genuine, whatever recent critics may say. Miss Moberly assembled the college and described the experience: how she and Miss Jourdain had both, separately and unknown to each other, seen Versailles as it was in the 18th century; seen for example a gate in the wall which was no longer there, and caught a glimpse of Marie Antoinette. They spoke with complete conviction and I cannot imagine that they would assemble the college to describe events of which they had any doubts at all.' Students were convinced of their gifts, and Beryl Beaver speaks of an elopement forestalled: 'Miss Jourdain and Miss Moberly were commonly supposed to possess second sight. Anyway, by some means they discovered that a young man was meeting a student at midnight in a certain spot in the grounds. Then they were to go to Gretna Green. So the Principal locked the girl in her room and went to meet the young man herself. I do not know whether it was Miss J. or Miss M. I do hope the latter. She was so very formidable.'

Belief in Miss Jourdain's psychic powers was firmly entrenched. The story of her vision of the College cat (to which she was allergic) sitting on her cushion in the Chapel, while she was at dinner, is related by a number of people. Another story which illustrates her powers is told by Ina Brooksbank: 'One evening we had a demonstration by a *Water Diviner*, which we found most interesting. Many of us tried the hazel twig, but the only person for whom it moved was Miss Jourdain.' Doreen Rogers thought, however, 'she was a creature of reason, and not the least mystical'. Many people attest to Miss Jourdain's musicality, and enjoyed her concerts in her drawing room. Cynthia Gamble tells us 'Miss Jourdain, a close friend of Ethyl Smythe, sometimes invited us into her study for informal singing.' She ran a musical society, which is recorded in Molly McNeil's letter of 25 February 1917. 'At 5.30 we had evensong in our chapel. It was the first time we have ever had it. Mr Cronshaw, the college chaplain, took the service, and *the musical society, taught by Miss Jourdain* [emphasis added], provided the anthem. She played hymns, and the other musical parts of the service, though we just said the Psalms. Joan Evans read the first lesson and Miss Ady the second. There was of course no sermon. It was a really delightful service. Mr Cronshaw did read the prayers so nicely, and we had several beautiful ones for soldiers and sailors.' Agnes Wayment tells us that the Prink [Miss Jourdain] held a hymn singing in her room once a week. This was a well-established custom, for Molly McNeill and a number of other students tell us this as well. There are a number of mentions of being invited to Miss Jourdain's room for a 'party'. Rosemary Volkert tells us of 'Sunday evenings we often went to Miss Jourdain's study and listened to her playing – a real pleasure. She also allowed me to

browse among her many folders of art, design and architecture.'
Molly McNeill describes a different sort of evening in great detail (5
November 1916):

> . . . I had to go to Miss Jourdain's party at 9.30. There were about a
> dozen of us and it turned out to be most enjoyable. We had a cup of
> coffee and some biscuits as soon as we went in. After that, Miss
> Jourdain showed us the most delightful postcards and engravings
> of Versailles and the Château Blois. The most interesting thing
> however was a French play that she had discovered. This last
> vacation she had been working in the British Museum on French
> Drama and she was looking up some old unimportant volume of
> short plays, when she came across one quite by accident which she
> discovered to be different from the others. It turned out to be a
> satire on the time of the French Revolution and it has got in it a
> great many new facts and opinions that haven't been known
> before. It is a most wonderful discovery. She has had it photo-
> graphed, each page of it, and she showed us the prints. It was most
> interesting. She also had some very old engravings of Paris that her
> people had brought over with them when they came from France.
> They were some of the Huguenot refugees who came over to
> England. She was telling us that there were two girls of them and a
> small brother. The two girls dressed up as sailors and put the
> brother in a barrel and so managed to escape. They came from
> Southern France. We left about 10.15, after a most enjoyable and
> instructive evening. I think it was awfully good of her to have us.

Doreen Rogers remembers Miss Jourdain's sermons as 'intellectual, and well worth listening to, and covered subjects such as
Einstein'. Some students, though, found the sermons boring – notably Dame Mary Cartwright.

Of tutors from the early years of St Hugh's, three stand out with
great clarity: Miss Ady, Miss Annie Rogers and Miss Evans. Miss
Ady was 'the "Baby don" who joined the college in my last year to
teach history. Miss Ady was very sweet, very pretty and very popular'
(Ethel Wallace). This opinion was not entirely shared by Felicia
Stallman, who describes her as 'nice, friendly, not pretty, rather
tactless, but a good scholar and a good historian in her own field'.
Molly McNeill was devoted to her, and the pages of her letters to her
mother are filled with references to Miss Ady, some of which show
the close relationship between Miss Ady and her students, past and

present. On 15 October 1916, Molly McNeill writes: 'If it wasn't for
Miss Ady, I don't know what I'd do. You'd think we had been friends
for ages and she seemed really glad to see me, and she was so nice and
sensible and kind. The poor thing was fearfully busy fixing up
people's work and she apologised for having very few wits.' On 31
January 1917: 'I was just going along the corridor when who should I
meet but Miss Ady, who wanted to know if I knew anyone who would
like her skates as she wasn't using them that afternoon. I didn't know
of anyone except myself, so I told her, and she was too sweet about it,
took me into her bedroom to see if they would fit.' On 21 January
1917: 'Eleanor Nicholas and another old third year, Muriel Holland,
are up for the weekend . . . Miss Ady is terribly excited about them.
Eleanor was a very special friend of hers . . . Miss Ady has asked me to
tea this afternoon to meet Eleanor Nicholas and Muriel Holland, isn't
that sweet of her.' Molly McNeill makes some illuminating comments about Miss Ady as a teacher: 'I am sure if I was doing the work
with anyone else I would be thoroughly depressed for I find it
frightfully hard, and Miss Ady says she is finding out how difficult it
is for me. One of my essays was "good", the other I hadn't done
enough . . . As usual Miss Ady was full of encouragement and I left
her feeling that I knew heaps more' (5 November 1916).

On another occasion she writes (10 October 1916): 'Miss Ady has
explained the whole thing. I feel ever so much clearer about it. Her
patience is almost as wonderful as her cleverness.' Molly McNeill's
other tutor was a Mr Stampa from Exeter College, and she compares
the teaching methods of her two tutors (February 1917):

I had my coaching with Mr Stampa, and he really is a terror for
work. After I'd finished reading my essay he said 'very good', but
whether he meant that the essay was good or that he was glad it was
over, I don't know. He gave me the impression that he spent the
whole hour in trying to find out exactly how much I didn't know
instead of how much I did. He is a perfect mine of information, he
seems to know the date of every possible event that took place in
English history, but all the same he seems entirely bereft of
originality and never attempts to discuss anything. That is what I
enjoy so much about Miss Ady. She is always eager to argue about
ideals and things like that, which appeals to me far more than facts.
I don't know how it is, when I'm with her she always makes me feel
quite clever, but Mr Stampa leaves me with a sense of utter
ignorance.

But she does also cast light on an adverse comment made by a later student, Doreen Rogers, who found Miss Ady 'uninterested in and not sufficiently well-versed in English history . . . I was somewhat shy and Miss Ady had nothing to say on English history and the result was an unproductive and terrible silence at tutorials.' Molly McNeill described a similar situation (22 October 1916): 'when I opened the door who should I see but Miss Ady and the Home Student sitting opposite one another apparently not speaking a word . . .' The Home Student was apparently 'just the sort of person who doesn't get on with Miss Ady for she likes you to answer questions and discuss things . . . '

Miss Annie Rogers is a jewel in St Hugh's crown. In the light of the more recent reminiscences, which are conscious only of her eccentricities, it is easy to forget how much women's education owes to her. She is a character, like Miss Gwyer later, who became legendary in her own lifetime. On her retirement in 1930, the *Chronicle* records that she 'authenticated with documents the well-known legend, hitherto deemed incredible in most quarters, of her having been offered an exhibition at Worcester College at the age of seventeen (the assumption being, it seems, that the top candidate in the "Senior Locals" list must be a promising boy)'. Dame Elizabeth Wordsworth, unable to attend a dinner in Miss Rogers' honour, sent a letter in which she wrote: 'To attempt to do justice to what we owe to Miss Rogers would be practically to write the history of Women's Education in the last half century', and with reference to one of her other 'multifarious gifts': 'If she had not been a great educationalist, she would have been a great gardener. "Si monumentum quaeris, circumspice" [If you seek for a monument, gaze around] – as was said of Sir Christopher Wren at St Paul's, and may with equal truth be said of her, and the garden at St Hugh's.'

Her merits, as a prime mover in the achievement of higher education and ultimately, degrees for women, were not, of course, the aspects which struck the students. To them she was first 'The Vampire of the AEW, the fell tyrant of the classical students, the bully of all beginners. She is a woman (?) who has brutality but not wit, force but no humour. (She has a nose)' (Dorothy Hammonds' journal, 7 November 1905): 'The classics tutor was Miss Rogers who was stout and plain and wore shabby clothes, thick boots and heavy woollen stockings. She was known as "the Rodge" and was a familiar sight in Oxford riding her bicycle' (Ethel Wallace). Her eccentric

A hurried sketch of the new Vice Principal (Miss Jourdain) at breakfast. Nov. 29, 1905.

Freeze, freeze, thou bitter sky!
Nov. 18, 1905.

Prof. de Sel.
Nov. 8, 1905.

Union Attitudes, November 30th, 1905.

From Dorothy Hammonds' Journal

clothes are a theme which recurs through the decades. A little later
Felicia Stallman describes her: 'Miss Rogers ... always used to wear
the same clothes – a long skirt, stiff shirt, and a hard felt hat, and in
the garden she wore stout boots, an old mackintosh and a kind of
trilby.' She 'had no idea of a student's appetite so when they were
invited to tea, they ate something beforehand. She became wise to
this, so when it was time to cut the cake, of which there was always
one, she would say "I'm not going to cut the cake, as I suppose you
had your tea before you came!"' (Ina Brooksbank).

Equally eccentric in matters of dress, but more flamboyantly and
with more style, was Miss Joan Evans, the Librarian.

The most dramatic member of the college was Miss Evans ... She
had been a student at St Hugh's herself and then in 1917 she
became the college Librarian with no qualifications at all apart
from her training in English, and a great love and knowledge of
books. She was very cultured, charming, but shy ... Miss Evans
wore medieval gowns and clanking chains, and owned some
remarkable jewellery – one of her other interests. (Felicia Stallman)

Molly McNeill was a student at the same time as Joan Evans, and
there are frequent mentions of her in her letters. She nearly buys a
cake-stand from her (price 2s 6d), to hand round cakes at her tea-
parties, but then decides against it; she is invited to meet an Irish
friend of Joan Evans and asked to dine at High Table; she goes for a
walk with her by the river; but the most interesting reference to her is
when she stands in for Miss Ady (who was ill) on a trip of the
Archeological Society to All Souls (February 1917):

In the afternoon the archaeological society was to be shown over
All Souls by Grant Robertson, and they were to meet at 2.30 ...
At 2.30 there was a regular bevy of womankind waiting at All Souls
lodge for 'himself'. Really college women, at any rate 'en masse',
are fearful. Miss Ady had a cold and didn't come, so the party was
in charge of Joan Evans. She had only met Grant Robertson once
before so to begin with the poor thing hadn't even a friend in the
crowd. It was awfully interesting and of course he knows every
detail of the history of the college, and he is immensely proud of it
... I was most frightfully sorry for him the whole time for there
was an awful crowd of us, and each seemed to look worse than the

other. Joan did bravely, but it was very hard for him not to have someone he knew. He was frightfully nice though and took no end of trouble to show us everything. All Souls is a gem among the colleges of course.

Miss Kirkaldy, the 'Kirk', receives an affectionate tribute from her pupil, Miss Wallace: 'a dour, old Scot, a tall thin, bony woman with a sense of humour, who eventually committed suicide. She lived in one of the very old higgeldy-piggeldy houses in Holywell over a coach house . . . I am indebted to her for more than my knowledge of zoo [logy], for her guidance, advice and care which made of me something more than a callow girl', and Ina Brooksbank remembers Miss Wardale: 'Dear, gentle Miss Wardale was my English Tutor, and wore her hat when she invited students to tea. I was much surprised to learn that she had written a book on how to tell character from ears.'

Miss Wardale, who was to be appointed to lecture for the Medieval and Modern Languages Faculty of the University in Hilary Term, 1914, recalls that in her time (from 1888) 'comparatively few lectures were open to women. Indeed in English and Modern Languages the difficulty was not to choose between lectures and tutors, but to find any.' And in 1908, this aspect of academic life is borne out by Ethel Wallace's experience. She had intended to read Botany at Oxford, but to her 'dismay and disappointment' found when she got there that 'old professor Vines was strongly opposed to women students and would tolerate only women who were quite certain of a First Class'. Miss Kirkaldy thought that, in the circumstances, it would be better to choose Zoology. During the war there were fewer problems, but with the return of the service men, while some lecturers and tutors took pains to accommodate all their students, other, more misogynistic lecturers reverted to their prejudices. 'When we returned to Oxford in January 1919, the University was a changed place. . . Dr Wright's English class, where instead of 3 there were 12 men students . . . We sped off to our lecture with Professor Raleigh at Magdalen, to find the Hall filled with men: all the seats were taken, some women stood, some sat on the floor. Professor Raleigh at once dismissed us until he could find better accommodation' but one History don 'dealt with the problem more speedily by announcing that he did not give his lecture to women, so the women had to walk out. Some male coaches refused to coach women again' (Ina Brooksbank).

Professor Raleigh receives several tributes: 'I remember best Sir

Walter Raleigh's lectures' (Ethel Wilson); 'I remember his unfailing courtesy, a worthy successor to his famous ancestor' (Ina Brooksbank); Ethel Strong says that he was 'beloved of all'. Miss Brooksbank recalls Professor Wright's 'lectures and classes on Gothic and Old English. He was a Yorkshireman who taught himself to read at 18, not having been to school for a whole day in his life . . . He and his wife had students to tea every Sunday, and I went several times. He amused himself by speaking in dialect to me . . . He used to take his Aberdeen terrier to classes, where it would sit under the table and chew my shoe laces. He was a great and lovable man.' Both Ina Brooksbank and Ethel Wilson had one term's coaching with J. R. R. Tolkien, but neither was particularly impressed. Ina Brooksbank also attended some lectures outside her own School: ' . . . Dr Montessori, and one on Einstein by Professor Turner, with lantern slides! I went to the Romanes lecture by Mr Asquith in June, 1918. It had been suspended in 1917. The Sheldonian theatre which as you will know, holds 3,000 people, was crowded.'

In Dorothy Hammonds' day, Professor de Selincourt was one of the most popular lecturers. She herself, though, is not madly enthusiastic! 'DMH *did* hear a lecture by Prof. de Sel. which wasn't bad, but what is such news as this among the possibilities of Varsity Life?' (Journal, 8 November 1905).

Molly McNeill is constantly referring to History lectures from Grant Robertson at All Souls: 'an excellent lecture at All Souls when G. Robertson excelled himself. He was also very humorous in parts. I don't know what Oxford would do without him.' Another student to remember Grant Robertson particularly is Dorothy Parr, whose name is linked with Molly McNeill's in another context, when they both decided that they must invite Mr Stampa of Exeter, their tutor, to tea. There is an amusing sequence in Molly McNeill's letters which reads thus: 'Dorothy Parr and I have just come to the conclusion that we'll have to ask Mr Stampa to tea this term, it will be rather awful' (25 January 1917); 'Dorothy Parr has asked Miss Jourdain if we can have Mr Stampa to tea on Tuesday, so he is really going to be asked, it's the sort of thing that won't get any easier by putting it off' (30 January 1917); 'Yesterday, I wrote the fatal note to Mr Stampa. I wonder if he will come' (1 February 1917); 'Mr Stampa is coming! This morning I got a very neat note saying he had great pleasure in accepting our kind invitation. I think that will be an occasion worthy of the fruit cake. We want to try and give him a good tea. I think a great pity of him living with a housekeeper and he feels the cold dreadfully' (2

February 1917). Alas! the letter recounting the tea party is missing, and sadly, Dorothy Parr cannot remember the outcome.

If Miss Brooksbank is representative, the students were most conscientious and disciplined in their work habits. She writes that: 'I did as much work as possible between breakfast and lunch with interruptions for lectures and coachings and again from 4 pm to 7 pm when we changed for dinner, and I sometimes got in an hour after dinner.' Certainly no one mentions the phenomenon of the 'essay crisis' or late-night working sessions.

This is certainly the pattern adhered to by Dorothy Hammonds and her contemporaries, by Molly McNeill (who also liked to take Saturdays off) and by Margaret Chilton, who writes: 'Work in morning, play in afternoon, work again when necessary.' Many students appear to have worked in the evening, unless there were some form of entertainment after dinner, and in view of the early hour students had to be back in College in the evening, and the shortage of chaperons, there frequently was. Unlike later generations, these earliest St Hugh's students relied a great deal for friendship and social contact upon events taking place in college – from Dorothy Hammonds' 'Sociables', story-telling and charades, to Ina Brooksbank's enormous garden party for 800 people in June 1919, to which Dr Bridges, the Poet Laureate, came and chatted with all the students. A perennial favourite was All Hallowe'en. Dorothy Hammonds' journal describes apple-bobbing, raisin-digging, chestnut-roasting, cake-cutting and story-telling (31 October 1905). Phyllis Davies remembers: 'We had a sort of Hallow'een party – with fireworks. We were all sitting there waving sparklers when Cecily Chorlton leapt up in flames – her cushion was on fire.' Molly McNeill attended a College fancy dress dance (see Appendix IV).

In a life that was hedged about with rules and regulations, 'the tea party', asking someone to tea, or going out to tea, was the main social event in most students' lives. Dorothy Hammonds' journal relates that there was 'an undergraduates' tea [in Dorothy Hammonds' day undergraduates were men, girls were students] in the garden of the House . . . the men were five in number, the girls seven, and all went merry as a marriage bell. They stayed till nearly six-thirty and then departed most reluctant – we have all agreed it shall not be the last of this type of entertainment!'

Molly McNeill derived a great deal of pleasure by going out to tea with various Irish Oxford ladies who kindly asked her, and in having people to tea. The provender was usually provided by generous parcels of cake and biscuits sent from home in Belfast. Here is a typical account of a visit by Miss Armstrong, a student from St Hilda's: 'Well, I got a lovely tea for Miss Armstrong. The spice biscuits, ginger cake, birthday cake all from home. Then I had the buns and the 1d cakes. She arrived punctually at four, and we started almost at once. The food at St Hilda's is wretched, so we both ate a grand hearty tea. I did enjoy the things you sent me. The ginger cake was excellent, it did me good to be tasting it again, and the spice biscuits too. We each had a piece of everything and several cups of tea. I'm beginning to think I'm getting quite good at afternoon teas.' The rules governing young men, or indeed men of any sort, coming to tea were stringent. To quote from the *Regulations* for 1919: 'All tea parties including men must be given in a common room or the garden by leave of the Principal. Parties on the river including men must be chaperoned and leave obtained from the Principal. A student may entertain her father or brother in her room, but if she is inviting friends to meet her brother, the party must be given in a common room.' Ina Brooksbank describes how she was at a loss because, although her brother could have tea, his friend couldn't. Joan Evans came to the rescue: 'Miss Joan Evans lent me her sitting room.' However, Dorothy Hammonds and her friend were allowed to go to Professor de Selincourt's for dinner with no chaperon (1906). Students were allowed to ask lady guests to dinner, and the custom seems to have been that the student with her guest sat at High Table. Molly McNeill describes a visit of her aunt: 'I took her down to the Common Room and I introduced her to Miss Jourdain, and then we all went in to dinner. It was most imposing, me following in the wake of all the dons up to the "high". Aunt Ina sat on Miss Jourdain's right, me on her left. We got on splendidly. Miss Jourdain talked very interestingly to Aunt Ina and seemed very interested to meet her. Aunt Ina enjoyed it thoroughly'(27 May 1917).

Cocoa parties formed a very significant part of College life, and appear to have been governed by strict protocol. Molly McNeill refers to 'the dreadful class distinctions'. This meant that 'a fresher might not invite a second year to a cocoa party in her first term' (Ina Brooksbank), but Ethel Wilson went as far as to say that 'a member of the first year could not be friends with a member of the 2nd or 3rd years, and if two people from different years were friends, they had to disguise it, and never be caught in each other's rooms'. 'The members of the three years didn't mix freely. They kept their own tables as a rule, and one sometimes felt to be an intruder if one found oneself in the wrong place' (Ina Brooksbank). Phyllis Deards recalls that in 1921, three or four freshers were invited by third years 'early on in the First Term'. Margaret Chilton remembers that there were 'cocoa parties, in which freshers were invited by 2nd or 3rd year students and often "scalped" (not called "Miss" any more, and allowed to use Christian name to scalper).' Molly McNeill describes a similar incident:

> A knock came at the door, and in came Mary Richards. She is a 3rd year history, and had been very kind to me all along ... I was always as friendly to her as I could be, knowing the dreadful class distinctions I didn't want to be presuming ... Going away, she said she thought she knew me well enough to call me Molly. Think of that — a third year, first of all actually coming and spending over an hour with a 'fresher' and then proposing to call her by her Christian name! (5 March 1916)

Ida Moberly calls the cocoa parties 'a very helpful institution, given by 2nd and 3rd year students to help the freshers along'. Dorothy Hammonds' journal, giving a second year view, states 'Two freshers more ticked off our account. We gave them good tea and good company' (8 November 1905).

Any visitors coming to see a student were first shown into the drawing room, the student was then fetched by the maid. Molly McNeill writes: ' ... I was just settling down to work, when I hear a knock, and in comes the maid with a card from Miss Maunsell who was down in the drawing room. I had not the faintest notion who this lady might be, but I'm getting quite used to these visitors now, so after giving myself a hasty brush up, I went down' (February 1917).

Ethel Wallace says: 'Even by Victorian standards, St Hugh's was strict and pernickety in its rules. To cross the road from one house to the other, one had to wear a hat and one was kept in the hall for the purpose in case you had forgotten yours.' 'The basic premise of the rules appeared to be that any young man, however well brought up, was a potential wolf: no young lady was allowed to go out with a young man or to entertain a young man alone in her very uninviting and uncomfortable bed-sit and certainly not to go to a man's room without a chaperon. A chaperon could be any married woman however young (and however irresponsible) or any senior member of the University' (Felicia Stallman). It was, however, 'only entertainments in the company of young men that were considered dangerous.

We were free to come and go in Oxford as we wished in the company of girl friends or on our bikes.' For some time, Miss Wardale recalls, 'we gave a mixed dance every three years, and we were the only Hall to do this, though members of all the others danced among themselves a good deal. One of Miss Moberly's many gifts was for playing dance music, and her piano was our entire band!' Margaret Westlake however, remembers that 'we were allowed to have dances, but of course not with men. I remember I decided to put on trousers and at once to my amusement the girls were delighted to dance with me!' A little later in the decade: 'Dances ended at 11 pm sharp when Miss Jourdain rang the dinner bell for the gentlemen to go' (Ethel Strong). After outside entertainments 'We were obliged to be back in College by ten o'clock . . . I never thought of being out late' (Ethel Wallace). Yet Laetitia Edwards writes: 'We applied for and were readily given late leave for Bach Choir rehearsals and concerts', and Katharine Dawson remembers 'climbing over the fence (not a difficult feat at the time) and meeting Miss Ady as I made my way back to college. Miss Ady said she supposed I proposed to climb in through somebody's window and instead used her own key to let me in.'

The rules affected the social lives of St Hugh's students in, for example, the segregation at the theatre: 'Male undergraduates went to the stalls but female ditto had to go to the gallery' (Ethel Wilson). This rule also applied in St Barnabas Church. Or again, in the Union, 'Women were not allowed in the Union except in the Gallery . . . ' 'College used to receive two tickets, plus one for a chaperon, but it meant that few people made more than one or two visits. I went in February, 1920, when the motion was the nationalisation of the coal mines. I don't know who was the President, but I remember hearing Beverley Nichols and Hore Belisha' (Ina Brooksbank). G. K. Chesterton spoke against divorce and several contributors remember attending this debate, among them Ethel Wilson and Margaret Hirst. Dorothy Hammonds and her friend seem to be more fortunate in 1905. They recount in the journal for 16 November 1905, 'An awful rumour reached us that there was no chaperon handy, and therefore no Union for us. Now we had tickets, and we wanted to go. However, E. J. [Eleanor Jourdain] arrives with the welcome news that we may dare "unchaperoned and gaze" upon the members of the school for British Statesmen.' They conclude somewhat tartly after they have been: ' . . . if the speakers of tonight are England's embryo statesmen, the prospects of the country are small indeed'.

In relation to the theatre, they may either have been more daring (or less tightly controlled) than their successors, for they recount: '. . . a party of six friends to attend the theatre. Supped off poached eggs at 6.45, scuttled out of the front door with stealth at 7, reached theatre at 7.15, got in early door by paying your extra sixpence, saw Martin Harvey it is true, but never a sign of a chaperon.' But for Ina Brooksbank,

> unless one was prepared to invite and pay for a ticket for chaperon, one had to be contented with a matinée, when we were allowed to sit only in the gallery which cost one shilling. We saw Fred Terry and Julia Neilson in *The Scarlet Pimpernel* and later in *Henry of Navarre*. We thought Julia Neilson overacted very much. We also saw Martin Harvey. Of comedies we saw *Charlie's Aunt* and *I killed the Count*. When the Carl Rosa Opera Company came we saw *Carmen* and *The Tales of Hoffman*. Our theatre secretary waited in a queue from 9 am to 3.30 pm for tickets. Before the war the undergraduates used to send a scout down at night to be first in the queue in the morning, when they brought him buns and coffee down for his breakfast.

The most notable OUDS production of the end of the decade was *The Dynasts* by Thomas Hardy at which the playwright was present. OUDS was not open to women students, but employed professional actresses. For those women who were interested in acting there was a flourishing tradition of college drama: '. . . each second year had to do a play – we did *The Importance of Being Ernest* in which I was Ernest with a most unsuitable plump figure' (Ethel Wilson); 'We . . . did *She Stoops to Conquer* in which I was Tony Lumpkin and *The Importance of Being Ernest* in which I was Canon Chasuble' (Margaret Hirst); 'St Hugh's usually put on a show of some kind for St Hugh's Day. In my first year it was a violent melodrama, in the middle of which the common room table collapsed because so many people were sitting on it. In one student play great excitement was caused when the hero stabbed his sword through the electric light' (Ina Brooksbank).

There was also interest in plays done by other women's colleges. Dorothy Hammonds' journal for 14 November 1905 describes a performance given by the Home Students of *She Stoops to Conquer*. 'They admitted none of the male sex *except*, and this seems to us to be drawing rather a fine distinction, except those who have reached the supreme position of *grandfather*. We sorrow to relate that out of a packed assembly only three lone grandfathers could be mustered.' She did not like the performance.

Molly McNeill becomes almost incoherent in her appreciation of *Arms and the Man*, by Bernard Shaw.

> After tea, I went down to St Hilda's with Dorothy Parr and Hilda Wood to see a play which they had got up. It was called *Men and the Arms* by Bernard Shaw, so it was really instructive. It really was the best amateur acting I have ever seen, really wonderful. There were only seven characters and they each one just suited their parts perfectly. It was very funny recognising girls who come to lectures with me . . . It was terribly melodramatic, and a modern kind of thing and they did it frightfully well. I was just sitting breathless for the next thing to happen. They had a collection in aid of the Prisoners of War Fund. (18 February 1917)

She also relates how the French students from Somerville came to St Hugh's, and with their opposite numbers from St Hugh's, staged some charades in French. 'It was the funniest thing' (November 1916).

St Hugh's attachment to the choirs of Oxford, and in particular the Bach Choir under its conductor Sir Hugh Allen, is documented from this period and many of the students attended Evensong in other chapels, especially New College and Magdalen 'which was candlelit' (Ina Brooksbank). Molly McNeill describes a service at Magdalen:

> Then we went straight . . . to Magdalen Chapel. I had asked Mr Stampa for an order for two of us. The service was *lovely*, such singing I never heard. We had two delightful seats with lovely cushions to kneel on, and a crimson cushion on the book board in front, with a great big prayer book, about the size of a family bible. There were several undergraduates there whom I knew by sight and a great many dons. There was one chorister with a heavenly voice and face to match it, just beautiful, and you could hear him above all others. We did enjoy it – I just was thinking of all the hundreds of men who have worshipped in that place, down to our own Prince of Wales. It is a great privilege to get in and a tremendous treat. (27 May 1917)

Molly McNeill was a very religious girl, and her letters are full of descriptions of services she has been to, and sermons she has heard. Particularly interesting is the information: 'Last night in chapel Miss Jourdain said there were going to be several meetings this term for women students as a sort of continuation of the National Mission. The Bishop of Oxford is to address one of them' (21 January 1917). She attended all the meetings, as well as a special 'intercession meeting for all women students in the Cathedral' held at the end of the previous term. The Church Missions to Oxford form a major part of undergraduate religious life, through all the decades.

There are references to a few societies: the Archaeological Society 'which explored many of the colleges and the castle. We traced the old town walls. Miss Evans took us on a most interesting tour of the Ashmolean with special reference to the discoveries her brother (Sir Arthur Evans) had made and the material he had brought home' (Ina Brooksbank); and the Literary Society, 'I was secretary ... and through my brother secured W. B. Yeats to come and talk to us' (Ethel Strong).

'There were facilities for sports, two or three tennis courts, a hockey team etc., but the only sport in which I indulged was rowing. No-one was allowed to take out a boat until they could swim and I was taught to do so in the Merton Street Baths: a small public baths which was open for ladies once or twice a week. One had to be able to swim fifty feet to be allowed to take out a sculler and fifty yards for a punt' (Ethel Wallace). Most students went on the river during their time at Oxford, in canoes, punts or sculls. The *Regulations* stipulated that 'in the case of those students wishing to boat, leave from a doctor to swim in cold water must be included (in the medical certificate of sufficient health required by the college for each student) and students must pass the swimming test required by boat club rules'. 'I enjoyed several picnics on the river and learned to punt without falling in. I could not get a doctor's certificate, nor pass the Boat Club's regulations for canoeing' (Ina Brooksbank). Margaret Haig fell in the river and with splendid insouciance 'put on a mackintosh we happened to have and dried my clothes on the bushes while we had our picnic!' Alice Peters relates, 'On May morning, pulled another student out of the river, who slipped getting out of a canoe.' Margaret Chilton descibes how 'One could pass a test and become a "sculling half captain" and then take out a boat with other half-captains. After another test, a full captain could take out a boat without any others. This applied to sculling boats, punts and canoes.' Another anonymous Senior Member, up in 1921, recounts that she and a friend had their 'own canoe and we were on the river all the year round'. The photographic records of the time show students reclining gracefully on the river bank in their long skirts and hats, with all the studied elegance demanded by Edwardian photography.

Lacrosse was in its infancy in the University, but Molly McNeill reports: 'There was a short meeting of the lacrosse club on Sunday when it was decided that it would be much better for people to wear tunics, isn't that good? The only objection is that the Principal of Lady Margaret Hall doesn't like them, but perhaps she will give in. You see all the women's colleges play together.' Ina Brooksbank played hockey, tennis and cricket and, when in 1919 an Oxford women's cricket team was formed, was a bowler ' . . . and perhaps at the age of 85 I may be allowed to boast that in local matches I took 4, 6 and 7 wickets. We bowled underarm, but the 1919–20 newcomers bowled overarm and appeared truly formidable . . . On the river and for cricket and tennis, white was always worn . . . we alway wore hats in the street as we had no academic dress.' Molly McNeill records skating on a frozen Port Meadow (30 January 1917).

Oxford was still almost exclusively a university town, but just on the brink of its industrial development and the bicycle was the main form of undergraduate transport: 'Mr Morris, later Lord Nuffield, was just beginning to transform the village of Cowley into a town full of workmen and their families, and the pavements were not yet crowded with household shoppers, and the multiple shops had not yet begun to creep down the Cornmarket . . . There was no litter problem . . . I had never seen so many bicycles in my life' (Ina Brooksbank). 'I was fascinated by the beautiful spires and colleges of Oxford and went in a small horse-drawn carriage which was just going out of fashion then. Undergraduates mostly went about on bicycles' (Margaret Westlake).

Florence Wyld, who matriculated in 1898, writing in the *Chronicle* in 1967 says:

> On one occasion, I had no money for my railway fare home, I sent my luggage by Pickfords', and I rode home on my bicycle – eighty miles. I had to ride over Salisbury Plain; there were no proper roads; just dust tracks; there were no indications showing which track to take, and you did not meet anybody for miles and miles . . . There were no cars; we went everywhere on our bicycles – if they wanted mending, or needed new nuts and bolts, we went to a little shop run by a young man with stubbly hair which stood straight

up. He did our small repairs for us . . . and his name was William Morris.

The students were not bound to Oxford by the rules, and were able to explore on bicycles 'the Oxford countryside and Woodstock, Dorchester, Bablock Hythe and all the places mentioned in *The Scholar Gypsy*' (Margaret Hirst). 'Sometimes we went to churches, Iffley, Dorchester; houses like Blenheim, villages like Bablock Hythe which was very pretty . . . Hinksey and Wolvercote . . . I found the flat country rather uninteresting after our Yorkshire hills and in one letter [home] I wrote "I'm going to Cumnor next week. I hear they've got a hill and I want to see it"' (Ina Brooksbank). From Molly McNeill we get a very full account of a walk to Wytham, passing an army camp and an aerodrome (see Appendix IV).

The war barely impinges on the pages of the *Chronicle*. It is noted that finances are strained, but that the number of students is still increasing rapidly. The College was designed for 70; by 1923, Miss Rogers informs us in her 'Historical Reminiscences', 'the number had risen to 150'. The *Chronicle* of 1916–17 acknowledges that 'The energy shewn by past and present members of the College in national work and war work of various kinds is most gratifying', and records that the 'Council has regretted the unavoidable absence for reasons of National Service of many of its members', and that of 1918–19 welcomes peace and looks forward to the return of the Council from war work. During the war, Miss Jourdain, the Principal, worked for the government, translating important documents, while continuing her other duties.

The women's lives were sheltered, but not to the exclusion of all reality. Although there are no political comments on the war or events of the period, and no outspoken suffragettes among the contributors (although the *Chronicle* for 1903–4 does mention a Miss Crick who had recently gone down as 'acting temporarily as secretary to Mrs Sidney Webb'), the effects of the war are clearly felt. Ethel Wallace was 'too involved in her work and in the delights of Oxford to be much aware of impending war: no-one really believed it was possible'. However, when war did come: '. . . the best college men enlisted for King and Country . . . and only foreign students remained' (Margaret Westlake); 'There were only three men at our English Classes and lectures – one was obviously unfit for the army, one had a wounded arm, and one had lost a leg . . . Some of us answered an appeal from the Churchill Hospital to take out wounded soldiers in wheeled chairs in the afternoons, and several students went regularly to Didcot to roll bandages' (Ina Brooksbank).

It is from Ina Brooksbank and Molly McNeill's letters that we get the clearest pictures of Oxford at war from the woman student's eye: 'I heard that Sir John French . . . had been inspecting some of the troops in the Parks today' (Molly McNeill, 5 November 1916); 'There were a great many wounded soldiers in Church today' (5 November 1916). 'This afternoon, the Master of Balliol [A. L. Smith] was talking about the awful loss of men in Oxford and Cambridge. Balliol College alone has lost more than ⅛ of the men she had in 1914' (10 October 1916). 'After dinner we had the first meeting of our work party. We are sewing shirts of butter-muslin for soldiers. They are steeped in some kind of disinfectant and then they are a protection against all kinds of vermin' (1 February 1917). 'Two aeroplanes are just passing. Yesterday I saw four altogether and the day before there were three flying over the town. There seem to be more than ever, and Oxford is simply full of soldiers of all sorts, though mostly cadets . . . Hilda Wood was saying that some time in February all boys over 18 are to be called up for Home defence' (28 January 1917).

Ina Brooksbank describes the aeroplanes:

Port Meadow was full of flimsy aeroplanes made of wire and matchwood, with, a fact this, wings of varnished linen, in which these men, who impeded our passage down the High [by marching across the road], were training to risk their lives . . . The city was full of soldiers, billeted in the men's colleges, Oriel being, I think, the only one unclaimed by the military. That was because it was the only men's college with baths, and that was occupied by the women of Somerville. Other Somerville women were in college lodgings near Pembroke, and many of them never lived in their own building, which had been taken over as a hospital . . .

Most sadly, the young man Molly McNeill was in love with was killed, in May 1917.

At College, the students suffered the domestic effects of war:

It was during the war and food was scare. Rationing had been introduced too late and unlike the second world war, the food which was available did not provide a balanced diet. I remember the unappetising yellow bread with a scraping of marge, the 2oz of butter which was our ration for the week, the sequence of inadequate meals. It was a time when to have a sardine was a red letter day! . . . One of the best sources of nourishment – not to be laughed at when you are being slowly starved – were the cocoa parties, accompanied by Captain's biscuits which were as hard as nails but quite filling. (Felicia Stallman)

. . . there were meatless days and rarely whole meat – it was usually mixed with something else . . . We had a meat mould at dinner which was called Jim Bailey, and a currant suet pudding at lunch which we irreligiously christened from the hymn 'Solid Joy' . . . The hall at college tea looked like an orphanage. There would be crockery, a teapot of tea, a jug of milk, a loaf of bread on a board and a knife. We had to take our own butter and sugar; jam if we had any. (Ina Brooksbank)

A very accurate idea of the typical menu is also given us by Miss Brooksbank: 'For breakfast there was always porridge, and egg dish, or sausages or boiled ham, or fishcake; for lunch, two choices of pudding and always some fruit; for dinner, soup, choice of second course, a rather light third course, and fruit for dessert.' Fairly substantial one would think, but Molly McNeill is always wailing pathetically how 'famished' or 'ravenous' she is! 'This morning I was so hungry I had to go out and buy a loaf and 2 oz of butter . . . it was standard bread I got. I made myself a really substantial lunch of Bovril and bread and butter' (16 February 1917). She is sustained by parcels from home. Ina Brooksbank also describes going to the Buttery on Sunday mornings to collect a 'half ration of butter and sugar, College keeping the other half for cooking'.

Food does seem to be a main item of expenditure in many people's reminiscences from this period, and Molly McNeill says: 'There is less food this term and more people . . .' (17 October 1916). But, despite the scarcity (and for some, the unappetising nature) of the food, the formalities had to be preserved: 'We had to dress up for our evening meal, and helped ourselves from the heated sideboard' (Margaret Westlake). But not only food is scarce. The lighting is turned off at 11 p.m. and Mary Wait remembers writing her essays by candlelight.

There was little heating. Coke was short in 1916, so 'We aren't to have any hot pipes this term except on the coldest days' (Molly McNeill, 17 October 1916). Many people complain about the cold in College, even in Dorothy Hammonds' day, long before the war:

This is the coldest morning we have spent as yet. Driven from our room by the depth of the temperature, driven from the common room by Kenney, we resorted to the Drawing, so called! There we found a gibbering company shivering round a fire which is being encouraged by a newspaper. MKM and DMH try to defy the elements by hustling together on the bed (sofa so called) wrapt in sundry blankets. We did not get warm, neither did we get through any work. (18 November 1905)

Margaret Hirst lay 'in a hot bath with my books on the bath rack trying to get warm', as did Molly McNeill's friend, Frances Savory, in January 1917. Molly McNeill herself used to retire to bed to work. The fires that students did have in their rooms, coal permitting, were greatly appreciated. Molly McNeill is always talking about her fire, and Phyllis Deards tells us: 'One pleasant memory was of lying in bed in the flickering light of a dying fire: each room had an open fire, which had to be cleaned and coal scuttles carried up daily by servants.' 'Those nice maids, brought hot water to our rooms in the mornings and laid fires with sticks and paper and coal – and how cold Oxford was in the Winter' (Frances Crossfield). Coal was rationed to two or three buckets a week, so the evening cocoa parties had a practical as well as a social significance – the coal went further.

Margaret Westlake recalls the anxiety caused by the blackout, and Miss Brooksbank describes an incident which brought the war as close to Oxford as it ever came:

During an ordinary dance in aid of Christian Union on the first Friday of term, all the lights went out. We were all sitting at the time and laughed, but in a few minutes the Fire Captain, who had been washing her hair, arrived to tell us all to go to the Common Room because a Zeppelin had been sighted over Oxford. We groped our way to the JCR and sat down, some under the table, most on the floor. Then someone found a book and read aloud to us by firelight.

A full account of an air-alert is to be found in Molly McNeill's letter for 5 March 1916 (see Appendix IV).

Descriptions of Armistice Day manage to capture both the exuberance of the undergraduates and the apparent aloofness of the Principal, tutors and lecturers: 'On that Monday morning of 11th November, 1918, we expected to hear news by 12 am ... About half way through the lecture we heard cheering and church bells ringing. Professor Raleigh said "Is that outside? I suppose the news is beginning to get about. I understand the armistice has been signed". Then he went on with his lecture . . .' (Ina Brooksbank). 'We were listening to [Miss Rogers] translating when the bells began to ring because the Armistice was signed. She wouldn't stop! At last we were freed and went and stood at Carfax listening to the bells and ringing our own bike bells' (Margaret Chilton).

> Everyone seemed to have brought flags, and penny trumpets and rattles. The undergraduates took charge of every vehicle that came along, from milk carts to motor cars. They crowded onto these and drove around the town in triumphal procession, waving flags and shouting at the top of their voices. Hurdy-gurdies were commandeered to add to the noise. The men climbed up the lamp posts, planting flags on top, or using them as platforms for street oratory . . . Miss Jourdain was very angry and gave a short sermon on the dignity of women students. (Ina Brooksbank)

The Principal's reaction is uncannily echoed in Miss Gwyer's own attempts to restrain the celebrations on VE Day twenty-seven years later. So too is Miss Stallman's observation on the effect of the war on the men who returned to continue their courses, typified by the new quality in the Union debates: 'The debates were first class when the men returned, older and more experienced than any ordinary undergraduates.'

Debating was a subject in which the 'young ladies of St Hugh's' took a deep interest. As well as holding regular debates with other women's colleges, they had within College the custom called 'Sharp Practice' (which so interested Clara Mordan). A number of students write about it. Dorothy Hammonds' journal is full of references to debates, Ina Brooksbank says that the debating society was 'compulsory attendance for the first years'. From Molly McNeill, there is a full description of the custom, as she describes it to her mother on 5 March 1916:

> After dinner we had the debate. I don't know if I ever told you that every Saturday night there is a debate. Some times there are set speeches and other times one of the girls goes round with a little pot [containing marked pieces of paper] and you draw, and whoever gets a piece of paper with a cross on it has to speak. There

are two speeches, one for and one against. Last night the motion
was 'Is capital punishment necessary in the present state of
civilization?' or something like that. So far I have never drawn the
cross, but Miss Wood has twice, last night and once before. She
spoke against it. I was for. After the two speeches then anyone can
get up. The point of the thing is to train people to speak without
preparation. Last night the debate was very good though before it I
thought the subject would be much too difficult, but people took it
quite seriously. Miss Ady made one or two good points. Miss
Jourdain never comes. The motion was carried by 17 to 16 votes, it
was a very good debate, but sometimes they are very stupid. For
instance last week it was 'That it would be nicer to live in pre-
historic times'. I think it's pure nonsense debating on that. [Other
debate titles included: 'A trade war after the war with Germany
would be wrong', 'That in the opinion of this house residential
buildings should not have been built within 3 miles of Oxford']

On 28 January 1917, she adds a little more information about the
whole custom:

After dinner we had a debate. I told you I was elected 'Up and
Down Girl'. That means that I have to see that the first years get the
chairs in their proper places and to count the votes. There is a
president and a secretary and I sit beside them. It's like this

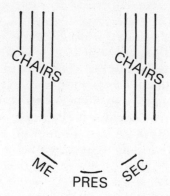

The debate was a very good one. The subject was that the
characteristics of which England is most proud are those which are
most dangerous to her. The proposer made a very good speech,
and it was rather difficult . . .

Inevitably, after the war there were changes, some minor and some of importance. From the granting of the franchise to women in 1918, for example, to the bobs and short skirts of the 1920s: 'In October 1919 two students returned with bobbed hair, one from choice, the other because she had been ill. The Principal advised the second to grow it again, the other was made to understand that the style was not approved, but more bobs arrived by degrees and then the "shingle"' (Ina Brooksbank). The most important development, in terms of the history of St Hugh's and of women's education was, of course, the granting of degrees to women, the culmination of a campaign begun by the Association for the Education of Women in Oxford in 1895. In Miss Rogers' words:

> In 1918 qualified women received the Parliamentary franchise, in 1920 the five Women's Societies obtained the right to present their students for matriculation and grad[u]ation. The Statute was passed with very little opposition and conferred privileges much greater than those originally suggested, or granted to women at Cambridge. Its success was no doubt an outcome of the War and the consequent political enfranchisement of women ... The examination already passed and the residence already kept were accepted, and on October 14th, 1920, women of the five Societies ... appeared in the Sheldonian Theatre to take their degree ...

Admission to the University did not make a great deal of difference to the student, Miss Rogers suggests, she 'had to pay more and to observe more rules, but she could feel that she really belonged to Oxford and Oxford to her ...' Certainly, it appeared to be of importance to, for example, Ethel Wallace: 'I went up to Oxford to get my degree on May 21st [1921] with some of the first women to receive them. How proud we were as we disported ourselves in our BA and MA gowns and hoods.' A fitting conclusion to the decade.

The euphoria evoked by the granting of degrees might have encouraged a stricter enforcement of the rules and regulations, as suggested by Phyllis Davies: 'Women undergraduates, only just admitted to full membership of the University, were expected to behave impeccably.' Ida Moberly recounts how Miss Jourdain made them rehearse for the ceremony of Matriculation, 'for she said that on our behaviour depended our survival as members of the University'. But it did not prevent the occurrence of the rift among the Senior Members which seriously embarrassed the College in 1923–4. After the expiration of the term of three years for which Miss Ady had been appointed tutor in Modern History, her appointment was not renewed. In protest, six members of Council and five tutors resigned. The 'unfortunate controversy which arose as a consequence of these events' might have done irreparable harm to the College, and did indeed disrupt the academic lives of those undergraduates up at the time, but at the request of the Council, the Chancellor of the University agreed to hold an enquiry which recommended the constitutional reforms discussed in the previous chapters of this book, including making provision for a Visitor. Lord Curzon's report in the *Oxford University Gazette* of 2 April 1924 mentions that 'for some time past relations between the Principal and . . . Miss Ady, have been inharmonious', but while he impugns the good faith of neither party, he exonerates Miss Ady from all imputations, written or verbal, and from any responsibility for the boycott against the College by the other women's tutors, and at the same time leaves it to the Council 'to consider what constitutional reforms are desirable' to secure 'a more defined and harmonious co-ordination among the College authorities' and whether 'such reforms should be accompanied by changes in personnel'. Miss Jourdain died suddenly, of heart failure, four days after the publication of the *Gazette*. She was succeeded temporarily by Miss M. E. Robertson, of Newnham College, Cambridge, and from Michaelmas 1924, by Miss B. E. Gwyer. From the reminiscences, it would appear that with Miss Gwyer's advent the turmoil abated almost immediately.

Those who were up in 1923–4 (or just before or after) nearly all make some reference to the 'Row'. Doreen Rogers admits: 'I may have unwittingly contributed to the so-called scandal . . . I went to Miss Jourdain to ask if it would be possible to change my tutor [Miss Ady], adding, I'm afraid, fuel to the fire of Miss Jourdain's personal dislike of Miss Ady.' Dame Mary Cartwright 'had the impression that Miss Jourdain was frightened of not being able to control things. After all things were changing, numbers growing and students less docile, and I don't think she had any idea how to adapt, but I have no real grounds for saying this . . .' Agnes Wayment 'admired both women for their different gifts and was very sad at the conflict between them'. Miss Ady was generally popular, she was 'always helpful, especially in my change of Schools (from science to history)'. 'My most vividly remembered tutorials are those with Miss – later Dr – Ady, in the friendly atmosphere of 40 St Margaret's Road. Besides making the people of medieval England and 14th century

Florence (for Dante Special) come alive, she was always interested in her pupils as people' (Lilian Sprules). A rather different picture from that drawn by Doreen Rogers. She was in demand as a chaperon, because she was nearer in age to the undergraduates than many dons, and she was 'extremely hospitable'. Margaret Field, for example, writes: 'I was taken out in Miss Ady's car frequently – fortunately there was not so much on the roads in those days, as she had a habit of taking her hands off the wheel and turning to speak to the passengers in the back.' She did not always preserve the distance which most tutors think necessary: Phyllis Davies recalls Miss Ady one evening attempting to fasten 'an endless row of tiny buttons' down the back of her dress with the aid of a long mirror on the landing. 'I did them up for her and this ritual was repeated every evening before dinner.' Certainly, it is recorded that her non-reappointment aroused strong feelings among the undergraduates: 'Miss Jourdain was very autocratic and she refused to renew the appointment of Miss Ady. This action stunned not only the college, but the whole university and strong views were expressed on both sides. We had many meetings of the JCR and most people sympathised with Miss Ady' (Agnes Wayment). For the other side Rosemary Volkert writes: 'I hated the way that Miss Jourdain, a gifted and brilliant scholar ... was hounded – I have no other word for it – at a JCR meeting.' Ruth Dean, an American student, was puzzled by the situation. 'Having come from USA where colleges and universities had "student self-government", I was struck by the question my friends at St Hugh's were raising: "Is the President of the J. C. R. a President or a Head Girl?" for I had not grasped till then that the Principal apparently equated her position with that of a Headmistress.'

Miss Jourdain was no longer the 'vivacious and far more approachable' don of Miss Wallace's day; she is remembered for her playing of the piano, 'a real pleasure' and her 'folders of art, design and architecture', among which she permitted her undergraduates to browse, for her psychic powers (attested by Lilian Sprules, and Phyllis Davies) and for her presence: 'I had met Miss Jourdain at my interview earlier in the year, and remembered her vividly, a short, compact, intensely authoritative figure rather like Queen Victoria' (Renée Haynes). The most vivid description of all is that of Kathleen Hobbs who writes:

I went to take leave of her (after coming up to take Responsions) before going to catch my train. She had just come into college and I remember that she was wearing a very well cut black coat and skirt, a lace blouse, and black velvet hat trimmed with shining cocks' feathers. This against her white hair dressed à la marquise, and very good skin gave a very handsome effect: although she was unduly pale and clearly showed the effects of a long period of worry . . . Mabel, the college parlour maid brought the afternoon post in just before I left. I only knew afterwards that in it was the letter from Lord Curzon who was the Chancellor of the University, putting the blame for 'the row' firmly on her shoulders.

Miss Jourdain died on Sunday 6 April, at 4 Norham Road, the home of her friend and old Principal, Miss Moberly. She had had an earlier heart attack a week before. She was in her room, and called for assistance, but death took place before the doctor arrived. She was sixty. One student to mourn her deeply was Phyllis Davies, whom Miss Jourdain had appointed college organist (at a salary of £15 p.a.). Miss Netherell, the Bursar gave her all Miss Jourdain's music 'which she wanted me to have' and also a studio portrait of Miss Jourdain, which still hangs over her bureau. Miss Jourdain left a letter to her executors (dated June 1921), which included a message for all who had worked with her:

I now send a final message of love to all the people I have loved and worked for and who have loved and worked for or with me. Please tell them all that I shall have thought of them in my last moments, and that I hope my prayers will be heard. Please say that the one thing worth living and dying for is the sense of something true and great which one puts before all selfish wishes; and if people have learnt that in their life at College I shall be glad. There is no need for pity or sorrow in this case. I have had a sufficiently long life full of activity; and the spirit returns to God who made it. In that hope I die. Much love to you all.
Yours affectionately,

E. F. Jourdain

The most serious effect of the 'unfortunate controversy' was the disruption of the education of those undergraduates whose tutors resigned in protest, or refused to teach members of St Hugh's. 'In my opinion, in retrospect, the loss of my French tutor, Miss Shaw, who resigned . . . and the hiatus in the Trinity term, caused by the death of Miss Jourdain in April 1924, had a serious effect on the standard of my work' (Eduarda Fowler). 'Our third year studies had been interrupted by the controversy between Miss Jourdain and some of the tutors who resigned in protest. Those who were reading French were taken on by two strangers from London, a man and a woman – an unsettling business' (Phyllis Deards). Not everyone, however, was affected: '. . . my second year was the year of "The Row". At the time I did not understand very much about it' (Ruth Dean); and Kathleen Hobbs shows how quickly the matter became history, while at the same time paying a warm tribute to Miss Gwyer's principal-ship: 'Some people', she writes, 'thought of us as the year that had to live down "The Row", but we did not see ourselves in sackcloth and ashes and behaved and lived normally . . . [the] happy atmosphere was probably the best way of burying the past. There is no doubt that Miss Gwyer played a very great part in this process . . .' But an anonymous writer says: 'The Row really did somehow overshadow St Hugh's, for how long, I've no idea. We felt, some of us, no idea what proportion, rather in disgrace, on probation.'

As time passed the rules became a little less rigid, the scope of activities and academic opportunities a little wider. Miss Rogers, retired as tutor of St Hugh's in 1921, is now associated almost exclusively with the garden and remembered for her eccentricities: 'I remember once going to see Miss Rogers, carrying my school hat. Although the rules governing the wearing of hats were relaxed by then, Miss Rogers was of the old school: "It is as rude", she said, "for you to enter my room carrying your hat, as it would be for a man to enter wearing one!"' (Doreen Rogers). 'I remember exploring [the gardens] rather fully once and finding Miss Annie M. A. H. Rogers, Custos Hortulorum, working where there is a little spring, we had to leave her talking, she showed no sign of stopping ever . . .' (Dame Mary Cartwright), and Ruth Haslop often spoke to her 'sitting on her camp stool tending her plants, and we used to have long conversa-tions. I learnt a great deal from her, not only about the plants.' The finishing touch 'was her hats . . . the pièce de résistance was an ancient black velvet hat, rather like a cap of maintenance that had been left in a trunk of old clothes in the attic some years. Round it was a wreath of very tatty small velvet flowers . . . she rode with complete disregard for any rule of the road' (Kathleen Hobbs).

Miss Joan Evans still 'wore the most wonderful clothes and glittering jewels' (Doreen Rogers). 'She was as thin as a lath then, and for dinner she wore dresses of rich materials, brocade and velvet, hanging straight from the shoulders with long earrings' (Dame Mary

Cartwright); and both Doreen Rogers and Dame Mary attended her Dante evenings at which they read *Il Paradiso*, with or without the help of 'a book with the translation on the opposite page' (Dame Mary Cartwright). When Phyllis Davies was unable to play the organ in Chapel, Joan Evans would sometimes 'stand in' for her.

Of other tutors: Miss Bullen, the Domestic Bursar, impressed Dame Mary Cartwright by her prompt and efficient appearance, with a bedroom jug full of water, to extinguish a fire discovered in the box room; 'My tutor was Margery Perham (reputed to have shot a lion and published a novel), young, energetic, full of vitality and enthusiasm for emergent Africa none of which qualities impaired her scholarly integrity' (Renée Haynes); the 'conscientious and interested Miss Seaton' cheered her pupils along 'with wise talk and tea' (Doris Saunders); while before she resigned, Miss Shaw discouraged any excess enthusiasm: 'After handing in my first essay to Miss Shaw, she said, bitingly, "Miss Volkert, at Oxford we do not hold with zeal!"' (Rosemary Volkert).

Outside lecturers and tutors are remembered:

Father Martindale – very thin, white-faced, black hair proceeded to translate the first poem (Catullus' love poems):-

'Give me a thousand kisses
Then another thousand . . .'

he squeaked. Sitting at the back, I could see the shoulders of the young men convulsed with laughter – The following week to my dismay only a girl from Somerville and I turned up . . .

Or in contrast, there were Maurice Bowra's lectures at Wadham which 'were sheer delight – He looked like a Greek God himself and was a vital person. He inspired us all' (Phyllis Davies); or 'lectures by Gilbert Murray, on metre, an unlikely subject to enthral one, but I recall that my interest never flagged even in the technicalities. To me he was "an amazing man"' (Helen Dixon). The 'remarkable Professor Joseph Wright . . . and his gracious wife' continued to extend their hospitality to undergraduates for Sunday afternoon tea (Phyllis Deards). Geoffrey Elton at Queens, tea and Turkish cigarettes with Dermot Morrah, Kenneth Bell, Nichol Smith, Professor Gordon and Professor Fiedler are all mentioned as particularly memorable. Amongst recollections of this galaxy of absurd, amazing or memorable academics, there continue to be a disquieting number of references to the misogynists: Professor Lindemann who 'disliked women' and 'used to glare' (Ruth Brown). For Agnes Wayment it was his learning rather than his basilisk stare which was frightening: 'I started work reading Science and was frightened by the learning of "The Prof", Professor Lindemann (Lord Cherwell), and in mathematics by the brother of Sir Oliver Lodge. Indeed so frightened was I by them that I changed to History.' 'At Keble, "Crab" Owen, as he was commonly called made the women sit at the back of the hall where, he hoped, he could not see them. He was, of course, a misogynist!' (Phyllis Davies). Or at Magdalen, 'C. S. Lewis's lectures. These were inspiring. We only went to a few because it was difficult to stand up to C. S. Lewis's dislike of our presence – as women . . .' (Anon). Male undergraduates, on the other hand, were more appreciative of women entering traditionally male preserves: 'My academic subject was Law – only two women, one Vera Galpin and I, went to lectures, and on the first occasion the men got up and cheered, which embarrassed us a bit' (Renée Haynes).

Even without the disruptions caused by 'the Row' and the subsequent boycott, or the misogynistic prejudices of some tutors and lecturers, some disciplines still had difficulty in finding adequate tuition. Dame Mary Cartwright, for example, reading Mathematics, was taught first by 'Alfred Lodge, brother of Sir Oliver, and recently retired from an engineering college . . . When he fell ill, no-one at St Hugh's did anything and we asked Mr Chaundy, but he had no time. After that a sort of moral tutor, Mrs Gardner, was appointed.' Dame Mary worked from notes on Mr Russell of Balliol's lectures, then after Mods was taught by Leonard Rogers, retired Professor from Leeds, and for one term by 'J. W. Nicholson, tutor at Balliol when Russell retired. He was already an alcoholic, but I went 11–12, the one time in the day when he was not in bed or drunk.' She was encouraged to attend Professor Hardy's evening class, which took place at 8.45 with 'tea and biscuits and conversation from 10.15 to 11 approx. So I had to have permission to stay out after 11.' Dame Mary, at least, was not held back by these difficulties – the *Chronicle* of 1923–4 records without comment: 'The results of the Final Schools in 1923 included the following:- Miss M. L. Cartwright, Final Honour School of Mathematics, Class I . . .'

In the late 1920s, the undergraduates seem to have attended lectures regularly and although some were clearly more organised than others, there are as yet no references to the 'essay crisis' and few to working late. A number of contributors refer to themselves as 'conscientious', though one adds; 'But I doubt if Miss Seaton did!' Another refers to her Ancient History studies as sheer delight. Attendance at Chapel and the churches of Oxford seems to have been equally regular. There are references to both Principals, Miss Jourdain and Miss Gwyer, in their capacity as officiators in Chapel, and particular mention at the end of the decade to the new vicar of St Mary's, Canon Frank Barry: 'I attended St Mary's, the University Church. I was there the first Sunday when Canon Frank Barry was the Vicar – there were 16 people in church at the 11 am service. Three years later if you wished to get a seat, you had to be in the church at the latest at 10.45' (Evelyn Jeffrey). 'When the Vicar (F. R. Barry) preached at Evensong, the church was filled . . .' (Theo Hale). Not everyone shared this conformity: one contributor went to the University Church because it 'was fun to try to understand the Latin sermons', but the voice which claims that not many felt much respect for the Chapel, is a lone voice, and any mild irreligiosity in other reminiscences suggests more the comfortable disrespect of familiarity and habit, than any deliberate rebellion.

In the second half of the decade, St Hugh's again expanded when the money left by Clara Evelyn Mordan to Mary Gray Allen reverted, in accordance with Miss Mordan's wishes, to the College. In her reminiscences, Annie Rogers said this was 'a sum larger than that which any women's College in Oxford has yet received from an individual benefactor' and it enabled the College to buy the freehold of the College, the Lawn and an adjoining house, and to add the Mary Gray Allen wing to the Main Building. The new wing was opened officially on Wednesday, 10 October 1928, by the Visitor, Lord Cecil of Chelwood. It is interesting to note that the theme of his speech was women as peace-makers. The *Chronicle* reports him as saying that it was the duty of the young, educated women of today to create a strong public opinion which would make war impossible, thus consummating the work which his generation had inaugurated. The number of resident undergraduates had been fixed at 150 by the Council before the University imposed a limit of 160, but the new building made it possible for more students to live in College.

Oxford itself in the 1920s 'was beautiful and very quiet with very few cars, but since it was after the First World War, there were a few motorbikes' and even these were subject to rules: '. . . It was necessary to appear before the Proctors on the apron outside the Sheldonian for the exhausts to be checked before they could be used – would that this rule were still in force!' (Doreen Rogers). 'Horse drawn cabs still met the trains ... I distinctly remember the embarrassment felt on the occasion of a visit from my ghastly Godmother when she hired a Victoria and I had to accompany her on a sight-seeing tour of Oxford' (Maud Prichard). There were stables in Merton Street, where one could hire riding horses. One or two undergraduates did own cars – Donald Baden-Powell, a friend of Dame Mary Cartwright's had a metallic sports car; and Ruth Johnson 'the lively daughter of a weathy industrialist' was the possessor of a car. A friend of Francis Crossfield possessed a car in the third year: 'Dorothy Rippon, one of the best and most delightful of companions ... in our last year had a car and she took Nancie Moller and me on to the Berkshire Downs and to her home at Abingdon.' As always, the majority of undergraduates had bicycles, although it is with something of a shock that one reads '... we collected our bicycles and proceeded to trim the wicks and check for oil in the lamps. I lighted them both and we set off ...' (Phyllis Davies).

By the last years of the 1920s, there are the first signs that bird song might soon be superseded as the preferred accompaniment to lazy, summer afternoons on the river. Patricia Talbot, for example, writes that it was: '... a delight to learn to punt (on the Cherwell). The number of portable gramophones was a background of sound – gentle.' The records she recalls are Fred Astaire's tunes, 'Ain't She Sweet' and, most appropriately, 'Bye Bye Blackbird'.

Descriptions of the river suggest an idyll: 'I found the nests of reed buntings, sedge warblers, reed warblers, whitethroats ... Once on a November dusk I hear a noise of tiny munching and traced it to water voles eating the red berries in a hawthorn hedge ... [they were] not alarmed by me, and neither were the kingfishers, fishing from twigs overhanging the river' (Margaret Whicher). 'Canoeing up the Cherwell past water-rats, purple loosestrife and scented river herbage ...' (Lilian Sprules). 'River picnics were very much the thing, suppers and even breakfasts, after going to hear the Magdalen Choir on May 1st' (Maud Prichard). The rules governing the river were still in force: 'We had to be able to swim 50 yards in order to qualify' as a Captain or half Captain. 'A half Captain could go out with another half Captain, but not with anyone unqualified' (Dame Mary Cartwright); and it was still necessary to have a doctor's certificate stating that one could stand immersion in cold water. Enforcement of these rules began to lapse, until during a League of Nations summer school, a punt capsized and 'about three people who could not swim were drowned, chiefly because they were caught in the weed, which was very thick in parts of the river, and dragged down before anyone could get to them. After that everyone had to learn to swim before they could go on the river' (Kathleen Hobbs). Ethel Brown records that she was not allowed to learn to punt as she was a non-swimmer, although she did go out on the river in a punt she and some friends hired for the summer.

A rowing competition between women's colleges was staged in 1928–9. 'We ventured into the slim boat, lent by one of men's colleges, about two weeks before the competition (speed, style etc.). Phyllis Hartnoll was the cox . . .' Of 1923, an anonymous contributor says: 'We also practised sculling in a "four" we kept on the Upper River, near Port Meadow. A young clergyman from St John's occasionally acted as coach. But we did not often request his assistance, as we found the afternoons more fun on our own.' A similar incident had been noted in Dorothy Hammonds' journal for 5 November 1905: 'The Second Year "pairs" practised this afternoon. It must be recorded that the Second Year has now put a boat on the river, which if occasion requires and with careful coxing should easily bump Somerville.' This last entry from the journal makes the next remark appear a little odd. 'We were not allowed to race as that was dangerous for women' (Ellen Reynolds). Phyllis Wallbank may throw light on the matter when she says that they rowed 'a timed race, as it was not considered good for us to race against each other'.

In the more conventional fields of sport, St Hugh's women continued to show considerable prowess playing hockey, netball and tennis. Two women in particular are singled out: Doreen Rogers is remembered as '. . . the outstanding sportswoman of my year . . . a triple blue in her first year ' (Phyllis Deards). Dame Mary Cartwright mentions both another aspect of women's interest in sport and another notable St Hugh's woman: 'We took considerable interest in the men's sports. We watched them practise. One of the year below (Rosemary Mitchell?) used to contribute drawings of football etc. to *Isis* over the signature TICH. We spoke of Little Tich and admired her success.' The men they watched included, for example, Lord Longford, the 'celebrated runner' and H. P. Jacobs, a university rugger star.

Not everyone was interested in sport, but every undergraduate seems to have enjoyed the theatre to some extent, whether involved in college drama or as a spectator of OUDs productions and the touring companies at the New Theatre. OUDS was still a male society, with

professional actresses taking the female parts, although Phyllis Hartnoll recalls being asked to audition for Miranda in *The Tempest*. She
was offered the part, but the opportunity was vetoed by her tutor.
Other students recall having crowd parts. *Antony and Cleopatra* was
produced by Bridges Adams with Cecil Ramage and Cathleen Nesbit;
Julius Caesar with Benson as Mark Antony; *Peer Gynt*; and most
memorable, Gyles Isham as Hamlet, to whom all the women undergraduates lost their hearts. 'The Playhouse started in our second year.
R. S. Smith, founder of the OUDS was in some of the early
productions and one noticed an unknown Flora Robson in Ibsen's
Master Builder . . . and we were electrified by the acting and speech
of a newcomer to the company . . . a young man named John
Gielgud' (Georgina Arrowsmith). Val Gielgud is also mentioned,
and Tyrone Guthrie. At the New Theatre, the regular appearance
of the D'Oyly Carte company was the signal for religious queuing
and devoted attendance – 'and why not? with Henry Lytton,
Darrell Fancourt, Bertha Lewis and Derek Oldham' (Maud
Prichard).

In College, most students seem to have seen and remembered, or to
have participated in, the productions of each year. Dame Mary
Cartwright tells of a play based on L. T. Meade's *Sweet Girl
Graduate*, in which the character of the Principal in the play de-
veloped into a caricature of Miss Jourdain, which must have caused
some embarrassment when she expressed a desire to see it. There was
a production of *If I were King*, in which Molly Challans (Mary
Renault) was the hero, and a production of *Captain Brassbound's
Conversion*, in which Helen Forth, praised in the local press for her
directing talents, is remembered for her performance as Drinkwater.
There were presentations of classics, such as *Friar Bacon and Friar
Bungay*, *The Beaux' Stratagem* and *The School for Scandal*, and plays
were written by undergraduates, such as *Ann Boleyn*, staged in
Michaelmas Term, 1922.

Interest in music was at least equal to, if not greater than, that
shown in the theatre, from Miss Jourdain who 'was an excellent
pianist and would sometimes invite a few of us into her drawing room
to play for us . . .' (Ida Moberly), to the performances of some of the
great names of the day – Cortot, Myra Hess, Moisewitsch, Albert
Sammons, Dorothy Silk, Dr Albert Schweitzer and Jelly d'Aranyi.
Athough one contributor writes that her 'favourite music was Bach
and rubbish' the works mentioned encompass chamber music, choral

music (both church and secular), orchestral music, classical and modern music. 'I remember a performance of *The Dream of Gerontius* in the Sheldonian and the shorter work by Gustav Holst, *The Hymn of Jesus*, its first performance in Oxford. I quote from my diary of 13th June 1920: "... it was very nice indeed. Holst was there himself a funny little man"' (Ida Moberly). The name which stands out above all others, however, is that of the conductor of the Bach Choir, Sir Hugh Allen, who was both loved and respected by the many St Hugh's undergraduates who joined the choir. 'We loved Sir Hugh, who could draw from us just the sounds he wanted. At the same time, we were in awe of him' (Phyllis Deards).

> Sir Hugh Allen was the conductor, a colourful character, much feared and respected. On one occasion choir and orchestra were in full swing with Sir Hugh conducting fortissimo, when the Vice-Chancellor's wife came crashing in late with her instrument ... the noise was terrific and our blood froze in our veins. Sir Hugh slammed down his baton and there was an ominous silence – then 'What the hell do you think you are doing, Madam?' he roared – Mrs. Farnell looked up calmly – 'I'm damned, Sir, if I know', she replied. (Phyllis Davies)

The awe and respect do not seem to have wavered, even in the face of two occasions when a lesser man would not have survived such a loss of dignity in front of an undergraduate assembly:

> conducting from a small platform in the Sheldonian at a concert in the afternoon (because lighting was forbidden in the Sheldonian for fear of fire), Sir Hugh suddenly vanished from our view. He had fallen off the inadequate dais ... the second concert took place in the Town Hall in the evening ... when at the end he turned his back to the choir to bow to the audience it was revealed that his trousers had split all the way down the back. (Phyllis Davies)

The general spectrum of interests is widening, but still limited compared to later decades. The local historical society's tour of Oxford city walls in the pouring rain is recalled by Dame Mary Cartwright; the college Classical Society which managed to arrange for Gilbert Murray to speak to its members by Phyllis Davies, and the 'Literary Society which on one occasion was addressed by G. K.

Sir Henry Wood

Professor Nichol Smith

Sir Hugh Allen

Ralph Vaughan Williams

From Ursula Dacombe's sketchbook (1924–27)

Chesterton whose advent was spectacular for he was then at his greatest girth' by Kathleen Hobbs.

> The first year was of course a time for being pressed to join student societies, like the English Club, where I saw the dazzling, dashing Vita Sackville West; the Music Club where I think I heard the Coffee Cantata; and a very solemn political science club where we worked out, through innumerable discussions, a written constitution for our country replacing the House of Lords by a body of Ealdormen (on no account to be confused with Aldermen). (Renée Haynes)

Phyllis Davies joined the 'OU Cambrian Society and was elected the first woman Vice-President – E. D. James of St John's was the President. It was a glittering affair as the young Earl of Cardigan was a member and he and his friends from the House always attended the meetings.'

The rules still made it hard to mix freely with the men's colleges, despite a certain amount of relaxation following the war when they 'were encouraged to be kind to the men returning: there were mixed games, tea parties at Corpus, and the rules of chaperonage were less strict' (Doreen Rogers); a little later and Eduarda Fowler writes: 'one could be sent down for going to see a friend in a man's college unchaperoned even if one went in the company of another woman undergraduate!' Only fathers, uncles or brothers could be entertained unchaperoned in College, otherwise one had to engage a common room and a chaperon and entertain formally. College dances were permitted. Mary Thorp remembers that 'Dances in College was 7/6d plus refreshments. They ended at 11pm.' However, refreshments were nothing stronger than lemonade – a request to Miss Gwyer for permission to serve a claret cup was firmly turned down: 'As we do not wish to make our homely little entertainments luxurious, sanction is withheld. Yours sincerely, B. Gwyer' (Ruth Haslop). And yet, Erica Barry met her future husband at a dinner party unchaperoned; Doreen Rogers went for long walks by the river, unchaperoned; others, unchaperoned, went to Commem Balls, danced the night away and then breakfasted at Blenheim; entertained men to a *thé dansant* at one of the College houses; and, despite the penalties (exacted in one case), at least one undergraduate admits climbing in when necessary. Donald Baden-Powell, friend of Dame Mary Cartwright's, seems to have walked roughshod over several of the rules and remained unscathed, and Doreen Rogers' husband, Edgar Lobel (then her fiancé) appears to have been equally oblivious to rules governing visits by men to the College: 'I was asked to remind Edgar that he must not just wander into the College without permission.' Beatrice Roberts was not really aware of any regulations, but discovered after she had gone down 'a regulation which forbade undergraduates to go up in balloons! a thing I had never contemplated.' The anomaly seems to be reflected in the undergraduates' widely different attitudes to life at College: 'Compared with wartime at school, Oxford was marvellous freedom' (Dame Mary Cartwright). 'I was disappointed with college life on the whole . . . it struck me as a continuation of school . . . the chaperoning rules were absurd' (Rosemary Volkert).

Money available varies considerably, though the amounts mentioned seem quite high compared to later generations: Dame Mary Cartwright had an allowance of £8 a term and Ida Moberly acknowledges the generosity of her 'good Godmother' who contributed £10 per term in addition to tickets for the Oxford subscription concerts. State scholarships were few and often conditional on teaching afterwards: 'a friend had one of these and dutifully postponed marriage for 6 years . . .' (Dame Mary Cartwright). To give some idea of the value of money, Helen Dixon says that theatre tickets were 9d for the balcony, 1s 6d for the gallery, and the University Dance Club dances were to cost 'not above 5/-' each. Several women sent their laundry home regularly. Incidental expenses included fares, exam fees, books, some clothes, soap, cigarettes and food. The College food was not noted for its excellence or its abundance – 'One dinner was soup, one stuffed tomato and a sweet. We habitually settled down to cocoa and buttered toast about 9 pm' (Dame Mary Cartwright); and Kathleen Hobbs relates that it even prompted a minor rebellion at one point. In the mornings the 'in' places to meet were the Cadena's upstairs café, as in the previous decade. Elliston and Cavells, Boffins (also mentioned before 1920), the 'Candied Friend' or the 'Super-Sin' (the Super Cinema) which served particularly delicious chocolate biscuits, and 'for afternoon tea we patronised the Northgate Café' (Joyce Robertson). Fullers, with its famous walnut cake, is also mentioned and, for lunch and dinner, the Randolph, the Mitre and the Clarendon. Only Kathleen Hobbs mentions any places outside Oxford: '. . . the White Hart at Dorchester; a pub at Yarnton; one at Godstow, where we ate and drank well, which one certainly did not in College'. Intrepid cyclists ventured out of Oxford to enjoy the country: 'My bicycle, Venerable Bede, besides clanking along to lectures, carried me in friends' company around the countryside as far as Dorchester, Burford, Great Tew – especially while waiting up for Vivas' (Lilian Sprules).

Women were now both full members of the University and enfranchised, but on the whole the reminiscences do not reflect any great interest in politics. The major event of the decade was the General Strike of 1926 and for those who were up at the time, this was the cause of 'much political conversation, some of it embittered; also the fulfilment for one or two male undergraduates, of a childhood ambition to drive a train' (Renée Haynes). 'Undergraduates from the men's colleges were recruited to go and help during the strike – they were welcome on the railways and in many other ways. Recruiting Offices were opened in Oxford High Street. We went in to some of them, but no women were allowed to be taken on for this sort of work. We were very indignant' (Margaret Clarkson). Apart from this major disruption there was little active interest. They listened to debates at the Union (still in the gallery only), when they could procure tickets, and at least one contributor, Marjorie Wilde, seems to have attended regularly: '11.11.26 to Union to hear motion on Coal Dispute. Lord Londonderry spoke.' '7.6.28 to Presidential Debate at the Union: Visiting Speaker Sir Herbert Samuels Maxton. (Stopford Brooke made President).' '2.11.28 to Union to hear Lord Robert Cecil . . . address the League of Nations Union.' '23.11.28 Went to hear Sir Boyd Merriman explain the Rating and Local Government reforms to the Conservative Association.' '28.11.28 went to the Union to hear Baldwin, then Prime Minister, address the Conservative Association.' '3.2.29 to Town Hall to hear Saklatvaala, notorious Communist: the diary records "pure curiosity – a remarkable man giving one the creeps."' Theo Hale remembers one of the best debates being 'on the respective merits of white and brown bread'. On the whole, though, Dame Mary Cartwright's amazement that any woman should wish to become a Member of Parliament, 'an idea totally outside my imagination', is representative.

By the end of the decade, the unfortunate controversy within the College in 1923–4 had become history and the position of the women's colleges in the University was secure. For many St Hugh's women of the day, more important, ultimately, to them than the events through which they lived were the friends they made. Sister Elsa Henry writes that 'one year, 1923–1926, kept in close touch by an annual newsletter for 50 years'; and Margaret Ratcliffe speaks for them all when she writes: 'The friendships I formed have been the most treasured result of my time at St Hugh's.'

THE 1930s

The 1930s were a period of consolidation for the College, but in Europe, one of disintegration, inspiring almost every undergraduate to unwonted political awareness and activity. The Hunger Marchers who passed through Oxford in 1931 met with active help and support from St Hugh's undergraduates; the men abandoned their courses to fight in Spain in 1936 on the side of the Communists; the fight against Fascism assumed the nature of a crusade, and the membership of the Labour Party increased accordingly. Discussions in the evenings were primarily political, and despite the overwhelming desire for peace, the shadow of war was all too palpable. It was a time for fervent belief and terrible disillusionment.

At home, despite the economic situation, the country was able to celebrate the Silver Jubilee of King George V in 1935. St Hugh's too, enjoyed a Jubilee, celebrating its first fifty years on 27 June 1936, with a thanksgiving service in the Cathedral, a garden party in the garden, and a Jubilee dinner in a marquee near the new Moberly Library. The College enjoyed 'a jubilee outing to Stratford for a performance of *King Lear* and a picnic lunch near Anne Hathaway's Cottage' (Luned Powys-Roberts); it was a most successful day despite a coach strike which threatened to upset the arrangements. The maids as well were given an outing – to Bournemouth. The Association of Senior Members collected the curious sum of £3135 1s 4d to endow a scholarship, and among the multifarious gifts received from Fellows, Senior Members and the JCR, Miss Gwyer gave the 'statue of St Hugh with his swan, an almost exact replica of the statue in one of the niches over the altar in the University Church and by the same sculptor, Mr Esmond Burton' which was placed on the Library stairs.

Though the number of undergraduates had been fixed, the College again expanded physically, when the death of Sir George Whitehead in 1931 made it possible to negotiate with St John's College for the purchase of the land behind numbers 74, 76, 78 and 80 Woodstock Road; and, as part of the arrangement, to buy the freeholds of these four houses, together with that of 82 Woodstock Road. By 1937, the Mary Gray Allen wing and the new Moberly Library had been finished on the site of 1 St Margaret's Road. Throughout these expansions, and while quietly noting, for example, the new Research Fellowship and lectureship made available at St Hugh's, or the academic distinction achieved by its own Fellows, and undergraduates such as Miss Adam (the first woman to achieve a First in Physics), or Miss McKee, given the unusual privilege of speaking at the Union, the *Chronicle* also documents the end of the old order. The decade saw the death of the foundress, Elizabeth Wordsworth in 1932, of Miss Jane Kirkaldy (1932), of Mr Ball (1937), head gardener from the opening of the first new buildings until 1934, of the first principal, Miss Moberly (1937), and finally of Miss Rogers (1937). From 1936, Miss Gwyer is aware of the '... critical period through which Europe is passing and the end of which no man may see' (*Chronicle*, 1936–7). In her report of December 1938, she refers again to the unsettled state of Europe and to such precautionary measures as the training of ARP Wardens among the SCR, Miss Salt being the first to earn her badge. In June 1939, emergency arrangements were made for the College in the event of war and the Principal's letter of December 1939 records the requisition of all but the 'Whitehead garden', the Lawn and 82 Woodstock Road, and the arrangements made to move to Holywell Manor, and Savile House, with thirteen undergraduates to be housed at St Hilda's. Her letter, in describing a party at Milner Hall, also records the difficulties caused by a combination of deplorable weather, the blackout and a shortage of taxis, but concludes that the blackout's most beautiful corollary, 'The moonlit High and Radcliffe Square with a star-strewn sky above, are a sight to dream of – none can lapse utterly into fatalistic views of man or of the universe who allows these sights to do their healing work within his soul.'

Miss Gwyer assumes a dominant place in the reminiscences for the era. In the words of a Fellow, once a St Hugh's undergraduate, Miss Gwyer was '... an outstanding figure in College life. The stories about "The Gwyer", her perception and wit, and firmness in dealing with undergraduates, were legion. Not a few undergraduates knew also her unsentimental, objective help and sympathy when they were in difficulties.' Miss Gwyer's wit has the quality of legend, and it is impossible to establish when her most memorable utterances were delivered. Joan Lake recounts the story that is apocryphal, attributed to many occasions: a student asked permission for yet another 'brother' to be permitted to have tea in her room. Miss Gwyer replied 'Miss X, I can only assume that your mother was a rabbit, or your father a Turk.' Kathleen Hobbs, who went up in the year that Miss

Gwyer was appointed (1924), records a tale about a first year, '. . . who wore skirts that were tighter and shorter than any seen before. Her hair was cut like a man's on one side and waved on the other and she wore some startling clothes. Once when she came up to bow to Miss Gwyer and go out, I was dining at High Table, and Miss Gwyer turned to me and said in her direct manner, "If Miss X wishes to wear trousers, I do wish she would wear a pair: that one will soon split."' Another dry comment found on a mantlepiece (in a ground-floor room in Mary Gray Allen wing), at the beginning of the Summer Term:

Dear Miss H,
The entrance to this room is through the door only.
Yours sincerely,
B. Gwyer

She was quite uncompromising, as is shown in an anecdote from Elizabeth Anscombe:

. . . I was had up before Miss Gwyer for not having dined three times in one week (three dinners a week was how we registered attendance). She said I must dine five times next week. I said 'Yes', but she asked me which days I would do. So I said, 'Can't I leave it to the time? Mostly when I go out it's on casual invitations from people I meet.' She said, 'Do not tell me, Miss Anscombe, that you are as flotsam and jetsam on the waves of circumstance.' So, I had to fix the days!

She was not without her weaknesses. Her partiality for crumpets and chocolate éclairs was known to everybody. Consequently, as it was the custom for each undergraduate to entertain the Principal to tea, she must have had a surfeit of these delicacies. Nor was she always sensitive or perspicacious. Beatrice Roberts, a member of the Unitarian Church, fell into the habit of attending the College Chapel, because she liked the service. '. . . one day, the Principal asked me to see her and suggested that as I attended so regularly, I might like to consider being confirmed and become a Church member. I was, no doubt stupidly, quite horrified and upset by the idea, and burst into tears, upsetting Miss Gwyer in turn . . .' Nancy Salinger found Miss Gwyer 'austere and cold . . .'; to her, 'scholarship and education were a high calling, a mission in remote lands, not an applied and disciplined study of the modern world, but of the classical, mythical, mediaeval world . . . so I felt alienated . . .'

On the other hand, Miss Gwyer is described by Eileen Mackinlay as '. . . a constant delight, for her kindness and wit: smoking a vacuum cleaner as the Caterpillar in Alice, or sailing into dinner on St Hugh's Night with a swan under her arm, and reading a poem of her own composition . . .' Stories of that kindness are legion. Ruth McKee describes her as 'a woman who found time for everyone . . . called me in to tell me that she had seen a report about my speaking in the Union (unusual in those days). I had earned her approbation and she had gone to the trouble of putting time aside to tell me . . .' Helen Roxburgh tells a tale of a different sort of kindness:

> Tostevin, a contemporary scholar, was summoned to see Miss Gwyer.
>
> *Miss Gwyer* We think that you should stay on an extra year to take a B. Litt. degree, Miss Tostevin.
>
> *Tostevin* I have no money, Miss Gwyer.
>
> *Miss Gwyer* But you have our affection and esteem, Miss Tostevin!
>
> She was ultimately granted a scholarship.

Perhaps the most important aspect of Miss Gwyer's character was her profound Christian belief. A Fellow writes of her: 'All that she did as Principal was inspired and motivated by her deep religious faith, and the Chapel was for her the heart of the College'. This ever-present Christian awareness shows frequently in her comments to undergraduates. Edith Temple relates a story which admirably illustrates the cast of Miss Gwyer's thought: '. . . a member of our year, who was out on the river with boy-friends, returned late, and when interviewed by Miss Gwyer . . . said: "It was natural!" To which Miss Gwyer replied, "My dear, we are not children of nature, we are children of grace".' One final story from Frances Lloyd demonstrates both Miss Gwyer's faith, and her sense of humour: 'she was inquiring of a graduate I was with, if she had seen a mutual friend lately. "Yes, in the Underground; but I was going down the escalator and she was going up, so we were borne inexorably apart". "Ah!' said Miss Gwyer, "I'm afraid that will be the case for many of us in the next world!"'

However, despite Miss Gwyer's sustained efforts to heal the ugly wound, the Row was not forgotten, although never officially mentioned. Katharine Harris recalls: 'The "troubles" at St Hugh's were before our time, but some undergraduates knew about them (probably from schoolmistresses) and told others. Miss Ady came regularly to Chapel.' This policy of 'official' silence has been kept until the present day, and has given rise to what a Fellow, appointed as a lecturer in 1949, refers to as 'some strange mythology'. Nancy Salinger mentions 'a tradition of maidenly good correct behaviour (because women were on sufferance in Oxford)'. It was not only the general position of women in Oxford which affected St Hugh's undergraduates. Because of the reputation gained by the College in 1924, every St Hugh's 'girl' was expected to behave with extra circumspection.

The SCR, again, is vividly portrayed in this decade: Miss Proctor, who was 'so reserved, yet so understanding, and so watchful of our interests and welfare' (Eileen Tanner); Miss Seaton, who was 'famous for putting on more and more layers of clothes as winter progressed until by February ("I consider February to be our coldest month") she would be wearing several cardigans over a woollen jumper, and woollen socks over woollen stockings' (Joan Lumsden), and who combined great scholarship with great common sense: 'It was a great relief to me when my tutor, Miss Seaton, looking up from what I had considered a competent essay, but which was in fact an appallingly dull list (it even bored me) of the main landmarks in the life of Donne, said, "Miss Thomas, would you now please write me an essay on So-and-So without one single fact in it?"' (Daphne Thomas); Miss Francis, who, despite the disruption of the move (on the outbreak of war) from College, was still to be found 'scattering hairpins, oblivious of time, so that tutorials were rarely bounded by the clock' (Frances Lloyd); and Miss Agnes Headlam-Morley: 'disenchanted with English studies . . . I transferred to PPE. Remember 1931 was the year of the Great Depression, going off the Gold Standard etc. I wanted to understand the background to all this rather than the origins of 19th Century poetry. Agnes Headlam-Morley had just been appointed PPE tutor and we were her first students . . . she inspired me to work and read voraciously . . . she was like Miss Jean Brodie in her effect on me at least' (Nancy Salinger). She was involved in family political affairs and 'usually arrived late for tutorials and sometimes not at all, but was so stimulating when we did have the privilege of a session with her that we could not resent the waiting' (Phyllis Crisp). '. . . there she sat, with one leg over the arm of her chair and smiling (I think), dismissing one's essay with modified approval, then proceeding to open up entirely new aspects of the subject of the essay, till one's head whirled and one felt utterly incompetent, but inspired to do better' (Eileen Tanner). And a little less reverent: 'Miss Headlam-Morley, delightful, interesting, easy-going. In one of my tutorials a message came that the police wanted to see her. She said "they should know by now not to come for me in the mornings!" (I think it was a parking offence)' (Edith Temple).

Undergraduates continued to appreciate the beauty of the garden, and particularly the terrace, graphically described by Mary Ker:

> One of my most cherished memories is of the flagstone terrace outside the main building of St Hugh's during the Spring and early Summer. Every bed was full of flowering rockery plants . . . In Spring the terrace was a mosaic of many colours, all the purples and mauves of aubretia, shading sometimes almost to pink, the bright yellow of alyssum, and the white of (I think) perennial candytuft, with every kind of green from the plants that would come into flower later on . . . As the season advanced, the colours changed, and I remember especially the rock roses that gradually unfolded in pink, white, cream, yellow, and a darker colour that I could only call rust, or perhaps, russet. There was a retired don, Miss Rogers, who did a great deal for the garden in her spare time, and could often be seen out on the terrace in earnest conversation with the gardeners . . . she is in my memory always as a part of [the] scene on the terrace.

Indeed, until her death in 1937, the timeless figure of Miss Rogers, *Custos Hortulorum*, was still to be found in the St Hugh's garden, undaunted by its increasing size, or the prospect of alterations which would be necessary when the Mary Gray Allen wing and new Library were completed. 'Miss Rogers on a blustery autumn day, wearing four coats, each shorter than the one beneath it, and a man's trilby hat, surveying the progress of some alterations with majestic dignity and judgement' (Anon). Variously described as 'mysterious' and 'witchlike' or as suddenly erupting 'from behind a bush to chase us away on our bicycles', she was as much part of the garden as the Wistaria or the terrace and for those who came near enough she was found to provide 'entertaining and instructive diversions, pausing in her walks to chat or show me some new plant she had acquired' (Eileen Mackinlay). She unwittingly provided some humorous diversions too, in her battles with her bicycle: 'It was said that she could dismount but not mount, and that her gardener used to put her onto her bicycle before she started and if she had to dismount on the way she had to walk the rest of the journey' (Helena Charles). This may have been an exaggeration, but Barbara Reeves remembers 'watching Miss Rogers in antiquated hat and long garments, trying to mount her bicycle usually about 10 times (in Banbury Road) each time looking round at the traffic before trying again'. In the end, it was on her bicycle that she met her death: 'Miss Rogers', the *Chronicle* of 1937–8 records, 'met with an accident in St Giles, which she was crossing on a dark, rainy night on her way to a meeting of the Archaelogical Society, and died early the next morning without recovering consciousness.' A memorial to Miss Rogers was put up just before the College was requisitioned in October 1939, in the form of a sundial.

The brass dial by Richard Glynn, the carved stone pedestal, and the plinth of two steps all date from about 1700 and came from Grove House, South Woodford, Essex. The College obtained them through Percy Webster, Antiquarian Horologist of Mayfair. On the upper step of the plinth is inscribed:

(North side)   Annie Mary Anne Henley Rogers
Custos Hortulorum
MCMXXVII–MCMXXXVII

(South side)   Floribus Anna tuis faveat sol
luce perenni

The inscription was composed by Professor Myres.

Outside the College, the lecturers who are particularly remembered are legion, showing both the calibre of the University at this time, and the greater diversity of Schools read by women undergraduates. Names which stand out include 'Professor H.T. Wade-Gery [who] was a striking figure, tall, loose-limbed, angular, with a shock of greying hair not always under good control'; 'Marcus Todd of Oriel, Reader in Epigraphy, a Wesleyan local preacher. There was a current rumour that once he had added "At the end of this lecture, if you will kindly open both phalanges of the door, it will facilitate the egress." But I cannot vouch for this, though it is exactly the kind of language he used' (Mary Ker); C. S. Lewis, no longer daunting to the women among his audience and universally admired for his 'Prolegomena to the Study of Medieval Literature', which was 'absolutely fascinating' (Joan Lumsden); Tolkien whose following is divided between those who found his lectures impressive and those who like Joan Lumsden found them dull, 'partly because they were above my head and partly because he would drop his head at the end of a sentence and mutter the last words to his waistcoat'; Einstein, whose lectures on relativity attracted students from every discipline; Professor Love 'who appeared to be aged 90 – and whose large white moustache was a handicap to a fellow mathematician, as, being slightly deaf, she needed to lip read! He was a fine lecturer, as was Mr Hodgkinson of Jesus. . .' (Phyllis Wallbank); Lascelles Abercrombie, whose lectures on versification are described variously as 'fascinating' but 'rather embarrassing to attend because hardly anyone went', and 'very poor'; Gilbert Murray with his 'beautiful voice'; Charles Williams, Brett Smith, Nichol Smith, M. R. Ridley, Enid Starkie and M. Berthon 'whom it was impossible to please. However painstakingly or brilliantly one achieved a translation into or out of the French language, he always found a "better rendering"' (Ingeborg Manger): George Kolkhorst 'the Spanish Reader, described in *Summoned By Bells* had a fine sense of humour. I remember his once telling me with astonishment "That's a very good essay! Did you write it?"' (Margaret Jackson). Professor W. J. Entwistle is remembered; and so is A. L. Rowse 'who lectured on Politics and Literature. He said, "The majority of people are fools, FOOLS"' (Dorothy Lovegrove); and that most notorious of misogynists, Dr Stallybrass of BNC: 'I remember Sonners (Dr Stallybrass) lecturing at BNC and introducing crude jokes and terms into his lectures in an attempt to show his disapproval of our being there at all, or to scare us away. The men used to go scarlet; we would laugh and run back to our dictionaries' (Mary Healey). A description of one of Oxford's most eccentric dons-to-be is given by Helena Charles: 'Donald McKinnon was an undergraduate at New College, and even then had a reputation as an eccentric. It was said that he used to dress in newspaper.'

Two St Hugh's undergraduates seem to have stood out particularly in the early 1930s: one, of course, was red-headed Barbara Betts (Castle), 'Marjorie Betts's little sister', and a girl reputed to be a White Russian, by name Vava Basilevitch (the spelling varies). Amongst many memories of her, Sylvia Goodfellow's stands out:

There was an outstandingly beautiful girl in the second year [1930] ... the story was told that she was pursued by the Bulldogs who served the Proctors, and they caught up with her late one night at the side door down St Margaret's Road: 'Your name and college, Miss?' they asked, presumably because she was not wearing a gown as required at that hour of the evening. But Vava Basilevitch had pressed the electric bell, and disappeared inside saying, 'I do not talk to strange men on the street'.

Within the College, things were now very different from the days of 'scalping': 'One of the best thing about St Hugh's was the friendliness between different "years"' (Lorna Clish). Other undergraduates were grateful for their new-found freedom: 'the sense of unbounded freedom, no compulsory lectures, no compulsory games' (Joan Lapraik); and to have a room of their own, however small, with few domestic worries: housemaids cleared the grate in the morning and laid the fire with paper and wood, and 'we did not have to do our own washing up – we dumped the things in the pantry and they were done by the maids' (Joan Lumsden). Financially, the recollections of Dorothy Sherwood give a picture of the time: 'I had an allowance of £12 a term. With this I paid for College Subs., Bach Choir membership (plus music) and riding lessons (*four for £1*) on Port Meadow ... I bought second-hand books but no clothes – these I bought at home during vacations. I don't think anyone could have managed on much less ... but I found it adequate and never felt "poor".'

Opinions as to the quality of the food vary, as any subjective assessments must, so Joan Lumsden and Betty Harris both pay tribute to its acceptability, while Zoë Grey-Turner remembers 'unspeakable breakfasts, and taking the statutory three dinners a week in Hall as near the door as possible so that one could sneak out early and off to a party and/or the George where one washed away the abominable Brown Windsor or Tinned Tomato which seemed the only soups ever contemplated by the college cook'. A further domestic detail is supplied by Naomi Papworth: 'The electricity was arranged so that we could use either the ceiling light or the table lamp' – an irritating economy in the same style as that observed earlier by Helena Charles, who found the food in Hall good 'though the lighting was poor. To remedy this, a Goethe Society was formed. The members all came into dinner in Hall carrying lighted candles. Miss Gwyer's only comment ... "How much candle-light improves their complexions".' However poor the lighting, or scarce the coal, it nevertheless seems that, at least, the bath water was always hot!

But, as in previous generations, the cold proved a problem, and Mary Ker describes

> after dinner we frequently gathered in the room of anyone who had a good fire, and talked ... until the hour grew late, or the coal supply was running low. Many of the science students often worked at the Labs until nearly time for dinner, and to them it was a great relief to be asked to share a neighbour's warm room until bed-time. Fires could be lighted only once a day – no more wood until the housemaid came the next morning, and this could cause problems for any of us on a cold day: between morning lectures, we would work in the College library, or in the Radcliffe Camera, or simply wrap up in a warm dressing gown in our rooms.

The rules had not relaxed in principle, but the attitudes towards them seem distinctly docile. 'We were irritated by being expected to wear caps as well as gowns to attend lectures' (Cecilia Todd); 'on the whole, College regulations e.g. signing-out for late evening shows, eating dinners in Hall, getting *exeat* permits etc. were usually observed because the reasons for them were recognised' (Nancy Rice-Jones); but since 'by the 1930s chaperonage had gone completely out of fashion' Pauline Brentnall says that the chaperonage rules were often ignored, and more people climbed in, for example, when necessary. 'There was a feeling that if one never asked to go to a man's room, the Principal would suspect that one was breaking the rules.' However, Phyllis Wallbank remembers that 'My policy was to ask permission when I knew it would be granted, but to refrain when the result was uncertain ...' Such pragmatism was useful for meetings outside College, but, within, it was still impossible to entertain young men with anything except rather daunting formality and prior planning: 'an Hon ... who came to call on me when I was still living in The Lawn ... on finding I could not entertain him either in my room or in the common room, sat with me on the lower stairs, holding my hand in a melancholy way. The friendship never recovered from the lack of welcome offered by The Lawn ...' (Shirley Sutch).

However, authority sometimes showed its teeth: 'One girl at The Lawn got sent down from staying out late with boys (I think!)' (Barbara Reeve) and another undergraduate, ingenious and brave enough to don one of her boyfriend's suits and go 'undetected to

Chapel and Hall in Keble' later 'stayed out late on the river ... the door left unlocked by an accomplice was locked by one of the "dragons" ... and [she] was caught emerging from bike shed where they had been forced to stay the night ... Mother sent for ... Sent Down ...!' (Margaret McDougle). The gate-book still had to be signed if an undergraduate intended staying after 9.30 p.m., under the eye of Miss Collett, the portress, and Betty Samuell writes: 'the lies we wrote in the book at the College Lodge when we were *ostensibly* going to the Union, or the Radcliffe' and ' "Covering up" for even less law-abiding friends'.

Alcohol, at the very beginning of the decade, was forbidden: 'It was an offence to have alcohol in our rooms' (Mary Milner), though this did not prevent a number of undergraduates keeping it there just the same. Sherry seems to have been the favourite drink, and Mary Milner, again, remembers drinking it out of tooth-mugs. On the other hand, Pauline Brentnall comments, 'I don't remember any of my acquaintances keeping alcohol in their rooms at St Hugh's but it was the era in which sherry parties were just becoming popular and I went to several in men's colleges. We still wore hats in those days and on one occasion I bought a black straw hat at Webber's in the High in the morning and wore it at a sherry party the same afternoon.' Rules or no rules, however, wine-merchants were obviously co-operative souls: 'A friend of mine ordering sherry to be sent to College, (legitimately as it happens) [presumably for a party for which permission had been given] was asked at the shop: "Would you like it disguised, Miss?" ' (Dorothea Bleasley). Nor did the regulations prevent special occasions: 'I shared a 21st birthday party in 1935 with Ingeborg Manger .. neither of us had much money ... we rather fancied riding the streets on an elephant to be borrowed from the local Zoo ... but ... settled for a greengrocer's horse and cart which took us and all our year who wanted to come to Port Meadow where we cooked sausages and jacket potatoes on a bonfire. Miss Gwyer referred to our party in one of her amusing St Hugh's Night speeches' (Dorothy Sherwood).

'The accepted idea was that we had come to Oxford because of our love of study and not in order to qualify for earning a living' (Naomi Papworth), but in 1932, a Women's sub-committee of the Oxford Appointments Committee had been formed for appointments other than educational, for an experimental year in which to prove its need, and though it was feared that the current economic crisis would militate against its success, it did in the view of the *Chronicle*, fully justify its existence within three years. An article written at the time of the St Hugh's Jubilee in 1936, which appeared in the *Oxford Magazine* (November 1936) comments on the diversity of interest already represented by St Hugh's graduates: 'The company included barristers, doctors, civil servants, missionaries, teachers, researchers, novelists, journalists, actresses, business-women, besides wives and mothers and voluntary workers of many kinds.' An impressive list, especially when one reads, for example, 'I was the only medical student in the college in my year. There was one in the year ahead and none in the year behind . . . There was only one other woman in my year (St Hilda's) and the 50 or so male students' attitude to us both was, uniformly, not to notice we were there' (Ruth McKee). One learns that Betty Harris was one of only two undergraduates in her year reading Law, and ultimately the only one. 'In 1934 there were two from Somerville, one other from St Hugh's and one from St Hilda's. At the end of the first year, one of the girls from Somerville had changed schools to History, the other law student from St Hugh's had vanished – I think she had been more interested in men than in Law.' She also comments on the fact that, as a Law student, she was allowed to use the Codrington Law Library at All Souls, but was there very much on sufferance, conscious that she must do nothing to offend. A little later and this concession is still regarded as notable: 'One great privilege that I enjoyed as a Law student – albeit female – was permission to use the Codrington Law Library' (Mary Healey). Oxford libraries in general are eulogised by Nancy Salinger: 'What riches there were for us. My real education took place in those libraries, and I'm grateful.'

Though few and far between, the women reading Schools in fields still regarded as predominantly male were none the less able to make their mark: 'By the last year when I was doing my BcL, I was elected Vice-President of the Law Society. The Society had been founded by an American, more used to women in positions of authority perhaps than his English counterparts. There were good dinners with interesting speakers, and when Philip Toynbee was President of the Union and the debate was on a legal subject, members of the Law Society were invited to attend and I sat downstairs with the officials – it was very rare for a woman to be invited to do so!' (Betty Harris).

By the middle of the decade the 'essay crisis' was becoming a recognisable feature of undergraduate life: '. . . four or five idle days followed by a frenzied period of sleepless nights . . . known as a "crisis" ' (Phyllis Crisp). 'Unobtrusive academics who worked

all the time were known as "bunnies" and considered boring ... [I]
worked late at night once or twice a week to finish an essay, known as
a "crisis" ' (Dorothea Bleasley); 'we worked, often late at night, but
never in the afternoon. The Oxford afternoon was sacred, sacred to
sport, to walks in the nearby countryside, exploring the colleges,
listening to records in (was it?) Ingrams and browsing in Blackwells,
to punting on the river or having anchovy toast by someone's fire'
(Sylvia Sturge). Nearly everyone remembers coffee, lunch or tea in
the cafés of Oxford: Elliston's, the Cadena, the Super, the Moorish,
the two establishments confusingly sharing the name Kemp, the Ship
Street Café ('Oxford was full in those days of tea-shops run by real
old ladies', Margaret McDougle) and even 'the old green-washed
Clarendon Hotel in the Cornmarket where ... we used to sit on the
stairs drinking coffee after the theatre'. The Clarendon, in fact (sadly
demolished after the war) with its urbane Georgian facade, was a
favourite, as also were the George and the Mitre for dinner. 'A
women's club was started in the High opposite BNC which had a
reading-room, coffee and snack room, overnight accommodation ...'
(Janet Bews). It was called the Pentagon 'because it was for the four
women's colleges and the Home Students' (Phyllis Brentnall). Here
they 'served very nice teas, with creamy cakes and sandwiches ...'
and 'though the atmosphere was perhaps rather prim' the tea was
remembered as a perfect antidote to a 'very daring film about
conception and child bearing' (Norah Cummins). Unfortunately,
although the Pentagon 'fulfilled a genuine need ... the authorities of
the women's colleges got together and decided to close it down'
(Elspeth Slimon).

Although 'men were not permitted to drink anywhere *out* of
college' (Shirley Sutch) and women were forbidden to drink even *in*
college, the same writer mentions pub-crawling, with the added
excitement of possible encounters with the Proctors and their Bulldogs and another contributor remembers 'being taken out by male
friends to country pubs for Sunday lunch, at the Swan, at Minster
Lovell, and the Rose Revived at Standlake', which illustrates both the
changing attitude to rules and the fact that there were more undergraduates with cars. Not all were men: 'a few men undergraduates had
sports cars, and I think Marghanita Laski at Somerville had one'
(Dorothy Sherwood). Earlier, 'Ruth Johnson (Johnson the Dye
Works) from Liverpool ... owned a smart green Buick and when
myself and two friends were in the Oxford [hockey?] team to play
Cambridge at the Newnham ground, Ruth drove us over there at top

speed . . . I sat in the dickey . . . we had to hang on going over hump bridges . . . the match took place in a snow storm and we lost . . . Ruth went up in a plane with a Cambridge chap . . . and I can't remember how we got back to College . . . but certainly not in the Buick!' (Elspeth Slimon).

The bicycle continued to be the more usual form of transport, however: 'I couldn't afford a new one, so I was pleased to get an old, probably sixth-hand one for four shillings (20p in today's currency) at the College sale. It cost me quite a bit in repairs but it became a priceless companion, and being so old was only "borrowed" once – and even then was recognised and returned by a friend' (Lorna Clish); and apart from being essential in Oxford, expeditions into the surrounding countryside were made by cycle 'to the Cotswolds . . . once we lost our way and cycled·70 miles, returning just in time for a Balliol Concert . . . and I remember that my legs continued to cycle . . .' (Elspeth Slimon). Or there were expeditions by bus and then on foot, with the aid of Ordnance Survey maps and sustenance provided by the College on Sundays in the form of packed lunches. Alone – 'I used to take a solitary Sunday walk with some coppers in my pocket for the ancient ferry-man who would oar me across the river' (Brenda Green) – or in groups, the undergraduates looked for fritillaries, or the places mentioned in the *Scholar Gypsy*; they pooled their re- sources and hired a punt for the summer term from which they enjoyed 'the scents and sounds of summer, warm earth, dry grass, May blossom in masses overhanging the banks, small river insects and animals busy in the water, the plop of punt poles, roses in the inn gardens where one called in for a beer . . .' (Shirley Sutch) or 'enjoyed watching the men fall in the river. Some with great aplomb would rise from the water with pipe still firmly clenched in the teeth' (Anon). Marcia Gillett, who says 'If music was the warp of college life, water was the weft', describes going 'over the tricky rollers at Parson's Pleasure in the half-light (no nude gentlemen disporting themselves at that hour) . . . the rowing addicts among us were ruled by the terms of our training; these were strict, as the College authorities considered rowing otherwise to be a health risk. At that time we used to race against Cambridge ("It takes the women to win the Boat Race" was the *Oxford Mail*'s acid comment . . .).' Katharine Hargreaves added variety by punting a canoe.

Oxford 'hostesses' continued to issue invitations to tea on Sunday, though these were not so appreciated as in previous decades. None the less, a high proportion of the contributors enjoyed their Sunday walks, or other outings either before or after attending church. Bryan Green and F. R. Barry are remembered as preachers, but for most attenders the decade was remarkable for the missions to the University of William Temple, Archbishop of York. From the Archbishop's niece, Edith Temple, who found his mission 'very memorable', to Mary Tamplin, who writes: 'Then in 1931 came William Temple's Mission to Oxford, and for me religion took on a new dimension . . . I have never before or since heard anyone with such a mastery of the spoken English tongue – no notes, no fireworks, but sincerity and a clarity of thought which left large numbers of us with no doubts at all as to where our allegiance lay.' The admiration for his addresses was almost universal: 'Some weeks [after his visit] . . . the *Church Times* published his addresses in full, so the circulation of that weekly increased amazingly for nearly two months' (Mary Ker). It was also a period when the Oxford Group was particularly active in the University: 'I was interested enough to enquire about their activities and this turned out to be a mistake. They . . . were terribly persistent. They would even march into one's room, fall on their knees and pray for one's conversion, which was embarrassing at best and highly trying if one were busy' (Joan Lumsden). There was, however, no official pressure put upon undergraduates and 'some never entered Chapel at all' (Mary Ker), while Nancy Salinger, for example, 'can't remember any difficulty with specifically Jewish observances or festivals or days like Day of Atonement'.

The theatre, too, was again rich in names – the Markova–Dolin ballet and the hardy perennial D'Oyly Carte; '. . . the OUDS *Othello* . . . Peter Fleming as Iago, Valentine Dyall as Othello and Peggy Ashcroft as Desdemona' (Elspeth Slimon); Gielgud as Hamlet, *Romeo and Juliet* with Peggy Ashcroft, who again, with Giles Playfair and Thea Holme is remembered in *Hassan* (by the OUDS) performed in February 1931. This was Dame Peggy Ashcroft's first association with the University of Oxford. She was made an Honorary DLitt in 1962 and in December 1963 became an Honorary Fellow of St Hugh's. Also recalled are Margaret Rutherford as Lady Bracknell; and later in the decade, Rosalie Crutchley at the Playhouse, and Pamela Brown as Hedda Gabler. The Experimental Theatre Club came into existence in the middle of the decade. Winifred Fox was one of the founder members under what Delphine Chitty calls 'the dynamic direction of Nevill Coghill'. 'Three outdoor performances were particularly memorable . . . *The Tempest* in the Worcester Gardens, with the storm-stricken bark in the opening scene gently rippling to shore from a very still lake; an enchanting *Midsummer Night's Dream* in Magdalen Grove, with Theseus and his huntsmen riding into view and the music of Mendlessohn drifting down from the trees; and our own College play, *Tobias and the Angel*' (Lorna Clish). College drama flourished like the green bay tree. Particularly memorable productions include *Maria Marten*, and *The Critic*, in which Brenda Green as Tilburina 'duly went mad in white satin with my maid doing ditto in white linen. This "maid", with her beautiful red hair and blue eyes, matured into The Right Hon. Barbara Castle MP, latterly Euro MP . . .' There was also 'a very ambitious parody of a Shakespeare comedy in blank verse', which 'so successfully exploited some of the tricks and occasionally the speech patterns of Elizabethan drama, that Miss Seaton told us . . . that she was omitting some of the material she had intended for her course on Shakespearean comedy as we had obviously grasped it already' (Joan Lapraik). The characters sound convincing: 'an Old Nurse confided to a Conspirator that in days gone by she had given birth to a single love-child no more . . .' at which point, Miss Gwyer, it appears, upstaged the actors by remarking crisply, 'And quite enough!' (Anon). There was *Nine to Six*, a play with an all-female cast, and a production of *Comus* in 1935, on the terrace in St Hugh's garden. Despite some reservations about the choice of site for the production, it is remembered by many people as magical. Marcia Gillett, describing her first clear memory of St Hugh's, says she woke on a foggy morning 'to hear a singer outside on the terrace; a rehearsal of *Comus* was going on and the Attendant Spirit was invoking Sabrina. Nothing could be seen however but the producer, wet-haired, hunched in a fur coat. Next the Rout went through their paces, and then the Shepherds. The sundial was found to be in the way. Could it be moved perhaps? It could not; what on earth would Miss Rogers say? . . .' A measured criticism in the *Chronicle* says that '. . . the various elements of the play – the long moralizing, the songs (beautifully sung), the Rout, and the country dancers – were admirably blended. The whole production showed evidence of a directing mind . . . ' The reviewer also praises the performance of Comus (Molly Gaminara), who 'perhaps gained our sympathy rather more than he should have done'. The performance of the Attendant Spirit (Dorothy Sherwood) was also highly praised: 'a beautiful performance'. These two performers both received letters of congratulation from Nevill Coghill.

Another St Hugh's production remembered by many contributors is *Twelfth Night*, 'costumed in black and white, in which Viola and

Sebastian suddenly and bewilderingly change roles ... ' (Marcia Gillett); and *Everyman*, which was accompanied by a string trio playing medieval music.

By now, cinema was competing with the theatre. Undergraduates went to foreign films at 'a little cinema in Walton Street', Naomi Papworth tells us; Dorothy Lovegrove remembers going to 'light-hearted musicals with Fred Astaire and Ginger Rogers, or zany ones with the Marx Brothers, or Greta Garbo showing us how to act ...'; while Lorna Clish 'went to see *Rebecca* and Daphne du Maurier was outside the cinema "promoting it". We saw *The Wizard of Oz* up at Headington and whizzed down the hill afterwards, singing at the tops of our voices ...'

The popularity of the Bach Choir, now under Sir Thomas Armstrong, continued unabated: 'The Bach Choir was a joy ... and we had a very full programme both for the Silver Jubilee of George V and the Coronation of George VI' (Katharine Hargreaves). 'One clear memory is standing for a minute's silence because Sir Edward Elgar had died' (Pauline Brentnall). In town, undergraduates again had the opportunity to enjoy some of the most eminent musicians of the day – Sir Malcom Sargent, Sir William Walton and Toscanini conducting, and the playing of the d'Aranyi Sisters, Solomon, Paderewski, Rachmaninov. Less formally, they enjoyed the St Hugh's carol concert, sung Evensong at Magdalen and New College, musicals such as *White Horse Inn*, and popular music by Cole Porter, Romberg and Paul Robeson among others, and Lorna Clish remembers Richard Tauber 'taking four or five encores for "You are My Heart's Delight"'.

The main preoccupation of the time was, however, politics. One contributor writes:

The run-up to the War and the rise of the Hitler Youth movement, Oswald Mosley and his Fascists, were the background in the 'thirties but we were sheltered and only casually aware of impending danger – those who were political animals were more aware – but there was little 'media' pressure from the outside world, no TV and limited radio communication. I can't remember any one in College having a private radio. (Dorothy Sherwood)

This is, nevertheless, a minority view. Lack of 'media' pressure may then have been as described, but as the decade progressed, with such publications as the Left Book Club, the politically-angled Penguin

Specials and the launch of *Picture Post*, there was plenty of written evidence of what was happening abroad, to say nothing of nearly two million unemployed at home, to ensure that the latter 1930s at Oxford were, politically, a fertile soil for left-wing attitudes. Though, again, there were exceptions among undergraduates who balked at what today would be called 'political trendiness': 'I well remember the enthusiastic reception of a speaker at the English Club who stated, "Nobody but a Socialist can write poetry". I left the English Club' (Phillipa Hesketh-Williams); 'I resisted (though not many did) the propaganda of the Peace Pledge Union' (Dorothea Bleasley).

On the other hand: 'the visit of Sir Oswald Mosley ... I was thrilled by his oratory. But I became totally disillusioned when his supporters threw hecklers down the steps of the Town Hall' (Helena Charles). And although 'The "October Club" was launched during my first year, and a group of us planned to join it for a joke ... those who did returned to report the manners of the officials had been so atrocious and the meeting such a waste of time they were not going again' (Mary Tamplin), the comments of Daphne Thomas seem nearer to catching the concern of those not committed to the left:

> For a couple of years I struggled uneasily in this ambience [the Oxford Group] of which I mostly disapproved but which I then thought was probably the alternative to Communism. As are all young people, we were deeply concerned with the way the world was going ... I remember writing urgently to my mother asking her to guarantee food and shelter to at least one Jewish couple amongst a score or so whom we were concerned with getting out of Czechoslovakia, and being astonished at her reluctance to give any such undertaking. Most of the people I knew were Communists, and some of them proudly card-carrying ones ... the shadow of the war we knew was to come really did hang over our days, particularly in the last year when there was a feeling, especially amongst the men, that it really did not matter what kind of degree one got, one would end up in one of the Services or possibly dead. Meanwhile Oxford was all the more enjoyed because of one's doubts about the future ...

At St Hugh's not everyone saw eye to eye with 'the fiery red-head Barbara Betts [Castle] even then determined on a career in politics' (Mary Milner) and whom Barbara Reeve found 'rather trying'. But '... my tutorial partner .. an Exhibitioner who provided much-needed intellectual ballast to our tutorials, the Zuleika Dobson of our year and a sparkling ornament of the Labour Club . . . was Edna Edmunds, who later married Denis Healey' (Daphne Thomas). The Labour Club was seen as the 'only really active political club (except the October Club) and its members helped feed and accommodate the hunger marchers, canvassed the town for opinions on military sanctions against Mussolini in Abyssinia, placed a white wreath on the war memorial on Nov. 11th at the close of a peace march . . .' (Janet Bews). In 1934 there was the 'famous King and Country debate in the Union and also, on 8 March 1934, a motion before the house listed as "The Trial of The Rt Hon Winston Churchill, in that he had constituted and does constitute, a menace to the world". It was proposed by Michael Foot and was passed by 175 votes to 55' (Ruth McKee).

Michael Foot, then a Liberal, was 'a quite good-looking young man and an excellent speaker. He has since been one of the great disappointments of my life!' (Pauline Brentnall). Other Union figures and speakers of the decade include Hugh Fraser, Quintin Hogg and A. P. Herbert (speaking on his 'own' topic of divorce). At the Labour Club some were moderately 'pink', 'others very "red" who saw the world in Manichean terms and cherished an ill-informed and idealised image of Russian communism . . . Some of the young men of my generation actually went to fight in Spain . . . when one or two of the men returned after seeing action . . . the girls were horrified by their accounts of air raids and bombardments and disconcerted by the often disillusioned and bitter conclusions they drew from their experiences' (Betty Brodie). At St Hugh's, the JCR instituted four bread and cheese lunches a term 'so that the money so saved may be sent to a distressed area', i.e. Republican Spain.

By 1937 Hitler was consolidating his power: the Rhineland had been occupied, Austria was threatened. Mussolini was conquering Abyssinia, the Japanese were invading China and the Spanish Civil War had broken out. The issues were clear . . . it was the duty of each and every one of us to do his or her bit to repel Fascism and by presenting a united front against the Nazis now, prevent the world war which would otherwise inevitably break out . . . many of my friends and I joined the Communist Party . . . [believing] that Fascism and Nazism were the last despairing convulsions of the capitalist system and when this final crisis was resolved, the great day of socialism would dawn . . . It is easy to say we were

simplistic, that we had illusions about the Soviet Union and it
would be true; but I do not think we can be shown to have been
wrong ... According to my book, Oxford communists of the
thirties have no apologies to make. (Shirley Sutch)

Despite the strong anti-fascist feelings among undergraduates,
several members of St Hugh's visited Germany during the decade on
singing tours, field courses or to play hockey. 'While with a Geography
School field course in Germany in the Spring of 1936, I saw the
German troops entering the Rhineland ...' (Helen Southern). Or
even closer to the outbreak of war: 'In 1938 the Hitler Youth invited
the University Hockey team to go and play in Germany ... We never
could get used to them lining up before the match and giving the
Hitler salute ... The whole atmosphere was very tense and we were
subjected to a lot of Nazi propaganda.' At Hamburg 'the match was
more like war than a game ...' (Nora Shaw). Back in Oxford, there
was an incident that summed up the uneasy times: at the German
Club the President was usually a German Rhodes Scholar: 'the
Rhodes Scholars were mostly anti-Nazi ... but one year we found
ourselves with a Nazi as the obvious candidate for the Presidency ...
the Germans had to be careful because if they voted against a Nazi
they might be reported back to Germany ... so it was decided that the
English, who outnumbered the Germans on the Committee, should
vote for the non-Nazi ...' (Pauline Brentnall).

War finally broke out just before Michaelmas Term, 1939. The
left-wing idealism and the fight for peace had been to no avail, and the
political activists either tactfully held their peace, or discovered a new
patriotism they had previously denied. An *envoi* to peace at St
Hugh's, meanwhile, is provided by Daphne Thomas:

What else do I remember? Eights week, on Brasenose barge. The
Old Red Barn superseded by the new Playhouse in Beaumont
Street. May Morning, and breakfast afterwards in the Market ...
I loved my work, and I loved Oxford; it all passed too quickly. My
last act as an undergraduate was to receive my degree from Gordon
of Magdalen who was then Vice-Chancellor. Almost all those
graduating with me were in uniform, and all but me were male. As
I waited for a friend outside, the Vice-Chancellor's procession
came out of the Sheldonian ... and the tall, handsome Vice-
Chancellor, recognising the one woman, lifted his square and
bowed to me, at which the Proctors did the same.

THE 1940s

The true beginning of the 1940s was Michaelmas Term 1939. The war had an immediate effect on St Hugh's. Undergraduates arriving that October found they had been dispossessed, among them Monica Melles:

> a letter to my Father, in late September – 'In view of alterations due to the war, St Hugh's is being assigned for military use . . . and your daughter will therefore be accommodated in Holywell Manor, St Cross Road.' A look at the map, and gasps of amazement: the Holywell site was shown as a *penitentiary*! Not so, of course . . . the site had been rebuilt as a new extension of Balliol. Their lucky men had had *two* rooms each, one very large sitting-room and a small, functional bedroom . . . we were allocated to share this accommodation between two, both sharing the sitting-room . . . and with one sleeping there on a divan . . .

The specific 'military use' to which St Hugh's was put was that of a hospital for dealing with head wounds. Its contribution to the war effort in that respect was both honourable and distinguished, but it was achieved at the cost of accommodating the undergraduates not only at Holywell Manor, but other houses including Savile House, The Lawn and 82 Woodstock Road. St Hilda's kindly came to the rescue with other accommodation in 1939–40, replaced later with leased houses in Canterbury Road and Holywell.

During that Michaelmas Term, Oxford, as did the rest of the country at the time of what was later called the 'phoney war', quickly recovered its composure when it was realised that the University was not to be bombed out of existence overnight (indeed, it most fortunately survived unscathed throughout the war). At the same time, the blackout was a new experience (already apostrophised by Miss Gwyer in the previous section). 'We had to learn to become blackout-conscious and navigate dark entrances and dimly lit halls before reaching the utter blackness of our own room across which we stumbled to draw the curtains before putting on the light' (Rosemary Tyrell), while outside, 'Oxford in the black-out (I was Librarian of St Hugh's by then) was ravishing, the moonlight uncontaminated by street lighting lying on the stone walls, unforgettable, and the stars became a reality to me for the first time. Mostly seen from a bicycle, the lights covered with two layers of tissue paper by order' (Philippa Hesketh-Williams).

By day, 'from The Lawn we could see everything, sadly. Perhaps those in Holywell Manor and other temporary accommodations were better off in this respect, for we could from our windows see the Nissen huts smothering the rose-beds and tennis courts (in the grounds of St Hugh's) and wondered whether things would ever be the same again' (Mary Healey). The only part of the College that remained open to its student body was the Library, and many reminiscences dwell on how the statue of St Hugh with his swan on the staircase was important in reminding the nomadic undergraduates that they really were members of St Hugh's College. 'The Librarian, Miss Hesketh-Williams ("Philippa" to us) . . . ruled her domain with chill efficiency, charging sixpence a day for each book overdue. I think most of us were more in awe of her than we were of our Tutors' (Sheila Ottley). Philippa Hesketh-Williams herself writes:

The Library . . . was also open to the whole hospital . . . it was not greatly used (by them) as the books did not appeal to the general reader . . . . . the big skylight filling the library roof was blacked-out making it seem very gloomy and the continual drip drip of rain through . . . holes in the roof . . . together with the cracking of wood panels which were still shrinking . . . produced an eerie effect. It was a wonderful opportunity for getting on with the huge back-log of work which had been built up through bequests to the new library just before I took over. The garden was being filled with hutments for the new wards, and with the construction of the operating theatre out of part of the garden and the angle of the corridor leading from the old building to the Gray Allen . . . the NAAFI was built in the courtyard . . . the Chapel was locked . . .

That St Hugh's remained an entity at all despite the disruption of wartime was in great measure owed to Miss Gwyer, who was not above doubling for an off-duty porter at Holywell Manor: 'it was her achievement to run the house as a college' (Ruth Andrews). As time went on, in fact, such was Miss Gwyer's achievement, there were undergraduates who were unaware that Holywell Manor was not St Hugh's proper. Certainly, ceremony, such as was possible, played its full part with a due place for prayers instead of Chapel, and Hall was made as much like the 'real thing': 'there were two dinners, an informal one at 6.45 and a formal one at 7.30 ... for the latter, everyone wore something decorous and stood waiting until the procession of dons had taken their places at High Table ... the Principal used to intone the long Latin grace starting *Benedic nobis* ... sometimes accompanied by a bugle call from the neighbouring barracks ... anyone who wished to leave early ... had to walk up to High Table, catch the eye of the senior don present and "bow herself out" ' (Sheila Ottley). In spite of this, a few regarded their experience at St Hugh's in wartime as embracing rather more of a general Oxford allegiance than one specifically to the College, but there are plenty of memoirs to the contrary. Outside Holywell Manor, many remember 'the gentle Miss Adam' (Rachel Franklin) in charge at Savile House: 'I remember that her room was next to the gate ... so one had to be very quiet in climbing in on the odd occasion when one had stayed out too late ...' (Mary Woodward). Other memories are of incidents and personalities which demonstrate that eccentricity, absent-mindedness and a certain presence-of-mind had not been evacuated from Oxford for the duration: 'While at Holywell, Professor Ida Mann would sunbathe in clothes which at our age seemed rather risqué for a middle-aged lady' (Rachel Franklin). 'Conversation with Mrs. Martin Clarke ... "Yes, Miss Brown, er, Miss Smith, er, Miss Robinson ...?" "May I have permission to stay up for the first week of the vac. please?" "You'll have to ask your tutor". "Er ... you *are* my tutor" ' (Jean Robinson). 'Two of my contemporaries at St Hugh's were married. One got pregnant and agonised for weeks about how to tell Miss Gwyer. When she finally got her interview, she found the Principal knitting a tiny white sock ... ' (Hon. Janetta Somerset).

With the curiously self-selecting nature of random reminiscences, many of the contributors in this decade were reading English. In St Hugh's, the names of Miss Seaton and Mrs Martin Clarke (of whom impressions appear elsewhere) recur most frequently. In the University, the lecturers who made most impact in the 1940s also seem to be those who lectured to this School: C. S. Lewis, Tolkien (who was apparently only audible when reciting *Beowulf*, which makes one wonder why his lectures were so well attended) and Lord David Cecil, who appeared to attract his audience as much by his appearance and charm, as by his learning and skill as a lecturer. Sheila Ottley provides a representative recollection of them all:

Miss Seaton lived at 18, Parks Road, a Ruskin-Gothic ... house owned by a family named Pusey ... there the eight of us reading

English in my year ... went in pairs for our weekly tutorials, reading our essays in Miss Seaton's stuffy, book-lined first-floor room with its bubbling gas fire in front of which ... stood a bowl of water to keep the air moist ... writing them was somewhat hampered by the fact that we were all set the same subject each week, and the Library had only one copy of most of the books that were recommended reading ... the tutor in English language ... slim, sharp-featured and usually dressed in twin-set, shirt, lisle stockings and court shoes ... Mrs Martin Clarke was always known by her Christian name, Daisy ... a Newnham graduate, she had a high regard for Cambridge's Professor Chadwick ... and insisted that we use his pronunciation where this differed from that in common use at Oxford. On an old-fashioned wind-up gramophone she would play a scratchy record of the Professor reciting the opening paragraphs of 'King Edmund' from Aelfric's 'Lives of the Saints', while we tried (not always successfully) not to giggle ... though a Quaker, she admired Winston Churchill greatly and followed the progress of hostilities on the radio in her ground-floor room at 82 Woodstock Road, with its reproduction of God Raising Adam over the fireplace ... Since the Examination Schools, like St Hugh's were being used as a military hospital, most lectures in the English Faculty took place in college halls, though some were given in the Taylorian ... by far the most sought-after lecturer ... was red-faced, untidily-dressed C. S. Lewis of Magdalen, who looked more like a farmer than a don. I remember attending his series ... 'Prologomena to the Study of Renaissance Literature' spellbound like the rest of the audience by his genially dogmatic boom ... almost as popular was Lord David Cecil, whom I heard speak in the hall at New College on 'Shakespeare's English Historical Plays' while fascinated listeners crowded every bench and even climbed on to the window sills ... Edmund Blunden ... although a tutor at Merton, usually lectured at the Taylorian in his OTC captain's uniform while his wife ... sat on the edge of the platform at his feet ... I did not attend lectures by Professor Tolkien. He did, however, set the Old English papers that we did for Pass Moderations in the Divinity School at the end of our second term. With typically impish humour, he set us to decline in Old English 'Three Blind Mice'. I declined it in both plural and singular, and realised my mistake just in time and did a bit of hasty crossing-out as the invigilator was about to take my paper ...

She concludes with a note which adds a further facet to the impressions of Miss Seaton:

English Schools were held in the Sheldonian ... the Examiners (Professor Nichol Smith, C. S. Lewis, J. N. Bryson of Balliol, Lord David Cecil, and Miss Dorothy Everett of LMH) took turns to invigilate, doing so in pairs. The weather was sunny and hot and, as we wrote, the chimes of Oxford floated through the open doors, urging us to write faster ... the first morning, Miss Seaton was waiting to greet all her pupils, pinning a freshly-cut rose on each girl's coat ... she was also waiting to greet us every day as we emerged into the hot, late afternoon, and to ask us how the day's papers had gone ...

Mary Healey, who read Jurisprudence, adds to the portrait of Agnes Headlam-Morley, who was her Director of Studies: 'My first recollection of her was most reassuring – she was sitting/lying with her neck in the bottom of the chair in her study wearing slacks and with her feet on the mantlepiece. A highly intelligent, and to me, a most reassuring person. I admired her more than any other.' To these well-commemorated names there were a few notable additions: 'Coghill would appear on the dais at Exeter dressed rather for dinner than his Shakespeare lecture ... we were ... exported for tutorials and classes, so met Dr Helen Gardner, Dorothy Everett, Mary Lascelles, and Katie Lee. The only tutor we found it difficult to work with was Mr Brett-Smith, who seemed to find it less embarrassing to talk about cricket than our essays. Pat Beer made up a nice clerihew about him:-

Mr. Brett-Smith is nice to be with—
He is rather, but not too much, like a father.'
                                        (Lorna Clish)

The Hon. Janetta Somerset, meanwhile, supplies a rounded picture of a figure already noted (in the previous decade) as an undergraduate, but who grew to full stature (and fame in Oxford) as an eccentric, in the 1940s:

Mr Donald MacKinnon, who dispensed philosophy at Keble ... lived in a den of a room, its central table piled with hoods, vegetable dishes, copies of the Oban newspaper, old examination papers, half-burned essays, broken pencils, bits of clothing and books. From time to time, as he paced back and forth, winding the curtains round his neck, little avalanches would fall off the table and dust would fly up. He would absently replace most of what had fallen and continue to expound. Yet whenever he wanted a book, he would put his hand into the mess, miraculously find the right book, turn to the page he wanted, read aloud, and thrust the book back into the tangle. He also had an alarming habit of sitting on the back of his chair with his feet on the seat, and swaying back and forth while you read to him . . . if he liked your essay he put it in the wood box, and if he did not, he put it in the coal scuttle, which is why so many of them got charred.

Also, from the same writer: 'There were few lecturers of note left in Oxford (A. J. P. Taylor was probably the best in my field) . . . there were a number of Great Men, like Sir John Myers, who rode a tricycle to the public danger in Canterbury Road, and Lord David Cecil, whose wife preferred him to go out with one of his little boys holding his hand, so he would not get run over.'

By early 1941, such was the lack of enemy action, Miss Gwyer was writing in the *Principal's Report*: 'University life has been permitted to continue in unbroken continuity. We have had a fair number of "Alerts", but no loss of life has occurred "within three miles of Carfax".' Oxford, however, was by no means isolated from the war, as numerous writers testify: 'Jeeps and tanks lined St Giles, and the ratio of men students to women changed dramatically. Soldiers in "hospital blue" were much in evidence, and brothers and boyfriends came to visit in uniform. Oxford took a lot of evacuees, and several of our English group went down with Mrs. Martin Clarke to help distribute clothing at a centre in St Ebbe's' (Lorna Clish). 'The news of the Fall of France came on the wireless at lunch-time on a perfect June day. Those of us who were living in 1940 at Savile House were just about to go off to Holywell Manor for lunch and crowded into the maids' room to listen to the news in grim silence while the sun shown brightly outside' (Doris Dixon). 'The most harrowing experience was in June, 1940, when we helped at the canteens and reception centres for our troops rescued from Dunkirk. They came in an endless line, hollow-eyed and grey with fatigue and practically speechless from their ordeal' (Mary Healey). ' . . . we all assembled in [Miss Gwyer's] sitting-room to hear the announcement (on my birthday!) of Hitler's invasion of Russia in 1941' (Ynys Scott). 'One limpid evening I was relaxing with some friends in a punt from Bardwell Road when wave after wave of aircraft roared overhead; we afterwards learnt that they were going to take part in the first 1000-bomber raid on Germany' (Sheila Ottley); and another note from Ynys Scott, which will seem all the richer to those who actually knew the accustomed dignity of those mentioned: 'My last year was spent ... at 1, Holywell Street, where Miss Procter and Miss Francis were the resident dons ... an air-raid warning (almost unknown in Oxford) sounded and immediately the two dons disappeared beneath the table ... to the amusement of those of us who had experienced the "real thing" in London.' Nevertheless, Edrey Peet reports, 'we had to carry gas-masks to lectures, and indeed whenever we went out, and the first air-raid siren was frightening to those who lived in quiet areas'.

Meanwhile, more parochially perhaps, St Hugh's had lost Miss Glover and Miss Gray to the Ministry of Labour and Board of Trade respectively. The inconvenience of the libraries, including the St Hugh's Library, closing at blackout time, was alleviated by an extension of 'daylight saving', and by the opening of the Radcliffe Camera until 10 p.m. All the St Hugh's houses, with the help of the City ARP authorities, were operating their own firefighting plans, and undergraduates were allotted duties in the houses, and also in certain University departments, with the leave of the College. There are many stories concerning this activity, and many stress the eeriness within the Bodleian on a moonlight night.

I was finding my way late one evening to the fire-watching room in Holywell Manor ... [and] came across Miss Gwyer fully dressed standing statue-like in a strategic corridor, perusing *The Times*. She asked me if I had seen Miss X, who was clearly out after hours, which were fairly early by present day standards. When I said I had not, she wished me a firm goodnight and turned back to *The Times*, clearly prepared to stand it out all night if need be ... Fire-watching was a voluntary affair outside college and since it was a paid occupation some of us augmented our grants with the odd small amount now and then. I went one night to the Chinese Room of the Bodleian to report for duty and was told I was expected over in the New Bodleian and was to go underground to get in. I walked alone with a small torch through the passageways under Broad Street to the New Bodleian, bravely attempting to eradicate from my mind the number of ghosts they had listed for me to meet, including that of Oscar Wilde. No bombs fell on us, except, I believe, for a few scattered incendiaries, which did little damage ... we of the fire-watch received instructions in putting out incendiaries at the bottom of St John's Garden, beyond the Archery Lawn. (Margaret Jacobs)

'I used to firewatch in the University Museum ... Notices on some doors indicated what important specimens were to be rescued if possible ... we were paid for firewatching a shilling a night' (Stella Hassid). 'There were concessions about residence during the vac in exchange for firewatching which ensured that the supply of fire-watchers always exceeded demand ... ' (Janet Gibbins).

Fire-watching apart, St Hugh's undergraduates undertook other forms of 'war work'. The *JCR Report* for 1941 records; 'To our usual forms of exercise, the war has added that of digging. A large number of people have taken this up, and have worked at allotments at Headington ... and on Port Meadow and in The Parks' (where potatoes were grown). Nor did the work cease at the end of term: 'Vacation activities have included nursing, tractor-driving, the sorting of Post Office mails, milk rounds, and all types of land work.' Mary Wright 'helped wash up at the Radcliffe Infirmary and to mend socks at the ... hospital based at St Hugh's'. Janet Gibbins recalls 'with horror ... washing endless greasy plates in the British Restaurant'; Anne Howard ' ... after trying to make camouflage nets, washing up in a NAAFI Canteen, and showing American troops round Oxford ... settled for firewatching in Bodley' and Margaret Jacobs recalls 'we ... had to do a certain amount of compulsory war-work, about two hours a week, I think ... I was on the Clearing Station at the British Restaurant, a central eating depôt at the Town Hall where, as in most towns and cities during the war, food could be bought fairly cheaply ... I am not sure that the war effort was furthered much by our exertions. Presumably this was a conscience-saving exercise in someone's mind.'

Not that the consciences of the undergraduates compelled to undertake the war work were made easy. Monica Melles recalls: 'I remember coming back to Holywell Manor after a seminar on *Paradise Lost*, to see a large group of soldiers, tired, hot, and travel-stained, being given tea and sandwiches by the main gate ... our academic efforts seemed a little out of place.' An anonymous contributor writes: 'We had uneasy consciences about whether we ought to be studying in the midst of a war', while Valerie Pitt puts it: 'we were [at Oxford] ... on a kind of ticket of leave, luckier than our contemporaries who were in the forces or the factories ... there was perhaps a shadow of guilt in being delivered from all that ... ' Ruth Andrews also wondered 'if we should be at Oxford enjoying ourselves so tremendously. We were, however, directed by the authorities ... to stay to complete our courses ... ' As ever, it took Miss Gwyer to provide some balm for this sort of heart-searching: 'There is no idea in Oxford of a University course as a privilege only or mainly, it is viewed as an indispensable preparation for forms of service many of which are already short of the trained personnel they need' (*Principal's Report*, 1942). Not everyone ascribed to the generally militaristic viewpoint. Edrey Peet, a Quaker, felt that she was part of an unpopular minority, but despite that, 'was thankful to be alive and felt privileged to be allowed to continue one's studies'.

These, then, were the chief circumstances, activities and attitudes that made wartime Oxford an abnormal (judged by peacetime standards) experience for the St Hugh's undergraduate. None the less, they do not prevent Margaret Blaker speaking for many when expressing, despite adversity, a love of St Hugh's and summing up: 'I count myself privileged to have known Oxford in wartime as a member of St Hugh's.' Nor the similar feelings of Penny Peters who, at the age of twelve, had been taken to the top of Radcliffe Camera and gazing at the spires as 'the bells of Oxford called the hours' determined 'that I would go there to learn, to become part of the magic'. Nor, despite wartime, was there any disappointment in this: 'Coming into Oxford by train was always a pleasure, even in winter. I used to watch the spires rise on the horizon, drawing closer as the train pulled in, and would think: "I'm home." ' Others drew pleasure at that same station from simply seeing the name OXFORD on the nameboard.

On the more popularly-remembered wartime stringencies, food and clothes rationing, the reminiscences do not dwell as much as might be expected (not as much, certainly, as in the immediate post-war years). Perhaps it was because they were so generally accepted at the time, but for whatever reason, there is only one note of any length about clothes:

Clothes were a serious problem ... still rationed ... and very dull. Some of mine were home-made or of upholstery fabric which was 'off-ration'. Particularly difficult was 'the long dress'. In my group of friends there were two or three long dresses, worn by everyone in turn without any consideration of colour or fit, but when a St Hugh's function required everyone in a formal dress on the same night, we were in despair. Women were not wearing trousers, apart from war-time uniforms, so we borrowed our brothers' heavy corduroy trousers and very lumpy we looked. (Joy Startup)

More serious rationing was that of food, and while some considered that St Hugh's fed them adequately, just as many have fairly trenchant criticism, much of it reserved for the dried egg: 'all I can remember of St Hugh's meals were the reconstituted dried eggs sitting like yellow rubber on the plates, and the part of the Latin grace that Miss Gwyer intoned that blessed the Lord and thanked Him for our repast *sumpturissime*' (Mary Woodward). 'The food was terrible in my third year 1941–42, soggy, watery bread-and-butter pudding with cheese sparsely sprinkled on it, was a frequent main course. But breakfast with our own rations was good' (Margaret Blaker). 'I remember blackened "cake" puddings, dried egg omelettes and pretty short rations at Holywell Manor. My mother sent me illicit tins of Ostermilk No. 2 which, mixed with cocoa, made an acceptable drink . . .' (Rachel Franklin). By contrast: 'War-time rationing did not impose many hardships . . . it was still possible . . . to dine quite reasonably at the Randolph and the Mitre' (Joyce Hepburn). Memories of other eating places and supplemented rations include: 'Coffee and buns at Ellistons very popular . . . we went out occasionally to restaurants . . . the Taj Mahal, the Kemp . . . mainly with boyfriends or visitors . . . ' (Ruth Andrews); 'buttered buns at Ma Brown's in the Market; cinnamon toast at the Stowaway; salads and cream cakes at the Kemp . . . ' (Daphne Tuck); 'British Restaurants where a two-course meal cost a shilling . . . ' (Stella Hassid); 'Morning coffee and walnut cake at Fuller's . . . ' (Mary Wright). But by far the most popular source of food outside the College, mentioned in almost every reminiscence, was Oliver and Gurdon's cake factory, to which there was a daily pilgrimage on bicycles in the early morning: 'The wherewithal for a tea party, our only form of entertaining, was achieved by cycling to Summertown . . . and queueing outside the cake factory for buns and cakes, the freshness of which compensated for their lack of such ingredients as butter and eggs' (Anne Howard). The factory, indeed, such was its popularity, earned itself a peculiarly Oxford distinction: 'We actually managed to get it called the Caker' (Patricia Wood).

Men, of course, were not officially rationed, but, in the jargon of the time they were certainly 'in short supply', a state of affairs to which frequent mention is made: 'Socially, men were at a premium. There were the Intelligence Corps, the scientists, the very young and the medically C3 rejected by the Forces' (Janet Gibbins). 'The only men around were medical students, sick people, ordinands and visiting servicemen' (Hon. Janetta Somerset). To these categories were added, in increasing numbers, short-course cadets, and American GIs of whom, in the latter years of the war, Oxford was full. Penny Peters remembers that it was 'great fun jitter-bugging with them at *totally* out-of-bounds dances at the Town Hall', while another undergraduate got a black eye colliding with a lamp-post as she fled the pursuit of a GI (not an uncommon occurrence) into the safety of St Hugh's. Round about the same time, also in the blackout, Miss Gwyer suffered a similar injury when she walked into a stationary bus. Margaret Jacobs recalls Miss Gwyer referring to the incidents in her St Hugh's Night speech: 'Miss X', she said, 'and I, have both had an accident this term – not, I might say, for the same reason.'

Financially, the members of St Hugh's ranged from those who had no complaint, to those (rather more) who had to exercise a good deal of management to make ends meet: 'I seem to remember that I had £3 a week, and was comparatively well off. I think I spent it on books, clothes when available, off-ration food, and do not remember having difficulty in managing. It cost ninepence [3¾p] to get a puncture mended at the cycle shop in Holywell Street, and this seemed to be a fairly frequent drain on resources' (Janet Gibbins). 'I was on a State Scholarship which paid (I think) £50 a term for tuition and maintenance. . . . my father allowed me £12 per term on top of this (. . . I lived free at home during vacations) and an older friend of the family£5, so I had £17 per term. This just about covered fares, books, subscriptions, entertainment and a few clothes . . . and was rather more than several of my friends had' (Ruth Andrews). 'We used to sell our books to Blackwells in order to buy more . . and our clothing coupons to each other, also to buy books . . . ' (Patricia Wood). Edrey Peet was allowed £20 a year 'for books, clothes, activities and holidays'. She found it hard to manage on.

Despite austerity, either financial or caused directly by the war, there was, hearteningly, much else going on in Oxford that was of a more reassuring nature, a still pervasive echo of the true Oxford, both within the fragmented College and in the University generally. The St Hugh's Dramatic Society had produced, in the hot summer of Hitler's invasion of the Low Countries, and of Dunkirk, a successful

Love's Labours Lost in the garden of Holywell Manor, kindly allowed by Balliol, and an ideal setting. Later there was a production of *The Trojan Women* and 'Gilbert Murray rehearsed us himself in his translation of a play by Menander, and I played opposite Monica Sims (who became Director, Radio 4) in Hsiung's *The House with the Western Chamber*, directed by Roger Lancelyn Green' (Patricia Wood). 'The Freshers' Play (*Alice through the Looking Glass*) at the end of the summer was in the garden at Holywell Manor and Humpty Dumpty fell off the wall and broke both arms ... ' (Yvonne Mead). Outside St Hugh's 'OUDS gave a *Measure for Measure* which looked like something out of Breughel and must, in retrospect, have owed some of its power to the young Richard Burton ... (then Richard Jenkins of Exeter College)' (Anne Howard). The same writer remembers: 'Nevill Coghill dominated undergraduate theatre, and Peter Brook gave a hint of future distinction by making, as an undergraduate, a film of Sterne's *Sentimental Journey*, which was shown in the Union building.' An anonymous contributor recalls 'Coghill's ... *Midsummer Night's Dream* in Magdalen Grove ... we disliked Puck as Jester ... but the setting as the actors came riding on through the Grove, was unforgettable'. The New Theatre 'used to have wonderful Shakespeare and Ballet sessions. The cheapest seats were sixpence and we used to queue for hours, sitting on little wooden stools working on our set books' (Monica Melles), while Mary Wilkins remembers 'excellent pre-London runs' and Anne Howard, 'Margot Fonteyn and Robert Helpmann dancing every performance'. The Playhouse 'had a quieter "ambience" but had many wonderful productions such as *The Ghost Train* and *The Cherry Orchard*. Pamela Brown made her debut there' (Monica Melles). 'I remember chiefly Shaw – Rosalie Crutchley as St Joan, in particular ... ' (Anne Howard). 'One of the most memorable performances ... was the Isherwood play *The Ascent of F6*. Yvonne Mitchell was the leading juvenile in the resident company, and her power and talent were outstanding. Isobel Jeans, Frank Shelley, Donald Houston were among the company ... Max Adrian ... as a guest artist ... was compelling and strange in the Ibsen play *John Gabriel Borkmann*' (Penny Peters).

At the cinema 'the most moving experience was the war-time *Dangerous Moonlight* at the Walton Street Cinema with a predominantly student audience. The opening scene of bombed buildings and devastation around a solitary pianist playing the Warsaw Concerto, was constantly and poignantly recalled during the summer term, for wherever one went in north Oxford, the haunting melody came through open windows . . . ' (Lorna Clish).

On a wider musical front:

Oxford musical life was rich. I remember Moisewitsch playing Beethoven sonatas, the Griller Quartet performing in RAF uniform, and, above all, Kathleen Ferrier near the beginning of her career, singing Messiah in the Town Hall and the St Matthew Passion with the Queen's Society . . . Sunday evening concerts in the hall of Balliol used to start in daylight and finish lit only by minute lights on the music stands. A memorable one was sponsored by John Masefield, with the old poet reading a poem to the memory of his dead son, followed by the Trout Quintet. (Anne Howard)

'Horowitz was our favourite pianist . . . I had a gramophone, the cranked variety. I took it on the river and played the Pastoral Symphony and had a passion for Brahms. The girl next door played nothing but Eine Kleine Nachtmusik. We could rent records – there was a lending library in the basement of the Clarendon building in the Broad' (Mary Woodward). Far from stifling musical activity, in fact, the war seems to have stimulated it, an impression confirmed by a *St Hugh's Chronicle* report (1942) on 'Oxford Music in War-time': 'Since the outbreak of war we have suffered, as have many provincial towns, not from having too little music, but rather we have been offered the opportunity of hearing too much. Who can hear Dr Sargent direct Elgar's *Nimrod* twice in one day, or leave the Sheldonian saturated with the artistry of Miss Farichi and Miss D'Aranyi to hear yet another admirable violin recital in Balliol Hall?' And it adds a telling description of packed Sheldonian Theatre and Town Hall alike resounding to community renderings of carols and oratoria excerpts conducted by Dr Armstrong 'with no equipment but a gasmask and a score . . . '. While mentioning Dr Armstrong, it is worth noting that, under his leadership, the Bach Choir maintained its hold on the enthusiasms of chorally-minded St Hugh's undergraduates: indeed this was an interest well maintained throughout the decade, from the reminiscences of Ruth Andrews in 1940 and others to those of Elizabeth Hunter in 1948. The latter remembers 'with joy and gratitude the experience of singing in the Bach choir. The tremendous emotional impact of singing the Bach B Minor Mass'. Also: 'Going up to London to broadcast Constant Lambert's "Summer's

Last Will and Testament" conducted by the composer. Singing a
summer concert in the ruins of Dorchester Abbey ... '

Theatre and music aside, Ruth Andrews remembers that despite
the war, 'activities of all sorts flourished. I belonged to the English
Club, Ballet Club, OU Music Club, Celtic Club ... and something
called the Five Arts Club', while Stella Hassid recalls the visit of C. E.
M. Joad (by then a celebrity of the BBC's Brains Trust) to the
Socratic Club where he 'seemed to me to set out to insult his
audience, regarding us at Oxford as a lot of snobs ... I (also) ... took
up ... campanology. In spite of the wartime ban on the ringing of
church bells there was a thriving University Society of Campanolo-
gists under the dedicated leadership of John Spice ... ' Petrol
rationing made car journeys outside Oxford a rarity: 'Having no cars
did restrict us to a smallish area but we went to London nightclubs by
train and came back on the milk train – all very illicit' (Patricia
Wood). The bicycle was a necessity (throughout this decade as all
others) and 'Cycling was not only the only real way to get about to
lectures etc. but also one of our great pleasures. On Sundays, we often
went quite far afield, to Lewknor, and the Icknield Way, to Nuneham
Courtenay, and the peacocks, and then to Dorchester (Oxon) where
we visited the Abbey and treated ourselves to a hotel tea' (Monica
Melles). 'The longest general exodus by bike that I remember was in
the year when the Boat Race was rowed at Henley (because of the
war) and we all went, hundreds and hundreds of us' (Patricia Wood).

> We cycled everywhere – to lectures and tutorials, rattling up all the
> little streets and alleyways between colleges, propping one's bike
> against a pile of other old crocks (no padlocks needed in those days)
> to dash into an early morning lecture in some college hall (the
> really early ones were still strong with the aroma of breakfast – did
> they *always* have kippers in men's colleges?) ... hardly anyone had
> cars in those days of petrol rationing, so Oxford was a much
> quieter and freer place for cycling and walking. (Mary Alexander)

Yet none of the activities so far mentioned rivalled the river, which
rolls through almost every reminiscence, as in other decades, like an
infinite thread of solace and pleasure, untouched by any wartime
restriction, an experience sublimely and uniquely Oxford: 'lovely
tranquil summer evenings, punting or being punted, from Timms
Boathouse in Bardwell Road ... pre-breakfast swims at Dames
Delight ... Eights Week with all the colour and gaiety of the college

barges . . . winter walks along the Cher or Isis, returning with glowing cheeks to toast and crumpets on the open fire in one's room' (Frances MacDonald). 'The upper reaches of the river were a joy. Some sunny days, I'd take a canoe, and my books, and paddle off alone, and, tied up among the rushes, which sighed in the slightest breeze, would pretend to work, but most of all, would enjoy being alone, in a world of sky, rushes, and whispering water' (Penny Peters).

In 1944, owing to a change in the regulations, which allowed prospective teachers to spend three years on academic work, and to a large entry of good candidates for the Scholarship and Entrance examinations, St Hugh's was having to find extra rooms for all the undergraduates expected to come into residence. Miss Gwyer reported a bequest of £20 000 over eight years 'to be applied to what we have never before been able to boast of – an Endowment Fund'. There were also relaxations in ARP and the necessity for 'war work', so that those who came up from 1944 onwards were relieved of these responsibilities.

Then in May 1945, came VE Day. It was, predictably, an occasion which is luminously imprinted in the minds of everyone who was at St Hugh's at the time, but, as Valerie Pitt observed: 'the Gwyer chose to take a high and mighty line about undergraduates returning to the College and their beds by 11 p.m. on VE day'. She continues:

> Everything was, of course, happening that day: the bells rang like water cascading out of the air, there was dancing and drinking in the streets, there were bonfires in the High. It was both an historic occasion and a continuous party. Nobody with any sense at all of what was in the minds of the young would have done such a damn fool thing – but, of course, the habitual reaction of that women's college culture was to look to the proper and respectable conduct of ladies – which was *not* dancing in the streets until midnight . . . I am surprised we all behaved with more common sense than our dons . . . we all signed in decorously and then slipped out (almost the entire college) by the usual routes (behind the bicycle shed at Holywell Manor, and across Lord David Cecil's garden at Savile House) and spent the rest of the night dodging the dons at Carfax and watching the young men leap in and through the bonfires.

An extract from Monique Viner's diary notes: 'V-Day, the day which we had waited for . . . for so long it seems quite unbelievable . . . evening, joined the throngs which coursed round Broad, High . . . an

absolute mass of humanity, singing, shouting, yelling ... danced
round Magdalen, round huge bonfires ... midnight, went off (with
some particular friends) on to punts on the river until 3 a.m. ...
climbed in very easily and of course, so late that no staff were about.'
Penny Peters describes other joyful and bizarre happenings:

> Some of us were having tea in a café above Taphouse's, the
> music-shop near the Randolph, when the news came through. We
> all poured out of the café, doing the conga, and picking up people
> as we went, until we had an immense line dancing from St Giles to
> Carfax. We formed a cordon across Magdalen Bridge, and every
> vehicle entering Oxford was given a piece of lavatory paper which
> they had to give up at Carfax. The G.I.'s thought they'd entered a
> madhouse! A bonfire was lit in the middle of Carfax, and melted
> the rubber blocks of which the road at that time was composed.
> People madly danced round it. Lord David Cecil and his family lit
> a bonfire in the middle of Addison's Walk. As fast as the porters
> tried to lock people out of the front gates of Magdalen, as swiftly
> were they let into the side-entrances. A trailer-pump was taken out
> into the middle of the river by Magdalen Bridge, and sprayed all
> passers-by with water; but, alas, the perpetrators ... sank inglor-
> iously, punt, pump, trailer and all. Everywhere was noise, chaos,
> rejoicing.

VE Day effectively marked the transition point of the decade for St
Hugh's as for the rest of Oxford. The war had another term to run,
but VJ Day occurred during the Long Vacation of 1945, and although
it signalled the end of all hostilities and, therefore, the *laissez-passer* in
official terms for a return to peacetime ways for the University, it
went unremarked. The end of the war in Europe had already, most
importantly, started the process; but that process was by no means a
return to 'normal'. As Miss Gwyer's successor, Miss Procter,
reported nearly two years later: 'Post-war Oxford is in some ways as
abnormal as was war-time Oxford.' The reason, of course, in large
part, compounded by the continuance of food and clothes rationing,
fuel shortages, and an austere mode of life imposed by the newly-
elected Labour government, was the return of demobilised ex-service
personnel, both women and men, to resume their interrupted studies
at the University. The first of these came back in Michaelmas Term
1945. They were the older ex-service officers, men and women, some

of them having left Oxford to join up as far back as 1939. In 1946 and 1947 the return became a flood; 1919 but on a larger scale, and included not only Scholars and Commoners who had completed, perhaps, no more than a year of their courses, but large numbers of short-course cadets, and an even greater number of 'new' undergraduates who, having joined the forces straight from school, were coming up to Oxford at an age when in normal circumstances they would have already gone down. It all had a profound effect on the life of the University and St Hugh's. Although, in common with other women's societies, the college did not receive back as high a proportion of ex-service students as the men's colleges, its life was none the less dramatically amended.

Social life in Oxford changed overnight. Everywhere was suddenly full of young men, old, perhaps beyond their years, many of them determined to forget the years in the Forces. The pubs were full – the Proctors almost had to give up, because no ex-serviceman was going to be prevented from drinking if he wanted to. The University Societies became full of mature minds; men with real opinions. The tempo of life quickened and, for those in the social whirl, life became hectic . . . of course, this incoming tide brought with it its problems . . . irresponsible drinking, a slightly anarchic attitude to authority . . . girls hitherto immured in boarding schools were frequently unable to cope sensibly. Sexual mores began to change . . . a girl was sent down from LMH for drunkenness; another for being found with a man in her room. (Penny Peters)

'In '45 we were probably two distinct groups [at St Hugh's] . . . those of us who had come up straight from school and those returning for a third year after war service, naturally much more mature and worldly – some of them had even heard of contraception!' (Marion Graham). 'Ex-servicemen were in the majority, and I felt sorry for the young men who had opted for university before national service (I believe this option was restricted to scholars). They seemed so immature, and socially they could not compete with men who had seen war service' (Margaret Mogford).

Physically, the most important obstacle to St Hugh's being a coherent entity was the continuing presence of the hospital, and the hiving off of the College into other parts of Oxford. This, fortunately, was soon to end. Indeed, the vacation of the St Hugh's buildings by the army medical staff was more sudden than anyone had hoped possible. Miss Gwyer wrote:

> As to our return, we had uncertainty hanging over us all through the Long Vacation, and then at a few weeks' notice ... were obliged to remove ourselves, our furniture and our books, into a College which needed cleansing in every corner, filled with broken furniture and worn-out equipment, and the essential services in dangerous disarray. Ready in a month? The first feeling of all who looked on the spectacle was of utter incredulity. But, by a feat of organisation for which the Bursar [Miss Thorneycroft] deserves the greatest credit, it proved just possible to receive students 'not earlier than 2 p.m.' on October 13th., 1945, (the first day of term). A hundred helpers, miscellaneous in character and antecedents, had been gathered together, including German prisoners-of-war (who proved effective cleaners), undergraduates and domestic workers of every grade, while electricians, plumbers, and emissaries of the War Office intent on their own mysterious business, threaded their way among the rest. All our buildings, with the exception of part of the Mary Gray Allen Wing and the Moberly block, which were themselves newer and perhaps were treated with more care than the rest urgently needed redecorations. (*Principal's Report*, 1946)

She spoke, too, of the prospect of 'demolition of the brick wards now ranged over the garden. The garden itself, even when cleared will take years to recover.' In the event the brick huts were to remain longer than anticipated, nor did the move back into College please everyone: 'We hated the move back into College in the autumn of 1945. The rooms seemed small after our spacious sitting-rooms, there were no locks on the bathroom or loo doors, and the beds were extremely hard' (Jane Langton). 'St Hugh's itself smelled of hospitals, having been vacated by the army about 10 days before term' (Marion Graham). 'That first dinner, the whole establishment was pervaded by the clinical breath of antiseptic and, indeed, there was still a large hand-basin in Hall itself' (Merrill Brady). But the *JCR Report* for the year takes a more balanced line:

> The Michaelmas Term was a memorable one for the JCR, none of whom, excepting perhaps those few whom we were proud to

welcome back at that time from the Forces, had known our own College building ... and though huts and passages could not be torn out of the once lovely gardens, nor a faint hospital odour removed from the central regions ... yet St Hugh's is once more a gracious and friendly building in which nearly all the members of the JCR are housed. Grateful as we were in our exile for the mellow, sheltering walls of the Manor, it is only now, reinstated after that exile, that we know the fullness of pride in the words: 'Our college, St Hugh's.'

The immediate post-war period brought changes other than in surroundings. In 1946, the long term of office of Miss Gwyer as Principal came to an end: she was succeeded by Miss E. S. Procter, who thus became only the fourth Principal in the history of St Hugh's. Mr Veale, the Chairman of Council (and University Registrar) paid generous tribute in his speech at the 1946 Gaudy to Miss Gwyer's achievements in twenty-two years as Principal: 'No more than thirty years ago, St Hugh's was an intruder in the sacred circle of Oxford Colleges, tolerated because of its insignificance. Today it commands an undisputed equality with the proudest of the old foundations.' In her reply Miss Gwyer saw herself as

the last of the amateur Principals. I did, it is true, get my degree by examination, but it is no use pretending that your retiring Principal ever published any research, ever worked in a Government Department, or sat on a Royal Commission, or indeed ever did anything whatever except play the modest violet ... All the other women Principals have done great things, and my successor is worthy to join them. Compared with such, you see before you a nobody! But nobodies, like mongrel dogs, have a way of getting themselves loved; all through today I have felt that, and have valued it more than I can say ... What it means is that we are moving out of the adolescent stage of Women's College life in Oxford. We produce among our Heads and Fellows women whose achievements place them on a level with the men who by their experience, richly placed at our disposal, have helped us till now, and continue to help us. I don't think even the most conservative of our male colleagues now feel they can do without the women. We see women more and more on University Bodies; and at our table tonight, there is that most distinguished member of her Faculty and our Professorial Fellow, Dr Ida Mann, while Miss Headlam-Morley is deputy during his absence for the Montagu Burton Professor of International Relations ...

(To bear our Miss Gwyer's point further, Miss Ady had been working in Naval Intelligence for three years; Barbara Castle, elected Labour MP for Blackburn at the general election, was PPS to Sir Stafford Cripps, President of the Board of Trade, while Mary Cartwright was shortly to be elected a Fellow of the Royal Society and, within a year or so, became Mistress of Girton, the first former undergraduate of St Hugh's to become head of an Oxford or Cambridge College.)

Meanwhile, undergraduates of the time, and earlier, had their own views of Miss Gwyer, not always corresponding to her own image as a 'modest violet': 'we were all very fond of her, though she seemed dreadfully remote ... I had the temerity to ask her why we had to be off the river by 10 pm, or whatever the rule was, and she replied, "There are *creeks*, you know, Miss Woodward, there are creeks" ' (Mary Woodward).

... the Gwyer (the title is significant) had been defined and mythologised for generations of undergraduates by an oral tradition of eccentricity and repeated anecdotes ('either your father was a Turk, or your mother a rabbit' and so on). It was in those terms that we encountered and remember her. She was part of a ritual game ... she had a magnificent episcopal presence ... indeed on high days she preached to the College rather better than most bishops, and her Chapel manner, in managing the sonorities of the Book of Common Prayer and the College Bidding Prayer, was exemplary. It was at the time very impressive to me. *Now* I have no doubt either that it *was* precisely managed or that she was fully aware of her reputation and played up to it ... she was unquestionably a gentlewomen of a variety now, I hope, lost, long-boned, long-necked, long-nosed, a sort of ladylike stick insect drawn by Tenniel for Alice and she had the two major characteristics which go with aristocracy of that kind: a capacity to be immensely rude and a total refusal to notice anybody else's right to moral privacy ... I was, of course, terrified of her, and so, I think, were others, though not everybody ... All third year undergraduates were expected to ask the Principal to tea – alone. It was rather like

entertaining God with whom, indeed, the Gwyer easily identified
... I was so rigid with unease that I can recollect only two bits (of
our tea-time exchanges) ... both *dicta* – a discourse on the moral
dangers of being in the Navy (how could she *know?*) and a
denunciation of the impropriety of Aldous Huxley's novels. It
came as a shock to realise that she was even aware of Huxley, and
that, I suppose, reveals that, innocent as we were, we did know that
she and probably most of our dons were light-years behind the
times. (Valerie Pitt)

Miss Procter's first year as Principal coincided with one of the
coldest winters in living memory. Much reminiscence is concerned
with describing the quite fundamental business (recalling the rigours
of the very early St Hugh's) of keeping warm in College. Some were
luckier than others: 'coming from South Wales, and having a full
coal-house, I had coal sent up so that I could keep a good fire for at
least some days in the week, and my room (in 82, Woodstock Road)
was quite popular with others ... in the house ... Because of the
bitter weather, when it eventually went, all the spring flowers came
with a rush and it was unbelievably beautiful' (Bertha Watcyn-
Williams). Outside: 'Oxford in the snow ... Gargoyles, spires,
turrets, towers, outlined in white against an iron-grey sky; streets like
frozen milk. Port Meadow was frozen, and Hannah Utitz (a former
Czech junior skating champion and my room mate at Holywell
Manor), taught me to skate. Port Meadow looked like some Victorian
print come to life' (Penny Peters). Even after the freeze-up, problems
continued: 'we had ... no central heating and ... were rationed to two
buckets of coal a week. This was quite inadequate (no fault of the
College) but it had the advantage of encouraging sociability ... a lot
of us had holes in the back of our gowns because we used them for
drawing up reluctant fires; however, the bathwater was always hot.
This was the great era of power cuts, and one simply adapted to
sudden blackouts' (Margaret Mogford).

Freshers soon became competent fire-kindlers. The first step was
to make your own bed and your scout would then smarm floor
polish on the firewood, which greatly facilitated ignition ...
Electricity, too, was provided only sparingly; it was impossible to
have the reading lamp alight when the ceiling light was on. This
gloomy situation could be remedied in five minutes by a simple

operation involving the switch and half a paper clip ... by the end of my third year, at least a dozen MGA rooms had been so doctored ... (Hazel Marsh)

With the cold, and unpredictable power-cuts, went food rationing even more stringent than in the war years: bread (and cakes) and potatoes had now been added to the list which still included, most seriously meat, sugar, butter – and chocolates. 'The Caker' continued to enjoy prodigious popularity, as well as a curious product mentioned by many, called NAMCO (National Milk Cocoa). Jane Langton remembers 'being permanently hungry ... bread and cakes were allocated by coupon, or bread units, known to us as BU's ... if a friend was coming to tea this entailed bicycling early in the morning up to the Cake Factory in Summertown to queue to buy cakes with our precious BU's.' The factory had an added attraction in that 'reject' cakes could be bought without coupons; but College food did little to stave the pangs: 'I remember College meals of "Spaghetti Stafford Cripps" (i.e. austerity – plain boiled), and marmite mould, a revolting concoction of marmite and a kind of blancmange' (Joyce Hawkins). 'St Hugh's grew quinces and all through Michaelmas Term we had quince jam .. if our thrice a week egg was bad there was rarely a replacement. From time to time there were large containers of NAMCO which made quite a pleasant drink. Some people preferred to eat the powder, there being chocolate rationing. Cooked breakfast sometimes consisted of a two-inch square of fried bread with a blob of meat paste on top' (Primrose Minney). 'Food in College was so awful that a mass walk-out of the dining room, after Grace, was planned – but the Principal heard of it and bought us off with a promise of improvement' (Elizabeth Monro). Even as long after the war as 1949, when Cecilia Green came up: 'The food was awful, and often insufficient – a particular memory is early evening dinner consisting of one pilchard and one apple ... I remember bicycling to the Cake Factory to buy a cake for Sunday ... our diet improved as the three years passed, and I helped to introduce the sale of beer and cider in Hall at lunch-time.'

In compensation there were gastronomic oases in Oxford and round about: 'The town was delightful in those days – coffee or a salad lunch at the Kemp, supper at Long John's or, cheapest of all, the Stowaway, a funny little place down a back alley off the High ... rather tatty but such a good meal for a few shillings. Rugger men liked the Taj Mahal because you got the most to eat there ... ' (Mary

Alexander). 'Trout at the George was the peak of gastronomic experience; a summer evening at the Perch across Port Meadow or the riverside pub at Godstow (the Trout) was a highlight' (Claire Isles). 'The Town and Gown was where we always had coffee after lectures or breakfast on May Morning etc. White's and the Mitre were where one was invited in the evening' (Diana de Rin).

Clothes, meanwhile, in contrast to austere conditions in College, were showing a sign of return to gaiety. 'The "New Look" had just burst on our coupon-ridden existence, and we somehow managed to produce the nipped-in waists, flared basques, and flowing skirts which few of us had any idea of how to wear successfully – but how it added to the excitement' (Rosemary Tupper); ' . . . it was such a thrill to be able to wear a "New Look" cotton dress, very soft and feminine after growing up in the austerity of wartime. To possess a Horrocks cotton dress was bliss. I remember the sensation caused by Brigid Brophy (or her friend Colette Finch) appearing in Hall in black silk pyjamas, which were considered highly improper. We were not allowed to attend lectures or tutorials in trousers, and of course no jeans yet!' (Mary Alexander). 'There were one or two fairly fashionable undergraduates, and a blue fingernail or two (Lois Stockley was always *interesting* to look at, and Daphne Deiner attractive in a Bloomsbury style) but the majority, as College photographs show, were "jerseys and pearls and sensible shoes" but without the pearls . . . ' (Lisbeth David). (Lois Stockley's blue fingernails, in fact, made such an impression, they are mentioned in other reminiscences, as well as meriting a mention in *The Isis*.)

Financially, the post-war years brought an unwonted affluence to some, but for most it was still a case of careful management: 'I seemed to be remarkably well off. Since tuition and maintenance were provided for by my Grant, the remainder seemed there to spend' (Joyce Hawkins). 'Money was certainly tight: you thought twice about spending sixpence [2½p] on a cup of coffee. But I was never in dire straits. I suppose it was mostly spent on books, writing paper and stamps, toilet requisites, food for a tea party and occasional tickets for performances' (Primrose Minney).

In 1947, a year after the retirement of Miss Gwyer, another link with the St Hugh's of the 1920s was severed, at least partially. Miss Seaton, tutor in English Literature since 1925, retired (to be succeeded by Miss Mahood). In the same year Miss Seaton was elected to a Research Fellowship. Many are the stories of this remarkable tutor, some of them already related, but Valerie Pitt (1943) adds a bright and affectionate impression:

Miss Seaton, I remember, when they gave her an Honorary D.Litt (and not before time) gave her old undergraduates permission to call her 'Miss' and not 'Dr.' None of that seemed unnatural. Dons were, you might say, not persons so much as a species of eikon, not exactly 'monuments of unchanging intellect' but certainly identified by formalised attributes like Miss Seaton's turban or Miss Francis's white hair and drooping mien. Mrs Martin Clarke was know to be addicted to bird-watching and strange strains of modern thinking ... Miss Busbridge talked, Miss Procter never did ... It's difficult to explain, in so different a context, that that impersonality did not preclude affection – a good many of my contemporaries were very much attached to their tutors. I was to mine. Miss Seaton at this distance exemplifies both the heraldic clarity and innocence we found in the place *and* my present sense that they were all arrested in time. It was said (was it Daisy Martin Clarke who said it?) that [Miss Seaton] was a cross between an Iceberg and a Nightingale. What I got was the Nightingale – and Darjeeling tea and cinnamon toast one winter afternoon when it was raining after a tutorial ... She was altogether behind her own generation in attitudes, approaches, dress ... Seaton's hair was taken up in a grey white bun and largely concealed in a woollen turban and she always draped herself in shapeless jumper suits (a mode of dress fashionable in the twenties and thirties) ... We thought ... [she] must have some affliction which compelled her to warmth and woollens because she not only wore thick stockings with this outfit but also wrapped herself during tutorials in layers of rugs and a foot warmer. ... she was the most learned person I've ever known ... I once asked Hugo Dyson (St Hugh's undergraduates reading English were frequently 'farmed out' to Mr Dyson in Merton) about an obscure French pamphlet whose author I didn't know. 'Ask Miss Seaton', he said, 'if she doesn't know, nobody will'. She knew ... ! We knew her to be devout in an old-fashioned Anglican manner (she'd once let out that she read a chapter of the Bible in *Greek* every day) but she was very sharp about Christians who went on about Christianity – she didn't care for it in C. S. Lewis or Dorothy Sayers, for instance, who were fashionable at the time ... I loved her and not merely as a teacher, and I think she would freeze me stone cold if she heard me say it.

Two other elections to Fellowships were made at the time (*Chronicle*, 1947–8): Miss Ida Mann who later resigned her Oxford appointment to become Director of Moorfields Eye Hospital, and Miss Betty Kemp, Tutor in Modern History. Miss Adam had been appointed University Demonstrator in Astronomy, Miss Busbridge, University Lecturer in Mathematics, and Miss Gray, University Lecturer in Homeric Archaeology. A further retirement, at the end of Trinity term 1948, was that of Miss Collett, who had kept the Lodge for the past fifteen years:

> Miss Collett, a grey-haired, bespectacled, be-bunned dragon . . . was the bane of my life all my time at St Hugh's . . . I had brought a male friend's dress suit back to Holywell to mend . . . I hung it over the end of my bed, as being the most convenient place to put it. My scout came early to replenish my coal scuttle . . . saw the suit, but said nothing to me. I was still in bed. The next thing I knew, there was a great commotion, and, without knocking, in steamed the scout, the Domestic Bursar, and Miss Collett. 'Where is he?' Where is he?' they shouted . . . 'Where's who?' I said, amazed. 'The MAN', they bellowed, 'the MAN you've got in your room'. Agape, I meekly said, trying not to laugh, 'There's no man here!' They even had the bedclothes off before they steamed out, not even apologising, looking like so many tigers baulked of their prey. (Penny Peters)

By 1948, food and fuel shortages apart, there were signs that St Hugh's was gradually settling to more of a peace-time existence in the generally accepted sense of the term. Gone now were the days, as described by Margaret Jacobs immediately after the end of the war, of

> the shortage of teaching staff as many of the dons had not yet returned to Oxford. It was rumoured that Ernest Stahl, my tutor at Wadham College, was teaching over 30 hours a week. There were often queues of people waiting to be taught. At the beginning of term those of us who were being taught by outside tutors for Modern Languages queued at the Taylor Institution to book our tutorials with dons who sat in Room 2 trying to fit us into hopelessly overcrowded timetables. But the bonus in those days was to have returned to a normal society with more mature men and women.

There was, however, pressure of another kind building up. The *Principal's Report* for 1948 outlined changes in the entrance examination system for St Hugh's, tracing the rise in the number of candidates entering for St Hugh's as their first choice from fewer than 200 in 1938, to a sudden and marked post-war increase: for the current examination the number had risen to 519 'of whom over half are offering either Modern Languages or English. With such numbers, the work of selecting candidates to fill about fifty vacancies becomes extremely difficult.' In the same report, the Principal gave details of the increase in the total number of women undergraduates. The four colleges were to be allowed a maximum of 180 each, and St Anne's 250, thus increasing the quota from 850 to 970. Until more accommodation could be provided (and this was not to occur until the 1960s on a large scale) numbers (at St Hugh's) could not be significantly increased from the limits imposed by the College buildings, including the houses – 'at most 150, ten less than our present quota'. On the subject of building Miss Procter gave, in addition, news of the huts in the garden. Far from being demolished, they had now been let to various University departments, and eyesores though they may have been, their demise had been postponed until 1951. The Shrubbery at 72 Woodstock Road, too, had been let (it was not suitable for undergraduate accommodation) and the Maison Française had made it their home.

In the same edition of the *Chronicle*, the JCR report commented:

> For the first time since the war it can be said that the Junior Common Room really belongs to St Hugh's again. Few are left who remember Holywell. Once again the College and houses represent a unity ... societies are growing and flourishing ... the Dramatic Society ... intends to stage an ambitious production of *The Antigone* in the Trinity Term ... the JCR held two dances ... one in May and one in February. Many undergraduates of St Hugh's will long remember June, 1947 for the gaiety of 'Commem.' week ... it was as though austerity was relaxed for a fleeting moment to permit the present generation to see what 'Commem'. Week used to be – and what it will be – like.

The appended *Games Report* also gave indications of the livening atmosphere of the time:

> After a considerable falling-off during the war, interest in games revived during 1947 in spite of the lack of facilities ... there are some followers of almost every sport in St. Hugh's at the moment,

although not in sufficient numbers in most cases to permit the playing of serious inter-college matches ... the large increase in membership of the OUWBC has made it possible to hold inter-college races in fours, probably for the first time since the College boat clubs ceased to exist ... three St Hugh's undergraduates were successful in gaining Blues last year ...

Already, in fact, the post-war period of the 1940s is acquiring its own particular character (so distinct from wartime that several activities already mentioned in the chapter require their own later definition). Several reminiscences note the fact: 'The late forties were "vintage" Oxford with so many people back from the war ... and making the most of everything Oxford had to offer. Many of our friends then are now shining lights in education, the law, journalism, politics, business ... A very special time to be there' (Mary Alexander); and

It is nearly impossible to convey to anyone who did not grow up in those years the full impact of the revelation that was Oxford. Always magically beautiful, those clustered pinnacles and towers seemed somehow an appropriate Coromandel for meeting the Strange Beasts who roamed at large in this most privileged of game reserves. Time has confirmed the outsize proportions of many of the Personalities I met there in their green and shooting state, and who have since grown great enough to bring out the envious Cassius in us all. Ken Tynan, usually to be seen in a plum-coloured suit, was merely the Great Bear among so many circling galaxies. Of course, I didn't meet, or even hear of him at once. I had many tamer social teas, and meeker meetings in the JCR (whither I once had the temerity to lure the already palely luminous Sandy Wilson) before I even encountered the Tynan phenomenon ... (Marion Farson)

Of all the 'personalities' of the time, Kenneth Tynan is the one most frequently remarked in the reminiscences whether 'horrid but memorable' or giving his name to what another calls 'the Tynan era'. There were, however, *others*. Jennifer May, though heading it with his name, gives a fairly comprehensive list of those who were well-known at Oxford then, and today: 'Norman St John Stevas, Robin Day, Shirley Catlin (Williams) ... Magnus Magnusson, Robert Robinson, Jeremy Thorpe, Peter Parker ... I knew Roger Bannister

quite well and saw his record-breaking four-minute mile at Iffley
Road.' Diana de Rin offers a slightly later compilation: 'I joined the
ETC – Michael Codron, Tony Richardson, Bill Gaskell . . . etc. were
the stars.' The earlier recollections of Penny Peters, apart from an
hilarious account of Will Shakespeare forgetting her lines in a St
Hugh's production of Clemence Dane's play of the same name, gives
a picture of the Oxford theatrical scene in the immediate post-war
period:

> Women undergraduates were still not allowed to be members of
> the OUDS, but during the war the Society changed its name to
> Friends of the OUDS, and used women students. Nevill Coghill
> was the very heart of the Friends . . . I threw my energies into the
> ETC . . . and was a Committee member . . . started as property
> mistress on a marvellous melodrama called *Castle Spectre* . . .
> progressed to acting . . . and singer and performer in Sandy
> Wilson's first two reviews . . . the outstanding theatre personalities
> of Oxford, prior to the advent of Kenneth Tynan and Sandy
> Wilson, were Celia Chaundy, the manageress of the Playhouse
> (always reeking expensively of Chanel No. 5 . . .) and the Parker
> Brothers. The younger brother, Kenneth, was a photographer . . .
> and the older brother Stanley, worked on the *Oxford Mail* . . .
> every Saturday night the Parker Brothers held a party in their flat.
> To this were invited the actors from the New Theatre and the
> Playhouse, and the undergraduate theatrical set drifted along as a
> matter of course . . . the rooms were darkened, and lighted by pink
> light. The music came from an amplifier which was disguised by
> the effigy of a negress's head, and draped with sequins; the drink
> was served out of jugs shaped like swans. It all seemed the height of
> decadent sophistication!

By far the best-remembered production of the time was Nevill
Coghill's OUDS presentation of *The Tempest* in Worcester Gardens
in 1949. Enthusiasm for it exceeds even that for the same play in the
same setting in the previous decade, and hardly a reminiscence does
not mention it with comments such as 'the most magical production I
have ever seen . . . ' (Marjorie Paine) and 'another enchanted evening
. . . most of the characters arrived and departed by barge across the
lake. Caliban laboriously climbed out of the water . . . dripping with
shining mud – magnificent. And finally Ariel ran *across* the surface of
the lake in a shower of sparks . . . ' (Mary Tindal).

There was also the highly popular series of Sandy Wilson's ETC revues with titles such as *Oxford Circus* and *High, Broad and Corny* in which several St Hugh's members took part, including June Burdett, Penny Peters, Barbara Dennys, Heather Couper and Elizabeth Zaiman; an outdoor OUDS production of *Epicoene* with John Schlesinger in the cast; the *Winterset*, also with St Hugh's representatives, which toured to Paris at Easter, 1948; *The Flies* in Magdalen Grove with Robert Hardy; an ETC production of *The Magistrate* with Michael Codron; and *Peer Gynt* produced by Tony Richardson; while Jeanette Johnson remembers particularly '*Samson Agonistes* put on in the University Church by Ken Tynan, and *The Castle of Perseverance* also in the University Church . . . '

Reminiscences of the Union in the latter half of the decade similarly yield an undergraduate cast which distinguished itself on going down from Oxford. Inevitably Ken Tynan 'provided regular Thursday evening entertainment' (Anon) and among those who later became famous or notorious or both the range is from Roy Jenkins and Anthony Crosland to Anthony Wedgwood Benn, Sir Edward Boyle, Dick Taverne, Robin Day and William Rees-Mogg. Bertha Watcyn-Williams belonged to

a Christian Socialist Group, and most of us joined with others who felt that the University Socialist Society was dominated by Communists and fellow-travellers. We set up our own Labour Club (a forerunner of the SDP?) and had an immediate success. We were soon 1000 strong and our first annual dinner had as its guest of honour, the Prime Minister – Clement Attlee . . . I remember Edward Boyle and Tony Wedgwood Benn as Presidents of the Union. The latter ended one debate with words which could sometimes still be employed when he has spoken: 'The House stands adjourned – and aghast!'

The late 1940s were equally remarkable for activity in a field not previously noted by St Hugh's writers of any generation: that of writing and journalism, and here again there are undergraduate personalities who later continued to make their mark. Not only that, *Venture* was founded, a magazine (noted in the *JCR Report*, 1948) written and produced for women undergraduates, and edited by a St Hugh's member, Lois Stockley. The literary scene is described by Marion Farson:

The great scramble was to become an *Isis* personality . . . those who
were going to get on certainly began there . . . as we all intended to
write, authors were in great demand. Somebody or other knew
Johnny Russell, a Scots poet with a real, if somewhat beer-stained
kilt; Johnny Russell knew Dylan Thomas, and brought the splendidly pursy Welsh genius to regale us all in Oxford bars. He was a
kind of fallen meteor, grandly accessible . . . Evidently Tony
Richardson recovered from being trounced (in print) by Michael
Croft over his reviewing style and lack of love of true theatre . . .
Naturally we all wanted to write for *Isis*, then edited by Alan Brien,
and he did in fact give me a mini-job on his Entertainments
Column. What a figure of awe and curiosity he was for us
girls – not only older, but Already Married. . . The male stronghold
in journalism certainly prevailed in the outside world; and within
Oxford. All but the most relentlessly talented found the posts
already filled by some calmly preening male god. Accordingly . . .
Lois Stockley decided we would start our own publication, to be
called *Venture*.

I remember Shirley Catlin (now Williams) breezed in, declared
she was bubbling with ideas, and rushed off to another meeting
before declaring what they were . . . of course, she was a Somervillian, so perhaps didn't feel the necessary allegiance to us St
Hugh's-ites . . . but at any rate we had to do without them . . .
Venture No. 1 was almost entirely written (by Lois) with a variety
of poems, reviews, and a short story with a cruel ending in the
Raymond Chandler manner. I turned in a short story or article . . .
and by that time she had chosen the paper, bemused the printer,
played with the founts available and had the thing set up in a
perfect herbaceous border of type . . . then, as now, criticism
adopted a critical, nay scolding, stance; and we were chided for
enthusiastic experimentation in page layout, and headings jostling
for attention . . . it was, of course, intended as an All-Women
Alternative. But in those days we had hardly had the New Look,
let alone been Liberated. Most of the products of Roedean and
Cheltenham, let alone Blogswich County High School for Girls
had not come to the oldest University to prove their womanhood
on the spikes of adversity, nor in all-women ventures . . . Accordingly, we foundered for lack of adequately fervent support. *Venture* folded after one further issue; we went off to play at being
journalists, or friends of journalists . . .

With all this activity, it is perhaps not surprising that not a single reminiscence of the time mentions an event of importance outside Oxford; and of public occasions in Oxford only one contributor recalls:

> Princess Elizabeth [now HM the Queen] visited Oxford in May, 1948, St Hilda's first then a garden party in St John's. I was there by virtue of being President of the JCR, and was – I think – the only person in a Commoner's gown ... Mrs Roosevelt came to tea at LMH on 13 November 1948, and again I was invited and presented, but Mrs R was looking over her shoulder and talking to someone else as she shook my hand (not the courtesy of the Old World!). (Lisbeth David)

Socially, it was a lively time with an abundance of parties and Commem. Balls, now recovering their glitter: 'Eights Week Balls and Commem. Balls in college gardens with marquees and lights and music and the dawn making it all look a bit tawdry, but not spoiling the magic even so. Once a group of us went out at the end of a Commem. in someone's open car to the Barley Mow at Clifton Hampden for the most wonderful summer breakfast ... ' (Mary Alexander).

> There were a great many delightful parties, on the river, in the men's colleges etc ... I remember giving a party (strictly against the rules!) in the cellars at St Hugh's, with a friend, which we called 'A Troglodyte Party'. Guests were met in the corridor to be escorted down and each was asked: 'Are you a Troglodyte?' To our horror one such person when approached, replied: 'Most certainly not. I am the Master of Balliol!' (Jennifer May)

It is hardly surprising that climbing in to St Hugh's, and its various houses, thrived: '... there was an extremely helpful policeman who patrolled St Margaret's Road ... always willing to give one a leg up to get through the upper half of a ground-floor window – I believe it was in Miss Procter's time that the bottom halves were nailed down. You had to be careful not to descend too damagingly on whoever might be sleeping with their bed positioned by the window' (Shirley Backhouse). 'Nimbleness was required and outside help an asset. I do remember winning a replica of the front-door key in a raffle run by its previous owner but never had the nerve to use it – I preferred the cleaner method of climbing in . . .' (Claire Isles).

In spite of all this, there is ample evidence that work also flourished, and there is a good crop of memories of tutors and dons, more than keeping their end up in competition with the more luminous undergraduates of the time . . . Coghill, Lord David Cecil, C. S. Lewis, A. J. P. Taylor are names still occurring frequently enough to suggest they were maintaining their positions as stars of the Schools and College lecture halls. In addition:

The open lecture system [once again] was one of the best things Oxford offered and I often went to more lectures out of the Geography School than within it. Especially I remember Kenneth Clarke at the Ashmolean on Rembrandt and on Henry Moore, Professor Galbraith ('A bad king is a good thing'), Helen Gardner . . . and Professor Seton Watson, who would come in to read at speed from his latest book on the Middle East and never appear to raise an eye to see how many undergraduates were in the room before he shuffled out with his head still bent. (Marjorie Paine)

In the Geography School, Helen Wallis remembers:

To my tutor, J. N. L. Baker of Jesus College, I owe my career in the Map Room of the British Museum, from 1973 the British Library. He was one of the most influential Oxford geographers from 1935 to 1960 . . . Our field classes in the late 1940s followed in the time-honoured tradition of regional geography. I well remember one incident. A. F. Martin of St John's was pointing out 'strip linchets', terraces following the contour of the hill, as we stood in a deep embayment of the Berkshire Downs near Faringdon. As Freddie Martin set out the various theories to explain the feature, a farmer ploughing the field nearby stopped to listen, and then chipped in, 'You're wrong, you know. It was the fludd'. 'Flood? What flood?' asked Freddie. 'Noah's Flood' was the reply.

Primrose Minney 'attended Professor Bowra's lectures on Greek poetry . . . and Sir Isaiah Berlin . . . I remember him as a mole-like figure getting very excited and waving his arms . . . I also went to some dreadful lectures at Balliol on Cicero's letters. Poor Cicero's sparkling prose was killed stone dead. We were given typed sheets of 22 emendations of *fabum mimum*, thought to be some kind of beanfeast ... the only memorable thing this lecturer said was that a Balliol servant had coined the perfect English hexameter, as he stood outside the bath-house – "Hurry up, gentlemen, please, there are other gentlemen waiting".' Finally, Mary Alexander: 'Alan Bullock "was" Gladstone for me, declaiming his speeches in ... the most memorable lectures I attended. Asa Briggs ran him a close second with his bubbling, infectious enthusiasm for the Chartist Movement.'

That description of Asa Briggs, in fact, could well serve as a summary of the end of decade. 'Bubbling, infectious enthusiasm' was the spirit of so many to whom the war was becoming a fading memory, as Oxford attempted to regain its stride. That, and the thoughts of Cecilia Green, repeated in different forms in reminiscences of the time: 'My outstanding memory is of happiness: I loved Oxford, I loved St Hugh's, I made many lifelong friends ... and summer is buttercups in an Oxford meadow ... '

THE 1950s

After the disruption and upheaval of the war years, the bonfires and fireworks of VE Day, and then the mad flowering of social life in Oxford on the return of service men and women, the 1950s, superficially, seem something of an anti-climax. It is not an altogether accurate impression. Although there is something of a feeling of inter-regnum before the eruptions of the 1960s and early 1970s when much that had been Oxford custom disappeared, there were significant changes slowly taking place. At the beginning of the decade, the last obstinate vestige of wartime, rationing, still existed; so did the ugly huts in the garden of St Hugh's. There were still four remaining ex-service undergraduates at the College. Only a year or two later, however, Valerie Kipping recalls 'the mature ex-service students had just ended and there was a sudden swing in leadership from people of 25-plus to raw school-leavers like ourselves.' In common with the rest of Oxford, St Hugh's was now reverting in at least some ways to habits and an outlook more akin to pre-war days. By the middle of the decade, the pendulum had swung perhaps too far, and there are frequent references in JCR Reports to St Hugh's members paying more attention to University rather than College activities and societies. The Dramatic Society, for example, had become moribund (it was revived a year or so later). Miss Procter had even more critical things to say, and took a disapproving line on the way things had gone.

Her 'State of the Union' speech to the 1953 Gaudy is particularly
abrasive. Following some remarks that have a notably historic ring to
them in the light of later events ('It is true that it is harder for a girl to
come to Oxford than for a boy, for Oxford is predominantly a man's
university and there are over five times as many male as female
undergraduates – and there are not five times as many boys as girls in
our schools') and noting 'we have now entered into what can be
considered a normal post-war period' she went on to criticise severely
the attitudes and habits of the undergraduates:

. . . the standard of undergraduate life has in some respects gone up
and this makes things still harder for the less well-off. More money
is spent in non-essentials – although expenditure on such essentials
as books is deplorably low. More serious is the blunting of the
sense of responsibility. We all value most that which costs us most.
University education is looked on too often as a right which the
Nation owes to its youth and a right which carries no obligations.
   It is not wholly a symptom of approaching old age that I am
convinced that undergraduates try to do too much and provide
themselves with too many distractions. Dances are far too numerous and there is far too much amateur acting. Women undergraduates now take the female parts, not only in the plays produced by
the O.U.D.S. and the Experimental Theatre Club, but also by
those produced by the dramatic societies of the men's colleges.
[This is not a phenomenon of the 1950s. Perhaps Miss Procter had
simply not noticed before she became Principal?] It is possible to
limit the number of dances a girl can attend or the number of plays
in which she can take part, and a very severe limit is, in fact,
imposed, but it is not possible to limit the number of societies she
can join, and societies have increased beyond bounds. They are
neither trivial nor frivolous . . . but even in the most serious the
social element seems on the increase; I am told that the Liberal
Club owes its popularity, not to its politics, but to the excellence of
its annual dance.
   Political clubs are on the whole less active and less time
consuming than before the war, but other interests have taken the
place of politics. There are societies concerned with every faculty
subject; with all the arts; ones which study every conceivable
current problem, or every type of philosophical question, or those
which purvey general 'uplift'. They tend to duplicate each other
and their number is staggering . . . in 1937 there were 72 [societies

registered with the Proctors]; in 1939 there were 95; in 1949 the number had risen to 150, and it is now over 200. Can you wonder that undergraduates on coming up are bewildered, and waste time in considering and sampling the claims of rival clubs?

Now I feel that behind all this immense undergraduate activity there is some change in the undergraduate's conception of the functions of a university, or at any rate a change in the stress laid on the importance of its different aspects. Our undergraduates tend to lay less emphasis on the pursuit of learning and more on making contacts, meeting people, enlarging their outlook and experience, on gaining a wide but sometimes superficial culture. There is something to be said for this conception of the functions of a university and it meets a real need of the times, but too hectic a pursuit of the 'fuller life of the older universities' may degenerate into something not far removed from a course of training in 'lifemanship'. The reasons for this change in emphasis are various but they may be partly due to the influence of such misguided educationalists as the one who wrote not long ago in *The Times* to ask how, on the maximum maintenance grants provided by the State, it was possible to *enjoy* Oxford. Whatever the causes may be I am sure the pendulum has swung too far.

Here, then, was one change, despite the fact that at about the same time the JCR was seeing itself as having had a quiet and unremarkable year, 'nice and not notorious'. In a broader sense, things were on the move. The decade began with St Hugh's, with the other women's colleges and St Anne's Society, subject to the quota. It was not long before the quota was increased, and in 1957 abolished altogether. Then, in 1959, with the other women's colleges, St Hugh's became, at last, a college of the University in the fullest sense. Internally, the beginning of the 1950s saw another important change. Council, the governing body of the College, which hitherto had Senior Members elected to it, had its constitution changed, and Senior Members were excluded.

Council, under the 1926 Charter, had consisted of the Principal, Treasurer, Miss Moberly and Miss Wardale ('as long as they shall desire to serve'), all Fellows (except Honorary and Probationary), six co-opted members, and three elected by the Association of Senior Members (ASM). Chairman of the ASM, ex officio, was the Principal, and its Secretary a Fellow of the College elected by the ASM.

In 1948, the Principal had become ex-officio Chairman of Council.

Then, in 1951, Council was reconstituted as Principal and Fellows
(excluding Honorary and Probationary Fellows). Up to this time,
several co-opted members had been strong advocates for the change,
in particular (Sir) Douglas Veale, Registrar of the University, and
Chairman of Council from 1937 to 1948. It was he who pressed that,
as a first step, the Principal should become ex-officio Chairman. The
later loss of the elected Old Students marked a greater break with the
past, for they were not 'outside members' in the sense that the co-
opted members were. There had been Old Students on the Council
since 1895, and elected Old Students' representatives since 1908.
Since 1895 Old Students had (if they wished) been 'members of the
College' and from 1911 to 1926 they had been, with Council members
'the College'. They became 'Senior Members' in 1926, having
through their elected members, a voice in the affairs of the College.
From 1951, this official involvement ceased, leaving the Senior
Members as an appendage to the College, rather than part of it.

Of course, decades are arbitrary periods with which to chart
progress. None, in all aspects, is all of a piece. Trends emerge,
flourish, then wither, sometimes overlapping the boundary which has
been arbitrarily marked. Just as there was no sudden end one
midnight to the Augustan Age, to give immediate place in the
morning to the Romantic, so we find that at one point the St Hugh's
Dramatic Society no longer exists, but a year or two later is very
much alive: 'The memory of a JCR is necessarily short: the present
one knows nothing of the time when dramatics and debating and so
on were organised on a college scale . . . ' (*JCR Report*, 1954–5). But
'Our own College societies are flourishing . . . the Dramatic Society
was lucky again in choosing almost the only week of cloudless weather
for its production with Worcester Buskins . . . ' (*JCR Report*,
1957–8). If there is a continuous thread in such reports in the 1950s it
is this inconsistency in College activity, matched by an equivalent
deploring of attention paid to University activities rather than those
specifically related to St Hugh's. Comments on these lines are
continuous from the early years through to 1958: 'Those whose
ambition it is to gain a certain renown have continued to seek it in
University rather than College activities' being a fairly typical example from a JCR report. Miss Procter's remarks thus seem all the
more justified, despite the fact that this was one effect she had not
noted, nor, indeed, envisaged.

A stronger thread of continuity within the decade, and with past
and future, is provided by the dons, and College and University

personalities, and, with retirements, new appointments, fresh faces and deaths, there is a perceptible shake of the previous decade's kaleidoscope. At St Hugh's, the best remembered is, fairly naturally, the Principal, Miss Procter; but there are frequent references to Miss Busbridge, Mrs Warnock and Miss Gray in particular, as well as the military figure of Mr Robey in the lodge. Jean Robertson remembers Miss Procter thus: 'Always wore flowing black. Never looked any girl in the face. Never smiled. Walked stooped forward. Exactly the shape of the Cumaean Sybil in Michaelangelo's Sistine ceiling: she never failed to remind me of her ... ' Yet: 'once I visited my fiancé in Cambridge and the coach didn't return till midnight. Miss Procter didn't like to keep the porter up late, so told me to go to her house at midnight, and she very kindly let me in with her own key. I was very touched by this kindness' (Valerie Kipping). Sylvia Hanson, who had stayed up during the vacation, went to see *Salad Days*, and though she left the performance early was still late returning to College, and was summoned to the Principal: 'Miss Procter listened to me with her habitual expression of detached benevolence – I can recall no other expression on her face – then she remarked mildly, and without any particular emphasis ... "Miss Hanson, this college is not run for the convenience of undergraduates". I left her presence staggered ... later, I understood what Miss Procter had meant ... that the convenience of undergraduates was of less importance than their good, the two being in no way synonymous.' There are many references to Mrs Warnock, who had been appointed as lecturer in Philosophy in 1949, and made a Fellow four years later. She obviously made a great impression on her undergraduates: '... an energetic young woman who seemed to us to be constantly pregnant or involved with very small children. She was at the same time a stimulating and inspiring tutor with time for all her pupils' (Marion Basco). '... Mary Warnock billowing up St Giles on her bicycle, exasperated at the beginning of my tutorial because Kit or Marius had, to be helpful, just put into the bath all the clean clothes that had been put out for them to wear. She was incredibly encouraging as a tutor ... and her enthusiasm for Logic was catching' (Primrose Cooper). Mathematicians at St Hugh's have equally striking recollections: 'Miss Busbridge was the outstanding lecturer ... She always enumerated the important points, and when she reached 100, the male undergraduates clapped and cheered. We waited, with bated breath, for the roof to fall in, but Miss Busbridge did not seem displeased ... ' (Enid Fortescue). 'Miss Busbridge had a tremendous impact ... each week ... she assigned more work than the week before, and each week we obediently did it, until one week (my tutorial partner and I) gasped in disbelief at our assignment. Miss Busbridge just smiled and told us that she had been trying to find out how much we could cope with, and now she knew!' (Clare Richardson).

Miss Gray's cat, George, features in the reminiscences as much as Miss Gray herself.

> My interview with her in 1948 I shall not forget. A particularly tricky question ... was punctuated by a coughing fit from George ... By the time she had attended to him ... that particular question had gone into abeyance and I found myself on easier ground ... months later there was cause to be grateful to George again. I had presented a very indifferent Latin or Greek prose with some trepidation, so you can imagine my surprise to hear her say à propos of nothing, certainly not of me, 'You've been as good as gold the whole time'. Once again George had deflected her attention in my favour ... I remember Miss Gray as exact in every way, saying 'If you care to remove your gown, may I give you a sherry?' (Primrose Cooper).

George apart, Jane Stothert recalls seeing her on one wet, windy night making her way across the garden on her way into Hall: 'She was a strikingly handsome woman ... dark-eyed, with a strong-boned face, and she wore a heavy cloak which flapped round her as she limped through the trees, leaning heavily on her stick, the lights flickering across the garden as the branches tossed in front of them. As she came towards the lights of the college, her eyes shining and her face glowing from the wind ... I remember it flashed across my mind that this is what the great god Pan must have looked like ... '

There was nothing Pan-like, however, in the demeanour of Mr Robey, who brought a whiff of the parade-ground to his administration of the lodge and a punctiliousness in keeping with his waxed moustaches. Jane Stothert again:

> the unforgettable Mr Robey, who delighted in locking the front door on the dot of 11.15, and if you arrived ten seconds late and frantically rang the bell, he took great pleasure in leaving you standing outside while he made his slow and ponderous way round

ALL the corridors, checking ALL the doors, windows or whatever, so that for 10 seconds only you ... would appear in the
signing-out book as 20 or 30 minutes late ... we watched him once
through the keyhole as he deliberately turned his back on the door
where we were ringing, and set off on his round ...

Back in the SCR, meanwhile, the 1950s saw many changes,
particularly with the retirement of several dons who have already
featured in the reminiscences of past decades. These included (1950)
Daisy Martin-Clarke, who, sadly, was to live only another four years;
Miss Thorneycroft (1951), who had been appointed Bursar in 1925,
elected to an Official Fellowship two years later, in 1946 became
Treasurer, and under whom the College had seen tireless expansion
and stabilising of resources; Miss Francis (1957) after thirty-three
years; and Miss Bickley (1958). Another retirement (in 1954) which
should not go unrecorded was that of 'Fred', the College Messenger
for forty years.

Among the new faces, Miss P. O. E. Gradon succeeded Mrs
Martin-Clarke; in 1951, Miss M. Jacobs (who had gone down from St
Hugh's in 1947 with a First in Modern Languages) was appointed
Cassel Lecturer in German, and took charge of the newly-leased 78
Woodstock Road; Miss M. M. Sweeting, who eventually became the
College's first Dean, was appointed lecturer in Geography in the
same year; in 1954, Miss M. R. Trickett succeeded Miss Mahood as
tutor in English Literature, and in 1957 Miss V. J. Daniel succeeded
Miss Francis as tutor in French; in the same year Miss Adam gave up
her tutorship in Natural Science and her Official Fellowship to devote
her whole time to work at the Observatory, where she was University
Demonstrator in Astronomy. The College elected her to a Research
Fellowship and she retained her seat on the Governing Body.

Since almost all the reminiscences in the book so far have been
provided by former undergraduates, those by Mrs Susan Wood, tutor
in Modern History and a University lecturer (herself a Somerville
graduate) possess the unusual merit of giving a vignette of SCR life at
the time:

As the Fellow now longest in office, I think it worth while to try to
convey something of what Senior Common Room life was like in
my first ten years here [at St Hugh's]. I came as a lecturer,
simultaneously with Mary Warnock, in 1949, when Miss Procter

had been Principal for three years; the College was still (until 1951) governed by a Council that included outside members, and there were only twelve Fellows.

The first impression for both of us was of an almost suffocating cosiness. Conversation was ladylike: concerned at its most intellectual with Jane Austen or the best detective fiction, otherwise with gardening and ornithology. My heart sank at being asked by Mrs Martin Clarke, at lunch on my first day, 'will you belong to the Bird faction or the Flower faction?' In the background was the Row, not then long enough ago to be viewed objectively or talked about without hurt. Indeed, one of us was taken aside and told by Miss Francis: 'You realise there are things we don't talk about.' In consequence, we and three appointed soon after us exchanged what 'information' we could collect from outside and acquired some strange mythology (it was almost like trying to discover the Facts of Life at the age of twelve). The impression of the Common Room collectively is not inconsistent with remembering individuals as full of character, learning and intelligence. Miss Procter, in particular, though unquestionably ladylike, was not at all cosy: she was austere, shy, formidably intelligent, with a sardonic sense of humour which she kept on a tight rein.

Mary was married shortly before coming to St Hugh's; I became engaged in my first term and married the following summer. Although our senior colleagues were wholly kind, we were made to feel we had done something slightly frivolous and, in my case, disappointing; and it was debatable whether, after our three years as lecturers, we could be elected as Fellows. The hesitation was unrealistic (for other women's colleges already had several married Fellows) but respectable, springing from a reasonable doubt whether married Fellows would give as much time and heart to the College, or indeed stay. (At the time it was generally assumed that a Fellow should be happy to stay for her working life: the departure of Molly Mahood for a chair at Ibadan caused a *frisson* as if a long-closed door had been opened to admit a cold draught). Later, to appear in College pregnant required some resolution; and older colleagues' friendly inquiries after one's children suggested that one had acquired a rather unusual kind of pet.

Governing Bodies were held on Saturdays, and it was almost unheard of to miss one; I remember explaining to Miss Procter, heart pounding with nervousness, that I was going to the wedding of a very close friend. The most dramatic absence was that of Olga Bickley from a beginning-of-term Tutors' Meeting, explained in a splendid letter full of the warm south (read aloud by Miss Procter in a voice frigid with indignation) about having to stay at Ventimiglia to tread her grapes.

There was Formal Hall every weekday, and most Fellows dined on most nights. We moved out of the Common Room to the High Table in strict order of seniority; whom one sat next to was thus almost predetermined, the only room for manoeuvre depending on a rapid calculation of which end of the table to make for – with the aim, often, of sitting next to Agnes Headlam-Morley (who would talk, enchantingly, about almost anything). The food was terrible and wine non-existent; even on St Hugh's Night there was only a wine cup. There were, however, Fellows who provided good wine when they entertained privately; Miss Procter herself was knowledgeable, and took a benign interest when, in 1958, some of us took the initiative in starting a Wine Cellar.

That innovation was part of a move towards more college entertaining, itself an aspect of a less cloistered, less unworldly style that was taking hold in the later 1950s. Fellows learnt to drive and bought cars. Our numbers were growing. Suez, over which we were sharply divided, irrupted with a hot blast from the outside world. We were at the beginning of a period of growth and change, with some loss of cohesiveness but larger gains, for Fellows and undergraduates, in openness and freedom.

Links with the very distant past of St Hugh were broken when (in 1952) Grace Parsons died, and, on 25 March 1958, Dr Ady. Grace Parsons had been one of the first four St Hugh's students. She read Botany – only two women had ever taken Science Honours before her. She took Finals in 1889 – 'the first woman admitted to this school. No other woman, or man, was examined for it this year' (*College Register*). Miss Ady had successively been Scholar (1900–3), tutor in History (1909–23), Research Fellow (1929–50) and Honorary Fellow (1950–8) as well as member of Council and Secretary of the ASM from 1932 to 1955. Her bequests to St Hugh's included nearly 400 books from her library and four pictures, including a drawing of a woman's head by Burne-Jones which became one of the SCR's most treasured and admired possessions. Her will also provided for a legacy of £10 000 for building a chapel or for payment of stipend for a chaplain, and although it proved impossible to carry out her wishes precisely, the money was applied towards the good of the existing Chapel.

Outside the College, the familiar ambivalence concerning lectures once again shows itself; so too the interest shown in star lecturers in schools other than an undergraduate's own. While Ann Morris writes: 'I rarely attended a whole series of lectures – too often they consisted of material better gleaned from the lecturer's books', there are plenty of references to popular figures, chief among them names from the 1940s still: 'I remember vividly the lectures of C. L. Wrenn on *Beowulf*, Lord David Cecil on Shakespearean Tragedy and C. Day Lewis as Professor of Poetry' (Mary Hare). There is another impression of lectures in Schools where 'Isaiah Berlin ticked like a great grandfather-clock swinging up and down the platform like a huge pendulum' (Primrose Cooper), and among frequent references to Helen Gardner, then tutor in Literature at St Hilda's, an anonymous contributor recalls that she 'strode on to the daïs and opened her lecture with a ringing "Dryden is a poet for maturity!"' It may or may not be significant that lectures yield far more reminiscence from the earlier part of the 1950s, but here is one from the later years: 'The legend of my day was Professor Wind. Most people enthused over his Leonardo series, but I found that Botticelli left a more lasting impression. I remember Miss Harvey's lectures on the Black Death, and her careful distinction between *Rattus Rattus* and *Rattus Norwegicus*; I know I went to Professor Galbraith's last series as Regius Professor, and Professor Trevor-Roper's first, but all I recall is the former's defence of King John because he was a good administrator!' (Anne Ward).

As already mentioned, the early part of the decade (surprisingly, perhaps, it may seem to later generations) was still subject to rationing: 'One of the jobs of the freshers was to deliver the butter rations. We took it in turns to deliver the weekly four-ounce portion to each undergraduate's rooms. It was a good opportunity to get to know the College and to survey the rooms with a view to choosing one's own for next year' (Elizabeth Browning). 'I think clothing coupons had just ended (in my first year). We were in any case a generation who had grown up with no frills ... After years of wartime white crockery, I was thrilled to be able to buy a cream coloured set with the luxury of gold rims' (Valerie Kipping). Yet the passing of rationing in 1954 is nowhere remembered in the contributions. Food, however, continues to be remembered, usually with distaste, although lacking the full-scale vehemence of wartime undergraduates and those immediately afterwards: 'I remember the truly awful (sorry!) food. In the early fifties catering in College featured lots of baked beans, something quite dreadful called lentil roast, and molten icecream which we had at least three times a week for dinner' (Mary Hare).

Despite Miss Procter's remarks about money being wasted on 'inessentials' at least a proportion of that money seemed to be spent on what seem to be essential forays to supplement the diet – from 'biscuits, cheese, salami and fruit' to meals in the increasing number of restaurants. The emergence of at least one pub as a pioneer in the now-common practice of serving food at lunch-time is well documented: 'I remember the rise to favour of the Welsh Pony which I think was the first pub to see the potential of "bar food" . . . You could get Scotch eggs and a range of pickles and salads etc. and it became very popular' (Jane Stothert). Another new 'in' place appeared to be a restaurant called variously, the Café de Paris or the Café de la Paix, 'where the female diners were always given a flower to wear, which then reposed on one's mantelpiece for a week' (Janie Moon).

Meanwhile, most of the familiar places of the previous decade receive honourable mention, with the Taj Mahal in the Turl (one of today's few survivors from that era) receiving most stars, for economic opportunity as much as standard of Indian cuisine: 'The Taj Mahal would let us order one pilao with rice and two plates' (Janie Moon). For breakfast, Ma Brown's in the Market (another survivor) continued its long-running success, as well as the Ross Café (upstairs in the High and popular for bacon and egg on Sunday mornings after buying the *Observer* at Carfax close by). There were cheap meals still at the Stowaway or the Lantern in the High 'where regulars paid two and sixpence [about 12½p] for lunch' (Ann Morris); and the same writer continues, 'Coffee bars were a later development. The Popina was one I remember in my third year – upstairs in the Cornmarket.' More established places for the lengthy Oxford pastime of 'coffee' were still the Northgate and the Kemp. For special occasions, still, the George, and also the Elizabeth; while outside Oxford an impressive list is contributed by an anonymous writer, including favourites such as the Bear at Woodstock, but others as far afield as Shipton-under-Wychwood and Kingston Bagpuize.

With clothes still on 'coupons' in the very early years of the decade there are still mentions of the 'New Look' skirts. Later, 'we wore very full skirts with nylon petticoats as described in Iris Murdoch's *Under the Net*. In winter, warmth was the main consideration, and we wore duffel coats, coloured woolly stockings, white ear-muffs and college scarves ... we were not allowed to wear trousers to lectures or tutorials or for dining in Hall, but I did acquire some denim jeans at the Army surplus store. I wore them on holiday in Ireland and was jeered at for my unfemininity' (Janie Moon). Later still: 'cycling wasn't easy in stiletto heels, and revealing that raw and draughty gap between stocking-top and pants bridged by a straining suspender' (Anne Ward), and 'Wide skirts over paper nylon petticoats ... unreliable strapless bras ... Marks and Spencer Orlon cardigans ... we used to get our stockings mended when they laddered, at a small shop in St Giles' (Fiona McKenzie). A final sartorial note, of a more unusual kind, is added by Mary Hare. She remembers Professor Wrenn 'as the only (the last?) lecturer to insist absolutely that we wore square caps to lectures'.

The huts in the garden were a further reminder of wartime for St Hugh's as for no other college. They came down, at last, in the summer of 1952, and revising for Schools at the time was, as several remark, punctuated by the crash of demolition. That they were pulled down at all was entirely owing to Miss Procter. An anecdote sent by Dr Busbridge emphasises this. In the late 1940s and early 1950s, when the wartime huts were still disfiguring the grounds of St Hugh's, preventing the return of the garden to its former beauty, and were occupied by several bodies, but chiefly the Department of Statistics, permission was sought to have the huts demolished.

Not only St Hugh's but the University, which had an alternative site already planned for the Department of Statistics, wanted the demolition. However, the Statistics people were perfectly happy where they were and had no wish to move; so much so that, no sooner had permission been given for the demolition by the relevant ministry, than it was peremptorily withdrawn, and it was conjectured that one of the resident statisticians had the ear of a statistically-inclined minister in the then Labour government. The Vice-Chancellor himself then wrote personally to Mr Attlee, the Prime Minister, on the matter; but to no avail. The letter arrived on the day, in 1951, when Mr Attlee had decided on a general election and he wrote back to say that nothing could be done. That autumn the Conservatives were returned, and permission was subsequently renewed. But that was not the end of the story. A Labour MP gave notice that the matter would be raised in the House of Commons, with the intention of once again blocking the permission. At this, Miss Procter acted (with Miss Thorneycroft, as Bursar, also deeply involved in the effects of the political wrangle). Miss Procter saw to it that a demolition company moved in, presumably after due notice had been given to the occupants of the huts (and certainly after squatters had had to be evicted from some of the empty ones). 'They used', says Dr Busbridge, 'a crane swinging a large metal ball, and every day were watched by crowds of little boys from the Dragon School.' By the time the MP had raised the matter in the House, his question, because of Miss Procter's courage and initiative, had literally become academic!

Dr Busbridge relates another, lighter, story from those days concerning the garden and the huts. The gardener, Mr Harris, one Christmas had raised in the greenhouse a particularly fine collection of cyclamen. He inspected them all on Christmas Eve, and they gave him great pride. But among the other occupants of the huts, apart from the statisticians, was the Bureau of Animal Population, and one of their assistants, possibly after an excess of Christmas cheer, neglected to secure the mouse-house which was part of their establishment. On Boxing Day, when Mr Harris next visited the greenhouse, not a single cyclamen remained! Not only that, St Hugh's was shortly overrun with mice, SCR included. By the time this came under control, North Oxford had also been affected, and the mouse problem was finally dealt with only when the City Council at last took action!

The demolition was hugely welcome, for once more, after years of deprivation, the great pride of St Hugh's, its garden, once so lovingly tended by Annie Rogers (*Custos Hortulorum*, a post and responsibility which Miss Procter had now taken over) could again be enjoyed by all. As the report on the 1953 Gaudy put it: 'there was tea out-of-doors on a fine summer afternoon. All rejoiced to see the College Gardens restored to their former serene beauty after the demolition of the wartime huts. The lawns bore hardly a scar, thanks to the skill of those who had watched over their recovery. May this success need no repetition.' A fuller account of the glories of the St Hugh's garden appears in Appendix III, but it is no accident that from this date there are few reminiscences that do not mention the pleasure it afforded throughout the rest of the decade as it came back to normal: 'Rock roses in June on the Terrace, revising for Schools under the beech trees, yellow autumn crocus, the blue wistaria over the garden door and the clematis on tree stumps . . . ' (Anne Heath). 'The garden is an abiding memory – the wistaria, of course, and the viburnum fragrans, which Mr Harris (the gardener) identified for me. He was delighted to answer questions. I remember the painstaking way he examined each twig as, on a bitter February afternoon, he pruned the rosebed' (Anne Ward).

Academically, the college maintained, throughout the decade, its record of steady success. On the field of sport, however, at the beginning of the 1950s, games do not seem to be much favoured and one contributor notes that to be 'hearty' was despised. Nevertheless by 1956–7 the *JCR Report* is recording no fewer than eighteen St Hugh's Blues!

With the return to a fully peacetime existence and an intake once again exclusively direct from school, several remark some social stratification: 'The grammar school girls settled into college much better than girls who had been to boarding school. The former were delighted to be away from home for the first time: the latter found college rules and regulations disconcertingly like the schools they had just left. Society was noticeably stratified into smart, rich public school girls and the rest ... I found the smart set self-satisfied and distasteful' (Jean Robertson). Cheltenham Ladies College and Westonbirt seem the schools most thought to have produced at various times 'cliques', but there were other views of St Hugh's society which naturally varied throughout the decade.

> We were, I think, a very friendly college but nothing was quite as it seemed and nobody ran quite true to type. The daughter of an Ambassador was the least snobbish and would readily lend her clothes and pearls to her friends, while the débutante took her work very seriously. The OUDS actress was the least 'posey', the kindest and most sympathetic listener, the girl whose passion was animals and spent her weekends beagling, later proved to have the most genuine insights into human behaviour; the chic, indeed the ultra-elegant American student was engaged in the pursuit of Bible studies; the Christian Union representative could say the most uncharitable things. Our rooms were left open. Somebody might occasionally borrow crockery or coffee. More often than not we would arrive back to find notes on our writing tables, small gifts, invitations, or a visitor seated in the only armchair quietly reading, awaiting our return. (Marion Basco).

Cliques or no cliques, work habits seem remarkably similar throughout the period and little different from decades immediately before and after, with 'This practice of creating an "essay crisis" ... a regular feature of college life' (Ann Tolansky). Bohuslava Necasóva records, somewhat wryly, that she had to be a conscientious student (she worked in Bodley most of the day), because she 'had to be good as the first Rawnsley Studentship was only £200 (it was my only income for the whole year).'

So too, was the manner in which St Hugh's undergraduates occupied themselves when not working. The bicycle continued as the most favoured mode of transport, although one anonymous contributor adds a note very much belonging to this particular decade: 'I think I was the first at St Hugh's to have a motor scooter (a little Vespa) and I remember adorning it with a black velvet bow as *"sub-fusc"* when it served to transport me to the Finals.' Another, later, anonymous contributor: 'usually used a car for going to parties or pubs/restaurants ... I had friends in North Oxford with a drive where I could park a car – so I avoided complying with proctorial regulations concerning cars'. The surrounding countryside, Abingdon, Woodstock, Minster Lovell and so on were explored assiduously, as by previous and future generations most often by bicycle, though also by bus and on foot. Anne Ward recalls in her first year 'exploring out towards Wytham. The boy-friend I was with gave me chapter and verse for "dreaming spires" – we had the classic view from that road. But already there were small white typed notices up, and I recall an argument as to whether Wytham should be allowed to keep its peacefulness, or whether Oxford's traffic should be relieved by a by-pass. I suppose we must have been the last generation to enjoy that particular view ...'

The river, too, continued to exert its never-failing spell, only the passing sounds from punts varying with the changing fashions in music and the latest hits:

We spent many happy hours on the river, punting and picknicking, and I used to have an old portable wind-up gramophone that we took along – we toned down the sound by stuffing the loudspeaker with my rather tatty commoner's gown. Recorders were coming back into vogue just then, and I remember one friend, now a prioress, I believe, who played her recorder on one such picnic, and the music floating across the water had a very sweet, sad, unearthly quality. (Jane Stothert)

and, 'once in the early post-May morning dawn, a man in dripping tails punted by, asking wrily, "Got a match?" ' (Anon).

The contributors suggest as strong an interest in music as ever, particularly choral music, and once again, the Bach Choir, first under Dr Armstrong, and later Sidney Watson:

> My best memories are of singing *Hodie* with the Bach Choir with Vaughan Williams himself in the seat of honour in the Sheldonian . . . my other memorable musical occasion was at Magdalen. David Lloyd-Jones, now musical director of Opera North but then an undergraduate . . . invited me to sing in a small choir to give a performance – the first in England – of a recently-discovered Haydn Mass . . . it was the foggiest, coldest, rawest November day I ever experienced in Oxford, and we knew that the critics of the National Press were due to come. To stop us shaking, for whatever reason, as we waited to go into the chapel, the leader of the orchestra tried to make us laugh by playing Hearts and Flowers – it was, of course, Dudley Moore! (who was organ scholar at Magdalen at the time)' (Anne Ward)

But though the reminiscences may be deceptive there was not, perhaps, an equivalent interest in the theatre until the very end of the decade with several members involved in the OUDS and ETC and a successful College production of the *Mask of Orpheus* by Philip Steer (1958–9). Much earlier, St Hugh's had provided (in 1950–1) the first woman President of the ETC, Diana Colman, and one of the few acting reminiscences dates from only slightly later:

> Two weeks after arriving in Oxford, I was offered the leading part in (another) college production of Anouilh's *Antigone* . . . however St Hugh's was somewhat more strict in its rules at that time than most colleges. Undergraduates were required to pass Prelims before they could take part in a Major Production. Bitterly disappointed I had to decline . . . hopeful that I had passed Prelims, I auditioned at the end of my second term for a production of *Romeo and Juliet* which Worcester College were ambitiously hoping to put on at the Playhouse. I could not believe it when I was offered the part of Juliet. At the beginning of the [next] term, although I had passed Prelims, I received a short, sad note from the producer (now an established BBC producer) to say that *he* had not and was therefore unable to continue with the production . . . (Marion Basco). [By coincidence, a former Juliet for the Worcester College Buskins had been Penny Peters, in 1946.]

Of public performances, Margot Fonteyn is remembered dancing 'like thistledown' in *Ondine* and *The Firebird*, and Sir Laurence Olivier giving a memorable performance in *The Entertainer*. Jennifer West witnessed an historic performance at the New Theatre – the pre-London run of *The Mousetrap*! But, though *The Birthday Party* is described as 'mind-boggling', nowhere are the Angry Young Men, nor their effect on the 1950s, in evidence. A few productions at men's colleges are remembered: *As You Like It* at Magdalen, with unrehearsed deer wandering across the stage, *The Merchant of Venice* in New College cloisters, and, directed by John Hale, a Masque in honour of Princess Margaret, involving two St Hugh's actresses.

Another Masque, which was at once even more of a St Hugh's *and* University occasion took place on and around University College barge in June 1950. It had been written by one St Hugh's undergraduate, Lois Stockley (already noted as the editor of *Venture*) in honour of the twenty-first birthday of another, Marion Farson. A total of 100 guests were invited, and 'about 300' turned up. In the cast were Shirley Catlin, and the editor of *Isis*, Robert Robinson. One uninvited guest hired a skiff and rowed against a very strong current throughout the entire performance hurling equally uninvited comments. This was the subsequent Chairman of British Rail, Peter Parker. Marion Farson herself gives some additional notes on the occasion:

Lois . . . had written her own Spenserian hymn to Mariana as a gift. It had a number of mythological characters of a Comus-like variety . . . and was crying out . . . to be staged . . . to be given the treatment . . . who else to produce it but Tony Richardson . . . who else to compose the music but Stanley Myers . . .who else the River God but the active and energetic Robert Robinson . . . that evening both invited and uninvited streamed, sauntered and boated to the river bank. A very chic chap called Paul something arrived by punt with Michael Codron, whom I'd not previously met. They were all charm and velvet lapels – . . . a remarkably under-rehearsed collection of water-gods . . . proclaimed their lines in the glistening dark . . . a lone figure was punted into the ring of light . . . it was Robinson the River God himself . . . declaiming those extravagant praises that the occasion demanded in a strong, relentless voice as the current tugged him doggedly away from the shore, pursued by a shower of votive pennies . . .

Another extravagant occasion is remembered by Isabel Greig: 'a party given by Ned Sherrin where I first tasted caviare . . . ' As a corrective to caviare, however, St Hugh's rules and regulations had changed little from the previous decade, and there is evidence of a subterranean rumbling of discontent with them – several references to attempts to alter the visiting hours for men and to extend College hours, but all firmly vetoed by Miss Procter. As a result, just as much ingenuity as ever was exercised in bending the rules, and the impression yielded by many reminiscences is of a generation ever lurking in the bushes round St Hugh's and its College houses waiting for an opportune moment, in the darkness, to climb in by a bewildering variety of routes. In the same connection, there was expertise of a high order in even more dubious arts, one of the easiest rules to break being that concerning the three obligatory formal dinners per week: 'A friend and I became expert forgers . . . the real blight on our lives was 11.15 pm (10.30 pm on Sundays) and I think THREE midnights a term, but all I remember doing was making mild complaints. We were very weak feminists' (Dorothy Fridjhon). 'If you lived in a college house . . . [you] had to be back to college by, I think, 10.30. I spent my first year in a downstairs room and was frequently asked if I would mind people unscrewing the bars and slipping in after a party or dance . . . for Commem Balls I usually arranged to stay with friends . . . Men weren't allowed in college for the hour before dinner. When I enquired why, I was told it was because it was the hour when people would be changing for dinner!' (Margaret Leighton). But, as usual, Miss Procter had the last word:

> I remember that once there was some pressure to extend the modest hours during which men might be entertained, and the Principal summoned us to a meeting in the Mordan Hall, an unprecedented occurrence for us. 'Your mothers and grand-mothers,' she said, 'fought for the right for women to come here; and you are only concerned with entertaining men.' We felt outraged, but I don't think we would have acted to resist her, though we were not far from a new generation who would have protested much more vigorously. (Rachel Thompson)

One reason, of course, why so many St Hugh's members sought ways round the regulations was the number of University societies, and their social whirl, for which Miss Procter reserved so much censure. The list cited in the reminiscences is almost endless; so, too, that of

Miss C. A. Moberly
(1886–1915).

Miss B. E. Gwyer, MA
(1924–46).

The Foundress, Dame
Elizabeth Wordsworth,
DBE, Hon MA, Hon DCL.

Miss E. E. S. Procter, MA,
FRHist.S. (1946–62).

Miss K. M. Kenyon, CBE,
MA, DLitt (Lond) FBA, FSA
(1962–73).

Miss E. F. Jourdain, MA
Doctor, Univ. Paris
(1915–24).

Miss M. R. Trickett, MA
(1973–   ).

Clara Evelyn Mordan
(1844—1915).

Mary Gray Allen
(d. 1925).

Dame Joan Evans
(1893—1977).

(a) Miss Gertrude Thorneycroft,
Bursar then Treasurer of St
Hugh's (1925–51).

(b) Miss Busbridge and Miss Adam (1936).

(c) Principal and four Fellows of St Hugh's College (Artist: Henry Lamb, RA).
From L to R: Miss Procter, Miss Wardale (Honorary Fellow), Miss Francis, Miss Gwyer
(Principal), Dr Ady (Research Fellow).
This portrait, painted in 1936, hangs in the Mordan Hall. (Photograph by Julia Davey).

First students at St Hugh's, 1887. Back row, L to R: Jessie Emmerson, Charlotte Jourdain, Wilhelmina de Lona Mitchell. Front row, L to R: Miss Moberly, Constance Ashburner, Grace Parsons.
Wilhelmina de Lona Mitchell joined St Hugh's in 1887. She stayed for only two terms and was not one of the original four students who joined in 1886.

St Hugh's, 1890. Miss Moberly, sitting second from the left, Miss Wordsworth, second from the right. Miss Wardale is in the back row, behind Miss Wordsworth.

(a) Miss Jourdain in 1915.

(b) Miss Ady, centre; behind her: Margery Lewis (L), Eleanor Nicholas (R). On either side of her: Mary Richards (L) and Muriel Holland (R), 1916.
(The last three girls are constantly mentioned in the text.)

(e) Molly McNeill, in witch's costume for fancy dress party, November 1916.

(c) Miss Ady in 1916.

(d) Gwen Vaughan, Norah Carter and Joan Evans, 1916.

The staff of St Hugh's, 1919.
Front row, L to R: Miss Ady, Miss Rogers, Miss Jourdain, Miss Wardale, Miss Evans.
Back row, L to R: Miss Spearing, Miss Shaw, Miss Bullen (Bursar), Miss Hind.

Girl in a canoe, 1915. (Photo by Thomas-Photos).

St Hugh's College, 1916.

1946, the first College photograph taken after the war, when St Hugh's returned to its own buildings.

The Ugly Duckling takes to the water, c. 1891. (Photo by Thomas-Photos).

St John's Madrigal Society afloat, 1947.
Four of the girls are from St Hugh's.

Studying on the river bank, 1956.

Nothing like hard work, 1985! (Photo by Thomas-Photos).

St Hugh's Hockey Team, 1915–16. Back row: Chappel, Varley, Davies-Colley, Cox.
Middle row: Baker, Holland, Nicholas, Perham, Richards. Front row: Hurry, Rhys-Davies.

Tennis at St Hugh's, c. 1916.

Skating on Port Meadow, 1958.

(a) Matriculation, 1920s.

(b) Degree taking, 1950s.

(c) The successful BA, 1940s.

(d) After Finals, 1950s.

(e) Taking their MAs, 1950s.

(a) Dorothy Rippon's car, 1925.

(b) The Proctor and his Bulldogs, 1957.

(c) Margaret Carpenter, 1967, a member of the OUOTC (Royal Signals) seen on exercise overlooking the Firth of Tay (1968) with a self-operating B.70 Radio.

(d) The Oxford Pastoral Mission to Sheffield, 1956. (Anne Heath, 1955, first right, back row).

Comus, 1935. Cast: Comus: Molly Gaminara; Lady: Margaret Burgess; Spirit: Dorothy Sherwood; Sabrina: Joan Yearly.

The Western Chamber, 1945 (at Holywell Manor).

St Hugh's Players, 1980. (Photo by Thomas-Photos).

Left: The early St Hugh's, at 17 Norham Gardens.

Below: The island site. (Photo by Thomas-Photos).

A student's room in the 'old' college, c. 1914.

An undergraduate's room in the 1980s.

Above:
The Proctorial Procession on 19 March 1980, when Miss Theodora Cooper was admitted to become Senior Proctor. This was the first time a woman became Senior Proctor. (Photo: *Oxford Mail*).

Right:
Dr Kenyon, the Principal and Mrs Mary Warnock assist at the ceremony of 'topping out' the New Building at St Hugh's in July 1965. (Photo: *Oxford Mail*).

(a) Miss Annie Rogers, 1930. (Artist: Leslie Brooke; photo by Julia Davey).

(b) George Harris, Head Gardener, 1972.

(c) The College Memorial to Annie Rogers, *Custos Hortulorum*, 1927–37.

(d) St Hugh's gardens – the Senior Common Room lawn, May 1937. In the deck chair – Miss Thorneycroft.

visiting luminaries: Dylan Thomas and Stephen Spender at the Poetry Society, Osbert Lancaster at the Heretics Club, F. R. Leavis 'giving a close reading of Yeats's Byzantium poems' at the Critical Society, Dudley Moore (still an undergraduate) 'in his Erroll Garner phase' at the OU Jazz Club (several enthusiastic mentions), the Erinyeans (joint St Hugh's and Pembroke Debating Club), the 1918 Club (all women and restricted membership), the Junior Mathematical Club (The Invariants), the China Society, the Liberal Club, the Cornish Society (which supplied pasties sent up from Cornwall which did not always arrive on time), George Barker, Roy Fuller, Kingsley Amis (not long gone down, but having just published *Lucky Jim*), Edwin Muir, Claire Bloom ... But if all these activities led to a certain waste of money, as noted by Miss Procter, not everyone deserved her criticism of 'deplorably low' spending on books. Ann Morris records the now all-but-vanished and much-loved phenomenon of Oxford bookshops with all their delights and treasure trove atmosphere:

> Bookshops in Oxford then were fabulous. The Turl Cash Bookshop had all four floors heaped with books. Thorntons even once let me go out to their shed at the back and take away books free! Parkers had a marvellous languages department and a second hand department where one could get great bargains for less than five shillings ... Blackwell's hadn't heard of Sociology then and had a marvellous foreign languages department innocent of any works in translation. I spent more hours in bookshops than in lectures.

Religion continued to play a significant part in the life of many St Hugh's undergraduates. One describes the religious interest of the time as 'enormous', and another writes: 'Religion loomed large at St Hugh's, and I went to 8 am chapel every Sunday. In my first year I went St Aldate's, but later became rather High and went to Pusey House which had only just admitted women to its services ... I heard Ronald Knox preach at the Catholic Chaplaincy and regularly heard the University sermons at St Mary's ... Austin Farrer, Chaplain of Trinity was the preacher I most admired, his sermons were works of art and I still enjoy reading them ... ' (Janie Moon). An anonymous contributor supplies an interesting footnote in the light of events of more recent times: 'David Jenkins was Chaplain at The Queens ... an eccentric character with interesting and erudite sermons ... ' Nor were lighter moments lacking: 'On one occasion, a visiting preacher, referring obliquely to "Hell" called it euphemistically, "The Other Place". He had to be told why the entire congregation collapsed into uncontrollable laughter!' (Anon) [To Oxford undergraduates, 'the other place', is, of course, Cambridge.] Anne Heath was involved in two long vacation Missions in the North of England, as were a number of St Hugh's undergraduates.

In contrast, St Hugh's, and Oxford in general, throughout the decade and particularly during the early part, do not seem very enthusiastic about politics or the Union. There are no star attractions to follow the Kenneth Tynan firework era, although Robin Day, Michael Heseltine and Brian Walden are mentioned, with visiting speakers Richard Crossman and Anthony Crosland (then a don at Trinity). The reason does not seem to be apathy, nor unawareness exactly, so much as a lack of the kind of fervour which characterised the 1930s and earned Oxford a political name – and perhaps a complacency in and around the Macmillan times. King George VI had died in 1952, and been succeeded by the present Queen, and perhaps Oxford reflected a general mood in the country as a whole. Things livened up a little in the middle of the decade: it was the era of Sharpeville, as one contributor notes, as well as Suez and Hungary, and the latter event caused a temporary renewal of political activity, and undergraduates leaving (in the same sort of spirit as for the Spanish Civil War twenty years previously, but with reversed allegiance), to volunteer help in that Iron Curtain country.

> I can remember only one friend, Sarah Myers, as an active political animal, but Oxford did change my political views. I had been brought up on the *Daily Telegraph* and the war propaganda, and when the Suez crisis started I signed a declaration of support for Eden's actions. By the end of the Suez episode I had been introduced to the *Guardian* and made to question my attitudes . . . the Hungary crisis was another political watershed, however, no communist attraction then, we abhorred the Russian action and went racing off to Hungary to 'help', or started knitting blankets for the refugees. Bulganin and Kruschev had visited Oxford at the beginning of one term, but I was writing a paper and missed them. (Janie Moon)

> Some people, of course, made their mark – we had one in particular involved with the rise of CND; another campaigning for the admission of women to the Union; some joined anti-racist groups

– this was the era of Sharpeville. I don't remember that we found party politics or philosophy as particularly relevant to these issues. My first vote at a parliamentary election was cast as a student. It was the Macmillan Never Had It So Good era ... Oxford was going through rather a quiet period, and somehow I think we were all conscious of it ... looking back, I realise that we were indeed in between some of the great struggles. We did not have to be suffragettes, and many rights had been won; and the later surge of Women's Lib was still only a twinkle in Germaine Greer's eye. I was dimly aware towards the end of my career that the College certainly, and possibly the University, was quietly consolidating its position ready for the expansion of the sixties – a wise policy, but not an exciting one to live through. (Anne Ward)

The need for expansion was indeed a College theme of the 1950s. since most of its income came from fees, there was a break-even number of undergraduates below which it could not survive economically, and above which it would gain more money and thus be enabled to expand its facilities. The obstacle was lack of accommodation. Even the expanded quota, before the figure was finally abolished altogether, could not be taken advantage of, for this reason:

The quota has been a definite discrimination between men and women and, for that reason, one is glad to see the end of it, but its abolition is unlikely to have much effect on numbers for some years to come ... Lack of accommodation limits numbers quite as effectively as a University Statute. Neither St Hugh's nor St Hilda's have yet reached the figure of 200 allowed them by the quota and both colleges will need to build before their number can be raised to that level ... For financial reasons undergraduate numbers of about 170 are not satisfactory and an additional 30 would be a great advantage. Educationally there would be no difficulty in increasing our numbers up to a total of 200. Anything above 200 would almost certainly require an increased teaching staff. The College should, however aim at reaching 200 within a reasonable period ... (*Principal's Report*, 1956)

To this end a Building Appeal had been launched in 1955. The object was to raise £20 000 which would provide another twelve rooms in college. Beyond that, the long-term objectives concerned securing possession of one of the houses of which St Hugh's was ground landlord (giving a further seven or eight rooms) – although separate houses had disadvantages. By 1957, the house (2 St Margaret's Road, next to the College) had been secured and converted and the following year work began on College extensions. This was the first new building at St Hugh's for more than twenty years and consisted of extensions to the East wing of the Main Building including dining hall, and to the West wing to make more undergraduate rooms. The money raised by appeal was supplemented by £5000 from the University Grants Committee for the dining hall extension. Beyond that, there were further plans for twenty-six rooms, and the College architects were examining the possibility of joining up some of the St Margaret's Road houses. One result of the completion of the Hall extension was that those who lived in the houses came into College for all meals. It was, perhaps, a suitable conclusion for College ambitions in this direction, and, like so much in the 1950s pointed the way to larger-scale activity to come.

The climax of the decade was, however, in Michaelmas Term 1959, the repeal in Congregation of Stat. Tit. XXIII 'Of Women Students' which since 1920 had governed the relations of the Societies of Women Students with the University, and thus St Hugh's, with other women's colleges, was granted the full status of a College of the University: an achievement so long sought, and something to justify the faith of Miss Wordsworth and the persistence and struggle of earlier generations.

THE 1960s

The 1960s, as a decade, has had more labels attached to it than any other so far in the twentieth century. While in popular retrospective imagery the 1920s unequivocally belonged to the Bright Young Things, the 1930s were the Years of Depression and the Rise of Hitler, and the 1940s predominantly the War Years, the 1960s have become stereotyped variously as the time of Flower Power, the Age of the Beatles, Hippy Culture, Students Against Authority and Pot Smokers Against The World, to quote only a few labels. Above all, the 1960s have been seen as Swinging.

That it was a time of turbulent change for young people, in general, is not disputed. But what is *not* included, as much as what is, in the recollections of St Hugh's undergraduates of the time, illuminates the fact that such labels, even taken *in toto*, do not necessarily summarise the entire 1960s experience for everybody.

There is, for example, not a word in any reminiscence about the Vietnam War (compare the St Hugh's equivalents of the 1930s and their continual reference to the Spanish Civil War and Mussolini's invasion of Abyssinia). Nor a single mention of LSD, cannabis or purple hearts. There is but one passing word (quoted below) about Aldermaston marches. The Beatles do slightly better. There are one or two references, one of them highly illuminating: 'While at home during the vacation, my parents (my parents!) told me about the Beatles' (Pamela Powley). Vivienne Brasier was told 'something about a group called the Beatles' by a friend who thought 'they'd got something'. The *JCR Report* for 1968 notes, rather distantly, that there had been 'widespread student unrest' (presumably in Oxford, rather than the excesses at the Sorbonne), but it 'had not penetrated St Hugh's'. There is one (rather vague) reference to participation in 'unrest': 'I think I did go to one demo, but I can't remember what it was about' (Anon). More typical is the comment of Susan Hope: 'Although I was up in the late 'Sixties, I do not recall any great political awareness among my contemporaries although there were various sit-ins and demos that I never came across'; and Vivienne Brasier mildly supported CND and took part in one demonstration at the time of the Cuba crisis. There is only one fragment of evidence that St Hugh's was witness to the newly-forged mass protest techniques: 'I recall we did protest actively on one occasion, arranging an Eat-In. I think this was because we were charged for meals whether we ate them or not, and reckoned that on Saturday nights the College banked on the non-attendance of two-thirds of the undergraduates. Unfortunately . . . someone must have tipped the College off, because they came up with enough food . . . ' (Judith Stevenson).

One quotation above all, perhaps, illuminates best the contrast between St Hugh's attitudes and the stereotype of the decade which has since been fashioned: 'We accepted so much in those days. We mostly did as we were told and student demonstrations were unheard of, though of course there was Aldermaston. I remember some people were asked their views on lecturers' techniques and the results of the "survey" were published in *The Isis*. We certainly thought we should be making this sort of assessment but it was considered pretty daring' (Pamela Powley).

Far more significant to St Hugh's in the 1960s was its own

expansion as a College. Miss Procter, in her *Principal's Report* for 1960–1, had concluded, as always, with the number of graduates and undergraduates in residence, and added a comment echoing her speeches throughout the 1950s: 'Numbers . . . vary a little from year to year but, until the College can increase its accommodation by building, it is unlikely that there will be any significant alteration in the total.'

That total, for 1960–1, was 214. By 1969, the equivalent total was 371, comprising 290 undergraduates, and 81 graduates reading for higher degrees, diplomas and certificates. The 'significant alteration' had been achieved, enabled by substantial additions to the College fabric (notably the Wolfson Building, opened by Princess Alexandra in 1968). At the same time, the Senior Common Room had expanded so that by the end of the decade it comprised the Principal and twenty-four Fellows, thirteen Honorary Fellows, three Emeritus Fellows and nine Lecturers (including three men). There had been a proliferation in the Bursar's Office, with the appointment in 1963 of a separate Estates Bursar (Mary Warnock) 'responsible for the planning of new buildings, for College property not in College occupation and for planning the use of College financial resources'; the following year a Deputy Bursar and two new Assistant Bursars were appointed. In 1960, a Dean (Miss Sweeting) was appointed for the first time, to take some of the administrative burden from the Principal. Such was the increase in the number of graduates that a Middle Common Room became necessary. And, hand in hand with expansion, by the end of the decade St Hugh's achieved the largest number of Firsts in Schools in living memory: a total of eleven (four in Modern Languages); while in one single year (1965), on the sporting front, there had been no fewer than twenty-three St Hugh's Blues.

Aside from these solid achievements, however, one of the best-remembered symbols of the 1960s does receive a good deal of attention, not to say exposure, in the reminiscences. This is the mini-skirt, which in Oxford as, perhaps, nowhere else, had a particularly striking effect: 'I remember one girl who combined extremely heavy false eyelashes with a skirt that was not visible beneath a Commoner's gown when viewed from behind. The sight of mini-skirts on bicycles was a source of great satisfaction to the male population of Oxford at the time. Rather chilly for us 'though – but wind-resistance was less with a short skirt' (Dorothy Wilkinson).

As might be expected, the 1960s saw considerable relaxation in what were increasingly seen as 'old-fashioned' regulations and customs. Towards the end of the decade the formal procession of dons to High Table was abolished; and then, 'Formal Hall became less so, as trousers could be worn, except on guest nights, and several JCR members accepted the SCR's invitation to dine on High Table during the year' (*JCR Report*, 1969). The beginning of the decade saw the start of greater freedom for undergraduates to come in late; 'the appointment of a night porter . . . made it possible for undergraduates in College to have midnight leave without having to ask for it specially' and towards the end of the decade, 'Another much-appreciated innovation is the late-night system whereby we can come in at any hour through the Lodge, instead of the romantic but uncomfortable route over the wall. St Hugh's is now by far the most enlightened [women's] college in this respect' (*JCR Report*, 1968). So ended a long tradition of climbing-in, but not the necessity still for climbing *out* of men's colleges:

> Amorous adventures . . . often used to involve considerable loss of dignity: for instance, having to be helped to climb out of Balliol at 2 a.m. in a snow storm over a six-foot wall by the chap I had just said I never wanted to speak to again, or spending the night in Wadham with someone I didn't particularly like because it was too late to get back into St Hugh's. I could never work out whether the college rules were supposed to protect our virtue from our boy-friends, or our belongings from burglars . . . (Christine Jones)

Earlier, the same writer described the St Hugh's gate rules as 'cumbersome' but they were not without some humanity in administration:

> One Sunday we had a meal out at Botley with friends who had a car which had seen better days. On the way back it broke down. The AA were so long coming it was clear we would not get back before the door was locked (11.15 pm on Sundays!) So we phoned College and were told that the door would not be left open for us, and no advice was forthcoming (in *loco parentis*) about this predicament. Consequently, when we did get back we were forced to climb in between some tennis-court-type wire netting and the new building – to find conveniently that the *back* door had been left open! (Celia Lowe)

Some progress was also made in a matter which the JCR had long thought irritant: that of hours in which men visitors were permitted. '... men visitors are now allowed into College until 10 pm – St Hugh's was the first women's college to make this extension, and the others have now followed suit' (*JCR Report*, 1964); and 'It was ... a great innovation when men's visiting hours were extended to 11 pm, so that escorts can now be provided with a quick cup of coffee after the theatre' (*JCR Report*, 1966). But even these extensions were considered inadequate by the very end of the 1960s: 'a contentious point was that of hours for visitors; a majority of returned questionnaires suggested they were too short' (*JCR Report*, 1969).

It is hardly surprising, perhaps, in view of greater nocturnal freedom, and the changing attitudes of the times, that sex is more freely mentioned in the reminiscences of the 1960s than in those of previous decades. One writer claims:

> I believe my generation pioneered ... genuine sexual freedom. Contraceptives became available from the college doctor in about my second year and the restrictions on visitors and coming in at night were lifted ... we were mostly virgins when we came up and my awakening to sexual experience was very, very slow and hence, I think, extraordinarily good. Again, it meant maximum intensity of feeling which I suspect must be lost when sex follows almost automatically from the first or second date. I am therefore very glad that I was so naïve when I arrived. By the end of my time at Oxford the sexual revolution was well under way and it became accepted for women to have sexual relationships when they wanted them, without moral censure or fear of pregnancy ... (Diana Manning)

Nevertheless,

> We were given a 'pep' talk in the JCR shortly after we arrived. I remember being astonished when, following a sombre warning from the Principal that anyone becoming pregnant would be sent down, the college doctor stood up and intimated that anyone finding themselves led into temptation had only to pay him a visit. Suitable contraception would then be arranged. This was in 1966 when women's magazines still adjured their readers to preserve their virginity for their wedding night. The advice was well remembered, however: nobody was sent down in my three years. (Dorothy Wilkinson)

On an allied topic, Diana Manning is again illuminating:

> I turned up at the interview for St Hugh's wearing a good quality,
> but unfashionablely long and dowdy suit with my hair in a bun,
> spectacles and no make-up, looking, quite deliberately like a 'blue
> stocking' and was amazed to meet one of the other candidates for
> my subject who wore a miniskirt and looked like a 'dolly-bird'. She
> even belong to the fan club of a pop group back home (Manfred
> Mann) and had a boyfriend! I immediately assumed that she
> couldn't be intelligent. After all, everybody knew there was an
> inverse relationship between a girl's brains and her looks . . . that
> was one of my first preconceptions to crumble . . . she got a
> scholarship and I was only a commoner! . . . This business of looks
> versus brains was one of the significant changes I witnessed during
> my four years at St Hugh's. I remember surveying the dining hall
> at dinner and thinking what an odd-looking bunch we were
> compared with a random cross-section of girls our age . . . By the
> end of those four years the average St Hugh's undergraduate was
> as attractive as any other girl.

Undergraduates were launching into matrimony during their three years at St Hugh's with an ease not dreamed of by their predecessors, but not without some obstacles. Wendy Davies recalls: 'Asking for permission to get married at the end of year two – considered highly irregular!! My moral tutor asked if my fiancé could keep me in the manner to which I'd become accustomed and the Principal told me I'd ruined my prospects!! Hiding my husband during year Three – he wasn't allowed to stay in college with me! I think my scout turned a largely blind eye . . .'

On a more weighty matter the decade witnessed a break with the past, going back to the 1920s, when in 1962, Miss Procter retired, and was succeeded as Principal by Miss Kathleen Kenyon. In her speech to the 1962 Gaudy, Miss Procter spoke of how the status of women had changed for the better since her first appointment to St Hugh's, and compared the life of undergraduates then and at the time she was speaking:

> Miss Gwyer in her speech at the 1946 Gaudy, spoke of women in
> Oxford 'moving out of the adolescent stage of women's College
> life' and taking their place on a level with the men. That had now
> certainly taken place and the Women's Colleges have attained their

majority and are mature institutions. The coming of maturity has been marked internally by the attainment of complete self-government and externally by changes in the relationship between the Colleges and the University . . . Two changes have taken place in the relations between the Women's Colleges and the University. In the first place, there is the abolition of the limitation of women students. In 1927, as a very young tutor I attended the debate in the Sheldonian Theatre in which the limitation was approved. It was certainly the most unpleasant of the many debates to which I have listened. The speeches showed clearly the amount of hostility to the women members of the University which was then felt and which continued to exist to some extent up to the war. The actual quotas (they varied slightly for the five societies – that imposed on St Hugh's was 160) did not cause any practical disadvantage at the time, as in every case they were larger than the number of undergraduates, but they underlined the fact that the women were in Oxford on sufferance. After the war the quota caused difficulty when pressure on places grew. It was raised slightly in 1948 when the proposal aroused some but negligible opposition. A further increase was allowed a few years later and in 1957 the quota was abolished. As the Men's Colleges had increased very rapidly, the proportion of women to men in 1957 was lower than it had been in 1927. The Women's Colleges are increasing their numbers slowly but lack of money for building is almost as effective a limitation as an arbitrarily imposed quota. Another change which came very quietly, without debate, opposition, or division, was the recognition by the University that the Women's Societies had full collegiate status and all the rights and privileges enjoyed by the older Colleges. This was in 1960 – 81 years after Lady Margaret Hall and Somerville College, the two oldest of the Women's Colleges, were founded, and 40 years after women were first granted degrees. The University cannot be accused of undue haste in its recognition of the Women's Colleges.

These are constitutional and legislative changes, but legislation normally follows public opinion, it does not form it. The question of women in Oxford was settled more than a decade before final recognition was granted. I do not think any of the post-war generations in either Senior or Junior Common Rooms have felt themselves to be in any way on sufferance, or have been treated as anything less than equals by their male contemporaries. The Fellows of the Women's Colleges have taken their full part in University teaching, lecturing, examining, and administration

– and may I here interpolate a tribute to the Fellows of St Hugh's. They are a very distinguished body and they fully merit the recognition they have received. Even that last stronghold of male exclusiveness, the Estates Bursars' Committee, has opened its membership to the Treasurers of the Women's Colleges although it has not yet invited them to participate in the archaic survival known as the Corn Rent Dinner.

Life for the undergraduate population is certainly very different now from what it used to be. Cloistered quiet has given place to a very strenuous social life and participation in innumerable inter-collegiate activities. Men and women mix freely. Equality is as much a characteristic of the fifties and sixties as inequality was in the twenties and thirties. The only inequality left is the numerical one, and this certainly adds to the distractions which beset the women. In its way the situation is almost as abnormal as the earlier enforced segregation, for nowhere else is the ratio of men to women 7 to 1, except at Cambridge where the disproportion is even greater.

The standard of life for the woman undergraduate has risen. State Scholarships and Local Education Authority grants allow most of them a greater margin for amenities than their prede-cessors had (even allowing for the change in the value of money). Although students everywhere are inclined to complain that their grants are not large enough, I have met with very few cases of real hardship in recent years. Undergraduates who have to support themselves throughout all, or most of, the vacation do run into difficulties, but these are exceptional cases and there is little financial stringency.

Although our women live a very full life, they also work steadily and well, as the class lists testify. The women do well in Schools and the great majority obtain Second Classes. They show a high standard of competency. For a period St Hugh's was rather short of First Classes, but the last three years have shown an encourag-ing improvement which will, I hope, be maintained. More of our undergraduates have been winning University Prizes and Scholar-ships and we are increasing our representation in the Senior Common rooms of the other four Colleges and in Universities throughout the British Isles. I have no doubt that St Hugh's has a useful, distinguished, and prosperous future before it.

Another weighty matter which marked the 1960s was that of building, earlier briefly referred to. The reminiscences do not make much of it, but St Hugh's for long periods during the decade, or significant parts of it, resembled a construction camp. In her first report as Principal (1963), Miss Kenyon gave the news that the proposal to link up the houses comprising nos 2 to 4 St Margaret's Road had been abandoned on account of excessive cost, and that 'at the beginning of the 1962–63 academic year, it was therefore necessary to start planning again from the beginning'. This resulted in an outline two-stage plan approved in principle.

... the new building will continue the College frontage along St Margaret's Road, replacing Nos. 2, 3, and 4 with a new block, with another block at right angles between the end of this block and 82 Woodstock Road; this block would thus form a fourth north–south wing, corresponding to the wings of the Main Building and the Library. For reasons of convenience, the north–south wing will be built first, since this will mean that the St Margaret's Road houses can remain in use meanwhile. An *ad hoc* planning committee was set up in the Michaelmas Term and an immediate tour of inspection of new university buildings in Oxford, Cambridge, and elsewhere was made. As a result, an architect was selected in November, and his preliminary scheme will shortly be received.

Each of these new blocks will accommodate about fifty undergraduates and two tutors. The increase in actual numbers with the first stage will not be great, as the present plan is to bring into College undergraduates in lodgings and from some of the detached houses, the vacated houses can probably be used with advantage for graduate accommodation.

These plans will, of course, involve the College in very considerable expenditure; a very rough estimate is that each block will cost about £100,000. It is hoped that help will be forthcoming from the Wolfson Trust, which has already given £100,000 each to St Anne's and St Hilda's. It is believed that it is the intention of the Trust to give similar sums to the other Women's Colleges, but it is not known when or in what order. In any case, the College will have to raise the other £100,0000, and in this connexion it will once more be necessary to call on the generosity of its Senior Members.

The Trinity Term of the same year:

J.C.R. activities have been, as usual, very varied. In Trinity Term the arrival of the plans for the new buildings and the architect's model of the first stage aroused a great deal of feeling. The majority of the J.C.R. liked the general ideas on which the building was designed – particularly the provision of a double aspect for each undergraduate room. There were, however, a number of objections to details, such as the large number of turrets and the over-emphasized entrance; and so it was decided to set up a special committee under the chairmanship of the President, to try to obtain a coherent digest of J.C.R. opinion. This committee produced two reports, on the outside and inside of the building, which were submitted to the architect via the Principal and the S.C.R. The committee was then invited to meet the architect himself and had a most stimulating afternoon's discussion with him which resulted in the adoption of some of the J.C.R. suggestions – the modification of the entrance and a reduction in the number of turrets amongst others.

Since these discussions took place the whole project has been gathering momentum – at the end of Michaelmas Term the J.C.R. set up a committee to organize a J.C.R. appeal for funds to correspond with that which is being organized among Old Students; and it is hoped that its activities will increase during Hilary Term 1964. (*JCR Report*, 1963)

Miss Kenyon's next *Report* (January 1964) gave the news that the plans had finally been approved, that fund-raising was going on apace with a 'magnificent response' from former members of the College, and 'we are . . . now proceeding with approaches to outside bodies'. Work was scheduled to begin in March 1964, with the building ready for use by the beginning of the academic year 1965–6. Meanwhile other, lesser, but none the less important building works had been going on. The Library was re-organised and expanded with money from Dame Catherine Fulford's legacy, and, taking in two additional rooms, gave an entire wing devoted to library purposes. In addition, the Mordan Hall was completed (when the dining room was extended in the 1950s, there were not enough funds to complete a similar addition to the Mordan Hall above, and the south end had therefore 'remained a bare shell, divided from the original portion by a temporary partition, and this original portion was left as a gloomy relic, not conveniently usable in any case because of the noise of traffic from the Banbury Road'). Now the Mordan Hall was resplendent with wood-block floor, double glazing to deaden the traffic noise, and 'through the generosity of an anonymous donor' equipped with an excellent stage. Said Miss Kenyon: 'The result is that St Hugh's now possesses an excellent and most attractive hall for use for social occasions, performances and lectures'. A further important addition was 'the coming into use in Michaelmas Term 1963 of 72 Woodstock Road as the Principal's Lodgings. It is a delightful building for the purpose, far more spacious than the Principal's Lodgings at any other women's college, and comparing favourably even with those of most men's colleges.'

Also in 1964, the Bishop of Oxford dedicated the memorial tablet to Dr Ady, from whose bequest the Chapel had been redecorated and refurnished two years earlier. In the following year there is one further piece of ancillary building to record before the 'main' new buildings were complete: the *JCR Report* for 1965 states:

The year 1965 has seen the fulfilment of the first stage of the College's building programme, with the completion of the Buttery and the new building, and both these new additions affect the JCR considerably. The Buttery [a one-storey building in the angle between the front door and kitchen wing] has been in use since October and is an enormous success. Besides relieving the pressure on Hall (which was becoming uncomfortably crowded last year) the Buttery is particularly welcome as being the first room in College where members of the SCR and JCR can meet informally at meal-times, and where non-members of St Hugh's can be entertained. Undergraduates receive two free meal tickets a week for use in the Buttery, but further meals can, of course, be bought, and the food is good and reasonably priced . . .

The new building (now known as the Kenyon Building), begun late in the event and held up by a brick shortage, was not ready until January 1966 and the *Principal's Report* for 1965–6 gives details of the scene:

The actual move came only at 9.15 pm on the Friday of the beginning of term. When the Bursar's office opened at that hour for the issue of keys, a wave of enormous activity began as the new owners, helped by a large band of male friends, moved in with all their possessions . . . Stage I in the expansion of the College is thus virtually complete, and we are now plunging straight into Stage II. In March 1965, the College was notified that the Wolfson Foundation had made a grant for the construction of a Wolfson Building. The College acknowledges this munificent benefaction with the greatest gratitude . . .

Plans had already been prepared for this building, providing forty-four undergraduate rooms, two Fellows' sets, and one lecturer's set, a comparatively low three-storey building, designed on the staircase system, and all rooms facing on to the garden: the completion being scheduled for Michaelmas 1967.

To make way for the Wolfson Building, numbers 2, 3 and 4 St Margaret's Road would be demolished, and this event was to provide some light relief in the siege of brick piles and contractor's huts:

A unique event was the 'Demolition Party' held by my French tutor, Miss Daniel, in my first year. She had a room at the top of one of three old Victorian houses that were to be demolished to make way for the Wolfson Building. My friend, Jenny, and I had already helped her to move all the flowers and shrubs from the garden of these houses to her house in North Oxford. She then prepared a party to say farewell to her beloved room. Jenny and I painted the entrance's walls black as a sign of mourning. A third year undergraduate painted a phoenix (the new building) rising from the flames (Miss Daniel was the expert on Valéry's poetry) and put up quotations from Victor Hugo (her other favourite). Various French and Spanish tutors were invited from different colleges, and the Principal . . . the gin bottles were wrapped in black crepe paper. The guests began to arrive: Giles Barber, an expert on the 18th. century at the Bodleian, arrived wearing gardening clothes and carrying a pick-axe. The Principal, an eminent archaeologist, brought her excavating tools . . . they were divided into teams and set a series of tasks such as ripping up a floorboard . . . it was hilarious . . . the Principal knocked down the banister rail, chopped it into pieces, and threw them through the skylight like darts . . . a row of worried undergraduates' faces appeared at the windows of the MGA wing as Giles Barber was hacking out a fireplace . . . my Spanish tutor still laments, years after the episode, that he did not think of ringing the Proctors and saying that vandals were destroying college property. (Susan Thurgood)

Not that this was the first time there had been DIY at St Hugh's:

Some members of the [Senior Members'] Association will have seen reference in the Press to the activities of the College during Michaelmas Term. The idea that undergraduates should be allowed to decorate their own rooms seemed to strike even *The Times* and its readers as novel ... one benefit derived from this publicity was that a firm of paint manufacturers, S. Bowley & Son Ltd., not only offered a very substantial reduction in the price of materials, but sent experts to advise on problems connected with the bad materials used in the post-war redecoration ... the first batch of undergraduates redecorated their rooms in the Christmas vacation, and though they were somewhat interrupted by press photographers, they all completed their tasks most successfully ... (*Principal's Report*, 1962–3)

In Michaelmas Term 1967 the second stage of St Hugh's great expansion was complete. Undergraduates moved into the Wolfson Building, and the College was now able to accommodate 244 undergraduates, and to provide rooms in College for all who wished to live in. The building would not have been possible without the generosity of Senior Members.

In May the following year the Wolfson Building was officially opened by HRH Princess Alexandra, an event mentioned in several reminiscences, not least an incident concerning the then Mr Harold Macmillan, who, as Chancellor of the University, was present with HRH: 'he talked to a group of undergraduates afterwards, but perhaps he had already picked his favourite. Standing in the Hall with the official party earlier, he watched a glamorous but unidentified member of the College pass by. "Zuleika Dobson?" the Chancellor was heard to murmur ... ' (Meriel Cowen). Also,

The College was given a special clean. The JCR was tidied out of all recognition and we were made to walk around with gowns on. We had a special lunch. The chef (this was St Hugh's first chef, not long appointed) took up the serving dish to High Table. We had never seen him come out of the kitchen before. He was very young and his face was redder than the salmon on the dish! We had, of course the [St Hugh's] pastry swans swimming on seas of green jelly for dessert. After lunch, Princess Alexandra visited the College and undergraduate rooms. We had been instructed to curtsey and say 'Madam' but she was so normal when she talked to us that I did neither, and was later called 'Incivilisée' by my French Tutor . . . (Susan Thurgood)

In the *Principal's Report* of 1961–2, Miss Procter had observed: 'The number of members of the College working for Research degrees is steadily increasing . . . It is to be hoped that ultimately, when the College has been able to increase its undergraduate accommodation, it may be possible to use one of the College houses as a "Graduate House", where some of those doing post-graduate work can live, and where all of them can have a Common Room of their own.' In fact the numbers referred to rose within only three years from the beginning of the decade from twenty-one graduates reading for research degrees or postgraduate diplomas to forty-four and in 1963, steps were taken to put Miss Procter's hopes into practice.

. . . three graduates (J. Cameron, A. Smith and C. Gverve) drew up a constitution for a Common Room whose purpose would be to provide a Middle Common Room for graduates in St Hugh's College . . . MCR membership has doubled in the last few years and there are more than ninety women in the MCR at the present time . . . more than half this number are graduates of other colleges or universities: among those approximately 16 per cent are from Commonwealth countries, 18 per cent from the United States, and 22 per cent from other countries including France, Germany, Spain, Greece, Italy and Czechoslovakia . . . Taken together, the fields of anthropology, archaeology, and geography occupy the largest number of graduates at St Hugh's. Research in English is a close second, followed by research in the sciences, mathematics, modern languages, medicine, and social and administrative studies, in that order.

The Middle Common Room is located in 12 Canterbury Road [it was originally situated in a room too small for its purposes in MGA] . . . The house adjoining it is also a graduate house . . . (First *MCR Report*, 1971)

There was early co-operation between the MCR and the JCR (with whom it shared certain facilities) and on St Hugh's Night, 1966, the President of the Middle Common Room, Hilary Turner (daughter of Louise B. Taylor, 1930) joined with the President of the JCR, Susan Scott (daughter of Nora C. Shaw, 1934) and together they made a rhyming speech of commentary on College happenings over the year, with many a mention of building activity, including the couplet:

New Buildings here, new buildings there
They grow and mushroom everywhere.

Thus one salient aspect of existence at St Hugh's in the 1960s was enshrined in verse. There were, of course, other pre-occupations and activities, and College life, as portrayed in the reminiscences, while distilling an unmistakable flavour of the decade, seems as notable for possessing an equally unmistakable continuity with the past. The same names as in the 1950s and the 1940s crop up (notably Lord David Cecil and Coghill) as well as new ones among lecturers and tutors, and attitudes to lectures show no sign of change: 'I remember cutting a few of my own lectures to attend some of Kenneth Clarke's at the Playhouse. They were marvellous and so much more interesting than Chemistry . . .' (Hope McIntyre). 'One statistics lecture started with more than a hundred attending; after about four, the attendance was down to fewer than ten (so boring)' (Anon). 'Most lecturers were competent but not inspired. One old Professor of Inorganic Chemistry was so incoherent that his audience finally disappeared . . . the women supported him for longer than the men . . . and I actually got something out of his ramblings' (Carolyn Herbert). 'Miss Trickett . . . she wasn't my supervisor, but how I wished she had been! I had Lord David Cecil, and from some obscure principle he never read a word of my thesis, or gave any help in constructing it at all. Whenever I consulted Miss Trickett – and I wish I had done so far more – she was a model of helpfulness, interest and sympathy' (Angela Leach). 'Kenneth Sandford's sepia slides of an amazing trans-Sahara expedition sometime in the 1920s, with people in solar topees, old Ford cars slung with entrenching tools and watercarriers, and totally nude natives washing clothes or cooking in the foreground of pictures which, in the background, illustrated obscure features of the arid landscape. They were the only geology lectures attended by non-geologists, who came entirely for the pictures' (Margaret Carpenter).

There was a great slackening of rules and regulations during the three years I spent at Oxford. At first we were not allowed to wear trousers for lectures at the Taylorian, but this changed after, I think, the first term. My French tutor, Miss Daniels, still objected to trousers, but did not insist on their removal as she did with boots. If an undergraduate wore boots (and they were the height of fashion) to a tutorial, Miss Daniels insisted that the boots remained outside the door. One felt somewhat vulnerable defending an already dubious theory in bare feet. (Beverley Swire)

As, perhaps, the most constantly beguiling and popular feature of almost every undergraduate's life at Oxford, the river yields many reminiscences, most of them reassuringly similar to those of every previous decade: 'Punting was a favourite pastime and there was a stampede to sign up when the lists were put up each week' (Margaret Bedwell). 'I remember thinking as I punted down the river on golden summer afternoons, always in love, that it was like a bad Hollywood B movie it was so romantic' (Diana Manning). 'One of my main achievements at Oxford was to learn how to punt really well . . . with some College friends, I punted up the Cherwell as far as it was possible to go, beyond the rollers, until the punt ground to a halt on the stones way beyond the North Oxford by-pass. I have already forgotten most of my degree course, but I hope I shall always be able to punt' (Marian Liebmann). However, at least one or two memories are adroitly of the decade: 'Once, four of us, clad in bikinis, were punting on the Cherwell through the Parks. There came the other way a punt laden with young men, piles of clothes, books, radios etc. As it passed, they crowded to the stern end to obtain a better view of us nubile young ladies. Inevitably, the front rose, the rear end sank, and the whole lot was deposited on the bottom of the river. We continued serenely on our way . . . Many of us have been immortalised on American home movies punting in scanty attire . . .' (Dorothy Wilkinson).

May Morning continued to be as well attended as ever, a delight to some, but a disappointment to others: 'I got up the first year for May Day, but was disappointed – couldn't hear the choir boys, no one fell in the river, and I couldn't find the Morris Dancers' (Beverley Swire).

A small minority of undergraduates now owned cars:

Quite illegally, I had a car up at Oxford during my first year. This meant that, unknown to anybody, I simply went home at weekends. Indeed, during my first term, my boyfriend was an Army Officer based down at Salisbury. He used to come to Oxford . . . and we used to drive down to London for the weekend. My social life was a round of Army balls and college balls supplemented

during the weekdays with visits out to pubs in the country . . . The
car gave me flexibility and freedom. But, alas, a sharp-eyed porter
realised that the sea-green Morris 1100 regularly parked in St
Margaret's Road must belong to some undergraduate. And very
soon I got summoned to see Miss Sweeting, the Dean . . . luckily I
must have been in [her] good books. She simply signed a letter to
the Proctors saying that she was permitting me to have a car in my
first year. And I duly went down to the centre of Oxford,
registered my car and got the famous green light to put upon it.
(Vicki Cohen)

Wendy Davies hid her car all her first year: 'inspecting carefully for
watching proctors before rushing up to it, leaping in and driving off!'
For the majority, however, the bicycle remained the *sine qua non* of
transport in and around Oxford: 'We cycled everywhere, including
on one Sunday afternoon to a concert in Dorchester' (Anon). 'I spent
a lot of time at weekends outside Oxford visiting churches, houses,
pubs, and walking. The chef in College would provide a packed lunch
on either Saturday or Sunday and, in Trinity Term, my friends and I
had a picnic lunch almost every weekend' (Ann Kennedy). But the
bicycle thief makes an unwelcome appearance and the usual bor-
rowers and maltreaters are still out in force: 'I remember my first
term. It rained every day – nowhere more dismal than Oxford in the
rain. My trunk got lost and didn't turn up for three weeks. I bought a
second-hand bicycle and had it stolen immediately because I didn't
think to buy a lock . . . ' (Pamela Powley). 'I knew one needed a bike at
Oxford and I duly brought mine from home, a sensible three-speed
model . . . within weeks it was scratched and the handlebars twisted, it
was plainly not up to the rigours of Oxford . . . I borrowed my
mother's bike instead. This was a 1920s German model very heavy,
huge basket, no gears and a back-pedal brake . . . I never bothered to
lock it, I knew the lethally unfamiliar brake would deter any borrower
. . . ' (Marian Liebmann).
   The worst snow and ice since the great freeze-up of 1946–7
occurred in early 1963: 'The first year I spent in 82 Woodstock Road,
and during that awful winter all the pipes and drains froze. Rather
awkward, as we were, of course, locked in at 11.15 pm. I can't
remember using a chamber pot; we must have controlled ourselves'
(Judith Stevenson). ' . . . there was thick snow and the Cherwell froze
solid. Lectures suddenly seemed irrelevant as we explored a new,
white, crisp, quiet Oxford . . . I spent several mornings trying to learn

to skate. I never did achieve this, but I did manage to stand up on the ice. I discovered that some intrepid spirits had skated to their lectures and one person had even *cycled* down the ice to Magdalen Bridge!' (Marian Liebmann).

Places to meet, with one or two additions, remained the favourite pubs and cafés of previous decades: 'The Elizabeth, the Turf, the Lamb and Flag' (Anon); 'The big treat when family visitors came, was tea in Fullers', (Elizabeth Jones); 'There are fond memories of tea gatherings at the Kemp and Cadena cafés . . . and we had memorable evenings at places like La Cantina . . . ' (Hope McIntyre);

> Wystan [the writer's uncle was Professor of Poetry at the time] used to have coffee at the Cadena where students could go and talk to him, and I did not go that often as I felt slightly self-conscious at Oxford about cultivating my own uncle . . . I used to be taken to dinner fairly frequently at the Fontana. Usually we had a daiquiri in the bar . . . the Elizabeth was another fashionable restaurant if you could spend the money . . . often we ate underneath the Fontana in the Cantina, the more informal and cheaper counterpart . . . tea I associate with the Mitre. They used . . . to produce the most delicious scones stuffed with an inch of thick cream and jam. The Randolph was another place people liked for tea . . . when my sister came up to St Anne's I often used to meet her at Brown's in the Market . . . (Anita Auden)

As far as clothes are concerned there is not much reported apart from the mini-skirt, previously mentioned, though at the beginning of the 1960s 'duffle coats and college scarves were popular. Dances were very dressed up, and the hairdressers specialised in back-combed lacquered "helmets" for these occasions' (Angela Crabtree); and *sub-fusc* received some embellishment: 'At exam time we used to go to town with *sub-fusc*. [Examinations at Oxford have to be sat in a dark suit, white blouse, black shoes and stockings, and black tie. On top of this is worn the cap and gown.] It was very good psychology. By the time you had put on that lovely blouse you couldn't really afford, arranged an extravagantly large velvet bow, made up carefully, sprayed on perfume, and pinned your boyfriend's rose in your hair, you approached Schools in a very different frame of mind to that of scruffy jeans and last-minute swot' (Marie Smith).

Each decade produces its own memorable parties and dances and the 1960s predictably were no exception: 'My friends and I organised a very successful Ball [at St Hugh's] – a Rose-Ball with vast arrangements of scarlet roses everywhere. I still have a ticket, with its Rose motif. David Wood (now a well-known writer of children's plays etc.) provided the cabaret' (Judith Stevenson);

> Perhaps my most memorable escapade was a Costume Party thrown by myself and a Chilean – Julio Retamal Favereau; we both had the same birthday and many mutual friends, whom we 'summoned' to a 'Carnival Fantastique' on 16 November 1963. He was dressed as 'Sun' and I was 'Night' – but we were fascinated at the wonderful costumes – there was Mike Emrys-Jones as James Bond–007 in just a towel and a revolver; Mike Johnson (now Mike York) as Lawrence of Arabia in the same white costume worn by Peter O'Toole in the film . . . one Spanish grandee and his lady, others in huge 'bear' costumes hired from London, cowboys, Indians; and a Viscount crashed the party in masked bandit costume . . . I remember going to my first Commem. Ball at Worcester College and twisting the night away at a smaller ball in Teddy Hall. The magnificence of the buffet, the champagne fountain . . . the splendour of the dawn as we left to go punting are still fresh in my mind. I remember seeing Cleo Laine dancing with her husband while his band played at the Magdalen Commem in 1964, and the Merton Septcentenary Ball also in '64. At the St Hugh's ball the previous year we had a Steel Band, which also played for the Principal's Party in October. (Hope McIntyre)

> Christmas Balls were . . . held by some colleges . . . I went to one in Merton. I have distant memories of braziers in the beautiful medieval quad, which was flood-lit and strung across with balloons. It was like something out of a fairy tale. (Susan Thurgood)

As for work: 'Our attendance at lectures fell off dramatically after the first few terms, but we were hard workers (almost "gnomes" as, for some reason, swots were known in our day) . . . life revolved around the once-a-week "essay crisis" with much burning of midnight oil' (Christine Jones);

> In my first year I was taught in College all the time. I learnt some useful things about punctuation, the presentation of work, the technique of sounding well-informed about books I had never

read. In my second year I had tutors exclusively outside College and learned to think for myself. I vividly remember the horror of my first interview with my tutor, when I was given an essay title and told to produce an essay a few days later ... I mastered a ... game of bluff, depending on grasping the essentials of the topic in three days, organising a neat and convincing argument, full of elegant phrases that made it sound as if you actually knew what you were talking about, adding a punch line at the end and a challengingly paradoxical introductory sentence, garnished perhaps with a personal reflection or two if it was an inspired day, and – hey presto! a gourmet essay, impressive and insubstantial as a soufflé. That technique of instant and condensed cookery even got me through Schools ... My real education was due more to the friends I made in Oxford and our wide-ranging conversations, than to any academic training I received, although without the latter I probably wouldn't have approached unrelated issues so critically. (Jennifer Duncan)

'Dr Busbridge worked us mathematicians very hard and during the first term I put on a stone because the only break from work was eating!' (Linda Knipe). Jane Boyce 'attended all relevant lectures and seldom failed to get an essay finished for a tutorial with the assistance of late nights and black coffee'; and Wendy Davies says that during her third year 'we were very disciplined about work: we had agreed meeting times for coffee and certain rooms and everyone worked conscientiously in their own room until the break-time. I found I had to have strategies for these 2/3 hr. work periods.... '

However secular the popular image of 1960s may now be, St Hugh's well maintained its adherence, for many undergraduates at any rate, to religion and churchgoing. 'I was a regular churchgoer throughout my years at St Hugh's, definitely one of the God Squad.' (This seems a popular phrase of the time: in another reminiscence describing involvement in lighting the Balliol Commem, Margaret Carpenter recalls: 'Various suggestions had been made, including a memorable one to flood the front quad and have an illuminated God Squad walking on the water ... ') 'I remember being very moved on hearing Archbishop Anthony Bloom during the university mission (1968–69) and being disappointed when Billy Graham came to Oxford in 1966' (Anon); 'I remember being quite amazed at finding standing room only at St Aldate's. I sat on a window sill and dangled my legs'

(Anon); 'The Congregational Society worshipped in Mansfield Chapel on a Sunday morning; the Methodists at Wesley Memorial Church. I attended Great St Mary's fairly regularly in the Sunday evenings and occasionally St Hugh's Chapel ... the Archbishop of York (Ramsey) held a mission to the University which packed the Camera and was a source of discussion for a week or two, but Father Trevor Huddleston impressed me far more – by his presence as much as by what he said ... ' (Carolyn Herbert). Meanwhile, the present Bishop of Durham, as Chaplain of The Queen's, consolidated his reputation for baffling the St Hugh's members of his congregation: 'Being in Queen's choir, I often heard David Jenkins preaching and couldn't understand him at all – invariably got lost after about five minutes' (Anon). Vivienne Brasier particularly remembers 'the freedom of discussion at meetings led by the chaplain, and gaining much from the College CU [Christian Union] Bible studies ... ' but Nandita Mukerji recounts how she was 'pinned down by some evangelical students who thought I might be a suitable target for conversion. Fortunately they knew nothing of Hinduism hence argument was easy ... '

As always, theatrical activity managed to produce undergraduate names that did not diminish on going down: 'an astonishing number of people I worked with then have become famous: Michael York (then Johnson), Michael Palin, Terry Jones, Sheridan Morley. A lot more people deserved success ... I recall *A Man For All Seasons* which Robert Bolt attended and said it was the best production of his play he had ever seen ... I was the props girl, later Stage Manager ... and we took the play to the Dublin Theatre Festival' (Judith Stevenson). 'While I was in my first year, Richard Burton and Elizabeth Taylor performed free in Marlowe's *Doctor Faustus* to raise money for the ETC. The rest of the actors were students, and the producer Nevill Coghill ... I paid the enormous sum of four guineas to see the performance (normally I went to cheap Monday evening performances at half a crown). It was fantastic, but apparently I was lucky not to have gone on the night Burton was drunk ... ' (Susan Thurgood). As for OUDS drama (offstage rather than on): 'Braham Murray lost out on the battle for the chairmanship: Mike Rudman got it, and did a rather weedy *Twelfth Night*. Braham worked wonders with the ETC. Both had begun with college productions – Braham's *The Hostage* was for Univ. but he had the Playhouse for it, and a very good press ... I played Teresa ... an enormously happy production' (Iris Woodford). At the Playhouse, 'Judi Dench was a regular performer' and Carolyn Herbert recalls '*Orpheus in the Underworld* and *The Wild Duck*'.

It was in 1963 that St Hugh's paid tribute to the professional theatre, by asking Dame Peggy Ashcroft to become an Honorary Fellow (she had just received an Honorary DLitt from the University of Oxford), an invitation that she was delighted to accept. There was no special inaugural dinner for her, but she was asked to a Fellows' dinner, shortly after. She was, she admits, rather awe-inspired at that dinner, and remembers, especially, one amusing moment, when a particularly distinguished Fellow asked 'if I had found it difficult to make the step between academic life and the theatre. At which, I'm afraid, I laughed a great deal, because, as I explained, I had never had any academic life, having left school at sixteen, without even taking any exams in my life; and there was, therefore, no question of a step at all!'

All in all, however, the theatre reminiscences of the 1960s do not produce the striking impression given in some other decades. Nor do those of the Union, surprisingly, perhaps, in view of the national political activity of the time and the fact that in 1965, Janet Morgan became the first woman Secretary of the Union, and in 1967, Geraldine Jones became the first woman President – both from St Hughs. Earlier, Carolyn Herbert comments: 'The JCR and Union were rather like national politics for me: something that other people did, although I took an interest in what went on.' Meriel Cowen also 'never took an active part in politics' but 'I did enjoy going to the Union regularly during my first term . . . Tariq Ali was President . . . there was also considerable excitement with massive demonstrations, when a group of American senators, led by Bobby Kennedy, came to Oxford.'

Even musical activity is not much reported. A solitary anonymous contributor 'Joined the Queen's Choir and the Bach Choir' and remembers 'Daniel Barenboim conducting and playing Mozart Piano Concertos in the Sheldonian.' Angela Crabtree 'went to a few concerts in the Town Hall and heard New College choir . . . also . . . I loved traditional jazz and went to the Union Cellars regularly on Saturday evenings at one time. I remember Vince Duggleby's jazz band, and how it played in the High on the day he finished his exams.' Anne Nuttall 'arrived as a music rebel as school music ended at Mendelssohn or thereabouts. The Beatles were far more interesting. But I heard some Shostakovitch . . . and so started what is now my major interest.' June

Boyce, herself a singer at the time, remembers James Bowman, and particularly 'Peter Pears coming to Keble to sing the Evangelist in a Schütz passion, and my singing Pilate's wife. I still have the programme with "Good Luck to Pilate's Wife" written on it.'

In the 1960s, then, it appears that at least in certain respects St Hugh's was not typical even of itself, let along the now over-publicised image of the 'swinging' decade. June Boyce sums up for herself and many of her contemporaries, when she says: 'I think I had a profound sense, however, of it not being the same world – that the undergraduate world was somehow different from the real world . . . '

THE 1970s

The College and JCR reports for 1970 indicate an abrasive start to a decade whose predecessor has a greater reputation in the public mind for student activity and unrest: 'The "participation bug" descended on Oxford in Hilary Term, 1970, with the Clarendon Building sit-in, the reactions to the Hart Report, the confidential files issue, and the first ever open meeting of undergraduates of the University. The whirlwind passed but student concern remains' (*JCR Report*).

'Events in the JCR have not been so exciting as might be imagined from the BBC and the Press. We have *not* had any "sit-ins" though it came closer than was comfortable, but swift and skilful handling by the Dean and tutors averted the danger . . . ' (*College Report*).

So the 1970s began for St Hugh's, for, 'at College level, the movement towards greater student participation culminated in the Governing Body's decision to invite two members of the JCR to attend its meetings to discuss matters raised at the Joint Committee of Junior and Senior Members . . . students want to be involved in decision-making and to contribute more fully to College life' (*JCR Report*). Yet the reminiscences give little indication of 'student unrest'. Only three writers mention it, one of whom, Gillian Gehring (Official Fellow and Tutor in Physics), was Dean from 1972–4. She introduced a system whereby, as a 'liaison officer' keeping the JCR and Governing Body informed about each others' mood and intentions, she entertained the JCR committee to coffee once a week after lunch:

then came my surprise; they suggested our coffee meeting should alternate between my room and one of theirs. I accepted this with pleasure . . . undergraduates are frequent visitors to dons' teaching rooms or sitting rooms but it is actually very rare for a don to be invited to an undergraduate room. All this was occurring rather soon after all the confrontations and sit-ins which had made the University an unhappy place around 1970 and so this gesture of friendliness and trust from our JCR was especially welcome. But then we do have a reputation for being a friendly college.

Two undergraduates of the time refer to the subject: 'I went up to St Hugh's in October 1969 which was a time of worldwide student unrest. Although I am no expert on such affairs I remember a certain amount of ill-feeling among students about "files" but none of this came anywhere near St Hugh's, as far as I was aware . . . ' (Rachel Thompson). 'I didn't participate in demonstrations, but my sister thought she saw me jeering at one in the High' (Jane Howard).

Yet the *JCR Report* for 1973 was observing: 'College seems to have had a stormy year . . . The political harangue in the Junior Common Room has been a constant feature of JCR meetings.' None the less, the report goes on: 'Many undergraduates feel that the JCR should remain apart from national student issues and would not lend support to proposals for a Central Students' Union in Oxford. The vocal and politically conscious minority in St Hugh's appear to be fighting a losing battle against the stolid majority.' By the middle of the decade the reluctance of the JCR majority to be 'politicised' seems well confirmed. 'One of the most pleasant features of the last year has been the fact that politics have played such a small part. The existence of the Oxford University Student Union has, despite its ineffectiveness, quietened the disruptive forces in the University, and our own JCR meetings have reflected a keener interest in that hoary chestnut, the state of the washing machines, than in Chilean solidarity' (*JCR Report*, 1975). Thereafter, and into the 1980s, politics continued to play a very minor role in JCR affairs, and domestic matters are the keynote.

One issue which crops up regularly is the still-vexed matter of men's visiting hours, which had been extended in the previous decade, but obviously not sufficiently to suit current taste. The *JCR Report* charts progress through the decade. In 1970 'a questionnaire . . . revealed an overwhelming desire of the JCR for longer visiting hours. Since then they have been extended, to midnight'. There was a further, experimental extension the following year, and this experiment, 'the extension of visiting hours till 2.00 am on Saturday nights ... remained in force, while a two-way key system has also been introduced'. In 1974, 'A campaign for the abolition of restrictions on visiting hours was conducted ... only to be turned down by the Governing Body. However, a very happy compromise was reached ... with the granting of extended visiting hours from 9 am till 2 am every day.' By the end of the decade most of what had been desired, indeed battled for, by undergraduates over the years had come to pass: in 1979, a 'JCR Referendum ... extended visiting hours to include overnight guests on Friday and Saturday nights'.

It is interesting to speculate what 'Gwyerism' might have been minted had this 'reform' been foreseen as little as half a century previously. It would be difficult to imagine, too, the comment that might have been made on another, earlier, 'major innovation' as the *JCR Report* (1971) terms it, and continues: 'the JCR Bar ... is being used to a considerable extent, and has brought new life to the JCR, which is more popular than it has ever been, and far less formal in atmosphere'. Members not even as old as those of Miss Gwyer's generation would also, no doubt, have their own comments on the further diminution of the institution of Formal Hall which took place the following year: 'Formal Hall now takes place only twice a week; undergraduates are not obliged to attend' (*JCR Report*, 1972). This measure was carried out at about the same time as another revision in the meals system, which had continued to cause irritation; and, still on the domestic front, by the end of the decade, the Buttery, one of the wonders of the 1960s when it was built and opened, had outlived its usefulness because of 'changing eating patterns among the undergraduates' (*Report to Senior Members AGM*, 1979) and was converted into a multipurpose room with a bar and snack service. It was later named the Wordsworth Room.

Despite the relaxation of visiting hours which progressed throughout the decade, it is obvious from the reminiscences that, particularly in the earlier 1970s, the practice of making a nocturnal exit over the walls of men's colleges had not yet been entirely swept away by 'progress'. Although one anonymous contributor writes: 'I can't remember any rules and regulations at St Hugh's ... ' and Fiona Ewart 'can't remember any trouble ... having one's own key was great – no nonsense about late passes or what-have-you ... ' there were other observations: 'we were allowed keys after my first year, which helped . . . I never had to climb in but various friends had to creep out – one came to know the night porter's routine, and when to make a run for it . . . but I was still caught once or twice as I was trying to get out of some of the men's colleges late at night . . . ' (Gill Wood); and 'Rules regarding men were strict – a spotlight on the front door to check who was coming and going late at night . . . ' But, increasingly, the rules were flouted: 'It was becoming not unheard of for men to manage to stay the night. They just had to keep out of sight until a reasonable time in the morning' (Liz Sayers) and 'Men were supposed to be out of the premises by midnight or 2 am, but often some remained . . . The sound of an electric razor in the corridors of Main Building on a Saturday morning was not uncommon' (Pamela Strong). Another reminiscence on this subject provides welcome reassurance that the solicitude of the Oxford constabulary, time-honoured, in helping undergraduates over college walls, was also not yet extinct: 'I went back to Worcester College with some friends . . . about 3.30 am we all got up to go but found the main door locked. We had to climb out . . . I was the last . . . when I got to the top of the wall . . . I saw two policemen on the other side! "Are you all right?" they asked. Assured that I was, and that I was the last, they wished us all goodnight and drove off' (Deborah Waterhouse).

On a much more serious note, the decade witnessed several retirements and a grievous number of deaths which signalled an enormous break with the St Hugh's of old. Dr Busbridge and Professor Headlam-Morley retired at the very beginning of the decade, and Miss Gray, after thirty-eight years at St Hugh's as Tutor in Classics, in 1973. In the same year 'the College said goodbye with regret and gratitude to Dame Kathleen Kenyon, Principal from 1962 to 1973, and wished her every happiness in her retirement to the borders of North Wales'. Sadly, Miss Kenyon's retirement was only a short one, for she died no more than five years later. Meanwhile, in 1973, Miss Rachel Trickett was appointed Principal.

Another retirement towards the end of the 1970s was that of Miss Betty Kemp, Tutor in Modern History since 1946: 'Her influence on her pupils had made her already distinguished scholarly reputation as a major eighteenth-century historian yet more widespread and effective . . . she was elected unanimously an Emeritus Fellow of the College . . . ' (*Principal's Report*, 1978–9).

Apart from the untimely death of Dame Kathleen Kenyon, the

decade saw the death in 1974 of Miss Gwyer and Miss Seaton and, in 1979, Miss Bickley – all of them the subject of reminiscence in previous decades.

Miss Francis, who had preceded Miss Gwyer at St Hugh's by a few months, gave the memorial address. She concluded her speech with the words: 'What I shall remember about Barbara Gwyer, and what I am sure other people will remember, is a rare combination of individuality and forgetfulness of self. She did not fear to censure things she thought wrong. But she never despaired, and she never lost her belief that with hard work and determination, these things would be overcome. This belief is her legacy to the College and to her friends.' It was not the only legacy, for gifts came to the College from Miss Gwyer's estate, including many books, Miss Gwyer's own desk and Miss Annie Rogers's work table.

Miss Seaton, at her death, left the College a large legacy for the endowment of the Fanny Seaton Schoolmistress Studentship, and for other exhibitions and scholarships. Miss Trickett in her memorial address refers to Miss Seaton's 'uncommon virtues'. Reminiscences of past decades have shown the respect, and indeed affection, with which so many of Miss Seaton's pupils regarded her; and they would all concur with Miss Trickett's words:

In her personal relationships and as a tutor she was neither possessive nor perplexed nor anxious. She never over-taught; she was cool, firm, and shrewd in her judgment of her pupils' work. Yet she kept up throughout her long life with most of them and forgot none. She was exceptionally generous with her time, her knowledge, and her opinions; she had that sort of lively intellectural curiosity which never failed to respond to news of old pupils' works and lives, or to novel ideas as much as to old forgotten works . . . Miss Seaton always assumed that her pupils and her colleagues, whatever their personal problems and difficulties, would go on inquiring and affirming. She would have taken this for granted in a way that our own hesitant generation seems sometimes to have lost. And her life, as we recall it, should enable us to regain something of that quiet confidence in the truth of the mind and the imagination which animated it until the end.

Professor Olga Bickley had left St Hugh's in 1958. She was made an Emeritus Fellow in 1960. In the same year she was appointed to a full-time Professorship in Italian at the University of Toronto, where she had been a part-time lecturer after leaving Oxford. When she retired, she made her home in Italy, though she would come to Oxford for part of each summer. Miss Procter, in her obituary notice in the *Chronicle*, said of her: 'Olga had great vigour and wide interests. She was adaptable and spontaneous. She made contacts easily and had a great capacity for friendship. She will be sadly missed by her many friends, especially her former colleagues and pupils who will remember her with gratitude and affection.'

The College also suffered a grievous loss in 1977, when Dame Joan Evans, Research Student of the College from 1914 to 1917, Member of Council from 1938 to 1958, and Honorary Fellow from 1958 to 1977, died. She had been one of St Hugh's most generous benefactresses. To do her work adequate justice would require more space than is available here; but she secured the early purchase of 82 Woodstock Road and gave it to the College, and in 1951, she enabled the College to buy freeholds which completed the acquisition of 'the island site'. She (anonymously) originated and later munificently augmented the Endowment Fund – and, in a characteristic gesture (after sleeping on a hard mattress), made a covenant providing new beds for the entire Main Building in 1953. Without her continuous and ready help, St Hugh's would have been a far different place.

Parallel with this wholesale change from the old order there seems to be, judging by the reminiscences, a dwindling of names and figures in University and College life – certainly fewer are remembered: 'I recall . . . going to the Sheldonian to see a friend get his degree and seeing by chance Tolkien getting an honorary something . . . but not realising it was he because [everything] was in Latin' (Anon). 'Dame Kathleen Kenyon was Principal . . . she was always held in great respect by me and my peers but there was always slight amusement about her large friendly dog. I was rather surprised that her sherry parties were generally unpopular . . . in spite of the fresh raspberries' (Rachel Thompson).

There are a few good pictures, however, of lecturers and tutors of the time: 'I only attended lectures on my subject [Zoology]. I can particularly remember . . . an ecology lecturer's booming voice which meant there was an even greater tendency for the back of the hall to be filled first, and no opportunity for anyone to sleep' (Anon). 'I would have liked to have taken advantage of the open lecture system but hardly ever had time . . . most lecturers were unobtrusive, interesting and able to communicate; one or two were quite awful, and one – Roger Mynors (??) was splendidly watchable, swooping and diving up and down in the Schools, horrid old gown all green with age, as he grew ever more informative on what Virgil was really all about' (Fiona Ewart). 'I will always remember Sir Rupert Cross's lectures on Criminal Law with his marvellous wit and clear, deceptively simple style ... we ... used to laugh at the ponderous lectures of Professor Dworkin on Jurisprudence. He spent the whole of eight lectures explaining: "X is the law, if and only if ... "' (Liz Sayers).

If there is a dearth of remembered lecturers, there is an even greater shortage of recollections about tutors, but the few contributors who have mentioned them do so mostly with affection: 'Marjorie Sweeting and Andrew Goudie – both... enthusiastic and helpful as well as knowing their subject extremely well' (Gill Wood).

> Mr. Wendon at All Souls ... he was a brilliant, stimulating man and teacher ... he was very sensitive to the fact that I did suffer a certain amount of culture shock at Oxford and it was he who helped me see that the advantages of being at Oxford can far outweigh any disadvantages ... two other tutors I remember with respect and affection are John Walsh at Jesus and Duncan McCleod at St Catherine's. They were both so human, and so down to earth, but dedicated and stimulating ... I'm eternally grateful to St Hugh's that it let us have outside tutors and that on the whole it endeavoured to give us the best teachers in the field. (Carole Strachan)

> I began to stop writing A-Level-type essays after Mods, chiefly with the guidance of the University's Ancient History tutor, George Cawkwell, who taught me the value of sources and how best to read them ... this was supplemented by Barbara Levick at St Hilda's, who taught me to read not just the sources but everything I could lay my hands on about the subject ... literature I learned to love later. Much of the syllabus loses its pleasure because one *has* to read it. However, Aristophanes survived the pressure, and so did Tibullus, Propertius and Martial ... (Fiona Ewart)

One memory of work habits is particularly significant, revealing as it does a practice that, common enough by the 1970s, utterly baffles older generations to whom silence when working is essential: 'Listened constantly to Radio One when writing essays or letters ... ' (Jane Howard). At the same time, the 1970s, perhaps, of all the decades, reveal a great enjoyment and zest for academic work, particularly in Oxford's libraries which provide several enthusiastic notes:

> I spent a lot of time in either the Radcliffe Camera, or the upstairs Bodleian Reading Room, or even the English Faculty Library. There I was so impressed, intimidated and overawed by the highly-intellectual-seeming inmates that I felt at the pulse of a nation's collected genius. Perhaps indeed I was. It was also peace, perfect peace in there. Nothing but the furtive turning of the odd page practically needing an apology, and the soft purr of retreating suede shoes as people sneaked out for the refreshment a true intellectual should surely be able to manage without . . . there was wonderful scope for dreaming. The Bodleian was best for that: because of the wonderful panorama of spires from the top floor, from All Souls onwards. It's incredible how long it can take a cloud formation to pass a line of spires if you really follow the process . . .
> (Joyce Hannam)

She continues: 'Inevitably, of course, there were library romances. It might seem an unlikely pick-up point but at times it seemed to me the library was more throbbing with emotion than a pulsating disco-theque. The darkened Radcliffe . . . intellectual's answer to a night-club.' 'It was always possible to find some peace in the [St Hugh's] library and most of my work was done there rather than in my room – partly because it was quieter . . the books were there . . . the tables were bigger and chairs more comfortable. In my room I tended to get diverted by tea and cake, friends and biscuits' (Gill Wood). Even Schools had their joyous side:

> I always enjoyed the carnival atmosphere of Mods and Finals. In the days of unisex jeans and T-shirts it was glorious to see everyone in their sub-fusc. I always thought that the organisers entered into the spirit as well by announcing the simultaneous start of two exams, one in the North Hall and one in the South Hall. The announcement meant that the three hours allotted had already started so there was quite a scrum of academic hopefuls pushing this way and that. St Hugh's provided special Schools lunches . . . superior to the meal of the day . . . I always thought that those who survived the rough and tumble of the Examination Schools deserved an extra qualification . . . (Anon)

Also an anonymous contributor remembers 'the distracting flap and tinkle of unbuckled sandals worn by an invigilator at Mods who swept the papers off your desk with his gown as he passed'. The weekly essay crisis continues to be a familiar part of the working landscape as in previous decades, and for science undergraduates in particular, perhaps, the comparatively recent practice of 'gnoming'.

Nobody outside Oxford really understands what 'gnoming' is . . . my working habits I guess followed those of most of my contemporaries. The days were filled with lectures, practicals in the laboratories and frequent 'farm visits' as I read Agriculture. The spare time seemed to belong to me and not to the preparation for the weekly tutorial. And so, there we are again, a work crisis for the nine o'clock tutorial on the morrow. Panic into the Radcliffe Science . . . find that corner hidden away from normal people . . . settle into the huge oak chair built for persons twice my size . . . and gnome. It was a perfect place to gnome . . . once someone recognised my bicycle outside. To it was pinned the following:

In yonder Radcliffe sits a gnome,
Who she is I do not know,
Perhaps she's working,
Perhaps she's sleeping,
I wonder when she will be free.

It was a cheerful little ditty and it came often to my drowsy mind in the library. (Charlotte Moss)

One science 'gnome' Margaret Moore says that, 'as a physiological sciences student my life was probably more organized than many. We had to attend, I believe, 80% of our practical classes to get signed up.'

One of the deep impressions that St Hugh's made on many of the 1970s undergraduates was the Interview before ever they came up. Several writers give graphic details:

I'd applied to Somerville, but after interview there was sent to St Hugh's. I remember sitting in the dark at the foot of the new tower building, looking up at the amazing lights up the steps and being impressed by the height and strength of the building and awed by the thought of the staff and students living there. The college was quiet, almost secretive . . . the interview was a frank, helpful affair, in which Miss Daniel brought to the surface the fact that I had never chosen to apply to Oxford but had been channelled into it. She asked if I would accept a place . . . when I next saw that same building, its awesome, secretive air had vanished, and it was just part of a college I came to be very fond of and very grateful to for shaping me as a person. (Anon)

I clearly remember the trauma of my interviews at St Hugh's. The telegram asking me to attend was delayed and arrived only on the morning I should have been in Oxford. I arrived . . . apprehensively a day late on a raw, late autumn morning in the middle of the blackouts of 1970. After a grilling by my prospective tutor, I set off to explore Oxford and to find the science area . . . after seeing the modern blocks at other universities . . . the gloomy depths of the Inorganic Chemistry Laboratory seemed to have come straight from the memoirs of Madame Curie . . . When I returned, the college was in darkness except for tiny night lights glimmering at strategic corners of the long corridors of Main Building and MGA. Dinner that night was by candlelight, the dining hall was warm and inviting, the conversation was lively and I began to enjoy myself . . . (Janet Chambers)

A more unusual memoir is provided by Jocelyn Seaburne-May:

It was not ideal to arrive in Oxford for my official interview on a bleak afternoon in February. But to arrive at Oxford at all at 50 was something of a miracle. It gave me a feeling of living life backwards . . . Because I belong to the generation who saw education as a very special privilege . . . I saw that Oxford was hallowed ground. Families of my generation who had a cash flow problem finished the basics as 14 . . . As I stood in the Broad, I remembered the frustration involved when I asked my father for financial help after I had won two successive scholarships in the pursuit of medicine. His reply . . . 'Young women always marry, and its an awful lot of money *just* for a girl'.

Later, she notes: 'Because I was so much older than the average undergraduate I suffered from some anxiety. Would the younger generation be prepared to accept someone who had been young before they were born? I need not have worried. They shepherded me here and there, and supervised my activities and even found the right page for me in Sweet's Anglo-Saxon Reader.'

Just as strong an impression is recorded regarding the St Hugh's garden, where Dr Busbridge had been *Custos Hortulorum* since 1962 'when she took over from Miss Procter, and she in turn is to be succeeded by Dr Honor Smith. The garden will always remind us of the care and devotion which Dr Busbridge, in collaboration with Mr Harris, has given to it in the past eight years' (*College Report*, 1970–1). Perhaps the garden after the ravages of wartime and building works had at last assumed a more settled appearance, but there is no doubting the unanimity of the 1970s undergraduates in praise for this abiding and pleasure-giving feature of life at St Hugh's – a unanimity which excels even previous generations who had been themselves lavish in their tributes: 'The St Hugh's garden is so marvellous – particularly the Magnolia Tree – and the "wild bit" kept deliberately wild for botanists to study' (Deborah Waterhouse); 'St Hugh's garden lingers longest in the memory. I am no gardener, but I was entranced by the quietness, the blossom and the gold of the seasons; later, I realised how lucky we were to have such grounds, neatly bordered by the roads and solid Victorian houses . . . ' (Fiona Ewart); 'I loved St Hugh's gardens and the evocative scent of Wistaria is a powerful reminder of my College days. Indeed, I vividly recollect descending the staircase of Main Building one hot summer's day in 1976 to be stunned by the overpoweringly rich perfume that drifted through the open window from the majestic mauve blooms of the Wistaria outside' (Stephanie Brand); 'The garden was lovely and much appreciated. I think later we came to look on St Hugh's as a bit of an oasis' (Sarah Barnes); 'the garden of St Hugh's – a haven of peace especially in the summer when central Oxford was hot, dusty, and full of tourists . . . ' (Pamela Strong).

Not every prospect pleased in St Hugh's, however, and one or two are highly critical. Caroline Bradbury offers a catalogue of what she did not like, and, too long to print, this is but a sample: 'Intimidating interview atmosphere . . . I disliked my room in MGA . . . big, north-facing, depressingly dark wooden panels, heavy dingy furniture . . . lots of fussy, dressy made-up women at breakfast, uncomfortable bitchy atmosphere; cold, unfriendly, under-used JCR – two silent rings of armchairs. Garden was beautiful but, again, silence of occupants gave it an air of mental institution. Domestic staff bad-tempered and officious. Too many petty regulations about tickets to eat . . . etc. etc.' Gillian Hanscombe, a postgraduate, thought:

The so-called 'Middle Common Room' was farcical: a room in an 'out-house' whose members were mostly women taking a teaching certificate course. There were no graduate seminars or any other academic gatherings, unlike the structures I had experienced in Australia when I prepared my MA thesis ... My greatest disappointment was my graduation. A history don (male) whom I'd never met was given the task of giving me (and some undergraduates) sherry and lunch after the ceremony. I would so have liked some effort at festivity; some appearance at lunch of the English dons; some feeling of pride that my effort to gain this degree (D. Phil) was appreciated by the College. But that must have been a childish fantasy. The grown-up women's world of St Hugh's remained true to my first perceptions; it was there for dons and for undergraduates. I had what I'd come for; why should I ask for or expect anything extra?

Milder criticism, and at least one interesting social observation, are made in the following: 'My room, (MB 2?) ... I was greeted by the head porter ... "MB2, Miss? Oh yes, the smallest room in College". He was right – it was not very salubrious, but it never worried me particularly' (Sarah Barnes).

I was given a small room in a college house, the Lawn, and was the only fresher there. I bumped into my tutor who told me the house was haunted, which did nothing to cheer me ... I was told that the front door was locked at night and I would have to find my way across the college garden and enter through the housekeeper's quarters ... I hated the housekeeper's corridor. Her alsatian sounded as if it was straining at the leash to get me, and a 30-watt bulb cast shadows on a Salvador Dali print. When I first saw the bathroom that catered for the whole house I resolved never to use it ... that summer the house was declared unfit for habitation and was out of action for a year while luxuries were installed: central heating and carpets. (Heather Downes)

I was rendered hideously self-conscious during my first few weeks by the amusement immediately evoked in most Oxford students by my Northern accent. Any incautious utterance was liable to be greeted by a resounding chorus of 'Eeh by Gum!' I rapidly adapted my accent, to the point where I spoke separate dialects at home and in college. I carried out this chameleon-like change so effectively that in the first conversation between my father and my boyfriend, each required several seconds pause for interpretation whenever the other spoke. (Jane Howarth)

On the other hand, the majority seem to have enjoyed their time without reservation and, as in previous decades, the overriding impression is that St Hugh's in the 1970s was still a very 'friendly' college: 'The atmosphere in St Hugh's was wonderful, very friendly and welcoming . . . the atmosphere generated by both tutors and undergraduates – one hardly saw the MCR members. I particularly remember the "college mother" system for freshers – a very good idea that made me feel much less lost on my first few days in college. I also remember that the Bursars, Scouts etc. were all very pleasant and helpful – very useful for someone as scatterbrained as me!' (Gill Wood). 'All in all, my time at St Hugh's was one of the best periods in my life, although I shall never like peach condé. I enjoyed the freedom, the socialising, the late nights working out the practical results and the opportunity to fit so much into such a small space of time. Every day was different and a new adventure' (Janis Kay).

Some informative pictures of College society and life at St Hugh's at the time also emerge:

well, you split into the normal and those with a bit more money, the sort of people whom a friend once described as 'the sort of people who go for lunch to country pubs in the week' i.e. they had a car and could afford not only to run it but to eat out as well . . . College did have its own social strata; there were, of course, those who did nothing but work (we called them 'gnomes') and then there were those who did anything but work, those who did some work and lots of acting (not to mention those who acted at working) and those who were forever involved in political societies and always exhorting one to stick up posters for this and that. (Fiona Ewart)

St Hugh's had some widely contrasting groups of undergraduates from very different backgrounds. As a Southerner, born in Surrey and educated at a public school, I was in a distinct minority . . . people were often divided by subject and tended to group together: the mathematicians and some of the biochemists were inseparable . . . like all undergraduates, I am sure a vast amount of time was spent in my room or my friends' rooms talking and drinking tea or coffee. We often sat around after dinner, delaying the time when one knew one should do some work. There was a television in College ... but I never watched it except to see [Princess] Anne's wedding. I don't recall that all those hours spent talking were devoted to very high-brow subjects. Rather we discussed every minute development in our social life and the social lives of those around us ... we were not at all very worldly-wise. (Liz Sayers)

But, if these reminiscences (television apart) might apply almost to any of the two or three previous decades, the unusually numerous comments on dress have, as might be expected, an authentic ring of the 1970s. St Hugh's at the time, apparently, was well endowed with various sets of snappy and/or eccentric dressers: 'I remember one eccentric dresser – Elizabeth (Liz) Moignard, who favoured a sort of green and white striped Victorian crinoline .. if Liz had legs I never saw a hint of them in three years' (Anon). The same undergraduate was noted by another anonymous contributor of the same year: 'she thought she was the bee's knees' and she 'cultivated an Edwardian appearance. She wore her hair plaited round her head and was perfectly made-up even at breakfast. Her skirts were long and she carried a parasol in the summer, with tailored blouses and jackets ... Ruth Chadwick who was then in the *Guinness Book of Records* for her number of O and A Levels ... rarely appeared in the same outfit twice (some were quite strange) ... Jo, who was Polish, wore black most of the time and had long black hair and a very pale skin. She gave my mother quite a shock when she came across her at twilight in 82 Woodstock Road'; 'There was a linguist who had a dress that looked like one from a Gainsborough painting and a long red velvet dress that she wore all the time. Bicycling must have been difficult, and sometimes she wore a totally black outfit of top and trousers, presumably when her "period" dresses were at the cleaners' (Victoria Medlin);

Laura Ashley arrived in Oxford and everyone floated around in her special creations, even on bicycles. Jeans etc. were often flared to follow the new bellbottom fashion, or, when they shrank, by inserting contrasting triangles of fabric into the split sideseams. This was most usual in my first year. Smocks came in and most of us must have looked as though we were pregnant. It was also a useful way to recycle the old minidresses which were then out of

fashion: one could wear them over trousers . . . everyone dreamed
of wearing the beautiful romantic frilly dresses designed by Gina
Frattini which were always displayed in the windows of the
boutique Campus in the High. I only knew one person who did . . .
she always dressed very elegantly . . . lots of expensive jewellery,
tailored suits . . . she never wore jeans or casual clothes. Copying a
couple of my American friends, I bought my first pair of Adidas
sneakers and wore them to a tutorial at Christ Church. My tutor
stared at them all through the tutorial and finally asked me: 'Did
you *run* down from St Hugh's?' (Liz Sayers)

But not all was high fashion: Gillian Gehring supplies a revealing
note: 'I learnt how a grant-conscious undergraduate copes with the
cold: she piles on more layers of clothes. On one occasion I went blue
with cold in a Wolfson room which was without heat in the middle of
the day while the undergraduates around me seemed perfectly
comfortable in their ankle-length tweed skirts, boots, and smocks
over sweaters over sweaters. One actually sees the same style of dress
in the 17th century Dutch paintings, so maybe their houses with the
tiled floors were as cold as St Hugh's on a winter day.' Also: 'One
example of changing times I can quote was an MCR formal dinner
which I went to with a group of friends. We were the only ones at the
dinner in evening dress, some of the diners even wore blue jeans.
That was roughly 1973. The food was spectacularly good on such
formal occasions. The hot chocolate soufflée was legendary' (Rachel
Thompson).

College food, from the depressive state of the 1940s and early 1950s
had by this decade undergone a dramatic change, as might be realised
from the previous reminiscence, and it is interesting to compare the
comments of those earlier years with those of the 1970s: from
'unremittingly awful', 'indescribably terrible', it had become, in the
entry written by Caroline Behr for the Macmillan student book:
'really terrific (domestic bursar ex-classy Cotswold hotel) and St
Hugh's girls are greedy. Dining-room is crowded at meal times with
famished hard-women-to-hounds and cosy girls in slippers and
curlers. Vegetarians are scrupulously catered for, and there's been
many a note in the JCR food-book praising the nut-cutlets.' At a later
date, 'I especially remember the wonderful College food of the mid-
70s which was renowned throughout the University for its high
quality' (Stephanie Brand). 'There was what we used to call "conver-
sation-stopping steak" on Saturday nights . . . the food in general was

very wholesome and well-prepared although ... not as exotic as in some of the men's colleges. We used to look a little enviously at what was taken up to High Table. But on guest nights and the pre- and post-Schools dinners the food was very good' (Liz Sayers). She continues with a home-catering note which, backed up by others, is illuminating: 'Most important of all, there was tea in one's room with friends or at tea parties. The best cakes came from the Straw Hat Bakery up the Banbury Rd. Crumpets were also a great favourite, toasted on the bars of an electric fire. Tea was often Earl Grey or Lapsang Souchong. Butter and milk and other perishables were stored on one's window ledge, or, very conveniently, on the balcony of New Buildings rooms. The local feathered wild-life sometimes had quite a feast'; 'I always had a stock of filter coffee from the Market (Brazilian was all the rage at the time, I recall) and some very choice pseudo-home-made biscuits. Time seemed to pass in jumping up for either a little coffee or perhaps a biscuit or two ... I don't remember most of my friends having anything much wilder than these luxuries in their rooms: we were far from stockpiling glue or marijuana in those innocent days' (Joyce Hannam). 'A friend and I who lived opposite each other in Wolfson Building for two years loved having dinner parties. It really is surprising how you can have a dinner party for 6–8 using a Belling "oven" with two hobs and a grill! Once we came into the kitchen to start preparing for a dinner party to find two of the other girls on our staircase in there already, skinning rabbits that they had just shot that afternoon!' (Deborah Waterhouse). And, in another food reminiscence, the cake factory, beloved of earlier generations, makes a welcome reappearance: 'The Summertown cake factory featured in our social life as they had a shop that sold slightly battered or overcooked cakes at reduced prices. The favourite was their chocolate Swiss Roll' (Victoria Medlin). And on a lighter note she continues: 'At one St Hugh's Night dinner (1972?) the chef had made heart-shaped table decorations out of confectioner's icing. They contained petit fours, and all through the Principal's speech there were noises like pistols going off as these "hearts" were systematically demolished and eaten, much to the annoyance of the chef, who had been planning to use them again.'

Religion continued to be a strong influence in the lives of at least a minority of St Hugh's undergraduates, the reminiscences indicate perhaps about 10 per cent. Miss Trickett preached the University Sermons in 1974 and revived the tradition of fortnightly sermons in College Chapel, which had been a practice of Miss Gwyer. Although

Fiona Ewart reports on religion: 'Avoided it like the plague. Nine years of school religion is enough to put anyone off . . . in fairness, the College chaplain was an extremely nice man, but I have to admit that we called the rather evangelical bunch of girls who ran the chapel, "the God Squad" '; there are more enthusiastic notes: 'Went to St Mary's most of the time and set up a discussion group for the younger members of the congregation . . . we always finished our meetings with sung Compline, soup and bread in that order . . . also helped to set up the Oxford Branch of the Jubilee Group . . . the Oxford Mission (1977) during my time was led by Cardinal Suenens and I shall never forget his compelling addresses to a packed Sheldonian' (Deborah Waterhouse). 'As a High Anglican I regularly attended Pusey House . . . and was always moved by the prayers for the dead and the choir's rendering of especial favourites . . .' (Jane Howard).

But if religion, compared with previous decades, appears to be diminished in popularity, sport, on the other hand, took an even firmer grip at St Hugh's. In 1975, out of ten athletics Blues, seven were from St Hugh's, and the college achieved a total of twenty-six Blues that year (*JCR Report*, 1975). The same report records that the St Hugh's Eight made 'the first bump ever on a men's crew – a still cringing Magdalen Eight. Even now, six months later, evidence of the victory remains boldly chalked, in previously exclusively male tradition, by the main door.' This was only the beginning of great success on the river for St Hugh's, and in 1979 'the first boat gained four bumps in Torpids and . . . attained the Head of the River position in Summer Eights. The continued good relations with the SCR were underlined in their support for the Boat Club's bump Suppers and the possibility of a new boat . . . ' In fact, rowing at St Hugh's might be termed the 'growth sport' of the latter half of the decade. Several reminiscences, not all of them serious, illustrate this:

My most treasured recollection . . . is from my second year when the girls were at last beginning to breach the rowing fraternities' defences. I was not fit enough to attempt the first Eight but a group of us decided we would try and get on the river as a fun Eight. We were the St Hugh's Bunny girls – not topless with bobtails – but black T-shirts with baby bunny motifs sewn on. While the first Eight rowed on and eventually bumped Magdalen IV . . . we unfortunately were not fast enough. We were praised, though, as the most stylish Eight on the river and our timing was magnificent. Our Pembroke College coaches were delighted and we were all very sorry when a separate women's division was started the following year. No more could we have the fun of competing directly against the men and even beating some of the less-well-co-ordinated Rugby Eights ... (Jackie Owen)

On the same event: 'Whilst we did not win the division we held our own and struck a minor blow for female equality – proving that a cleavage and a 24″ waist did not prevent a decent performance in a "muscular" sport' (Jane Carroll). Meanwhile, on St Hugh's rowing in general and describing the founding of the St Hugh's Boat Club in 1973:

At the end of Trinity 1973, Jenny Greenwood, Judy Bartlett and I decided that the next term we would make a sustained drive to get a college boat going ... the main problem as I remember was finding equipment to borrow. This meant that the duties of Captain of Boats were not just to row ... and to teach novices ... and keep up enthusiasm ... but to spend long hours chatting up young men from other colleges to persuade them to coach and let women use their precious equipment. I seem to remember I tackled this problem by buying them large quantities of beer in the newly-opened St Hugh's bar and introducing the young men to a succession of young women all briefed to flatter them. We were very lucky in getting help from people in BNC ... there was certainly some prejudice against women rowing in those days, ranging from ribald cries from the bank to mutterings from elderly boatmen that our doctors would tell us that we would do nasty things to our insides ... and there was a strong feeling the OUBC would like us off the river, but we also got a lot of support from other areas, not always from other girls at St Hugh's, a number of whom found us something of a joke, and one could hear frequent comments on butchness and big muscles. To be fair, in those days anyone of either sex who was involved in organised sport was a bit odd, although that was beginning to change. (Julia Winterbotham)

Other sporting memoirs illustrate that rowing was not all: 'I seem to recall a tug-of-war in the Parks and a football match played against Jesus College Second XI on the rugby pitch in the pouring rain. I think we won 2–1, though I daresay the referee was biased' (Janis Kay).

Nor was rowing the only activity taking place on the river. There is an abundance of more traditional reminiscences: 'I took part in the May Day celebrations for all three years. The first year, I slept on a friend's floor in Main Building because my room was in 82, Woodstock Road, and we were not sure that I would be able to get through College at 5.30 am . . . we cycled down to Magdalen Bridge, where we joined the group of dancers that progressed up the High. We went back to College for breakfast, and then continued to our first lecture still in our dancing finery, long dresses and with flowers in our hair . . . ' (Victoria Medlin); 'My fondest memories remain those of punting on the Cherwell. After Finals, my boyfriend and I bought strawberries and cream, and champagne, to while away a sunny afternoon picnicking on the river bank. The champagne suffered on the trip over the rollers, and showered me in foam on release of the cork. It fitted with the mood of the day – a last taste of the carefree times in Oxford' (Jane Howarth); '. . . I punted, fell in, ducked trees and missed swans, and, talking of water, discovered all for myself the canal that runs up from Jericho, an unexpected haunt of wild-life by the railway, with water-rats and swans' nests. Most of the time, however, was spent watching others fall in, or cycling along the canal to Osney, or watching the activities of Eights Week' (Fiona Ewart); 'In the summer . . . we used to punt to the Vicky Arms' (Gill Wood); 'On warm days Parson's Pleasure usually had a few customers. We ladies usually studied the opposite bank carefully. Once I spotted a water-vole and before I could stop myself, had exclaimed "Oooh, isn't he gorgeous!" no doubt causing an appropriate reaction on the opposite bank' (Anon).

In contrast to the previous decade, the strong interest in music in St Hugh's, particularly choral work, is once again a constantly documented feature of life. No more the Bach Choir much patronised and loved in former years, perhaps, but instead 'St Hugh's now provides an overwhelming majority of the membership of the Kodàly Choir, whose performance this term was Elgar's *The Music Makers*. No wonder the corridors of College, darkened by the electricity economies, resound with singing!' (*JCR Report*, 1973). There are many other reminiscences: 'I joined the Jesus College choir. In the days when all the colleges were single sex, most of the men's colleges had to entice females from the women's colleges to provide sopranos and altos. Jesus did this by providing a substantial tea before chapel and dinner in Hall afterwards . . . On St David's Day the service was entirely in Welsh and we had Welsh lessons for weeks beforehand after dinner on Sunday' (Anon);

I was by training a string player, but couldn't get into any orchestras, so I found instead that sight-reading ability was just as useful in choirs. I sang out of College, but was perfectly happy to sing in the College Chapel when needed by the organ scholar. I joined a chamber choir based in New College which is how I met my future husband and why I spent so much of my time listening to New College choir. I had a stereo set of my own – a small one on which I could play my rather odd selection of records (mainly rock and roll it was then, with a smattering of early and classical music). (Fiona Ewart)

'Joined innumerable choirs, including St Hugh's Chapel Choir (under the superb leadership of Cathy Ennis, a year ahead of me) and eventually helped to found a choir called Nova Capella. We sang little-known works, ancient and modern, including a number of pieces specially written for us by young Oxford composers (undergraduates). We also took the choir on tour in the Midlands' (Deborah Waterhouse);

I was a member of the Kodàly Choir . . . it was the only reasonably good choir at the time which you could join without having to endure an audition. The result was that it was full of untrained enthusiasm . . . there was a time when St Hugh's was positively swinging to the Brahms Requiem. The conductor was Edward Lambert who is still conducting at Covent Garden I think. He inspired tremendous dedication and loyalty from his down market choir . . . and our high point was our memorable performance of the Brahms in Merton Chapel. It was winter, cold outside, and we were all dressed in brightly coloured dresses and DJs . . . the entire work was performed in flickering candlelight with only the shadows of the audience's faces visible down the dark hall of the chapel. I think there was hardly a dry eye in the choir when the last string note died away into the silent audience . . . (Joyce Hannam)

'I joined a Madrigal group which met in Corpus Christi. The female voices were all recruited from St Hugh's. We punted up the Cherwell one evening, singing madrigals as we went. This sounds very good in theory, but the punts kept drifting apart and so the parts got rather out of phase and the result was more comical than beautiful' (Victoria Medlin); 'Perhaps my greatest debt to Oxford remains the love of music which Oxford encouraged and nurtured . . . and introduced me to opera in which I have made a career . . . I sang in the Isis Singers, the New Oxford Chamber Choir, in two Opera Club productions, Oriel College Chapel Choir and various other *ad hoc* musical events . . .' (Carole Strachan). Sara Cavalier 'played the violin in four regular orchestras and countless ad hoc groups. We also formed a College quartet . . . we had an enormous amount of fun playing for pleasure and at small functions.'

Drama, like music, also revived and exerted a strong hold on St Hugh's, both in and out of College, and in Oxford outside the University: 'On the dramatic side, as ever, a large number of St Hugh's undergraduates have been involved in college productions, both on stage and backstage. Clare Howard was Secretary of OUDS . . . she played Ophelia in Jonathan Miller's controversial *Hamlet* which showed in London at Easter . . . St Hugh's pulled off a fine hat-trick in Michaelmas Term when three girls took the three major parts in Congreve's *The Double Dealer* . . . Clare Howard, Ruth Parsons and Margaret Hill all gave marvellous performances' (*JCR Report,* 1971). Individual memories are fairly prolific:

drama . . . I did a lot of that: in various college productions and even once or twice at the Oxford Playhouse. There certainly were prima donnas, although I remember the male versions of them as being more obstreperous than the female versions. There were several young men deeply in love with their own talent . . . a couple of productions are worth mentioning. Mark Morris (Jan Morris's son) directed a production of Isherwood and Auden's . . . *A Dog Beneath The Skin* at the Playhouse, in which I had a small part. Auden himself actually came to see it and came on stage to shake hands with Mark . . . [who] had collected a star-studded cast of university prima donnas . . . Another memorable production was one of *Twelfth Night* . . . it so happened that . . . real-life drama got entangled with the show. The director (a guest up from the West End of London) had made the best possible use of the lake in Worcester Gardens. Viola and Sebastian appeared separately from it, as did the sea-captain. It was lit with fairy-lights . . . In the final scene the happy couple disappeared over the lake to the dying strains of *If Music Be The Food Of Love* . . . One night this dreamy scene was interrupted by sounds of frantic splashing. A member of the cast had fallen seriously (and literally) for the girl playing Viola (who was indeed a phenomenally attractive girl with the most beautiful speaking voice). Spurned by her before the performance, he had made a suicidal plunge into the lake, hoping, no doubt, for some change of heart from her. History does not relate who pulled him out of the weeds ... Undergraduate love is a thing you take lightly at your peril! (Joyce Hannam)

'The three outdoor Shakespeare's were magical ... *Love's Labours Lost* in Wadham Garden. How trendy we were then i.e. we had a streaker! I was Rosaline, and the Princess had just been told that her father, the King of France, had died. We ladies solemnly walked towards her, our frolics and teasing of the gentlemen cut short, when suddenly a padding of bare feet whisked behind me. A gasp, a titter from the audience. Oh, how I itched to turn round, but ... ' (Monica Kendall). She continues: '*Pericles* with the [Playhouse] stage covered in banks of sand ... we took that Hilary Term production to London that summer (1975) to Sam Wanamaker's Bankside Globe ... then, Viola in *Twelfth Night* to be directed by that lovely lady and actress Yvonne Mitchell, whose daughter, Cordelia, was at St Cath's. Sadly for us she got a part in a film about Sarah Bernhardt and could only *help* direct us – but her weekend appearances were an exciting breath of fresh air.'

Oxford introduced me to the theatre for the first time and I became a serious playgoer and a broad-minded one at that. Memorable evenings ranged from seeing Diana Dors in a thriller and the Actors' Company in an Alan Ayckbourn play both at the (then) New Theatre, to *The Foursome* by the ETC and *Pericles* by the OUDS at the Playhouse, to stunning outdoor performances of *Cyrano de Bergerac, Love's Labours Lost* and *Oh! What a Lovely War*. I will never forget Matthew Francis's mesmerising performance as Cyrano, and I remember feeling that Richard Attenborough's film version of *Oh! What A Lovely War* was not as powerful as that Oxford undergraduate production. (Carole Strachan)

While not strictly drama, meanwhile, it is worth recording in the 'performance' field, frequent mention of St Hugh's consistent success in the TV programme *University Challenge*, on at least one occasion battling their way (the team in 1973 including an MCR representative) to the quarter-finals, beating Girton, Bedford College, London, and Churchill College, Cambridge on the way (but on another occasion going out in the first round to Keele University).

Apart from music and drama there was activity in all sorts of societies, including the Union:

> There were ... hundreds of societies and clubs to join ... I was involved through others ... and as Treasurer to the JCR – but it was not a political year, perhaps because the previous President had been ... very political, and the college mood was for something more muted. We went at irregular intervals to the Union and always wondered if it was the stars there who would star in later life ... (not yet though – the first contemporary to become an MP at 28 was renowned at Oxford for being rowdy and hearty – raucous parties rather than intelligent Union debating). (Sarah Barnes)

'My parents paid for my Union subscription and I went along to the first debate of term and squeezed into a place on the floor because it was so crowded. I was very impressed by the evening dress and buttonholes and amazed by the standard of debating. David Warren was President in my first term and he appeared very efficient and organised ... ' (Heather Downes). Altogether, however, these brief references apart, neither the Union nor politics in general, seemed to be the burning affairs they had been to some previous generations: nor indeed are any outstanding personalities remembered.

In contrast, other, more timeless Oxford features are well documented, including several flamboyant parties:

> I remember a couple of marvellous parties that were like something out of a Waugh novel and not at all part of the 'seventies. Hilary Term, 1972, the party of the term was Emma Lubbock's 1930s Party. Finding the appropriate vintage was quite a feat and I don't believe that I owned a thing I was wearing, it was all borrowed ... in the summer of 1972 I recall an Edwardian Punt Party that was also a re-creation from a bygone era. All the guests went punting on the river, dressed in style and this was followed by a magnificent picnic ... there was a whole smoked salmon, a very large turkey and a great deal more. Typical of reality (rather than the novels) the weather was very unsettled and overcast, so the picnic had to be inside. There was enough champagne to float the entire British Fleet ... My friends and I gave a quadruple 21st Party for about 100 people in Lincoln College. It was supposed to be quite a dressed-up affair, with finger food as well as wine, punch

etc. The disco was late and one of the punches tasted a lot more innocuous than it really was. We had a very motley collection of friends ... there were a few too many men, not to mention a light show that sent cavorting pink elephants across the panelled walls and fine architectural details of the room. (Liz Sayers)

As in previous decades the 1970s produced favourite eating-out places, alongside old favourites: 'The Nose bag: the best place for tea, coffee etc. especially the chocolate cake. A great place to reward oneself and one's friends after having survived a tutorial ... La Sorbonne, the Elizabeth: where everyone aspired to eat and seldom did ... I really ate out very little. Most men asked you to dinner at their college, not at a restaurant' (Liz Sayers); ' "In" places ... Brown's (in the Market), King's Arms ... ' (Anon); 'pubs on the river at the weekends, the Perch, reached by walking across Port Meadow, the Trout, further up, reached by bicycle, cream teas at the Wickham, usually the prize for a bet ... ' (Pamela Strong). Fiona Ewart also supplies a note on coffee habits: 'one tended to meet in specific locations. Classicists met in the Ashmolean Library and wended their way across Beaumont Street to the Playhouse Coffee Bar, or one could join the exodus from the Bodleian c. 11 am and have coffee at the King's Arms. If you went at 11.30, licensing hours seemed to have begun, but pre-prandial indulgence did impair performance in the library.'

The bicycle, as ever, trundled on timelessly:

I well remember reading 'Undergraduates will find a bicycle useful at Oxford,' I certainly did. Not only could I zip around Oxford quicker and easier than cars and park without difficulty, I also used to explore the surrounding countryside. On the day we finished Mods I set off, and, spotting a sign to Binsey, cycled down a pretty country lane. Unfortunately it was farther than I expected and as we were planning a celebration party I had to return, promising myself that, God willing, I'd return after Finals. My friends knew nothing about my 'Appointment with Binsey' when two years later I set off. Imagine my surprise to find it had been a place of pilgrimage. I signed in the Visitors' Book and was amazed when, the next day, four friends said, 'We see you went to Binsey.' I felt I'd been followed! (Margaret Trelfa)

The same writer contributes an appropriate 'Oxford is ... ' saying:

'Oxford is . . . crouching in the dark with your bicycle lamp between your knees trying to undo your combination lock.' Bicycle locks by the 1970s were certainly an entrenched feature of life:

> what scope for amusement there was in the bike racks all round the Radcliffe Camera . . . someone used to arrive, slip the front tyre neatly or otherwise into the rack, and, in the same liquid motion, detach their bike clips from their inevitable cord jeans. Then they would stand up and stretch luxuriantly. That done, they would unstrap their books from the back of the bike or from the straw basket at the front (if female) and place them on the ground beside the bike. Then the padlock procedure would start: there were all sorts and kinds of these from the simplest to the smartest, but they were unfortunately extremely necessary in my day. By this time, the watcher from inside the library had built up an entire personal history and personality type of the cyclist. Good fun. (Joyce Hannam)

Bicycles apart, 'I had a great bunch of friends . . . we all had mo-peds (a couple had cars) – a great boon . . . ' (Sarah Barnes). But more typical, perhaps, was the sight of 'strings of cyclists on the Banbury Road setting off to lectures or streaming back for lunch . . . arguments with buses as we fought to share the bus lane . . . stacks of bicycles several deep propped up against the Science buildings . . . ' (Pamela Strong).

Other Oxford sights and places are remembered: 'I loved Port Meadow at sunset and went there a lot especially in my Schools' term. I even went there the night I finished and we walked back from the Perch after dark while larger-than-life cows loomed ahead' (Heather Downes). 'I remember . . . finding Arnold's spot for the dreaming spires . . . and [this peculiar to the decade] . . . being deprived of Magdalen Tower for most of my time' [It was hidden by scaffolding and partially dismantled] (Anon).

So the decade passed. Whatever happened outside Oxford is largely unremarked, except for one reminiscence: 'To a certain extent the outside world did not impinge upon us, although I remember the postal strike, the candles during the miners' strike, and the introduction to decimal currency' (Janis Kay). Financially most undergraduates seemed able to make ends meet: 'I always had plenty of grant money and managed to spread out my spending on things fairly evenly' (Rosamund Hughes). Certainly no one complains of hard times: indeed, good times seem the keynote of the 1970s, which, in many respects, seem far more carefree and lively, though just as hard-working, than the decades that had gone immediately before.

Of events not so far recorded, St Hugh's anticipated the entry of women into men's colleges, and vice versa, and kept up its academic standards: more than seventy undergraduates were awarded Firsts during the decade. The *Principal's Report* for 1971–2 states: 'Some men's colleges at Oxford are also proposing to admit women' [from Michaelmas Term 1972, three men's colleges had already decided to do so. By 1982, only Oriel of the men's colleges, Somerville, St Hugh's and St Hilda's of the women's, on the undergraduate side, remained single-sex.] 'The women's colleges are agreed that they must accept that this will happen. To the extent that it will increase the number of vacancies at Oxford for women, and that women will be eligible for fellowships at men's colleges, with all that implies financially, we must welcome this, but we are doing our best to ensure that the result will not be too disastrous to the women's colleges . . . ' Nearer the end of the decade St Hugh's itself made a change in its statutes: 'In January 1978 the Queen in Council gave her consent to a change in College Statutes which opens all College offices and Fellowships to men. Dr John Morris (Tutor in Medicine) and Mr John Wilkinson (Tutor in Geography) are the first male Fellows of the College to be appointed' (*Principal's Report*, 1977–8).

As noted above, these were not the only changes: the old order among dons had swiftly changed through many retirements and more grievous losses. But the continuities of tradition and atmosphere in the College and in Oxford in general remained, possibly, the striking features of the 1970s, each summed up, in their own way, by writers of reminiscences from the time:

'Never will I forget Oxford at 6.30 in the morning. I would never have seen it had it not been for the rowing. It epitomised everything that was Oxford for me. The romanticism of the spires, the bells chiming in the morning peace, the feeling that the sleep was about to break with the splash of oars on the Isis. The vibrant undercurrent of University life getting ready for another day as it had done for centuries and I pray will do so for centuries to come' (Jackie Owen); and, lastly, from Janet Chambers: 'I had four eventful and happy years at Oxford from 1971 to 1975 and remember St Hugh's with great affection.'

THE 1980s – A POSTSCRIPT

This final section of the chapter is necessarily short; partly, of course, because the 1980s have still some way to go, and had even longer when the book went to press; and partly because only one representative of the decade sent in her (unsigned) reminiscences. Extracts from these are printed later.

The decade had a melancholy beginning. 1980 witnessed grievous losses in the ranks of those whose connections with St Hugh's went back for more than half a century, and who had significantly helped the College in its expansion and success. Miss Procter, Miss Francis, Miss Gray and Miss Wells all died. So heavy was the loss felt to be for the College, that the Professor of Poetry, whilst delivering the Crewe Oration, made mention of the deaths at St Hugh's, and expressed sympathy to the SCR.

Miss Thorneycroft had been Bursar from 1925 to 1932; she combined this office with that of Treasurer until 1946, and then was Treasurer from 1946 to 1951. She had been an Emeritus Fellow for twenty years until her death. In the address given in the College Chapel, Phillipa Hesketh-Williams said of 'Thorney': 'To those who responded to her friendship she offered legendary hospitality and lifelong concern. She knew all the hundred and fifty undergraduates at College during her twenty-six years of work here, and their children who came to College after them. They were her family and in this she included all who worked for St Hugh's. College was her home, and to it she gave her whole-hearted love and loyalty.'

Miss Wells had succeeded Gertrude Thorneycroft as Treasurer in 1951. She had been responsible, with Miss Procter, for organising the demolition of the huts. She was then concerned with the extension of the College, and with the redecoration of the Chapel. In her memorial address, the Principal said of her: 'Priscilla knew the College from end to end. More important, even than that, she knew every member of staff, domestic, administrative, gardening, and understood their problems, and fought for their rights . . . I would want us to celebrate her, and to remember her as a reconciler and a peacemaker.'

Miss Procter, having been appointed assistant tutor in History in 1925, and elected a Fellow the following year, succeeded Miss Gwyer as Principal in 1946, and in 1962 retired, giving place to Miss Kenyon. The previous reminiscences have already given a picture of how the undergraduates of her day saw her, and extracts from her detailed and often outspoken Principal's *Reports* in turn have shown how she saw *them* and how the College was progressing, as well as giving an insight into her own character. Miss Procter is remembered as having a certain shyness and reserve when dealing with people albeit she possessed considerable wit and charm; that she had determination and strength when required has also been seen.

In her long memorial address, given in the University Church of St Mary the Virgin, on Saturday 7 June 1980, Miss Trickett dwelt on this strength, and refers to her as a 'formidable adversary . . . tenacious, meticulous in every detail, unsparing in her stubborn opposition to any trespass on the College's independence'. She also described her as 'This scrupulous woman, through a life dedicated to scholarship, meticulous exactitude and attention to detail in the conduct of everyday existence, and in the wider context of thought and belief, demonstrated her quality by a complete devotion to truth . . . Her loyalty to St Hugh's was the predominant passion of her life, and she put aside her research to devote herself to its care and administration.'

In her retirement, Miss Procter was, once again, able to devote herself to scholarship, and at her death, the corrected proofs of her completed book, *Curia and Cortez in Leon and Castile*, were on the desk in front of her, as she sat, *The Times* crossword on her lap. She was eighty-two.

With Elizabeth Francis's death, the last remaining link with the early years of the College was severed. Appointed as tutor in French by Miss Jourdain, in 1924, at the time of the Row, she became a Fellow of the College in 1926, and an Emeritus Fellow in 1960. Those who have written of her in their reminiscences, have done so with affection and amusement, for like the White Queen in *Alice Through the Looking Glass*, she was always scattering hairpins, seemingly wreathed in a cloud of impenetrable vagueness. Miss Trickett, in her memorial address on 6 July 1980, refers to that 'entirely characteristic manner of speech' as having 'periods of such Proustian complexity, such serpentine structural involution, that at first a crude or inattentive listener might imagine that her mind was cloudy or her responses vague . . . it was a warning that the matter in hand was more subtle, more complicated, more interconnected than might at first be evident to a less perceptive mind and imagination than hers. Everything, she gave you the impression of thinking, was less simple than it seemed, and she was generally right.' Miss Trickett talked of Miss Francis's scholarship and humour, and her kindness:

The number of pupils who loved and kept up with her is itself proof of her natural kindness, a kindness towards all sorts of people

which was wholly unassuming and sprang from her imaginative
sympathy with, as well as her curiousity about, other human
beings ... Elizabeth Francis was a modest women, but always an
intriguing one. A fine scholar, a devoted tutor and friend, one who
enjoyed fastidiously but genuinely the pleasures of good living and
good learning ...

It might have been thought that Miss Trickett had had her fill of
celebrating lost colleagues, but remorselessly, death continued to
haunt St Hugh's. In 1981, Miss Mary Lunt, Fellow and Tutor in
Biochemistry since 1959, died tragically at the early age of forty-nine,
of cancer. Remembering her, Miss Trickett said:

There is no doubt that her interest in her work was maturing and
intensifying towards her premature end. She spoke to me often,
when she knew the danger she was in, of the decisions she must
take, and it was at once painful and inspiring to see her make these
choices, relinquishing her rôle as a brilliantly effective Senior
Tutor who had fought successfully for women scientists' appointments, and for scientific appointments in women's colleges, in
favour of the interests of her pupils and her research.

Her early death was a great loss to St Hugh's. A memorial fund was
later inaugurated.
1983 saw the death of Emeritus Fellow, Miss Dorothea Gray,
Fellow and Tutor in Classics from 1935 to 1973, about whom a
number of memories have already been recorded. Crippled by a
childhood attack of polio, she had not in any way allowed her
lameness to incommode or embitter her. She was an outstanding
teacher, and her pupils had the warmest regard for her. Miss Trickett
said:

They knew that she would hide their delinquencies, cover their
shortcomings, scold them and sympathise with them, and they
knew that she was always on their side.
  Her relations with undergraduates living in the Lawn who were
not her own pupils were equally warm. She would open the locked
front door to latecomers (for she was always later than anyone
else); like a benevolent despot in her own house she would disobey
college rules if it suited her, but only for the convenience of her
undergraduates, never for her own ... her colleagues and pupils

found other inspiration, too, in her dedication to her college, and her subject, and in her generous spirit and her tenacity . . . she will be remembered as long as anyone who knew, or met her, or was taught by her survives.

Between 1980 and 1983, the deaths also occurred of Mary Glover, Fellow and Tutor at St Hugh's from 1927 to 1945; of Honorary Fellows Dame Ida Mann, Emeritus Professor Dorothy Russell and Lady Wolfson. In 1982, Dame Margery Perham died. She had been a Scholar at St Hugh's in 1914, acquiring a First in History at the end of the First World War. She is remembered by contemporaries as a formidable hockey player. She returned to St Hugh's as a Fellow and Tutor in History in 1924, but to quote from the memorial address delivered by Dr A. F. Madden, Reader in Commonwealth Government, Oxford University, and Professorial Fellow, Nuffield College (where Dame Margery was a Fellow),

her heart was not in undergraduate teaching. Lothian's intervention in 1929 gave her a break – twelve months' travel at Rhodes Trust expense to study 'native problems'. In Tanganyika almost a year later two cables arrived: one from Lothian offering a second year's travel: the other from St Hugh's, that she must give up her Fellowship if she did not return to teach. She sent off two one word cables: 'Accept' and 'Resign'. 'I now had to sit down and consider as calmly as I could how best to use this glorious gift of time.' This seemed to be answered in one word – Africa.

From that moment, she devoted herself to African affairs, writing innumerable articles on Africa for *The Times*, as well as books in the field of African Studies. In 1939, Dame Margery became the first Official Fellow of Nuffield College. She was elected the first Reader in Colonial Administration in the same year. To quote Dr Madden again: 'Indeed her reputation – based on her excellent book on *Native Administration in Nigeria* (a skilful interpretation which even half a century later stands as a classic analysis of empire on the spot), her regular letters to (and leaders in) *The Times*, and her lobbying of Westminster, Great Smith Street, and many Government Houses – was widespread. She had made Colonial (African) Studies a respected area of study, and had become a name to conjure with in high places – a name sometimes to be afraid of . . .' Despite her earlier resignation, she became an Honorary Fellow of St Hugh's in 1962.

Nor were the Senior Members without their distinguished losses. Mary Renault, remembered by her contemporaries for her acting, and by the rest of the world for her novels, died in 1983. She was to have written the introduction to this book, but her illness prevented her. In her will, she has bequeathed St Hugh's, on the death of her companion, and also of her sister, a sum of money to 'assist arts students to travel anywhere throughout the world in order to carry out research work connected to their studies'. Another death recorded in 1984 is that of Molly McNeill, whose letters home, sent to College by her sister are quoted extensively in the early part of these reminiscences and in Appendix IV. Of her, the obituary in *The Irish Times* says:

> her understanding of Ireland's problem of the two traditions first grew out of the work of the Irish Christian Fellowship, and deepened as a founder of the work of the Irish Association. She became increasingly immersed in the historical background and wrote several books, one of which, *The Life of Mary Ann McCracken* is considered a valuable contribution to the study of the history of the period. She was awarded an Honorary MA Degree in 1961 by Queen's University. In her last years she was working on a biography of Frederick Hervey, the Earl Bishop of Derry.
>
> Handsome and striking in appearance, and with an infectious laugh, Molly McNeill was an enthusiast. She had an unusually discerning eye and an innate feeling for quality, whether in the clothes in which she took such delight and which she wore with such style and elegance, or in the books and works of art with which she loved to surround herself . . .

But death fortunately was not the sole facet of existence at St Hugh's in the 1980s. Fellows retired, among them, Miss Gradon, University Lecturer in English Language, who had succeeded Daisy Martin-Clarke thirty years previously; Miss Romney, Tutor in Philosophy; and Mrs Russell, Official Fellow, Tutor in History, and Librarian, whose 'universal competence, her warm and cheerful temper' said Miss Trickett, 'will be greatly missed'.

Some signal honours came to St Hugh's during the early 1980s, the most outstanding being those to Mary Warnock (one-time Fellow and Tutor in Philosophy), Senior Research Fellow, who was awarded the DBE in 1984 and was then elevated to the peerage in 1985, becoming Baroness Warnock in the City of Westminster. She was also elected to be Mistress of Girton (a position once held by a St Hugh's Senior Member and Emeritus Fellow, Dame Mary Cartwright). Honours of a different nature have been achieved by Dr Jane Glover, Mary Glover's niece. She came up to St Hugh's in 1968 to read Music. She was appointed as a Lecturer in Music in 1976; in 1982 she became a Senior Research Fellow. Now, also, she is Musical Director of Glyndebourne Touring Opera, and most recently, Director of the London Mozart Players. In a speech at the 1984 Gaudy Dinner, she expressed her gratitude to St Hugh's for the tolerance, understanding and practical help that she had received from the College over the years, and which had been so essential to her in establishing her career. Her great success adds lustre to the long years of musical tradition at St Hugh's, so much a part of College life from the days of Miss Jourdain.

An unusual honour came the way of St Hugh's in the first year of the decade: Miss Theodora Cooper, Tutor in Economics and University Lecturer, was admitted as the first woman Senior Proctor in the history of the University. Miss Trickett commented in 1981 that she 'appeared to enjoy very much her first term of office'. In the same year, Miss Marjorie Sweeting, the Vice-Principal (Official Fellow, Tutor for Geologists, Lecturer in Geography and University Reader in Geography), was awarded the Bush Medal of the Royal Geographical Society. This was for scientific research and discovery recognising the importance of her work on limestone.

To come to more general College affairs, in the autumn of 1979, an ambitious development appeal had been publicly launched, with the object of raising £2 million by the Centenary Year, 1986. In 1980 the fund had already reached £530 000 following a great deal of activity including a jumble and book sale which raised the remarkable sum of £1600, an evening of readings and music at the Playhouse by Dame Peggy Ashcroft, and George Rylands with Blanca Bartos which provided a further £1000, and the visit of Miss Trickett to the United States, where former members of the College had greeted the Appeal 'with warmth'. By the following year, the fund had passed the £1 million mark, thanks largely to gifts from four Hong Kong donors (S. H. Ho Foundation Ltd, Ho Tim Foundation Ltd, Mr K. K. Leung and Wideland Foundation Ltd) of £100 000 each – this money to be spent on renovating and recovering possession of houses on the College site, with four houses to be named after the donors. The year after that, the St Hugh's connection with Hong Kong progressed further with the arrival of the first undergraduate under a new Hong Kong Studentship scheme. Then, in 1984, Miss Trickett was able to report: 'With two years to run, the Development Appeal reached approximately £1 586 807, by the end of January . . . this includes the largest single benefaction ever received by the College, an anonymous gift of £280 000 in honour of Dr Busbridge, to endow a Fellowship in Mathematics named after her, and graduate and undergraduate scholarships . . . it also includes a substantial bequest from Miss Gray . . .' The Appeal was also swelled by numerous gifts and bequests to College, among which were legacies from Miss Procter, Miss Bickley, Miss Lunt and Dame Margery Perham. Among Senior Members to remember College in their wills, Miss Mollie Ratcliffe (who matriculated in 1935), and Miss B. G. Hutton (in 1919), both left legacies to endow special scholarships. The former wished the interest from her bequest 'to be used to help students in financial difficulties', preference to be given to those reading Classics or other Humanities; and the latter, to endow an E. F. Jourdain Memorial Scholarship, in memory of Miss Jourdain, a further memorial to whom was presented by Miss Betty Kemp, Emeritus Fellow of the College, in the form of an oak bookcase which had belonged to Miss Jourdain.

Nor was the garden forgotten. There were many gifts and bequests, with which to buy trees and plants. There were gifts of benches and jardinières. Most importantly, it was decided to build an ornamental pool, north of the Wolfson Building, as a fitting memorial to Miss Procter, whose love and care for the garden during her term as *Custos Hortulorum* did so much to restore it after the ravages of wartime. In 1984, the gardens were placed on the Register of Historic Gardens, and are now open to the public under the National Gardens' Scheme.

An ambitious redecoration scheme for the Chapel had been completed, and its new organ was dedicated by the Bishop of Oxford on Ascension Day, 1980; there was also news of two notable mechanical acquisitions, one ancient, one modern: in the course of 1981–2 St Hugh's acquired both a computer and harpsichord, the latter being installed in a newly decorated Music Room in the Principal's Lodging and made available there for musicians to use.

The Library, from its humble beginnings in St Hugh's Hall, by 1984, had reached a total of over 53 000 items, including non-book materials. The Library stock has been augmented recently by generous bequests of books from Miss Gray, Miss Lunt and from Sir Rupert Cross, and by other smaller gifts and legacies.

But, despite the growing success of the Appeal, and the general atmosphere of expansion and growth in College, there have, nevertheless, been grave anxieties. For instance, it has been necessary to re-assess the whole admissions procedure. In 1984, the Dover Committee (which included Mrs Smart, Fellow in Law at St Hugh's), produced a report on the matter. Although the aim was to achieve 'a more ordered and equitable method of admission to Oxford', it was obviously going to take some time before all the colleges (among them St Hugh's), decided whether to proceed on its recommendations or not. Mrs Susan Wood, Fellow and Tutor in Modern History, commented on entrance procedures, and on the related subject of academic standards:

Some years ago, the college was incorporated with one of the 3 groups of mixed and (originally) men's colleges, instead of the women's colleges forming a group on their own and setting their own papers. (There was an intermediate stage when we co-operated with the first five mixed colleges.) This change both enlarged the scope for looking at other colleges' candidates (and they at ours), and gave us more sense of the general standard. The Essay was dropped from the entrance exam. a long time ago; the General Paper common to all subjects is currently giving way to a diversity of General Papers. There are losses and gains in this. We admit up to one third of our entry by conditional or matriculation offers, instead of by examination: this works quite well.

Standards at entrance, apart from widespread inability to punctuate or (less important) spell, have changed slightly in the matter of languages. For subjects other than Modern Languages, we do not nowadays get many really good linguists; language requirements have been dropped for some subjects, diminished for others (The History Prelim. has recently been changed, so that only one foreign language text need be offered, although two may be). Many Comprehensive Schools find it difficult to provide two languages; more disconcerting is the weak grip on even one, from all types of school. It is difficult to make any general judgment about standards over an unbroken period of more than thirty years, but I have an impression that the very best of my pupils now have more sophisticated perceptions but less analytical clarity than the very best of my earlier pupils.

Another issue, which caused considerable concern in 1982, was the question of what cuts would have to be implemented at the behest of the University Grants Committee, acting on government policy. A decrease in undergraduate numbers had already been imposed; fees had to be raised; only by 3.8 per cent, it is true, but this was enough to draw forth the following comment from the JCR: 'Other momentous happenings of the term included the usual discussion about fees – to which every JCR President looks with fear and apprehension: how much will they want for a glass of orange-juice this year . . . etc.'

In the JCR, the *Report* for 1980–1 serves as well as any for a representative picture:

> 1981 has been a busy and successful year for the JCR which continues to dispel any illusion of the apathy it has been accused of in the past. The St Hugh's Players continue to enhance their reputation as one of the best drama societies in Oxford and the Music Society are well pleased with their new acquisition, claimed to be the best harpsichord in Oxford . . . our Boat Club, now sharing the Oriel boathouse, has more members than ever before with five Eights on the river in Trinity [Term]. Unfortunately our success of previous years was not repeated by the first VIII although the second VIII were top of their division . . . on the social front, such ventures as SCR/JCR darts matches, Cheese and Wine evenings and joint discos with Oriel and Trinity have been highly enjoyable . . . an informal JCR meeting showed that an overwhelming majority still feel that St Hugh's should remain single sex. Members stressed the positive qualities which would be irretrievably lost should St Hugh's follow the example of LMH and St Anne's.

This last opinion re-inforced the vote and referendum, held in 1980, where the JCR voted 'overwhelmingly to maintain our single-sex status'; and in 1984, the President of the JCR expressed the undergraduates' views on the issue to the Governing Body. Susan Wood makes the following comment on the matter: 'St Hugh's, of course, is *not* a single-sex residence. About one third of the Fellows are men, and two or three of them live in College, or do so in term-time. The College is unique in Oxford in being single-sex as regards junior members and mixed as regards Fellows. There is much to be said for this half-way house, but perhaps not enough for us to stay in it.'

As the 1980s progressed, the St Hugh's Boat Club continued its remarkable success, re-establishing itself at the top of Division I in

Summer Eights, and by 1984 being able to report: 'The Boat Club beat everyone in sight . . .' On a slightly different sporting level, the JCR *Report* for 1983–4 also offers a significant item of news: 'The new JCR Committee's term began in Hilary Term; one of our first actions was to instal a pinball machine (!), the surprisingly large proceeds of which we were able to give to charity.' By coincidence, it was exactly thirty years since the JCR dealt, but rather differently, with similar matters. The JCR *Report* for 1954 contains the following item: 'members voted overwhelmingly against buying bagatelle and darts boards . . .' And so 'the whirlygig of time' brings in its changes.

The academic year 1983–4 saw the JCR, and the College, much in the national newspapers. The College decided to take the unusual step of admitting as an undergraduate a young girl not yet in her teens – Ruth Lawrence. She was awarded the Clara Evelyn Mordan Scholarship, for Mathematics. She has since justified the College's faith in her ability, by passing Honour Moderations in 1984 with a First. (It is rumoured that the marks she attained were the highest on record ever to have been attained in the Mathematics School.) Nevertheless, her presence has caused some problems for the JCR, whose President reported in 1984: 'Michaelmas Term saw also the inauguration of a women's group at St Hugh's, and self-defence classes for those who wished to take advantage of them (possibly to fight off the "Gentlemen of the Press" who were trying to worm information about Ruth Lawrence out of them; we all held out of course).' She was allowed to take her finals early, and passed with a starred First. She hopes to do a research degree.

It is time now to include the final reminiscences of the book:

I have only just done Greats this year . . . so these are very recent impressions of College . . . I never did like reading out my own essays . . . and latterly handed my script over on arrival for my tutor to read to himself, asking questions and making comments as he did so. The one disadvantage was . . . that [I] could watch the expressions of long-suffering, weariness, horror, or disbelief fleeting across my tutor's face as he read . . . Sunday evenings in the first year spent around my four-slice toaster, when there was no meal provided in Hall, friends bringing cheese and homemade blackberry jelly, and large tins of assorted biscuits brought back after the vacation and demolished in record time . . . flopping down in D's room and soothing away the vexations of a demanding class with cups of coffee, and, always, Don McLean's *American Pie* album ... the tantalising smell of bacon as we rowed past the houseboats moored on the Isis on early morning outings ... peaceful and comforting yellow haloes of light shining out in the library's evening darkness from the desk lamps and a clear bright crispness of a fine layer of snow in the street light as I cross the Banbury Road on my way home from finishing a philosophy essay one night at 2.30 am ...

Thus the single personal memories of the present decade; but alone as they are, a reminder of St Hugh's and Oxford as they always were, echoes of the past as strong as the unmistakable sense of the 1980s. To paraphrase: present and past, contained both in time future – this has been evident in so many of the hundreds of reminiscences from which this chapter has been distilled. It remains only for Monica Melles to write a postscript to them all: 'We said we'd never look back ... and yet, how could we help it? ... part of "me" will always be at Oxford ...'

LIST OF CONTRIBUTORS

Following is a list of all the people who have written in. Not all have sent reminiscences, as time did not permit. Nevertheless, their names have all been included. Some people who went up to St Hugh's in the last years of a decade obviously belong in two decades. Such people are marked *. Although they have been placed in one decade (e.g. someone who went up in 1939 will be listed under the 1930s), if they have been quoted, it is likely that their words will be found in the next decade. People marked ** are Fellows of the College. Those who are former undergraduates of St Hugh's are listed with their contemporaries. Others are placed in the decade about which they write.

Pre-1920s

Beaver, Beryl E. 1918
Brooksbank, Ina 1917
*Burnett, Helen D. 1919 (Mrs Laybourne)
*Cartwright, Dame Mary 1919
Chilton, Margaret 1918 (Mrs Power)
Edwards, Laetitia 1916
Dawson, Katharine M. 1918 (Mrs Evans)
Gamble, Cynthia 1917 (Mrs Harris)
Haig, Margaret 1917

Hirst, Margaret 1917
Holland, Muriel 1913 (*dec.*)
Parr, Dorothy 1915
Peters, Alice D. K. 1919
*Prichard, Maud E. 1919 (Mrs Bown)
*Rogers, Doreen 1919 (Mrs Lobel)
Stallman, Felicia 1917
Strong, Ethel 1919
Wallace, Ethel 1908
Westlake, Margaret 1916 (Mrs Charman Westlake)
Wilson, Ethel 1917
Wyld, Florence 1898 (*dec.*)

1920s

Arrowsmith, Georgina 1922
Barry, Erica 1922 (Mrs Thompson)
*Bell, Lucy 1929
Brown, Ethel 1927
Brown, Ruth 1921 (Mrs Pledge)
Chattaway, Mary H. 1920
Clarkson, Margaret 1923
Crossfield, Frances 1922
Dahl, Camilla G. 1927 (Mrs Campbell)
Dalglish, Maisie 1920
Davies, Phyllis 1922 (Mrs Eliot)
Dean, Ruth J. 1922
Deards, Phyllis 1921 (Mrs Cooper)
Dixon, Helen 1926 (Mrs Lamb)
Ervine, Margaret 1926 (Mrs Aitchison)
Field, Margaret 1921
Fowler, Eduarda 1922 (Mrs Farrar)
Gent, Hilary 1923
*Green, Brenda 1928 (Mrs Insley)
Hale, Theo 1927 (Mrs Peacey)
Hartnoll, Phyllis 1926
Haslop, Ruth 1927
Haynes, Renée 1924 (Mrs Tickell)
Henry, Elsa Margaret 1923 (Sister Elsa OHP)
Hobbs, Kathleen M. 1924
Hutton, Edna 1921 (Mrs Hastings)
Jeffrey, Evelyn 1927 (Mrs Thom)
Lake, Joan 1927
Moberly, Ida C. 1920 (Mrs White)
Morton, Gertrude M. 1923
Power, Esther 1925
Ratcliffe, Margaret 1926
Reynolds, Ellen W. 1926 (Mrs Bowman)
Roberts, Beatrice 1926 (Mrs Colman)

Robertson, Joyce 1922
Roxburgh, Helen 1926
Saunders, Prof. Doris 1922
*Slimon, Elspeth 1928 (Mrs Thomas)
Sprules, M. Lilian 1921
Stave, Liesa 1925 (Mrs Macdonald)
Talbot, Patricia 1928 (Mrs Thackwell)
Taylor, Dorothy C. 1924 (Mrs Dacombe)
*Thorp, Mary 1929 (Mrs Fleet)
Volkert, Rosemary 1921 (Mrs Glenny)
Wait, Mary E. 1920
Wayment, Agnes E. 1921
Welch, Flora 1925
Whicher, Margaret J. 1921 (Mrs Sykes)
Wilde, Marjorie 1926 (Mrs Wrottesley)
Williams, Gwendolen M. 1924

Unsigned: 12

1930s

Allun, Mary 1933 (Mrs Lines)
Anscombe, Prof. Elisabeth 1937 (Mrs Geach)
Baker, Joyce 1935
*Blaker, Margaret 1939
Bews, Janet 1932 (Mrs Leonard)
Bleasley, Dorothea 1934 (Mrs Bott)
Brentnall, Pauline 1933 (Mrs Pelham)
Brodie, Betty 1936 (Mrs Bethenod)
**Busbridge, Dr Ida 1936 (Emeritus Fellow)
Charles, Helena 1930 (Mrs Sanders)
Chitty, Delphine 1936 (Mrs Flash)
Clerk, Margery 1932 (Mrs Thornton)
*Clish, Lorna 1938
Crisp, Phyllis 1932 (Mrs Warr)
Cummins, Norah 1932 (Mrs Hall)
Dixon, Doris J. 1938
Forster, Doreen 1937 (Mrs Shelbourne)
Fox, Winifred 1934 (Mrs Gray Debros)
Fursdon, Jennifer 1936 (Mrs Lidwell)
Gernos-Davies, Catherine 1938 (Mrs Morda-Evans)
Gillett, Marcia H. 1935 (Mrs Marsden)
Goodfellow, Sylvia 1930
Grey-Turner, Zoe 1932 (Mrs Johnson)
*Grove, Stella 1939 (Mrs Carlisle)
Hargreaves, Katharine M. 1934 (Mrs Buxton)
Harris, Betty J. 1934 (Lady Johnston)

Harris, Diana 1932
Harris, Katharine M. 1931 (Mrs Cartledge)
*Healey, Mary 1938 (Mrs Kershaw)
Hesketh-Williams, Phillipa 1933 (Librarian of St Hugh's, 1938–50)
Hesketh-Wright, Winifred 1930 (Mrs Charlesworth)
Jackson, Margaret 1934 (Mrs French)
Jackson, Mary 1930 (Mrs Fletcher)
Ker, Mary 1930 (Mrs King)
Keast, Dorothy 1933 (Mrs Crawshawe)
Keenlyside, Grace I. 1938
Lapraik, Joan 1930 (Mrs Campbell)
Levinson, Adeline 1936 (Mrs Hartcup)
Lewis, Mervyn B. 1934
Lloyd, Francis E. 1938
Lovett, Margaret 1933
Lovesgrove, Dorothy 1935 (Mrs Walton)
Lumsden, Joan 1932
MacDonald, Frances 1936 (Mrs McCallum)
McDougle, Margaret E. E. 1933
McKee, Ruth 1932 (Mrs Ghey)
McKenna, Diana 1934 (Mrs Fearon)
MacKinlay, Eileen 1934
Manger, Ingeborg 1933 (Mrs Hickinbotham)
*Melles, Monica 1939 (Mrs Dobbs)
Milner, Mary 1930
Morton, Annie M. 1931 (Mrs Carruthers)
Mossop, Gwen 1937
Papworth, Naomi 1934
*Peet, Edrey 1939 (Mrs Allott)
Powys-Roberts, Luned 1934
Reeve, Barbara 1930 (Mrs Oxford)
Rice-Jones, Nancy 1932
Salinger, Nancy 1930 (Mrs Burton)
Samuell, Betty 1931 (Mrs Ellman)
*Scott, Inys 1939 (Mrs Johnston)
Shaw, Nora 1934 (Mrs Scott)
Sherwood, Dorothy M. 1933 (Mrs Knight)
Southern, Helen J. 1934
Sprules, Alison 1933
Sturge, Sylvia 1933 (Mrs Lewin)
Sutch, Shirley 1935 (Mrs Smith)
Tamplin, Mary 1930
Tanner, Eileen 1932 (Mrs Miller)
Taylor, Hilda M. 1930
Temple, Edith 1930 (Mrs Hoare)
Thomas, Daphne M. 1936 (Mrs Lennie)
Todd, Cecilia M. 1931 (Mrs James)
*Tyrell, Rosemary 1939 (Mrs Kenrick)
Wallbank, Phyllis 1931 (Mrs Touch)

*Yeats-Brown, Gertrude 1939 (Mrs Cossanteli)

Unsigned: 8

1940s

Alexander, Mary 1947 (Mrs Gill)
Andrews, Ruth 1940 (Mrs Fuller)
Backhouse, Shirley 1944 (Mrs Wilson)
Brady, Merril 1945 (Mrs Sylvester)
Brassington, Jeanne 1942 (Mrs Higginson)
*Cooper, Primrose 1948
David, Lisbeth 1946
*de Rin, Diana 1949 (Mrs Gosling)
Eade, Elsie 1940 (Mrs Howarth)
Easter, Muriel 1943
Farson, Marion 1947 (Mrs Gair)
Fortescue-Foulkes, Jocelyn 1942 (Mrs Hemming)
Franklin, Rachel 1941 (Mrs Waterhouse)
Gamon, Jill 1941 (Mrs Weston)
Gibbins, Janet 1942 (Mrs Grieve)
Graham, Marion 1945 (Mrs Milligan)
*Green, Cecilia 1949 (Mrs Barton)
Hassid, Stella 1942 (Mrs Strawbridge)
Hawkins, Joyce M. 1946
Henderson, Brenda 1945 (Mrs Hall)
Hepburn, Joyce M. 1940
Howard, Anne 1942 (Mrs Scott)
Hunter, Elizabeth 1948 (Mrs Rowlinson)
Isles, Claire 1948 (Mrs Scott)
**Jacobs, Margaret 1942 (Official Fellow and Tutor and Cassel Lecturer in German)
Johnson, Jeanette 1944 (Mrs Cockshoot)
Langton, Jane 1944
*Lawton, Dorothy 1949 (Mrs de Salis)
Levett, Megan 1948 (Mrs Allen)
Marsh, Hazel S. 1948 (Mrs Rossotti)
May, Jennifer 1948 (Mrs Chorley)
Mead, Yvonne 1944 (Mrs Lothian)
Minney, Primrose 1947
Mogford, Margaret C. 1947 (Mrs Duncan)
Monro, Elizabeth 1947 (Mrs Bowlby)
Oakshott, Ann 1945 (Mrs Burton)
Orton, Mary 1943 (Mrs May)
Ottley, Sheila 1940
Paine, Marjorie 1946 (Mrs Betton)
Peters, Penny 1944 (Mrs Waterman)
Pitt, Valerie 1943
Robinson, Shirley 1943 (Mrs Sampson)
Robinson, Jean 1943 (Mrs Cardy)

Rogers, Christine 1946 (Mrs Golding)
Somerset, Hon. Janetta 1943 (Mrs Ridgely)
Startup, Joyce 1944 (Mrs Brookfield)
Thomson, Patricia 1940
Tindal, Mary 1948 (Mrs Rentoul)
Tuck, Daphne 1944 (Mrs Painter)
Tupper, Rosemary 1947 (Mrs Kelly)
Viner, Monique 1944 (Mrs Gray)
Wallis, Helen 1945
Watcyn-Williams, Bertha 1946
Wilkins, Mary 1940
Wood, Diana M. I. 1946 (Mrs Scarisbrick)
Wood, Patricia 1943 (Mrs Crampton)
Woodward, Mary L. 1941 (Mrs Stewart)
Wright, Deaconess Edith M. 1941

Unsigned: 8

1950s

Albery, Jennifer M. 1958 (Mrs Draffan)
*Auden, Anita 1959 (Mrs Money)
Basco, Marion 1952 (Mrs Maitlis)
*Bedwell, Margaret 1959 (Mrs Nicholas)
Bennett, Ruth M. 1958 (Mrs Bullivant)
Browning, Elizabeth 1952 (Mrs Crossley)
**Busbridge, Dr Ida (Emeritus Fellow)
Byrne, Naomi 1957 (Mrs Collyer)
Claye, June 1953 (Mrs Wenban)
Colombo, Madeleine V. 1958 (Mrs Constable)
*Crabtree, Angela 1959 (Mrs Thorpe)
Dale, Mary K. 1950 (Mrs Pate)
Daniel, Deirdre 1953 (Mrs Baker)
Davies, Margaret 1953
Dight, Carol 1953 (Mrs Haines)
*Duncan, Jennifer A. 1959
Fortescue, Enid 1950 (Mrs Walbridge)
Fridjhon, Dorothy 1954 (Mrs Sefton-Green)
Gildea-Evans, Patricia 1957 (Mrs Wackrill)
Greig, Isabel 1951 (Mrs Moyes)
Hanson, Sylvia 1957 (Mrs Reitinger)
Hare, Mary 1951 (Mrs Bradfield)
Heath, Anne 1955 (Mrs Clarke)
*Herbert, Carolyn 1959 (Mrs Keep)
House, Anna Mary 1950 (Sister Mary Edward)
Hurst, Barbara 1950 (Mrs Burns)
John, Sylvia 1950 (Mrs Lyons)
Kelly, Sheila 1955 (Mrs Friend-Smith)
Kipping, Valerie 1952 (Mrs Griffiths)

*Leach, Angela 1959 (Mrs Bull)
Leighton, Margaret A. M. 1952 (Mrs Parsons)
McKenzie, Fiona 1956
Moon, Janie 1954 (Mrs Cottis)
Morris, Ann 1953 (Mrs Ridler)
Morton, Pam 1950 (Mrs Cooper)
Necasóva, Bohuslava R. 1954 (Dr Bradbrook)
Oates, Sheila 1957 (Mrs Williams)
Richardson, Clare 1954 (Mrs Friedman)
Robertson, Jean 1954 (Mrs Jones)
Seeviour, Greta 1951 (Mrs James)
Smith, Elizabeth 1955 (Mrs Alberti)
Stock, Mary 1952
Stothert, Jane 1950 (Mrs Smith)
Thompson, Rachel 1954 (Mrs Moriarty)
Tolansky, Ann 1957 (Mrs Saunders)
Ward, Anne 1956
West, Jennifer 1951 (Mrs Barbour)
**Wood, Susan (Official Fellow, Tutor in Modern History; see also 1980s)

Unsigned: 7

1960s

Asher, Clare 1967 (Mrs Gillies)
Brasier, Vivienne 1962 (Mrs Rowson)
Boyce, June 1962 (Mrs Tillman)
Carpenter, Margaret 1967 (Mrs Joachim)
Cohen, Vicki 1964 (Mrs Harris)
Cowen, Meriel 1965 (Mrs Buxton)
Davies, Wendy M. 1967 (Mrs Down)
Hope, Susan M. 1967 (Mrs Branch)
Irish, Margaret 1968
Jones, Christine 1968
Jones, Elizabeth 1967 (Mrs Whitehead)
*Kay, Janis 1969 (Mrs McGowan)
Kennedy, Ann S. 1968
Knipe, Linda 1964 (Mrs Wycherley)
Liebmann, Marian 1961 (Mrs Coldham)
Lowe, Celia 1963 (Mrs Hodson)
McIntyre, Hope 1961 (Mrs Stewart)
Manning, Diana 1966 (Mrs Clift)
*Moore, Margaret 1969 (Mrs Payne)
Mukerji, Nandita 1962 (Mrs Ray)
Nuttall, Anne 1961 (Mrs Conchie)
Powley, Pamela 1960
Smith, Marie 1962 (Mrs Jelley)
Stevenson, Judith 1962 (Mrs Pitchon)

Swire, Beverley 1967 (Mrs Tebby)
*Thompson, Rachel 1969 (Mrs Angus)
Thurgood, Susan 1965 (Mrs Paez)
Wilkinson, Dorothy 1966
Woodford, Iris 1961 (Mrs Rogers)

Unsigned: 9

1970s

Barnes, Sarah 1973 (Mrs Sassoon)
Belt, Tertia 1978
*Bradbury, Caroline 1979
Brand, Stephanie 1975
Behr, Caroline 1971
Carroll, Jane 1973 (Mrs Wilkinson)
Cavalier, Sara 1978
Chambers, Janet 1971 (Mrs Bratley)
Church, Anthea 1976
Downes, Heather 1973
Ewart, Fiona 1973 (Mrs Hodges)
Garlick, Susan J. 1976
**Gearing, Gillian (Official Fellow and Tutor in Physics, Dean, 1972–4)
Hannam, Joyce E. 1971
Hanscombe, Gillian 1974
Howard, Jane 1970 (Mrs Howard-Griffiths)
Howarth, Jane 1976 (Mrs Bains)
Hughes, Rosamund 1977
Kendall, Monica 1973
Medlin, Victoria 1971 (Mrs Davidson)
Moberly, Elizabeth 1972
Moss, Charlotte 1972 (Mrs Martins)
Owen, Jackie 1973 (Mrs Barns-Graham)
Sayers, Liz 1971 (Mrs Hall)
Seaburne-May, Jocelyn 1970 (Mrs Whittaker)
Strachan, Carole 1973
Strong, Pamela J. 1974 (Mrs Williams)
Trelfa, Margaret 1972
Waterhouse, Deborah 1974 (Mrs de Haes)
Winterbotham, Julia 1970 (Mrs Cresswell)
Wood, Gill 1971 (Mrs Smith)

1980s

Unsigned: 1, 1984

There are four contributions which are unsigned, and which are, also, impossible to date.

5 Origins and Outcomes

Sarah Curtis

Who are the 'ladies of St Hugh's'? What families and schools have sent them to the College over the 100 years of its existence? What did they do with their time at Oxford and how have they used the degrees they were awarded?

St Hugh's has been described in various ways: as the sporting college, as the place where girls went who were not clever enough for Somerville or well enough born for Lady Margaret Hall; or simply as too far down the Banbury Road to matter. These and other descriptions have as tenuous a relation to reality as jokes about women undergraduates in general.

As far as women graduates are concerned, few studies have been undertaken to analyse their backgrounds and careers, or to see what factors increased or limited their choices in life. Did the early pioneers meet intense opposition at every stage? Was the choice for nearly everyone who graduated before the Second World War to teach and remain single, or to marry and devote herself exclusively to her family? Has there been a change in the last two decades, not only in the kind of jobs open to women, but also in their attitudes and expectations about their futures?

It was to answer questions like these and to pull aside the web of conjectures and false assumptions that I suggested a survey of St Hugh's graduates. Between 1886 and 1983, St Hugh's produced 5000 graduates. In June 1984, the 3000 for whom the College still has addresses were sent a questionnaire asking for information about their school and family backgrounds, academic careers, life at St Hugh's and Oxford, subsequent employment and family circumstances. Most of the factual information was put onto a computer, but the questionnaire was planned in such a way that those who replied could extend their answers and give their views on related topics. As well as analysing the overall results I made a detailed study of the seventh year in each decade, from 1916 to 1976.

Nearly a quarter of those who have ever been at St Hugh's

244

responded, a total of 1180 graduates, 39 per cent of those sent
questionnaires, with an even spread of replies for the period 1930 – 59
(Tables 5.1 and 5.2). A response of this size to a postal questionnaire
is good, but it is important to note that what follows is an account of
the lives and views only of those St Hugh's graduates who replied.
They do not form a sample from St Hugh's and were not selected at
random. We must, therefore, be cautious in generalising from their
answers, even though it is clear from comparison with College records
that they were a representative group in the subjects they read,
degrees they gained and grants they received.

What prevents some people from keeping in touch with their

Table 5.1 Replies to questionnaire by decade

Decade	Total St Hugh's entry	replies from questionnaire
1900–9	116	2 (2%)
1910–19	242	22 (9%)
1920–9	523	107 (20%)
1930–9	523	159 (30%)
1940–9	532	160 (30%)
1950–9	594	174 (29%)
1960–9	859*	192 (22%)
1970–9	1 055	276 (26%)

*May include a few graduate students.

Table 5.2 Replies to questionnaire by mid-decade years

Year	Total St Hugh's entry	replies from questionnaire
1919	24	1 (4%)
1926	56	15 (27%)
1936	51	17 (33%)
1946	58	21 (36%)
1956	59	17 (29%)
1966	86	27 (31%)
1976	114	32 (28%)

former college? To judge from the number of questionnaires returned from overseas, residence abroad was not an obstacle. Countries from which St Hugh's Senior Members replied included Canada, the United States, Australia, New Zealand, France, Belgium, Spain, West Germany, Finland, Mexico, Columbia, Guadeloupe, India, Costa Rica, Korea, Hong Kong, Jamaica, Indonesia, the Philippines, the United Arab Emirates and Vanuatu in the West Pacific (formerly the New Hebrides). One St Hugh's graduate in New Zealand photocopied her questionnaire form for her daughter, a St Hugh's graduate living in Paris, as she knew her daughter would not be on the address list. A questionnaire from Nigeria was too late for the computer deadline, but it is worth recording that the respondent was the first Nigerian woman to gain an Oxford degree. She became a headmistress in Lagos, a member of the board of directors of the Bank of Lagos and first National President of the Nigerian Council for Women.

Those who replied included both the highly organised who filled in the questionnaire the day it arrived and those who set it aside for when they would have time, sending it back months after the closing date. Many said they enjoyed completing it, but perhaps some non-respondents were like one Senior Member who complained it reminded her of an Inland Revenue form. Another disliked what she saw as feminist overtones, believing that the 'battle for equality' was won long before she became an undergraduate in the 1940s. There are, in addition, always some people who do not want to retain links with the past. No one said the questions intruded on privacy and the commentary on the answers as far as possible avoids identifying individuals.

The computer finally processed 1092 questionnaires. Those who had studied at St Hugh's only as postgraduates were omitted, because their careers were not strictly comparable; those who entered the College after 1979 were too few to form a representative group and had not had time to establish their lives after Oxford; questionnaires received after 24 October 1984 were too late, but all views were noted. In what follows, where a date appears in brackets, for example (1941), it indicates the year the respondent entered the college. As memories of St Hugh's are recorded in Chapter 4, this summary of the survey concentrates on the lives of St Hugh's graduates before and after Oxford and gives only a little of the information obtained about them as undergraduates.

FAMILIES AND SCHOOLS

Families

The study confirms differences in the way men and women were educated in the past and shows that change took place only slowly.

We find that 434 of the fathers of those in the survey were graduates, of whom 121 went to Oxford; and 345 of their brothers were graduates (131 at Oxford). As might be expected, the totals for mothers and sisters were smaller, 186 mothers and 280 sisters (117 at Oxford). The percentage of mothers who were graduates increased over the decades, from 6 per cent in the 1920s to 25 per cent in the 1970s, but the percentage for fathers increased by nearly as much, reflecting the general rise in numbers attending universities. So although the total proportion of parents who were graduates increased, the gap between the type of education received by fathers and mothers was only slightly closed over the years.

The first in the study to record a mother who was a graduate entered the College herself in 1918; the first whose mother had been at St Hugh's in 1925; and the first whose daughter subsequently went to the College entered in 1921. In total there were 21 respondents with mothers who had been at St Hugh's, 54 with sisters and 18 with both mother and a sister at the College.

Since four out of ten fathers were educated at university, it is not surprising that until the 1940s most were in middle-class professions. From the beginning, St Hugh's had a strong association with the church. One reason why it attracted the daughters of clergymen on modest stipends was that its fees were lower than those of the other women's colleges. The earliest questionnaire returned (1905) is from the daughter of a Church of England canon who explained, aged 99, that she was sent to St Hugh's because there would be 'other clergymen's daughters and not too wealthy'. In 1916, St Hugh's was chosen for another canon's daughter because it was 'a church college'. There were 35 daughters of clergymen among these St Hugh's graduates in the years till 1939, all but four from the Church of England. But as well as doctors, teachers, lawyers, civil servants and others in professions, there were some fathers in trade and industry. The year 1926, for example, included a flour factor, a coal dealer and a tyre salesman.

When we reach 1946, we find more entrants whose fathers did skilled or manual work (a coalminer who became a postman, a foreman warp-dresser in a textile mill), but professional and white-collar jobs predominate to the present day. The breakdown of fathers' employment for the 1976 year is as follows: three civil servants, two university teachers, a headmaster, a stockbroker, a Member of Parliament, a chartered accountant, a marketing operations manager, a barrister, a solicitor, a physicist, an ecologist, a teacher, an engineering technician, a technical director, an electrical engineer, a doctor, a design engineer, a minister of religion, a bank manager's assistant, a grocer, a master baker, a farmer, a business man, a cabinet-maker, an electrician, a painter/decorator, a bricklayer, a contracts manager and a manual worker. Only three unskilled jobs are included.

It is known from research in health patterns that girls are more likely to imitate the behaviour of their mothers and sisters than that of their fathers and brothers. Does the information about the employment of the mothers of these graduates tell us anything? Two-thirds of the mothers of the 1926 intake were housewives, looking after their families and homes, as was normal for middle-class women at that time, but it is interesting that a third had worked outside the home, mainly as teachers. By 1946, over 60 per cent had worked outside the home and, by 1966, three-quarters. In 1966, the mothers included a doctor, a textile designer, an architect, a solicitor's clerk, shop assistants and clerks, offering their daughters a wider range of experience. In 1976, as many mothers were teachers as were house-wives.

Schools

A few of the older graduates had been taught at home in their early years, but everyone had attended a school at some stage. If those schools which until recently were direct-grant are counted as fee-paying, only just over a third of these St Hugh's graduates were educated at state-maintained schools (Table 5.3). A total of 442 respondents described their schools as grammar schools and only 34 said they went to comprehensives. Only 75 attended co-educational schools.

The predominance of girls from fee-paying schools fits the parental backgrounds of this group of St Hugh's graduates but is at odds with the reputation of St Hugh's as a college where girls from poorer

Table 5.3 Type of school

State-maintained	384 (35%)
'Public'	299 (27%)
Direct grant	259 (24%)
Privately owned	116 (11%)
Other, or no information	34 (3%)

homes found a place. In 1936, only one girl came from a state-maintained school. However, if the type of school is looked at from decade to decade, a shift is seen with the proportion of public school entrants diminishing from a peak of 38 per cent in the 1930s to 21 per cent in the 1970s when almost half came from state-maintained schools.

The contribution of the former direct-grant schools in sending girls to St Hugh's is significant. Although the schools had independent status, many pupils had assisted places which removed or lowered the financial barrier to an academic education. In order to encourage more schools of every type, and particularly the new comprehensives, to send candidates to St Hugh's, the College since the early 1970s has held open days with Junior Common Room participation, for headmistresses and headmasters, for girls considering applying to Oxford and for girls specifically interested in St Hugh's.

Did the types of school differ in relation to the universities to which they sent pupils and the range of subjects offered to the level of university entrance? Nearly half the replies said that their schools sent pupils regularly to Oxford and to study most subjects; a further 14 per cent said that their schools sent pupils regularly to universities in general for most subjects. But only a fifth of those schools sending pupils regularly to Oxford to read most subjects were state-maintained, compared with over 40 per cent of the public and direct-grant schools. The state-maintained schools had the highest proportion going to universities other than Oxford and offered a more restricted range of subjects.

The general policy of the school is one of the factors influencing an individual's choice of university or college. The questionnaire asked 'What made you decide to go to university/Oxford/St Hugh's?' and 'Did anyone in particular influence your choices?' A frequent reply was 'the school had a St Hugh's tradition', often followed by the information that either the headmistress or a favourite subject teacher had been at St Hugh's. In 1936, three out of 17 were drawn to St

Hugh's through a direct link of this kind, three out of 21 in 1946, eight out of 17 in 1956, ten out of 27 in 1966 and eight out of 32 in 1976, when some respondents say they made the choice for themselves after a visit to the College. In all, 402 said that their choices were influenced by teachers, 207 by other adults including parents, and 156 by both teachers and parents. A third said that they already knew someone at St Hugh's when they came up.

The next most frequently cited reason for trying St Hugh's was the reputation the College had in various subjects. Mathematics, Geography and Classics were most often mentioned. In addition, St Hugh's at some periods offered unusual subjects or allowed new subjects, before other women's colleges. For example, it was one of the first colleges at Oxford, Cambridge or London to allow women to read Law as a first degree; it offered Geography early in the School's development, and as late as 1976 was chosen because it was one of the two women's colleges with a tutor in Biochemistry. Some reasons were less positive. Its lower fees, in the days when there was little state financial support, have already been mentioned. 'It had some small rooms', explains a 1917 entrant, and these cost less. In every generation, St Hugh's was chosen by some because it was seen as a less formidable fortress to storm than Somerville or Lady Margaret Hall.

There were also logistics concerning the timing of the entrance examinations. In the late 1920s, St Hugh's was teamed with St Hilda's and their joint examination took place after that of Somerville and Lady Margaret Hall, giving an extra term for preparation; by 1939 it preceded that for the other pair of colleges; but whichever way round it was, the timing of the St Hugh's examination suited some people better than that of the other colleges. One respondent chose Oxford in 1929 because Cambridge did not give full degrees to women. It was not until 1947 that Cambridge made women full members of the University, but in 1920 the newly matriculated undergraduates of St Hugh's watched their past and present principals, Miss Moberly and Miss Jourdain, take their degrees.

The questionnaire also asked whether St Hugh's graduates had met surprise, encouragement or opposition when making their plans to go to Oxford. It is commonly assumed that, certainly until the Second World War, girls had a hard time convincing their families that it was right for them to go to university. The education given to sons and daughters in the same families was different, to fit the different roles they were expected to play in life. As the emancipation of women became accepted, boys had priority for education fees if money was short. Thus in her essay *Three Guineas* Virginia Woolf talked about 'the daughters of educated men' who received a proper education themselves only if there was enough money left over from 'brother Arthur's Education Fund'. The reference was to Thackeray's *Pendennis*. 'You who have read *Pendennis*', she explained, 'will remember how the mysterious letters A. E. F. figured in the household ledgers. Ever since the thirteenth century English families have been paying into that account.' Although the Board of Education from 1912 paid or lent fees in exchange for an undertaking to teach for a number of years, grants were neither usual nor generous.

It is, therefore, interesting to find that three-quarters of this group of St Hugh's graduates met nothing but encouragement. Comments like 'My father believed that daughters should have as good an education as sons' (1927), and 'My mother held that girls could not be certain of a husband who would be able to support them and that money invested in education was never wasted' (1940), were more typical for the period than 'In middle-class, philistine and non-conformist Birmingham it was considered outlandish "to want to be a blue-stocking". I was told no one would want to know, let alone marry me' (1933) and 'I had some opposition from aunts who said "Men do not like it"' (1921).

There were, of course, some parents who divorced theory from practice: 'My father thought girls should have the same educational opportunities as boys, although this did not extend to sending me to as good a school as my brother' (1942). Occasionally a girl had to be really determined: 'My father was against university education for women. I paid the fees with a legacy from my grandfather and a grant from my school' (1943). It is also clear that for many 'the decision was not mine'. Young women fell in with plans made for them, and most of those who reached St Hugh's in the early years were fortunate in having enlightened parents and teachers. However, the fact that 782 met encouragement in their endeavours, compared with 23 who met surprise, 18 who met opposition and 184 who came across a mixture of attitudes, does not imply that it was easy for all women to reach Oxford or university. On the contrary, the privileged circle was small. The problem then as now was to make the circle grow to encompass far more girls, families and schools.

When surprise and opposition were expressed, it was often for other reasons than an objection to women going to university. 'Surprise was expressed on class grounds, that an ordinary village girl should think of going to Oxford' (1933). The most cases of outright opposition and of mixed attitudes were recorded from the 1970s, not the early decades, and as coming from schools. Sometimes a school said that a pupil was 'not Oxbridge material', so that she had to fight to prove herself. Others operated an inverted form of snobbery or self-abasement: 'Girls from this school don't go to Oxbridge.' Sometimes parents and teachers opposed girls reading certain subjects: Theology, for example. Others had no idea why their schools had opposed their trying Oxford, like the 1976 entrant from a co-educational grammar school who says: 'My headmaster gave me no help at all and seemed deliberately obstructive – why I don't know.' Luckily her parents, who were both civil servants, gave her every encouragement and her grandmother was 'an inspiration'.

AT OXFORD

The Academic Record

Women are traditionally associated with subjects like English, History and Modern Languages, with the arts rather than the sciences. However, a quarter of these St Hugh's graduates read science subjects or Mathematics, with 95 mathematicians leading the field. Only a few read Engineering or Agriculture. The proportion in the study reading Science or Mathematics correctly reflects the balance at St Hugh's over the years, since 22 per cent of all St Hugh's graduates have read Science or Mathematics. On the arts side, English, Modern Languages and History certainly dominated, as Table 5.4 shows.

Three-quarters of the graduates in the study came up to St Hugh's as Commoners, 14 per cent as Exhibitioners and 10 per cent as Scholars. Selection procedures are under closer scrutiny than ever today and the idea of awarding special status to certain undergraduates on entrance has lost favour. It is interesting to see, however, that the dons at St Hugh's were good at predicting academic success. Only 6 per cent of the Scholars ended with Thirds in their final examinations and over a quarter won Firsts, compared with 11 per cent of the Exhibitioners and 5 per cent of the Commoners.

In general, what kind of degrees did they acquire? St Hugh's has never been near the top of the Norrington table, which for over twenty years has ranked Oxford colleges according to the results in

Table 5.4   Arts subjects studied

English	174
Modern Languages	170
History	169
Geography	79
PPE (Philosophy, Politics and Economics)	75
Literae humaniores (Greats)	67
Theology	32
Law	25
Oriental Studies	10
Music	6
Other arts subjects	5
Total	812

the class lists each summer. The five colleges founded for women have tended to be bunched together near the bottom – and in 1984, St Hugh's came last. The degree classes of those who replied to the questionnaire are given in Table 5.5. Overall, three-quarters were awarded Firsts or Seconds. The scientists did better than those reading arts subjects, both for winning Firsts and avoiding Thirds. In the subjects read most frequently the highest percentage of Firsts was won by mathematicians (18 per cent), although they also scored high on Thirds (19 per cent). The small Law School produced the highest percentage of Firsts on the arts side (16 per cent), followed by Theology, Modern Languages and English. The most Thirds were in PPE (33 per cent), History (31 per cent) and Greats (27 per cent), followed by a quarter of the English School.

Table 5.5   Degree classes

Class	Total	Sciences	Arts
Firsts	87 (8%)	33	54
Seconds	734 (67%)	191	543
Thirds	224 (21%)	39	185
Fourths	20 (2%)	2	18
Other	27 (2%)	15	12

Many of those who were awarded poor degrees, or who just missed Firsts, still regretted what had happened, pointing out factors that had worked against them. An Exhibitioner from the late 1920s writes:

I was very disappointed getting a Third, for I know that I have some ability and I enjoyed my work. Something had gone wrong ... chiefly it may have been the result of falling in love. I was unable to cope with two great emotional involvements at the same time ... if I may be allowed to put some of the blame on others I should pick out not any of my teachers at St Hugh's but the discourteous man who did not try to help me in my last term.

This Senior Member is not alone in speaking of a 'great emotional involvement' with her work. Whatever degrees they were awarded, a very high proportion (88 per cent) said they enjoyed reading their subject and only a few (4 per cent) said they disliked it. Someone with a First in English from the early 1930s describes her commitment to her subject as 'a life-time's love affair'. Continuing interest in their Oxford work was not confined to people who used their subject directly in teaching, research or their profession. In total, two-thirds said they had used it directly in employment and a quarter that they had used it indirectly. But many explained that they continued with it in some way now for their own pleasure, mainly by reading. This was easier for those who had studied arts subjects. Most had chosen their subject at school because they liked it best, or showed most talent in it, and their early enthusiasm remained.

The tutorial system was on the whole much praised. Nearly everyone was taught out of College at some stage and all but a few by men as well as by women. Some, reading subjects like Theology or Geography when the College had no tutor in them, were taught exclusively outside the College, a system which could cause difficulties, as in the 1920s, when the tutor in charge of the PPE School was a medievalist. On the other hand, some of the minority taught entirely within St Hugh's said they envied the variety of teaching enjoyed by their contemporaries in others Schools. Other criticisms included: 'There was negligible opportunity to be counselled about the appropriateness of the course for one's talents/aspirations, or to change course, and lectures were not geared to the syllabus' (1946); 'I do not think I was helped sufficiently over expressing myself lucidly or tackling my subject' (1947); 'Looking back I do not think any don understood how little an eighteen-year-old knows or can "place"' (1948). Such criticisms were, however, rare. Most of the St Hugh's graduates would probably agree with this comment: 'Sometimes I came away from tutorials feeling like Harriet in *Gaudy Night*, as though my brains had been given a thorough spring-cleaning and restored in top working order.'

In the 1950s, St Hugh's had dons who combined their academic careers with marriage and motherhood, 'timing the additions to their families for the long vacations'. They impressed their pupils and other undergraduates by their success in their two rôles and also by showing that such success was not achieved without some conflict: 'I remember her saying that sometimes she convinced herself that she had to bake a cake rather than work at philosophy. I continually have this kind of problem now and it's comforting to think of her remark.'

Attitudes to College

'It was the experience of Oxford that was significant to me rather than the experience of St Hugh's', writes a graduate of the early 1930s. In total, a third of those who replied to the questionnaire agreed with this verdict. Most thought of themselves as being at both Oxford and St Hugh's and only a handful as being first and foremost at St Hugh's. These proportions were constant over the decades, although it might have been expected that the earlier students would have identified more exclusively with the College, since they were debarred from participating in many university activities.

Perhaps because of the restrictions of the chaperonage rules, 80 per cent of graduates from the 1920s mainly drew their friends from St Hugh's; but by the 1970s, 81 per cent said their friends were drawn both from St Hugh's and other colleges. Many life-long friendships in all generations were made at St Hugh's, through mutual interests, propinquity and being young and independent in the same society. They were probably reinforced until recently by the curfew rules about visitors, and the comparatively isolated position of St Hugh's in Oxford. Most people reported still seeing or communicating with friends from St Hugh's, even if they now lived in remote areas. As a third of these St Hugh's graduates married Oxford graduates, they often had a common circle of Oxford friends with their husbands.

Various questions were asked about activities in College. Did they play any College sport, belong to any College society, attend Chapel, go to a St Hugh's dance? A difficulty here was the fallibility of human memory, demonstrating yet again how careful historians must be in assessing primary but not contemporaneous evidence. 'What societies?', writes one Senior Member. 'There weren't any at St Hugh's in my day.' Yet someone else in her year claims to have belonged to the St Hugh's debating society. 'I don't think there were any dances when I was up', says another, whose exact contemporary thinks she was on the dance committee.

The details about College societies, Chapel, sport and the rules are not given here as they are covered by many reminiscences in the previous chapter. In general, however, a third said they played College sport, although more than that were involved in the early years, and fewer in the 1970s. This hardly makes St Hugh's primarily a sporting college. Once attendance at Chapel became voluntary (and attendance in College was monitored by signing a register at dinner in Hall), the religious commitment of many St Hugh's members was still evident. A third of those from the 1950s attended Chapel regularly. Although only 9 per cent attended regularly in the 1970s, over a third still attended sometimes.

As far as rules are concerned, if you read through the question-naires in chronological order, it is apparent that as soon as one set was modified the next, which would have seemed liberal a few years before, felt equally oppressive. Each generation pushed the boundar-ies further. The final word on chaperonage must go to the Senior Member of 1927 who commented, 'The chaperonage rules were unnecessarily strict. They were not needed by those who kept them and not kept by those who needed them.' A graduate from the late 1970s found it most hypocritical to ask male visitors to leave by 2 a.m. 'Presumably if an undergraduate is to be corrupted', she says, 'it can only happen after 2 a.m.' Exactly the same argument was put forward from the 1950s, only then the disputed hour was 6.30 p.m.

Half of those who returned the questionnaire had at some stage lived out of College, those in earlier decades in the College houses round the grounds, the latest graduates in digs, flats and houses all over Oxford. Before the Second World War, most people preferred the convenience of College. As late as 1961, an undergraduate 'loved being looked after, all meals provided, my room cleaned, my tutor knowing everything I did, having a doctor in the college, going to chapel every day, close friends', but by that time the majority viewed such cosiness as claustrophobic. They preferred fending for them-selves, self-catering bringing choice as well as chores. For all those now aged over forty who look back at their Oxford days as the only time in their lives when they have been free of domestic responsibilities, there are as many under thirty who found communal provision of food and lodging both a restraint on their independence and too expensive.

St Hugh's in Oxford

In a speech to the Gaudy of 1953, Miss Procter, who was at that time Principal of St Hugh's, said that the number of undergraduate societies had grown from 72 in 1937, to 150 in 1949 and over 200 in 1953.

This proliferation of societies is confirmed by the number mentioned by St Hugh's graduates who returned the questionnaire. As Miss Procter said, they joined them with enthusiasm. Most took part in more than one activity; over a quarter had three interests and a fifth more than three. Subject-linked societies (like the Invariant Society for mathematicians, the Herbertson Society for geographers and the Wireless Society for physicists) and religious ones were most favoured, with politics strongest in the 1930s. A modern linguist, who entered the College in 1936, explains her political activity as 'stemming from passionate support for the Republican cause in the Spanish civil war and an ill-informed and idealistic idea of Russian communism'. Music always interested over 40 per cent, but drama was a minority taste. As for dances, 65 per cent in total went to a Commemoration Ball or dance at a college other than St Hugh's. About a fifth took up new interests, others developed interests they had before Oxford.

According to their answers, Miss Procter was on less sure ground in believing that in the 1950s girls took part in more extra-curricular activities than previous generations. Before the Second World War, many societies, including some linked to subjects read, were closed to women. In 1928, for example, only men could join societies associated with the Greats course or the organisation for Roman Catholics at the University. But the proportion of St Hugh's members in the study who belonged to several Oxford societies was the same in the 1930s as in the 1950s. Miss Procter acknowledged that most of these societies were 'neither trivial nor frivolous' but she detected a change in the undergraduate's conception of the function of a university, or at any rate a change in the stress laid on the importance of its different aspects. 'Our undergraduates', she said, 'tend to lay less emphasis on the pursuit of learning and more on making contacts, meeting people, enlarging their outlook and experience, on gaining a wide but sometimes superficial culture.'

There were, of course, different degrees of intensity with which people engaged in their Oxford activities. An interest in music ranged from singing in the Bach Choir, as many from St Hugh's did, to going to an occasional concert. Similarly, an interest in drama could be as spectator, actress, wardrobe mistress or secretary of the Experimental Theatre Club. To gauge such differences the questionnaire asked whether St Hugh's graduates had held office in or been on the committee of any Oxford society. The answers indicate not only a measure of their involvement in Oxford life but also how many wished, and were able, to achieve positions of responsibility.

In all, a third held office or were on a committee, but, in the mid-decade years which were studied in detail, very few actually headed a society. In 1936, there was a co-editor of *Cherwell*, and the Captain of the University Women's Squash Club; in 1946, the President of the Jewish Society, who comments, 'as a refugee girl this was "ethnic Jewish" rather than religious'; in 1956, the Captain of OU Women's Netball; in 1976, the President of OU Middle Temple Society, and the Chairman of OU Riding Club. Sometimes a society had more than one committee member from St Hugh's in the same year, as did JACARI (the Joint Action Committee Against Racial Intolerance) in 1956, shortly after it had been founded. The purpose of JACARI was to fund a black student from South Africa at Oxford. A St Hugh's undergraduate was one of its first joint chairmen.

Those who were at St Hugh's during the Second World War were in no doubt that it was the war which opened opportunities for women to participate in more aspects of Oxford life. As the College buildings were used as a hospital, most of the undergraduates lived in Holywell Manor, where they felt 'nearer to the centre of things'. A comment from 1942 marks the shift specifically: 'In war-time Oxford women were prominent in the organisation of activities and societies.'

Certainly until the Second World War, there was a feeling that in some ways women were second-class citizens. 'I resented the low esteem in which women were held. The highest compliment was to be taken for sisters or visiting friends' (1930), and 'We were condescended to by male dons and undergraduates who thought of the women's colleges as hatcheries for schoolmistresses' (1934). The resentment was about the material privileges men enjoyed, their superior numbers, the ease with which they could enter Oxford, that they could read for Pass degrees whereas women had to take Honours, that they had laxer rules and paid less stringent penalties if they broke them. The double standard for sexual misdemeanours was particularly noticeable, with women, unlike men, nearly always being sent down at the least whiff of scandal. But anger about these differences was to a large extent dissipated by the gratitude most women in every period felt for being at Oxford at all. This outweighed the pinpricks of sometimes being disparaged, of not being fully accepted in the University, and not being allowed membership of prestigious organisations like the Oxford University Dramatic Society (OUDS) and the Union Society, which to the outside world often symbolised Oxford undergraduate life.

As early as 1924 a Senior Member regretted that she was unable to join the OUDS and in 1934, her chagrin was echoed by another graduate who was on the committee of the newly founded Experimental Theatre Club. The first complaint about exclusion from the Union Society comes from 1933, but after that the Union is not specifically mentioned till 1954. The bar from membership was particularly invidious for those who were active in politics and could not take part in the Union's political debates. This point is illustrated with reference to the debate on the 1956 Suez crisis, to which a St Hugh's graduate could not contribute, although she was president of one of the university political clubs.

In 1962, debating membership of the Union was extended to women, but they still could not hold office. Full membership was at last won in 1963, and St Hugh's soon had not only its first committee member, but, in 1967, the first woman to be elected as President. Geraldine Jones (she cannot remain anonymous) modestly says that by that time the election of a woman was inevitable. 'I like to think that I was a good enough speaker to be elected even if I had been male but obviously, when I was elected, more fuss was made of me.' A number of graduates from that period testify to the gradual change in the climate of opinion and to the hard work of many in bringing it about. Membership of the Union is mentioned by six replies after 1967, including one from a graduate who, as well as being Secretary and Librarian of the Union, was also Wardrobe Mistress of the OUDS, President of the Edmund Burke Debating Society, on the committee of OU Conservative Association and cartoonist for *Cherwell* – and she got a Second.

The final question about life at Oxford asked for any comments on the sexual mores at the time. We are told that in the 1920s, despite chaperonage, there was 'plenty of opportunity for companionable, non-furtive, happy relationships with members of the opposite sex'. Someone, who in the early 1930s was engaged to an undergraduate at Queen's, says she was able to be with her fiancé as much as they had time for and wanted.

On the whole, the answers to this question showed there was variation according to the circles in which people mixed. In 1930, 'There was a fast set but I think most of us were chaste and romantic.' In 1931, sexual mores 'were our main topic of discussion. Should you sleep with your boyfriend? How could you avoid getting pregnant? We were afraid of pregnancy but eager to have experience. Several people had abortions in my year.' In 1935, 'The public school young men divided women into those you slept with (from the town) and those you didn't (their friends' sisters). In the Labour Club we approved of steady one to one relationships. Many of them became lasting marriages.' In 1936, 'Of homosexuality I knew little. I never consciously met a Lesbian until I was in the WAAF and I do not remember such males at Oxford although there must have been many.' The individual nature of such observations is shown clearly by two comments from the same year in the 1940s: 'There were few, if any, virgins left by the time of graduation', and 'Having sex though not married was considered avante-garde.' The truth was probably told by a third in the same year who said: 'It was vastly different person by person. People made their own codes of conduct.'

The verse of Philip Larkin that

Sexual intercourse began
In nineteen sixty three

is not altogether applicable to St Hugh's. On the contrary, the contraceptive pill, which by then was available at clinics, was still considered to be 'rather brazen', and two girls with unwanted pregnancies were not allowed to continue in residence. In 1966, however, contraceptives became available from the College doctor, who told the new students on their first evening that if they wanted the pill or advice on birth control they were to visit him, not trust to luck. As before, undergraduates acted in accordance with their own principles and those of their friends. We are variously told, 'To have sex with a serious boyfriend was the norm', 'More was talked about than happened' and, 'Each category assumed everybody else was behaving like them.' Fortunately, there seems to have been tolerance on all sides and in all generations.

St Hugh's as a Single-sex College

In January 1978, the Queen in Council gave her consent to a change in the College statutes which opened all College offices and fellowships to men. The JCR was invited to give its opinion on going 'mixed'. The report in the *Chronicle* for 1977–8 says that there was surprisingly little interest; less than a third of the undergraduate body replied; although over half of those who did favoured co-residence, only 25 voted for immediate change. In 1980, the JCR voted overwhelmingly that the College should remain single sex and, in 1984, it was one of the three women's colleges still to be so. Somerville also retained an all-female Senior Common Room.

The questionnaire asked for views: should St Hugh's remain single sex at undergraduate level, offering an alternative for those girls who did not want mixed residence but risking the loss of others who preferred a mixed environment? A number of Senior Members thought the issue should be decided by the present generation, but many were willing to give their opinions and to take sides. The most frequently expressed fear was that, if the College remained single sex, many talented girls would be attracted by the traditions, buildings and academic reputations of the mixed colleges with ancient names, leaving St Hugh's with less able candidates, a fear aggravated by the College's 1984 performance in the class lists.

On the other hand, others argued that as long as there was an imbalance in the numbers of men and women at Oxford (and men still outnumbered women by six to four in 1984), there was a strong case for retaining as many places as possible exclusively for them. Some thought that women still needed nurturing in Oxford to increase their confidence and to give them experience of responsibility in their own community. Others countered that women would be more equipped to compete with men in the wider world outside Oxford if they had experienced co-residence. Would it be easier for a girl 'to find herself' in a single-sex college? Would there be pressure on girls in mixed colleges to excel socially or to take on a domestic rôle with their boyfriends, washing their socks and cooking them meals? Feminists would not approve, as a reason for the College remaining single sex,

Table 5.6　Fees

Paid	1910–19	1920–9	1930–9	1940–9	1950–9	1960–9	1970–9
Total by state	1 (5%)	17 (16%)	28 (18%)	76 (48%)	119 (69%)	168 (88%)	230 (83%)
Part by state	2 (9%)	22 (21%)	36 (23%)	17 (11%)	12 (7%)	3 (2%)	18 (7%)
Total by parents	13 (59%)	51 (48%)	76 (48%)	54 (34%)	38 (22%)	13 (7%)	21 (8%)
Other	5 (23%)	16 (15%)	19 (12%)	13 (8%)	3 (2%)	6 (3%)	5 (2%)
No information	1 (5%)	1	0	0	2 (1%)	1	2

Percentages sometimes do not total 100 because of 'rounding' of decimal points.

Table 5.7 Maintenance

Paid	1910–19	1920–9	1930–9	1940–9	1950–9	1960–9	1970–9
Total by state	1 (5%)	3 (3%)	18 (11%)	51 (32%)	62 (36%)	53 (28%)	67 (24%)
Part by state	0	23 (22%)	35 (22%)	25 (16%)	51 (29%)	96 (50%)	146 (53%)
Total by parents	18 (81%)	61 (57%)	87 (55%)	66 (41%)	54 (31%)	36 (19%)	50 (18%)
Other	2 (10%)	18 (17%)	19 (12%)	18 (11%)	5 (3%)	5 (3%)	10 (4%)
No information	1 (5%)	2 (1%)	0	0	2 (1%)	1	3

Percentages sometimes do not total 100 because of 'rounding' of decimal points.

embarrassment at having to appear at breakfast without make-up on the face, but this view was expressed, as was its mirror image: 'I hate seeing scruffy men at breakfast.' Others noted with regret that the identity of the college they knew would be fundamentally altered.

A rough count of views given by those in the mid-decade years – and it had to be a rough count since Senior Members often demonstrated trained minds and judicial detachment by rehearsing arguments on either side – reveals a shift over the years towards the College changing to co-residence, but even those from 1976 were almost equally divided.

The one aspect on which there was unanimity, among the considerable number who mentioned it, was the inconsistency of the Senior Common Room being mixed while the undergraduates remained all female. Between 1978 and 1984, there were eleven male Fellows appointed and only six female. Although graduates replying to the questionnaire appreciated the wish of the Governing Body to appoint the best possible scholars and tutors, they thought the appointment of so many men robbed undergraduates of the opportunity of seeing women in responsible positions, as well as making preferment harder for female scholars, at a time when some positive discrimination could still be justified.

Fees and Maintenance

Who paid for the education of these St Hugh's graduates? The fees of 69 per cent were paid in some measure through the state system and for 59 per cent totally. The figures for maintenance show parents contributing more: they paid all the fees for 25 per cent, but all the maintenance for 34 per cent, with the state contributing to the maintenance of 57 per cent. The shift of financial responsibility to the state over the years is clearly shown in Tables 5.6 and 5.7.

Before the 1962 Education Act made grants at Oxford mandatory subject to a means test of parental income for maintenance contributions, various types of state financial aid were possible. A graduate who entered St Hugh's in 1919 explains the system whereby the Board of Education gave grants, or in some cases loans, to students who promised to teach for five or seven years after graduation. The scheme, which was taken up by many at St Hugh's, began in 1912 when the form of indenture was remarkably strict and had to be legally witnessed. In 1922, it became a declaration of intent, rather than an undertaking, and the scheme continued in various guises till 1952. Women were released from their obligations on marriage. Until the Second World War, they normally had to resign from teaching on marriage. There were also state scholarships, awarded through the examination system, from 1924, but at first only 200 were awarded each year for the whole country.

Finding the money was a real problem for some. One graduate from the late 1920s had her fees paid partly by the Officers' Families Fund which helped families in which the father had been killed in the 1914–18 war, but the Kitchener Fund was not at that time open to women for educational purposes. A moral tutor at St Hugh's, in the 1930s, is remembered with gratitude for letting her pupil fit a four-year Honours course into three years because of her limited financial circumstances. At that time, too, 'a cloud of anxiety' was at the back of the mind of a student from a state school, who lived in a depressed area. 'Should I get a job?' she used to wonder. 'Would it enable me to lend a hand at home?'

By the 1950s, the number of state scholarships had increased to over 2000 and by 1951–2, out of a total of 165 undergraduates at St Hugh's, 52 held state scholarships (including some automatically given to the holders of College awards), 56 held local education authority awards, which were also available on examination results, although the generosity of the various local authorities varied. Only a fifth had no financial assistance of any sort. Miss Procter, speaking at the 1953 Gaudy, said that although she thought the financial barriers which used to stand between the child from the poor home and the university were now demolished, she suspected that parents whose incomes were not much above the upper income limit, and who had sons being educated at public schools and universities, could not afford a university education for their daughters – 'Arthur's Education Fund' again. Thirty years later, there is still the problem that some parents cannot, or will not, make up the gap between the state grant and what their children need at university.

The pattern for undergraduates taking paid employment in the vacation showed similar changes over the years. Before the Second World War, such work was actively disapproved, both by the College, whose permission had to be asked, and by most parents, who believed that their daughters should spend the vacations working at their books. There were a few exceptions of undergraduates who, for financial reasons, had to take jobs. One 1921 entrant worked in two long vacations to cover her maintenance. Only 15 per cent of those from the 1930s had vacation jobs, but 44 per cent from the 1940s, 64 per cent from the 1950s, 67 per cent from the 1960s and 77 per cent from the 1970s. The main reason for taking jobs after the Second World War was still financial. Sometimes undergraduates took work such as mail delivery at Christmas to earn extra spending money, especially for travel, but often it was to buy essentials like books, or to lift the burden from their parents. Modern linguists worked *au pair* abroad to improve their languages. In the 1970s another reason emerged: to gain experience of the outside world and to prepare for employment. Those wishing to enter industry tried work with appropriate companies to see if they enjoyed it and to give themselves an advantage if they applied to that company or a similar one.

AFTER OXFORD

The Transition

How did these St Hugh's graduates find employment after they left Oxford? For employment they did find, not just the majority, but virtually all of them. Only 17 of the 1092 had not had any paid employment since graduating. We shall see how marriage and child-bearing changed the pattern of employment for many, but after marriage two-thirds worked outside the home for some, if not all, of the time. The argument that it is a waste in economic terms for women to go to university, because they do not give enough back to the public purse, is refuted by the work record of St Hugh's graduates.

Those who were sure of their profession often immediately took a postgraduate professional qualification. At least 240 held the Post Qualifying Certificate for Education (PQCE) or its equivalent, though a minority took it on deciding to teach in later years. Similarly, 22 held a social work diploma, 18 at some stage took library or archive qualifications, 20 took legal qualifications, and others diplomas in theology, marital and family therapy, the fine and decorative arts, senior secretarial work and surveying. Among those who had changed their profession in the course of their careers, or who worked outside the main categories, were over 100 with some kind of postgraduate qualification. By the mid-decade year of 1976, the proportion taking teaching qualifications had fallen from the high of 29 per cent in 1936 to 19 per cent. Instead, 16 per cent of this group who matriculated in 1976 took accountancy qualifications, planning to work in business, industry and the City.

In addition, over a fifth (220) had a higher degree, ranging from medical qualifications (27) to the PhD, MSc, BLitt, BSc and other advanced degrees, at Oxford, and elsewhere. They were not only held by 69 per cent of those with academic careers, but also to further non-academic careers, or for personal satisfaction. The mid-decade years show a third with higher degrees in 1956 and 1966, reflecting the increasing importance attached to them by employers and increased competition for academic preferment. (However, one senior lecturer at a polytechnic, who subsequently took a higher degree, believed she was given her initial appointment because the head of the department thought the Oxford MA was an extra, earned qualification.)

Whether or not the St Hugh's graduate was armed with a higher degree or professional qualification, she still had to find her first job. A third did so through advertisements. Many would-be teachers found their posts in the pages of *The Times Educational Supplement*. A fifth were personally recommended for posts, a further tenth found theirs through professional recruitment and 17 per cent through the University Appointments Board, now the Appointments Committee. Only just over half said they found the job they really wanted.

The University Appointments Board receives stringent criticism from graduates of most periods. It was used most in the 1950s and 1970s, when a quarter found jobs through it, but the first attack comes from a 1934 Senior Member: 'The University Appointments Board was quite useless.' She answered advertisements and became a library assistant. In 1946 they were 'unhelpful' and in 1947 'they pushed all the "don't knows" in the direction of social work'. They found someone in the mid 1950s a post as an investment adviser and manager, but usually took a more restricted view of possibilities at that period: 'When I went to the Appointments Board, flushed with triumph at my results (a First), I was asked "Do you want to teach or do secretarial work?" When I replied "Neither" I was asked "Then why did you do modern languages?" Dejectedly I took a six months intensive secretarial course, the most miserable time in my life.'

It is easy with hindsight to criticise the Board for its timidity. It went at the pace of the rest of society and was not prepared to encourage girls to risk entering fields where they might not be welcomed. Women in general were still pictured in supportive roles. What could be more useful than a secretary with an Oxford degree, who had 'the ability to take responsibility, make decisions and act for the boss in his absence'? In her 1953 Gaudy speech, Miss Procter reflected the cautious view based on the experiences of recent St Hugh's graduates: 'There is still next to no future for a woman barrister; there are more openings for a solicitor provided there is a family firm in the background. There are also administrative and advisory posts in which knowledge of the law is an asset.' Such sound analysis, but discouraging advice, still has the effect today of keeping doors shut. The most common reason given by industry and the professions for the dearth of women in them is that women do not apply.

The Careers

Over 400 of these St Hugh's graduates (38 per cent) had devoted their careers to teaching in schools, passing knowledge to the next generation, as was the intention of the College's founder, Elizabeth Wordsworth. Over 70 per cent of the teachers had a First or Second class degree. A further 99 Senior Members have taught in universities, polytechnics or other places of further education, or undertaken research. The range of careers can be seen in Table 5.8. The final category, 'other', covers a variety of careers in industry: jobs as different as owning an horticultural business, working with the

Table 5.8 Professions

School teaching	418 (38%)
Higher education and research	99 (9%)
Journalism, the arts, translating	50 (5%)
Secretarial and general administration	46 (4%)
Civil service	35 (3%)
Librarianship, archives	31 (3%)
Medicine	29 (2%)
Social work	28 (2%)
Law	25 (2%)
Advertising	5
Other and mixed careers	337 (31%)
Never employed	17 (1%)

United Nations Food and Agricultural Organisation, or being an inspector of historic monuments. It also includes many graduates who have at some stage taught. There are teachers who have become educational psychologists, systems analysts, civil servants, company directors, an adviser to the World Bank, the first woman programme organiser for a BBC local radio station and ministers of religion. The other way round, to quote but a few, a BBC news trainee went into teaching, as did a press library assistant and a market researcher.

A 1922 graduate explains that: 'I never really wanted to teach but it was the only job open to ordinary women in those days.' Certainly it was one of the few jobs open to women then, although a graduate from as early as the 1921 year entered social work, there was a paid political organiser in the late 1920s, and someone from the 1923 year who entered advertising comments: 'There were several St Hugh's graduates working in it.' The first civil servant recorded in the replies entered the College in 1926. She was compelled to resign on her marriage in 1936. The marriage bar in the civil service was not removed until 1946, and most teachers had to resign on marriage, until the shortage of teachers in the Second World War made their continuing service essential. An informal marriage bar also operated in most other fields. A graduate from the mid 1920s who went into publishing was sacked by her employer when she married.

But in considering the large number of St Hugh's graduates who entered teaching, it would be wrong to think that most of them did so *faute de mieux*, or that those who could not find another career disliked teaching. Many came to St Hugh's with the explicit intention of entering teaching, and not just those who were being paid for by the Board of Education's grants. Teaching was the profession of many of their parents. For others it turned out well: 'In 1954 very few industrial firms employed married women. If they had I would never have become a teacher – which would have been a pity as I enjoy it and am a good teacher.' In all, 85 per cent of teachers said their employment had given them job satisfaction (and 68 per cent adequate earnings).

There is no doubt that the range of careers open to women has widened. Among those who matriculated in 1966, one graduate became, before the birth of her first child, the section leader of an actuarial division of a leading industrial company; another, still single, used accountancy qualifications to become a tax specialist in a merchant bank and is now a tax adviser with a leading industrial company; a third, who began as a systems programmer and engineer, is now director of an industrial firm. Among the 1976 intake are a graduate on the scientific staff of the Royal Aircraft Establishment, Farnborough, an auditor with a leading City company, a computer programmer with Ferranti, a combustion engineer with Rolls Royce, a marketing and credit officer in the private banking division of an American bank, an agricultural analyst, several chartered accountants, a barrister and others in jobs previously held only by men. But we do not yet know how far they will be able to proceed up the managerial ladder, or what choices, if they have children, they will make with their husbands or partners.

The shift away from teaching is marked after the 1950s. In the 1950s, 43 per cent of St Hugh's graduates taught; in the 1960s, 32 per cent; so far only 19 per cent from the 1970s have chosen teaching. In 1953, Miss Procter pointed out that scientists and mathematicians were tending to go into industry: 'Unless more of them become teachers', she said, 'the flow of candidates in these subjects will dry up for lack of specialists to prepare them.' What will be the consequences, not just for the universities but in general, now that fewer highly qualified women graduates are entering teaching?

There are still some careers closed to women. A graduate from the late 1940s, who is a specialist in heraldry, points out that there are no women in the College of Arms. If the Church of England decides later this decade to admit women as priests, a number of the first privileged to serve may well be from St Hugh's. There were replies from 36 Senior Members who were in some capacity professionally involved with the Church, including six ordained ministers (the Baptist and United Reformed Churches were specifically mentioned), four deaconesses, seven nuns or former nuns, and five lay readers and preachers. Ten commented on 'the perpetual frustration as a qualified woman in the Anglican church' (1940), and there was even one Senior Member in the interesting position of being a part-time Director of Ordinands, who could not herself be ordained.

The overall figure for both job satisfaction and adequate earnings was 60 per cent, with another fifth saying their employment had given them only job satisfaction. The adequacy of earnings obviously depends on the individual's definition of needs, and some qualified their answers by phrases like 'for my modest requirements'. A more satisfactory measure of financial security was obtained for single women by asking them if they owned their own home. The answers showed that 59 per cent of single women did own their own homes, half of whom had bought them entirely from their own earnings.

On the subject of pensions, another measure of whether a job gives adequate financial rewards, there was grave dissatisfaction except among those who had worked continuously and full time in one profession. A third said they did have a satisfactory occupational pension, but there were frequent comments on the unfairness of present pensions systems. A single woman from the late 1930s at St Hugh's, who had worked first as a teacher, then during the war in nursing, then as a librarian, and who had ended in medical social work, explains: 'After twenty-nine years in the NHS my occupational pension is only slightly more than my old-age pension. I would be living on an income way below the current earnings average if it were not for some inheritance.'

The solution most often put forward by Senior Members, for both women and men who change their jobs mid-career, was 'portable' pensions, through which the contributions accrued in one organisation's pension fund can be transferred to that of another. Alternatively, individuals could be given the choice of placing their employer's contributions in a personal pension scheme similar to those available to the self-employed.

Other reforms suggested to improve pensions include a flexible retirement age for both sexes, especially now that the gap is narrowing between the average ages at which women and men die. More fundamental is the right for widowers or other nominees to be eligible for a pension from a woman's contributions when she dies, just as at present all pensions provide for widows. A few pension schemes in industry, like that of the Shell Group, were cited as already having introduced this change.

Reaching the Top

How many of these St Hugh's graduates have reached the top of their professions? This question is not intended to decry the achievements of many who did not, nor to suggest that reaching the top of a profession should be everyone's aim. It is asked only to see if there are any barriers to success which could be removed to help those in future generations with that ambition and ability. It certainly does not follow that, because a profession is open to women, they will automatically enter it or rise in it. Since 1930, most posts in the senior civil service have been open to women, and in 1946, the marriage bar was removed. In 1983, 12 of the administrative trainees appointed were women, compared with 33 men, although almost equal numbers (1340 women and 1418 men) had applied. In January 1984, there were no women Permanent Secretaries (40 men), 5 women Deputy Secretaries (131 men) and 23 women Under Secretaries (482 men), a marginally smaller percentage than in 1976.

Among the 418 St Hugh's teachers were 39 headmistresses, including one former President of the Headmistresses' Association. Most worked in schools with an academic reputation, many in the former direct-grant schools. Nine of the headmistresses had married, six had their own children and two step-children. Until the Second World War, teachers normally resigned on marriage, and it is still difficult for a woman who has taken time off, when her children were young, to reach the top of the teaching profession. In 1984, only 16 per cent of head-teachers in secondary schools were women, although they formed 63 per cent of teachers on the bottom pay scale. However, a graduate from the early 1950s, who is a headmistress, and also married with children, says that the greatest barrier she had to overcome was not fear of her domestic responsibilities, but suspicion because she had been educated at a well-known public school. A 1930s graduate, who was interviewed for headships, remarks that 'a great stress was put on the daily corporate act of worship which it was assumed that, as a Jew, I could not conduct'.

The group who returned the questionnaires also contained academics at over 70 universities and colleges, including six Oxford colleges, and universities all over the world. In politics, there was one former Cabinet Minister, who is now a Member of the European Parliament (Barbara Castle – her achievements identify her); in the civil service, a former Under Secretary for Housing and Local Government, and an Assistant Secretary; in the National Health Service, a Consultant Psychologist, a four-fifths time Consultant in Child and Family Psychiatry, and a Senior Lecturer in Paediatrics. Others included an Assistant Director of a Social Services Department, a Queen's Counsel, a BBC producer, who like many from the 1930s rose from the typing pool, an Associate Professor, who was the first editor of *Social Trends*, the first woman to be appointed a cathedral organist, and successful authors of academic works, novels and other books.

Some of those listed above married and raised families, others were single. Marriage as a factor in careers, and the modern woman's balancing act between her career and her home, will be considered next. In discussing such choices, two Senior Members quoted Cassius in *Julius Caesar*:

> The fault, dear Brutus, is not in our stars
> But in ourselves, that we are underlings.

Marriage, Families and Work

St Hugh's graduates in the survey had fewer marriages and fewer divorces than average for the general population, as is shown in Table 5.9. A small number of those at present married had previously divorced and the single women include 13 from the later years, who said they were cohabiting. One asked 'Why does this questionnaire not include cohabitation but assumes marriage as the sole stable form of relationship and rearing children?' According to the 1982 General Household Survey, one in eight women aged between 18 and 49 is cohabiting. It would be interesting to chart this and other social trends in a wider study.

Table 5.9 Marital status

Married	608 (56%)
Single	353 (32%)
Widowed	78 (7%)
Divorced	36 (3%)
Separated	11 (1%)
No information	6 (1%)

The marriage rate increased sharply over the years. From the 1920s, after so many potential husbands had been killed in the First World War, 45 per cent were single, from the 1930s, 37 per cent, from the 1940s, 16 per cent, from the 1950s and 1960s, a fifth. About half the graduates from the 1970s had married by 1984, despite the trend towards cohabitation.

The first indication that marriage and having a family would significantly affect the patterns of careers came from answers to the question about why job changes were made. The highest percentage for any single answer (17 per cent) was for those who said that they changed to suit their husband's career or family commitments. (The next highest was for those who wanted to improve job satisfaction.) Mobility was one problem: 'I really made it difficult for myself marrying a professional soldier' (1936). The importance of the husband's work another: 'I did from an early stage accept the dominance of my husband's career. He has always been extremely busy since for most of our married life he has been establishing or pursuing a political career. My job has always been secondary to his and abandoned, temporarily or permanently, to suit his needs' (mid 1950s).

On the other hand, sometimes the partnership of marriage liberated a graduate. 'Marriage made it possible to pursue a writing career subsidised at first by my husband – for many years my earnings would not have been enough to support a family', comments a successful novelist who was at St Hugh's in the 1940s. Another graduate from the 1940s, now a Fellow of an Oxford college, writes: 'If I'd not had to stay at home with the children we would never have written our definitive work and maybe never have moved back to Oxford. And I'd never have discovered that I enjoyed writing books much more than research articles or even doing experiments.'

Two-thirds of the married women worked, although only 146 had kept up continuous, full-time employment. The family was given as the reason for their choice by a third of the part-timers. The phrase used in this context by a graduate from 1918 was 'home duties'. The words differed for subsequent generations, and possibly the overtones, but the implications were the same.

In total, half of the graduates in the study had children. By examining the mid-decade years, it was possible to see the size of their families and how long they had to establish any careers before their first children were born. The average number of children was just over two each, except for the 1946 year who had just over three each. Only six of the married graduates in the mid-decade years (excluding 1976) had no children. It is interesting that although the interval between graduation and marriage was longer for the married graduates from 1926 and 1936, they had their first children after the same number of years from graduation as those from 1966. The gap between graduation and marriage was seven years for those from 1926 and 1936, and under four years for those from 1966, yet their first children were born on average after eight years for them all. The graduates from the 1960s had married earlier, but, with the choice available through improved methods of contraception, had postponed having children until their careers were better established or their marriages more financially secure. The overall average interval between graduation and marriage was just over four years. In 1946, it was only six years between graduation and first child, and, in 1956, only five.

The amount of time mothers spend out of employment may also depend on the number and spacing of their children. The interval between the birth of the eldest child and the time the youngest reached compulsory school age was greatest for the graduates from 1946, because they had the most children. For them it was twelve years. It was ten for those from 1926, eleven for those from 1936 and nine for those from 1956 and 1966. The way most careers and professions are structured today, nine years is a long time to be absent. The St Hugh's graduate who is a Queen's Counsel, and who has four children, says she succeeded only because she worked at the Bar full time for eight years and then continued part-time, never giving up her practice.

There is plenty of testimony to the difficulties these St Hugh's graduates met in their careers through the suspicion that they would be bound to leave because of marriage and having children. 'There was always the suspicion that family life would tempt me away – they were right' (1973); but a graduate from the 1940s, who was turned down for one post on the grounds that she was a married woman and therefore bound to have children, points out that it was seven years before she had a child. Training as a branch manager in a bank was refused a St Hugh's graduate as late as the 1970s, because it was thought she might have children. On the other hand, women in business and industry in the last decade have had the advantage of 'visibility': 'It helps to be unusual, you are remembered and it's easier to make a good impression' (1978).

The agonies, the rewards and the conflict inherent in working, while bringing up children, were dramatically brought to life in the pages of the questionnaires. Senior Members were asked: was it practical in their case to combine employment with bringing up children? Was it enjoyable, was it unavoidable? Most of those who answered said it was a mixture of these elements and in addition it was very hard work: 'It is perfectly possible to bring up a family and have a career so long as you don't mind working a sixteen-hour day and a seven-day week' (1956). It was often unavoidable because the family needed the money. In addition, most graduates wanted the intellectual stimulation of work without having to hand their children's upbringing totally to others: 'I wanted to rear my children myself. There were no nursery schools or play-groups. We were too poor to afford help. It was tough. I worked at night in adult education for that reason. I worked hard' (1931), and 'It is wearing but I have to do work beyond child-rearing' (1944). A Senior Lecturer in Paediatrics pulls these strands together when she argues that part-time work should be encouraged. It strengthens the family because it relieves boredom, whereas full-time work, in her view, induces stress.

The difficulty lay in balancing needs. We hear: 'I think I was a better mother once I got back to work' (1951); 'Earning my own living has been the key to my freedom within marriage' (1948); 'Some sort of work is essential to me, partly because we need the money, but more importantly because I need to make money. I cannot bear to be a dependant and I need the contrast from domestic work but I would not want to work full-time while my children are young' (1966); 'Part-time work allows one to see one's children and yet not be bored by their constant company' (1952); and 'I am now permanently exhausted but content' (1972). On the other hand, 'My children always said I cared more about my pupils/students, and gave them more time than I did them' (1944); and 'I always felt guilty, either about the children or about the job' (1941).

Some were sure that such conflicts were not for them: 'Full-time Mum suits me best – I hope it suits the family' (1966). No one from the 1940s or 1950s cited interpretations of the work of child psychiatrists like John Bowlby as having influenced them in wanting to stay at home, but some simply saw the rôle of mother as full time: 'I could not and cannot leave the children while they are young. It is my responsibility to look after them and my joy to watch their development' (1967), and 'It meant delaying my professional development but that was my choice – I did not want to delegate the care of my children' (1945). Others found the prospect of organising a dual life too much: 'I never can understand how anyone can find time to combine family responsibilities and work – I never have enough time for the family' (1954).

How did those who tried to do both manage? Few (53) had full-time, resident help. A 1960s graduate, who did have a resident nanny for a new baby, was working four days a week, but found it stressful. The location of work was shown by many to be important. Teaching is an obvious choice for mothers, in that the hours and holidays coincide (usually) with those of the family, but it is no good teaching at the far side of a big city if your children are still young: 'Teaching is the ideal job and my school was ten minutes' walk away. We all came home for lunch, a salad meal. When holidays did not coincide, a neighbour or friend helped' (1938). Similarly, a general medical practitioner with domestic help can take a full workload if her practice is near enough home for her to return, when necessary, between surgeries or visits. Only ten people used day nurseries for small babies. For as many as employed paid help in the home, or took their children to child-minders, there were others who had arrangements with relatives or neighbours, or whose husbands worked hours which complemented their own. Once a child reached school age, many mothers contrived to arrive home in time for the end of the child's school day.

Husbands

It is often said that behind every successful man there is a supporting woman. The reverse may be equally true. Every study of married women who work (for instance, *Women in Top Jobs, 1968–79*, by Michael Fogarty, Isobel Allen and Patricia Walters, Heinemann Educational Books, 1981) shows that the husband's attitude is crucial. Graduates who answered this questionnaire agreed: 'It is essential to have a co-operative husband/family and a reliable back-up' (1933); and 'Working is enjoyable but it could result in conflict without the support of your husband.' Sadly, from the 1960s: 'I separated from my husband largely because he believed I should be at home, not working.'

The husbands of these St Hugh's graduates were nearly all graduates themselves (82 per cent) and nearly half (48 per cent) were Oxford graduates. The questionnaire asked whether the respondent was primarily responsible in her household for the shopping, cooking and cleaning. A graduate from the 1940s, who felt the questionnaire was influenced by the feminist movement, marked the question about domestic responsibilities as 'silly', although she herself had recorded that one aspect of College life she particularly liked was 'the freedom from domestic duties'. Is it silly to ask such a question when shopping, cooking and cleaning (not to mention gardening and home-decorating, which some Senior Members added to the list) take so much time and energy? It is not that they are in any way demeaning activities. Indeed, many find cooking creative and cleaning therapeutic, but they limit choices for those who have to do them, when they would prefer to be doing something else. If graduates from one of the men's colleges were to fill in this questionnaire, their answers might be different on many counts, but it is unlikely that 62 per cent would be primarily responsible for all the chores in their household, and 77 per cent for all except the cleaning. Most would have someone else organising their lives for them in these respects.

If it is accepted that domestic responsibilities take time, and that working wives need supportive husbands, did these husbands give their wives more than moral support? There is a sliding scale of participation by husbands in the work of the household from the earlier decades ('my husband did not expect to take on an additional role in the house though he appreciated my wish to use my qualifications' (1932)), to the 1970s when a fifth of husbands shared all chores. Statistics may not tell quite the whole story, as the following comments show, but sharing had begun: 'My husband prepares breakfast and says I should add that' (1964); 'They are a joint responsibility with my husband but obviously when I am not working outside the home this falls mainly on me' (1972); 'My husband is under the impression that he shares this but in fact I do most of it' (1973); 'I organise and delegate half the tasks. My partner is willing but only rarely shows initiative on domestic chores' (1976). A 1972 respondent offered a traditional domestic vignette: 'My husband took down the answers to this questionnaire whilst I ironed'; but ironing was the speciality of one 1974 husband.

Children

In summing up her views on combining work with rearing a family, a graduate, who entered the College in 1941, said: 'I do not regret having regarded the bringing-up of my four children as a virtually full-time job. All are now quite distinguished people in their various professions and although I have no means of proving that my making them my "career" was a large factor in that success, I think it well may have been.' To have looked at what happened to the children of these graduates, and at factors affecting their development, would have been a different project, but the questionnaire did ask whether any sons and daughters had gone to university or intended to do so.

We have seen that 39 per cent of the fathers of those in the study were graduates compared with only 17 per cent of their mothers. A marked change is shown in the opportunities open to and taken by girls in their children's generation. The numbers of their daughters and sons going to university were almost equal. There were 220 graduates with daughters who had been or were currently at university (38 of them at St Hugh's) and 236 with sons. Ambitions for younger children were the same for both sexes. In general, the number of their children who attended university, calculated for those who had grown-up families, is evidence of the transmission of academic ability and expectations. It suggests that, despite the fall in the birth rate, there will be increasing pressure for university places as each generation of graduates raises children with university aspirations, joined, it is to be hoped, by newcomers.

The Future of Part-time Work

'There is no solution', writes a St Hugh's graduate from the 1950s, 'to having your children, enjoying them and continuing with a man-type career.' One question before future generations of St Hugh's graduates, and other women, is whether the majority of careers will continue as now to require the full-time commitment which most men at present give them.

The compromise many St Hugh's graduates with families have reached is to work part-time, most of them (85 per cent) in similar work to that which they would have done full-time, and most (80 per cent) till recently saying it was easy to find. But they vividly document the frustrations of part-time work as it is organised today. 'There is equality of opportunity in medicine if a woman is prepared to pursue her career as singlemindedly as a man', we are told. 'However, to try to combine this with marriage and children is a daunting task' (1955). Another St Hugh's doctor explains that medicine is still 'a man's profession', with the top National Health Service consultant posts rarely, if ever, being awarded on a part-time basis to women who want to spend the rest of their time with their families. This is despite the fact that they are awarded part-time to men who want to spend a proportion of their time on private work outside the Health Service.

The disparities within teaching are still more striking and it is tempting to suggest that a new marriage bar has been erected, preventing part-time teachers attaining positions of responsibility. From the headteacher's point of view, the scene may appear to be of part-timers who want to arrive at school after they have deposited their own children at their schools, who want to leave in time to fetch their children home, and who never stay late to organise out-of-hours activities, or to see parents. But the part-time teachers who returned this questionnaire had a different tale to tell: 'I am still on scale 1 (the bottom scale) although I teach for four-fifths of the week and despite my qualifications and experience' (1950), sounds very like 'I had to give up my permanent teaching post when I married and continued as a "temporary" doing exactly the same work' (1926), or 'As a married woman I was not considered for head of department. These posts were reserved for single women or men' (1938). A complicating factor recently has been the reduction in the number of all-girl schools which previously had female heads: 'Being an Oxford graduate does not outweigh the disadvantage of being a married woman. Deputy heads and department heads in mixed schools in the seventies all went to men' (1957). There is some contrary testimony: 'I have met a part-time head of department in a GPDST school' (1955), but the general feeling is: 'However great the effort one puts into one's work as a part-time teacher, there was no sense of "career" at all.'

Such individual instances are supported by figures from the National Union of Teachers. In *Promotion and the Woman Teacher* (1980), published by the NUT, it is shown that, in 1976, there were over 34 000 women in part-time teaching, of whom 60 per cent taught the same subjects at the same level as they had before their break for maternity. In the same way as the St Hugh's graduates, many had spent about eight years with young children, but still had a long working life ahead. Out of 55 local education authorities surveyed, only 12 said part-timers were eligible for posts above the bottom scale. Part-timers were often paid only for the hours they taught (not for preparation or marking), were not given holiday or sick pay, and had no security of employment.

The position is similar in other professions. A university librarian (1950) writes: 'When I became a part-timer I lost official status and promotion prospects, although doing exactly the same job and receiving salary pro rata, three-fifths for a three-day week.' Only 24 graduates said they could reach a senior post in the organisation in which they worked in the same way as a full-time worker. To sum up: 'Part-time work does not allow full-time commitment' (1950).

Are there compelling reasons why those who work part-time should not have as satisfactory conditions and prospects as full-time workers? There are two central issues. First, part-time work should be recognised as a permanent alternative type of work for some people. This would entail contracts which recognise the right of the part-timer to be paid pro rata, to receive holiday and sick pay, to have normal security of tenure, due notice for dismissal and redundancy rights, and a pension in proportion to the hours worked. If pensions become portable, as it has been argued they should, then there is little reason why the principle of portability should not be extended to allow employees and employers to build pensions for the requirements of part-timers.

The second issue is harder to resolve, but is at the heart of the difficulties experienced by all but the most determined or fortunate women with families. It is the argument that really responsible jobs must be full-time and cannot be broken down into smaller, equally responsible units. There are some jobs, like that of Prime Minister, which obviously demand a twenty-four hour commitment. But are they so numerous? 'One accepts the part-time availability of one's doctor at his surgery, why not other professionals?' asks one graduate. Occasionally, St Hugh's graduates in senior positions have been able to negotiate part-time contracts. A Principal in the Treasury managed to work part-time between 1966 and 1977, with no work and no pay in the school holidays. She was in the historical section, but could not such arrangements apply to most sections? Even the most dedicated civil servants and businessmen take leave during the year and the conduct of the nation's affairs continues.

Job-sharing, which is often cited as a theoretical solution, is rare in practice but could be extended, especially for specialist teachers. There were only two examples of job-sharing among the replies from the questionnaires. A wife (early 1960s at St Hugh's) and her husband shared a post co-ordinating a support scheme for victims of crime. Their experience, organising 50 volunteers, has not been free of problems, and in order to work this way, sharing the care of their child, they had to take a post which is not as well paid as either of the posts they held previously. In the other case, the St Hugh's graduate (1970) shared a job at the British Council with another Oxford graduate, each working two and a half days a week, and, with two young children at home, this was ideal for her requirements.

The verdict of another St Hugh's graduate is: 'It would help if both sexes could choose to work part-time instead of part-time work being a second-class option for the married woman' (1952). Indeed, it could be argued that the underlying reason for the lack of change is that politicians, and the trades unions in particular, view part-time work as a women's problem. It is true that 93 per cent of part-time workers in the 1982 General Household Survey were women, but there are signs that more men want flexible working lives, and that men as well as women resent having to choose between a successful career and close involvement with their children. Modern technology will allow more work to be based at home through the use of computers. With employment opportunities shrinking for everyone, it would make sense to encourage part-time work, so that couples can together earn enough for their needs, while leaving some time for other concerns. The myth that women work for pin money dies hard, but most of the St Hugh's married women indicated that their salaries were essential to the family budget. The trouble at the moment is, it seems, that 'Too many women are condemned to poverty or the slavery of two jobs' (1952). Responsible part-time careers for more women, and for more men, could be an answer.

Other reforms were suggested to give a full spectrum of choice. Tax allowances for paid help for dependants, whether young or old, would enable more women with families to work if they wished. Just as important, a complementary tax allowance, for the person in the family who stays at home to do the caring, would recognise his or her contribution, and give everyone a real choice.

Voluntary Work

Four out of ten of these St Hugh's graduates undertook some form of unpaid work outside the home in addition to, or instead of, paid employment. 'At this time of high unemployment, if the husband earns enough to keep his family, then the wife should not take paid work but use her talents to help others on a voluntary basis' (1959), was one view, and certainly it was the married women who were able to undertake most voluntary work, 346 of those who had been married compared with 105 single people, undertaking some. Again, as might be expected, older women had more time for voluntary work. The range of their activities summarised from the mid-decade years includes service with church groups, on the bench as magistrates, as school managers and governors, on parole boards, on charity committees; work with old people, the housebound, the bereaved; for conservation, adult literacy, mental health, the Samaritans, community relations, youth groups, theatre and musical groups and politics. Sometimes younger women found active participation thrust upon them by their circumstances: 'I had to found playgroups in two different villages to ensure that my children had pre-school education and play' (1955).

Finally, 15 per cent of these St Hugh's Senior Members, mainly in the older age groups, had supported or helped financially a member of their family other than their husbands and children. Most of those aided were parents, but some contributed to the welfare or comforts of aunts, uncles, nieces, nephews and godchildren.

IN CONCLUSION

The study has thrown light on the backgrounds of over 1000 St Hugh's graduates, their perceptions of St Hugh's and Oxford, and their lives after university. Only a study which compared their replies with those of graduates of another Oxford women's college, or another university, could show that they had characteristics which belonged specifically to St Hugh's. Their families were perhaps more affluent than the stereotypes of St Hugh's suggest. Many did share the religious devotion of the founders of the College and, for various reasons, many did become teachers. Nearly all enjoyed their academic work and used it directly or indirectly in paid employment. But it is the influence of Oxford rather than of St Hugh's that most of them acknowledge, like the graduate from 1956 who says: 'Being at Oxford was the most significant thing that has happened in my life so far.' St Hugh's for many was the means by which they entered Oxford, not a separate experience.

Although there is no typical St Hugh's graduate, those in the study reflected the typical dilemmas of women of their generation. As individuals, most met encouragement rather than opposition on the road to Oxford; but after Oxford they were confronted with choices that most found difficult to make. For many life has been a compromise. If they married and had children, they had to balance their own wishes and society's expectations about their rôle as women, against their desire to develop as individuals and to contribute to society through a career. The study shows that changes in attitudes take place only gradually, whether in schools, employment or marriage. But changes are taking place, even accelerating, and it is clear that eventually these changes could increase choices for everyone, men as well as women.

6 Women's Education and its Future

Baroness Warnock

A hundred years ago, to secure education for women was the most important goal of the Women's Movement. A decade or so after the death of J. S. Mill, his belief in the power for good of education was probably more influential even than his belief in the right of women to vote. The great founding age of the new girls' schools, the Girls' Public Day School Trust schools, and many others, was coming to an end, and the universities were everywhere opening up. The aim was to break down the barriers and allow women access to the very same kind of education (though not in the same schools and colleges) as men. No enlightened person questioned that this was what women deserved and should have, both for their own sake and that of the world at large.

Today, in the 1980s, it is still impossible to consider the future of women's education without taking into account whatever is the driving force of feminism. For it is by no means the case, as the pioneers would have hoped, that the battles are all won. Where will feminism lead us in the next 100 years? To predict in detail would be folly. But it seems justifiable, all the same, to distinguish two possible ways forward, corresponding to the two different kinds of feminism discernible at the present time. We may refer to them as the radical and the conservative feminism.

Radical feminism was, in the beginning, especially associated with the United States and Australia, and was first publicised under the banner of Women's Liberation. *Spare Rib* and many other shorter-lived publications were the outcome, in the late 1960s and 1970s, of the new radicalism, whose politics were left-wing, more because of an emotional affinity with the left, than any necessary conceptual connection. There have been many different versions of radical feminism, and many different forms of expression of it, perhaps most notably in the visual arts and photography. The work of the American, Judy Chicago, for example, received a good deal of publicity, especially, in this country, her *Dinner Party*, a set of ceramics with explicitly genital themes was the subject of a television programme of some interest in the early 1980s. Her theory was that, since painting and sculpture are not cerebral but physical arts, the product not of mind alone but of body, it follows that women's art must show itself to be different from men's art, as the female body is different from the male. In men's art, women are seen always from without. Painting women is, for men, necessarily a spectator sport. Women, on the other hand, must express what it is like being the flesh portrayed by the Great Masters. In the same spirit, Mary Kelly, an Australian artist, put on an exhibition illustrating childhood; not the conventional externalised vision of the mother and her child, but a record of the child, his nappies, his weight chart, his diet sheets, everything about him that preoccupied the mother from his conception until the day when he went off to his first school, and became separate from her. This kind of work was, of course, partly designed to shock. But it was partly a perfectly serious attempt to establish the difference between conventional, aesthetic objects including women, and objects presented from the standpoint of a woman, seen with her eyes and constructed by her hands.

For in whatever form it has expressed itself, and to whatever ridicule it has quite intelligibly been subjected, the essential message of radical feminism is the separateness of women from men. And it can easily be seen that such a message has important educational consequences. The radical feminist argues that, once the consciousness of women in general is raised, they will see not only that they are exploited and used by men, but that the standards of success and failure, the criteria of what is and what is not worth doing, are all of them established by men. What is to count, for instance, as worthwhile knowledge, what is to count as a valid argument, what is the proper subject-matter of history or of science, what is the most valuable advance in medicine or engineering, all these things are determined by men in their own interests. The expression 'It's a man's world' takes on a new sense: not only do men do better in their professions, in industry, in sport, in art and music and literature, but it is inevitable that they should, since they created the world, and the language through which we think of the world, for themselves.

It is no use arguing against the radical feminist that some standards are absolute or that a valid argument is valid whichever the sex of the person who employs it; that biology, chemistry, physics, history . . . all have their own internal standards proper to the subject, whoever practises it. For the feminist will reply that this is precisely the masculine point of view, the ultimate confidence-trick played on women by men. And if it is a woman who puts forward the argument, it simply shows the subservience of the female to the male. If the question is raised, 'What will the new female-dominated biology or mathematics actually be like?' the answer is that we don't know till we have given it a chance to come into being. If women had 'space' to try, they could re-invent history, philosophy, literature and, most probably, the wheel.

Now it may well seem that all this is exaggerated, and very unlikely to affect the future of women's education one way or the other. And certainly to engage in conversation with some of the more extreme radicals is to come near to dismissing the whole thing as a mad aberration, a lunatic pimple on the otherwise smooth surface of women's university education. Nevertheless, though many of the radical suggestions of separatism are impractical, the very existence of such theories may have a very marked effect within the universities and one which, in my view, would be depressingly retrograde. Even after the first battles to allow women to enter the university were won 100 years ago, it was many more years before separatism, that is to say *educational* separatism, was altogether eliminated.

It is essential to distinguish what I here refer to as separatism from the different issue of single-sex or mixed education. The question whether girls should be educated by themselves, in single-sex schools or colleges, may have some importance, and historically it has certainly had some educational significance. But it is predominantly a social, not an educational matter.

But in the early days of higher education for women there was a strong lobby for a different *kind* of education for women, and this lobby had to be defeated, if any kind of educational equality was to be achieved. Equality of educational opportunity, the goal towards which the pioneers struggled, entailed that girls should study the same subjects as boys for the same length of time. It entailed their sitting the same examinations and getting, at the end, the same degrees. All these ends have, to a greater or less degree, been achieved in this country, though by no means world-wide. The ideal of radical feminism is in danger of putting this educational achievement in jeopardy.

We may consider, as an example, Women's Studies. In many universities, including Oxford, there has been a demand for Women's Studies to be instituted as a regular part of the curriculum. Is this something we are to expect in the future? There is a good deal of confusion about what is meant by the expression, which is indeed ambiguous. If one examines programmes of Women's Studies where they exist, they seem to be mainly historical. They consist in social history, with an emphasis on literature and the other arts. They are concerned with women as they actually were revealed, perhaps in diaries, or as they were seen in novels or plays or as the subjects of paintings, whether through the eyes of men or of other women. It is obvious that there is a great deal of valuable work to be done on this kind of subject, and there is much material, only now being published, of great interest to historians and sociologists, and even to political theorists. Indeed there are probably many quite new aspects to be explored. But the name 'Women's Studies' carries a suggestion that it is not a study *of* women so much as *for* women. And though it is doubtless true that men could teach such courses, and may do so, and that men are not excluded from taking them, it is still the case that, mostly, when they exist they are taught by women and to other women. So, whatever the intention, they tend to seem like special women's courses. They may begin to be thought of as soft options, where women are especially likely to succeed, and to be contrasted with 'hard' subjects. They will count for less in the eyes of the world.

And Women's Studies might be the thin end of a separatist wedge. If the radical ideal were to be put into practice, there would begin to be Women's Philosophy, Women's Physics, Women's Mathematics. All these subjects, whatever their content, would tend to be taught by women to one another. They would be separate from 'proper' Philosophy, Physics and Mathematics.

To show how genuinely radical such proposals are, I can best quote from Dale Spender's book *Invisible Women* (Chameleon Press, 1982). She argues that Women's Studies should not be one isolated element, fitted into the pattern of the existing curriculum at school or university. For if it were, it

> could come under male control and become another academic subject in the same mould as . . . conventional subjects . . . And we would be back with the descendants of Aphra Behn who were allowed to learn Latin and Greek, and the descendants of Mary Wollstonecraft who were finally permitted equal access to men's education: we would have gained little . . . Women will simply have made some ground on men's terms, and will be no closer to gaining our autonomy, to gaining . . . control over our own education. Only when women decree half the terms will women have their own education and be receiving equal opportunity . . . If men's mean-

ings are to co-exist with women's (and it seems to me that there is
no other way that equality can be realised) . . . then at a . . .
fundamental level, men will have to abandon the concept of
objectivity which they have erected and appropriated for themselves, and accept the limitations of their own subjectivity. If there
are to be men's 'truths' which originate in men's subjectivity, and
women's 'truths' which originate in women's subjectivity, then it
is obvious that there must be more than one 'truth', and this will
have to be acknowledged and taken into account.

Every true proposition, whether of history, chemistry, mathematics or sociology, thus becomes relative to the gender of the
person who utters it. For any statement to be accepted, it is necessary
first to ascertain the sex of the utterer. A women will accept the
statement of a man only at risk of subordination; and presumably, in
the future envisaged by Miss Spender, the reverse will also hold.

Even if such suggestions seem fantastic, I think it is necessary to be
cautious about the deep anti-rationalism implicit in some of the
radical demands. For the hallmark of the new subject-matter is to be
its bringing together of Reason and Emotion, its exploration of a new
way of thinking which does not rely, or not exclusively, on argument
and proof. Now it is undoubtedly true that much conventional
nonsense has been talked as a result of the kind of Faculty Psychology
which absolutely distinguishes Reason from the Passions. It is also
true that, in education as a whole, we may expect to see more
emphasis than before on the education of the emotions and the
imagination. And this will be greatly to the advantage of everyone,
men and women alike. Nevertheless, there is danger in the suggestion
that the world has gone wrong because of an exclusive pursuit of
Reason, and that it is men who have led it thus off course. Such
arguments were put forward, for example, by Dora Russell, now
something of a heroine of the radical feminist movement. She
believes that men have always been unduly fond of mathematics and
engineering, and have therefore found themselves dominated by
their own inventions. All the economic, social and political ills of the
world can, she holds, be ascribed to this cause. Women, because of
their different and, on the whole, less mathematical way of thinking,
would never have invented the machines in the first place; and if they
had, they would never have allowed them to become more important
than feelings of generosity, sympathy and love. Men have valued only
one kind of knowledge, and have been prepared to search for it

Women's Education and its Future 289

anywhere and at whatever cost. Women would never have done so, since they are able to value other things than science and scientific truth. Such is Dora Russell's dogma. Such a conventional and sentimental view of the difference between women and men may be thought unworthy of further consideration. It may be seen at once to be absurd. But if the radical feminists are prepared to suggest not only that women are irrational (an accusation women have long been accustomed to), but also that they prefer to be so and even have a duty to be so, then there seems to me to be a danger in the doctrine. For, in the name of the proper education of women, this doctrine may issue in a kind of isolationism of which Women's Studies would be only the first step. If the educational isolation of women, their separateness from men in the matter of knowledge and learning were to spread throughout the university curriculum, then women would indeed be in the kind of ghetto from which they so painfully emerged before the First World War.

But there would be an important difference. Then it seemed clear, at least to most women, that there was a battle to be fought; and they had the will to fight it. Radical feminism, on the other hand, undermines the spirit; for it may seem disloyal to the Women's Movement to object to the direction in which it seems to lead. There is a dilemma: if women do not support separatism, they are betraying one another. If they do, they are betraying the standards of scholarship, of evidence and of academic rigour which they have been at such pains to acquire and adhere to.

In the early years of the century, it was practically impossible for women undergraduates to forget that that was what they were. It was not only that they were so few, but that they and others had continuously to call into question their rôle, to justify their presence in the universities, to protect themselves against ridicule or other forms of attack. Later, between the wars and for what seems like a long time afterwards, it became possible for women in the universities simply to get on with their lives. Though still greatly outnumbered, they were able to take a rest from reflecting constantly on themselves and their rôle. Both junior and senior members were accepted, and respected, as a part of the scene. Though women were conscious of obstacles remaining in some of the professions, and though many of them felt that their educational opportunities were not perfectly equal to men's, there was, all the same, a sense that steady progress could be made, by going on in the same direction. Radical feminism, in my opinion, is in danger of putting the clock back. It has reintroduced a kind of persuasive self-consciousness among those women who embrace it. What had seemed like progress suddenly came to be represented as a more subtle defeat, a more complete and total surrender to the enemy, Men, and this when the university had at last come to seem a comfortable place for women. The radical feminist's mission to raise the consciousness of all women, translated into university policy, could lead to a demand that the separate nature of women's cognitive processes (a belief on which this feminism is founded) should be given instititutional recognition. This I believe would be a blow to education itself.

I sincerely hope, therefore (and indeed believe) that radical feminism will be rejected by the universities as a whole. For a preoccupation with the question what it is like to be a woman in higher education, though doubtless of some interest, is not the best background against which women should get on, more and more of them, with the business of education, with learning and teaching. Let us turn, then, instead, to conservative feminism. Though the principle of this feminism must be formulated, publicised and held with faith by anyone interested in the education of women, it is nevertheless a principle so general and so simple that it will not require much elaboration. For it is a version of the principle of justice itself: that no one should be at an educational disadvantage, if that results from baseless discrimination. Women are human; and if higher education is among those good things from which humans benefit, and to which they may even be thought entitled, then women should have as much of it as men. This principle should be taken for granted. Whatever kind of education is held to be enlightening, useful, good in itself, women should have equal access to it.

Conservative feminism, then, does not seek to revolutionise the world. It seeks merely to ensure that, in the world as it is, women are not treated with injustice. It would appear to follow that, whatever the education on offer in the next decade or so, the demands of feminism would be satisfied if this education were fairly and equally distributed, among men and women alike. And this is, on the whole, true. But things are rather more complicated than that. For the goal of genuine justice in education is still some way from being achieved, despite all the advances of the twentieth century; and in the course of achieving their aim, it may be that women will have to contribute to some reforms in the educational system itself, even if they do not seek to revolutionise it.

In the pages that follow, I want to suggest what some of these reforms may be, and how they may be brought about. By no means all the changes will come as a result of action by women, or by their foresight. For all kinds of different reasons, the face of education as a whole will change. But women will be more fully integrated into the education of the future (and in higher education will certainly be more numerous). They will therefore, if they so wish, be in a better position than ever before to initiate change, and to influence the educational pattern of the future.

It is necessary to look first at the areas within which educational equality for women have not yet been fully achieved. It is a cliché of the 1980s that the problem lies largely at school. It may all start as early as primary school. A great many books have been written in recent years showing that teachers tend to pay more attention to boys in class than to girls, when classes are mixed; that girls are, and are expected to be, 'good at most things', able to get on by themselves, orderly and quiet. They will not need much help. Boys, on the other hand, tend to demand and get attention, and though some of them are backward compared with their female contemporaries, they are held to be more likely to produce brilliant, eccentric or imaginative work. Such seem to be the assumptions of many teachers, and of course such expectations are, as we are frequently told, largely self-fulfilling. And the attitude of teachers will tend to reinforce unspoken assumptions often found at home, that the education of girls is of less importance than that of boys. Such asssumptions are astonishingly widespread and difficult to eradicate, and are made just as much by women as by men.

More serious trouble may arise at secondary school. Once again, this aspect of the sociology of education has been well documented. Certainly discussion has been widespread, and not merely in feminist publications. For all children, girls and boys alike, have to make important educational choices as early as their third or fourth year at school. They are then no more than fourteen years old, and it is a bad time to make decisions which will affect their whole future. For the unselfconsciousness of childhood has been left behind, and rôle-playing is at its height. Pressures on girls are peculiarly strong at this age, especially from the popular press, advertising and romantic stories. They must at all costs be 'feminine'; they must have and hold their man; above all they must be attractive. The belief that boys do not find clever girls attractive is widely held, certainly by girls, and perhaps also by boys. As for competitive or ambitious girls, they are thought the worst of all. And so there is a tendency for girls to fall

behind their male contemporaries at this stage, and to be less
ambitious about their futures.

This tendency is the more marked as boys become increasingly
engaged with electronic gadgets, computer games and other technology at home. Much more money is spent on this kind of hardware for
the sake of boys than of girls; from a very early age, boys may have
been playing computer games of which all the programs are concerned with conventional 'boys' subjects, such as war or soccer. Thus
ancient presuppositions are reinforced by modern means, and this
shows up at school in the greater competence of boys in the whole
field of science and technology.

There can thus be seen to exist two related trends, one for girls to
give up all academic aspirations, and settle to leave school as soon as
possible; the other, if they propose to seek higher education, for them
to choose arts subjects, not science. Obviously this means that, in the
first place, many girls who would enjoy higher education and benefit
from it, and from whom the world in general would gain, if they were
educated, are lost altogether to education, because they themselves
rejected it, early in their school careers. Equally, many girls who do
apply for places in institutions of higher education either fail to get
places, because there are too many applicants in arts subjects, or do
not very much benefit from their degree courses when they embark
on them. The urge to read English or History or Modern Languages,
felt at school because those were the subjects in which they did best,
may not survive the scholarly demands of a university course.

Such trends as these will not, I think, change by themselves. Nor
can they be changed by any edict of central government, more and
more prone, as it seems, to intervene not only in the financing of the
universities, but in the balance of the student intake and the nature of
the subjects to be studied. The only thing which could begin to
reverse the tendencies described would be a general change in
attitude to the education of women, a change which must stem from
the attitudes of women to themselves. I am not suggesting that a day
will ever come when girls will choose predominantly scientific or
mathematical subjects at school. I doubt if this could happen, given
that girls are emotionally ready and eager, on the whole, to enjoy
literature and language at an earlier age than boys, and are likely
therefore both to excel in these sorts of subject at school, and to love
them. Nevertheless a change in women's beliefs about themselves, a
greater confidence in their own ability to master and control the
physical universe and, above all, a greater belief in their own

independence and autonomy ... these changes could have a great effect.

It is for this reason that I believe it is necessary to analyse the central concepts of feminism in order to predict the likely future of women's education at St Hugh's or any other university institution. I have suggested the ways in which a radical feminism might damage the prospects of education for women. I shall now try to show how a conservative feminism may be able to help remedy the remaining educational disadvantages under which women still suffer.

The premise of the argument is the very proposition that the radical feminists most vigorously deny, namely that true education and learning is a common ideal. Whatever forms education may take, whatever the enormous variety of subject-matter and of method to be found in the universities, within every range of studies, truths may be discovered indifferently, by any student. It is in this faith that both teaching and research proceeds at the universities. No one who, as the outcome of his research, claimed that what he had set out was true only 'for him' would have reached a respectable or even an intelligible conclusion. The purpose of research, as of learning and teaching, in universities is to make discoveries, to explore new ways of thought which may then be shared and communicated. One of the great changes in education during this century has been towards wider and wider communication. Historical and scientific discoveries, philosophical or sociological methods, all have a far larger potential public than they used to. This is not simply a phenomenon of the media. It is part of the democratisation of education itself. It is all the more important, therefore, to reject any kind of higher education that would reintroduce barriers now beginning to be broken down. The female ghetto of the radical feminists runs wholly counter to the spirit of a common learning.

For education is becoming demystified, and will, I believe, become ever more accessible in the next years, even though it is often said, truly, that the concepts of, say, physics, biochemistry or economics get more complex all the time. Those women, then, who are anxious to see genuine educational justice, our conservative feminists, have a central part to play in this process. In the first place, women have always been good at demystification. In the old days when they had to fight for the privilege of learning Latin and Greek, they did so, at least partly, in order to penetrate the mysteries with which their brothers were occupied at school; then knowledge of the Classics turned out after all not to be mysterious, but simply an enormously fruitful source of enlightenment and pleasure, in which anyone could share if they wished. Rather as rituals and private languages, clubs and hierarchies, the life-blood of the nineteenth-century boys' schools, tend to wither away once women are admitted, so a more realistic, less elitist concept of learning has already come into existence in the universities with the advent of women. Forty or fifty years ago, a girl reading Classical Mods would feel herself to be at one with the grammar school boys, however smart and private her own school, because together they were struggling against the effortless superiority in knowledge of Latin and Greek of the boys from Winchester and Westminster. At least in the case of Mods and Greats, there was an educational class war, and the girls did not belong to the upper classes, hardly to the middle. Now this war is over. Generally, girls are increasingly able to think of themselves as the educational equals of boys at university, whatever subject they are reading.

Obviously the changes within schools, and the higher proportion of pupils from state schools who form the university population, have a great deal to do with this change. But it is within these schools, many of them newly sending pupils on to higher education, that, as I have suggested, women need to be especially vigilant on behalf of girls.

Schools themselves are becoming democratised. The virtual disappearance of the grammar school, with its tradition of preparation for higher education, has meant an even greater need among pupils for definite and positive motivation, if they are to persist with their education. And, in addition, there has recently been a tendency (already, I suspect, on the sharp decline) for teachers to be more concerned with the less able child than the academically distinguished, more eager for mixed-ability teaching for the sake of the slow learner, than for sets and streams for the sake of the quick. The enthusiasm for the integration of handicapped children into ordinary classes, though perhaps more marked as a matter of theory than of practice, may further distract attention from the academically ambitious, and especially from those many girls who need only a bit of encouragement before they *become* ambitious. There is an increasing danger within the genuine comprehensive school that girls may slide into the soft subjects, the easy options, or join the group who wish only to leave school as soon as possible. I do not believe that such an outcome for girls is a *necessary* consequence of the comprehensive system. It simply needs more vigilance to prevent it than all teachers are prepared to give.

Moreover, with the democratisation of education at school, we are almost certain in the next few years to see a radical change in the system of examinations at school. Indeed reform of the system is on the way. Though it would be rash to try to predict in detail what changes there will be, it is likely that there will be less specalisation in future, and that a wider spread of subjects will be studied by everyone in the sixth form. In the past, the universities have always objected to this kind of reform, on the grounds that students would simply know less when they arrived at the university, and would need an extra year to achieve the standard they now reach at their final examinations. I have never entirely believed in this argument, largely because what is learned at school for A levels is often immediately forgotten; and much of it is better forgotten. There is a lot in the theory that a generally sharp wit and a readiness to work, combined with a general knowledge of how to read intelligently and how to discover things, are the best preparation for university, even where what is to be studied there is, say, a language or a specific area of science. But in any case, whether this theory is correct or not, I believe that universities will have to accept in future that students will come up with less specific knowledge, though perhaps more general competence than before, and courses and methods of teaching will have to be adapted to fit. More than ever, university teachers will have to interest themselves in communicating with their pupils. It is sometimes held that in order to make such teachers effective they ought all to undergo training. I do not think that this is either necessary or acceptable. I hope that it will always remain true that a teacher at a university will be distinguished from a teacher at school by his commitment, for at least a proportion of his time, to research; and that such a teacher can learn to teach out of the depth of his own understanding of his subject. After all, he does not, or not usually, have to face the problem faced by school teachers of teaching the reluctant, the delinquent or those who would much rather be anywhere else on earth than where they are, in the classroom. It is to woo those pupils, and make education tolerable to them, that teachers need to be trained. But it is likely that, with or without training, university teachers will in future have to take their own teaching more seriously than before, and will have to begin, if they have not already done so, to think of their subjects as essentially to be shared and communicated. The old-fashioned 'academic woman', who despised simplification as vulgar, who pretended to assume that all her pupils were as scholarly as she, or, if not, were failures . . . this woman will have no place in the new university. The new teacher, on the contrary, must be prepared to explain the general principles of her subject to complete beginners, and to explain the different directions in which the subject can develop. It is likely that to cater for the new, more generalist pupil, universities will offer more and more combined courses, or more options within particular single courses, and to help students to make sensible choices when they are already at the university will become an increasingly important part of the university teacher's rôle.

And so there is another risk that should be faced: just as now, at school, there is a tendency for girls to choose the easy options, and leave the 'hard' subjects to boys, so at university the more choices there are, the more vigilance will be required to see that for various social reasons, or from lack of self-confidence, girls do not get into the way of choosing soft options, that they do not avoid those subjects in which they feel that they will not be able to compete with boys or do not wish to. Obviously, the more successful schools have been in avoiding such sex-linked choosing, the easier the task will be at the university level. But it is something that should be watched.

There are faint signs that in the next decade or so polytechnics, originally supposed to provide vocational and technical education to a high standard, may be about to revert to this rôle, or rather to begin to fulfil it (for they never developed in the way intended by the planners). If the bipartite system of higher education continues, but with the polytechnics growing in esteem, and specialising more and more in fashionable subjects such as biotechnology or information technology, then there will be a new battle for the feminists to face. Not only will they have to make sure that, within the university, girls are not allowed to drift into 'soft' subjects, but they will have to fight to ensure that girls have genuinely equal chances with boys to enter the polytechnics, if this is where their interests lie. Entry to many polytechnic courses is already extremely competitive. Such competition is likely to increase. Once again, the main burden of ensuring that girls have a proper chance in such competition must fall on the schools.

It is clear that changes at school must not only be reflected in universities, but must to some extent be engineered by universities. In the future, the relation between the two parts of education, always important but somewhat uneasy, will, I believe, have to be closer, better articulated and more genuinely co-operative than in the past. And here our conservative feminists have a crucial role. If they have reflected on their own place in society, and on the education they have had, and how it might have been improved, then they are less likely than men to take the status quo as unalterable. They are more likely to want to initiate change in schools that will result in change in the university. Those of them who enter the teaching profession are likely to be alert to the kinds of disadvantage which girls may suffer from and, as parents, they are likely to insist that their daughters are taken as seriously, in terms of education, as their sons. The very self-awareness, the so-called raised consciousness, which in the radical feminist constituted a danger, in the conservative will constitute a strength. It will give to the educated woman of the future a critical attitude to the educational system as a whole, which can lead to positive improvements, always within the framework of the assumption that education is a benefit, to be fairly distributed. Equality of opportunity will remain the goal of this feminist, just as it was the goal of the feminists 100 years ago.

There are two final points: in the next few years, as we enter the twenty-first century, it will, I suppose, become increasingly clear that we shall never return to a time of full employment. This is a difficult view for the educational establishment as a whole to come to terms with. For it seems to demand two contradictory responses. If there are fewer jobs, then competition for them will be greater. Therefore it seems only fair to pupils, whether at school, university or polytechnic, to prepare them as energetically as possible to compete. This line of thinking leads to an increased emphasis on vocational education. The applied will always be preferred to the pure in educational terms. On the other hand, if a considerable number of people, when they leave school or university, are never going to have full-time employment, or are never going to be employed in the kind of work they would ideally choose and enjoy, then it is all the more important to educate them so that they may find their lives enjoyable apart from work. To this end the 'pure' subjects, like history, music or philosophy, may seem increasingly valuable. Opinion swings between these two perspectives.

Whichever way schools or universities go, women, whether specifically feminist or not, are peculiarly well-fitted to open the eyes of politicians and educationalists to the new world of mixed employment. In this world, people will work partly at home and partly outside; men will be as likely as women to be at home looking after the children; jobs may be shared; the old and the young, the male and the female, are very much more likely to be in roughly the same boat. Women have for years been accustomed to this kind of mixed life. They have never, traditionally, felt that if they were not paid for doing something it was not worth doing. Generations of women cleaning the house, doing the cooking, looking after the very young and the very old, as well as generations doing their embroidery or painting in watercolours have accustomed them to value what they do in a quite different way, and to distinguish work from non-work differently. So women have often been readier to value education just on the grounds that life is more enjoyable with it than without it, even if their education didn't, as they say, 'lead' anywhere. In this kind of attitude to education women will, I suspect, have to be the leaders.

Secondly, in the new world, universities and polytechnics, as well as the sixth forms of schools, will somehow have to dispose themselves to accept students at any age, and at any stage of their careers. They will also have to arrange for part-time and evening students, who can work for degrees or professional qualifications. Women have so far been better than men at seeing the advantages of this kind of education. To reorganise universities to accept it as a normal part of their commitment will be administratively extremely difficult, but not impossible. Women may well have to be pioneers in this sphere, and individual colleges, perhaps especially women's colleges, could give a lead within the university.

I have been guilty of many generalisations in the foregoing pages. I have suggested that women, as a class, are liable to this, prone to that. I have spoken of trends and tendencies affecting all women and all men. There is obvious danger in this. Men are different one from another, and so are women. Is there anything that can be said of *all*? If I were dealing in psychology, I would hesitate. But there are facts, sociological and historical facts, illustrated, among other places, in this book itself, which can make it necessary still to talk about the education of women in such general terms. I have argued that there are still battles to be won. But even if all the fighting were over, the education of women would still be something worth analysing, both how it has been and how it is. Moreover, even the most conservative of feminists would not wish to deny that men and women are different; and their educational *style*, in learning, teaching and research, may always remain distinct. Whatever may happen in the next 100 years, one certain prediction is that the difference between the sexes will remain an interesting topic. Our question is not whether such differences can be eliminated, but how they can best be used. It is to this question that I believe the conservative, reforming feminist must supply the answer.

Select Bibliography

HISTORY OF ST HUGH'S AND ITS MEMBERS

Apart from various brief items published in *St Hugh's Club Paper* and *St Hugh's Chronicle*, the only published account of the history of St Hugh's is an article by Miss E. E. S. Procter in *The American Oxonian*, vol. XLVIII, no. 1 (January 1961), and this only gives the bare outline.

Dame Elizabeth Wordsworth

Wordsworth, E., *Glimpses of the Past*, 2nd edn. (Mowbray, 1913).
Battiscombe, G., *Reluctant Pioneer* (Constable, 1978).

Miss Moberly

Moberly, C. A. E., *Dulce Domum* (Murray, 1911).
Moberly, C. A. E. and Jourdain, E. F., *An Adventure*, 4th edn. by Edith Olivier (Faber & Faber, 1931).
Moberly, C. A. E. and Jourdain, E. F., *An Adventure*. 5th edn. by Joan Evans (Faber & Faber, 1955). (This book inspired quite a lot of literature, too extensive to be listed here.)
Olivier, E., *Four Victorian Ladies of Wiltshire* (Faber & Faber, 1945). (Chapter 2 is about Miss Moberly.)

Women in Oxford and Women's Education

Bailey, G., *A Short History of Lady Margaret Hall* (Oxford University Press, 1923).
Brittain, V., *The Women at Oxford* (Harrap, 1960).
Butler, R. F., *A History of St Anne's Society*, vol. 2 (Oxford University Press, 1949). (This has some information about Miss Rogers and forms a sequel to: Prichard, M. H. and Butler, R. F., *The Society of Oxford Home-Students* (Oxonian Press, 1930).)
Howarth, J., section on women in Oxford in the early days forthcoming (c. 1987) in part of the *History of Oxford University*, general editor T. H. Aston (Clarendon Press).
Rogers, A. M. H., *Degrees by Degrees* (Oxford University Press, 1938) (this contains a brief appreciation of Miss Rogers by Miss Gwyer).
Victoria County History of Oxford, vol. III, contains articles on the women's colleges.

Appendix I: Women and Science in St Hugh's and the University

Dr Mary Lunn, Vice-Principal, St Hugh's

Over the years, science within St Hugh's has grown and flourished, nurtured by some determined women scientists, Dr Ida Busbridge, Dr Madge Adam and, more recently, Dr Mary Lunt. Since the fellowship has been opened to both men and women, the College has profited from several of the many new science posts created within the University. The total number of tutorial fellows in science (including Mathematics) is now 10 out of a tutorial fellowship of 25, at October 1984. This move has been paralleled by an increase in the number of girls studying science within the College, and by a wider coverage of the science subjects on the Governing Body.

In the University at large, the number of women undergraduates has grown and is still increasing. As the figures below show, much progress has been made in the eight years from 1975 to 1983.

	Total applications	% women	Total acceptances	% women in first year intake
1975	5 298	28	2 719	25
1983	7 563	41	2 853	40

The biggest jump in the percentage of women accepted (28 per cent to 36 per cent) came between October 1978 and October 1979, when a large number of men's colleges became mixed. As can be seen above, men still achieve a higher acceptance rate than women. Two factors partially affect the rates, the higher percentage of men from public schools, and the higher percentage of pre-A-level candidates among the women.

To evaluate the effect on women in science, we must examine the entrance examination for November 1983, when the girls comprised 30 per cent of the science applicants and, again, a rather lower percentage of acceptances. Within science, the numbers of girls applying in the various subjects fluctuate enormously:

Applications in science

Overall	30%
Medicine	44%
Biochemistry and Biology	40%
Mathematics	29%
Chemistry	23%
Physics and Engineering	14%

A brief look at two particular subjects clarifies the current position.

Overall numbers of women applying to read mathematics

Year	Total women	Total	% women	
1971	97	Not known		
1979	108	400	23	entrance examination only –
1981	133	504	26	does not include other
1983	139	480	29	methods of entry.

The percentage of girls currently reading Mathematics is about 25 per cent.

Number of women taking engineering science finals

1970	1971	1972	1973	1974	1975	1976
2	2	3	4	4	0	3

1977	1978	1979	1980	1981	1982	1983
2	3	6	5	6	9	10

This growth has been maintained within the year currently in the University, and represents a significant increase in a school of just over 100 students. There has been a corresponding growth within St Hugh's.

One of the major constraints on numbers in very recent years has been the imposition, by the government, of an overall quota of home and European Community students for each university. Of the current quota in Oxford, 40 per cent are science students (includes Mathematics). This in turn has led the University, with the colleges' agreement, to impose a quota on each individual college. For 1984–6 St Hugh's has a quota which splits into 36 per cent science students, 64 per cent arts students. The percentages and total numbers are calculated on past numbers within each college. The quotas are difficult to achieve in the light of the growing number of offers made on A-level results. Further, they represent a new constraint on each college.

The prediction for the future is that the increase in the number of girls studying science within the University will continue, and that the numbers within the College will remain at least steady.

Appendix II: St Hugh's College: The Acquisition of Property and Progress of Building from 1886 to 1981

Susan Clear

The following details show how St Hugh's College has grown over the last century from one small hostel in Norham Road, to its present size.

1886   No. 25 Norham Road was rented by Miss Wordsworth, at an annual rent, initially for one year. It was then rented for a further year.

1887   No. 24 Norham Road was rented for one year.

1888   The leasehold of 17 Norham Gardens was acquired by Miss Wordsworth, and this house replaced Nos. 24 and 25 as accommodation. The leasehold was transferred to the Trust in 1895.

1892   A new wing was built on to 17 Norham Gardens, adding students' rooms, a dining room and a separate room for a Chapel.

1901   The leasehold of 28 Norham Gardens was acquired.

1909   Fyfield Lodge, in Fyfield Road, was rented.

1912   The leasehold of The Mount on the corner of St Margaret's Road and Banbury Road was acquired.

1914–16 The Mount was demolished, and the major part of the Main Building was constructed.

1919   The leasehold of 4 St Margaret's Road was acquired, and the building came into College use.

1924   Dr Joan Evans bought the leasehold of 82 Woodstock Road, and gave it to College for their use.

1927   The freehold of the site on which the main College building stood was purchased. Later, 1 St Margaret's Road and 89 Banbury Road were also purchased.

1928   The first stage of the Mary Gray Allen Wing was completed.

Late
1920's   No. 3 St Margaret's Road came into College use.

1931   The freeholds of 2, 3 and 4 St Margaret's Road were purchased. No. 2 was still subject to an existing lease.

1932   The freeholds of 74, 76, 78, 80 and 82 Woodstock Road were purchased. No. 80 now came into College use, alongside No. 82. The remaining properties were still subject to existing leases.

1936   No. 1 St Margaret's Road was demolished. Extra rooms were added to Mary Gray Allen, and the library extension was completed.

302

1943   The leasehold of 72 Woodstock Road, The Shrubbery, was acquired.

1951   The freehold of 72 Woodstock Road was purchased (since its derequisition in 1946, as it was not suitable for undergraduate use, it had been let to the *Maison Française*). No. 78 Woodstock Road came into College use. The freeholds of 85 and 87 Banbury Road, and 9 to 13 Canterbury Road were obtained. Although these properties were all subject to existing leaseholds, their purchase meant that St Hugh's now owned the entire island site, over 14 acres, bounded by Banbury Road, Canterbury Road, Woodstock Road and St Margaret's Road.

1957   No. 2 St Margaret's Road came into College use.

1958   The two south extensions to Main Building were completed, together with a small extension to the kitchens.

1963   The College took over the use of 72 Woodstock Road from the *Maison Française*, and the house became the Principal's Lodging.

1964–7 During 1964–5, the New Building, now called the Kenyon Building, was constructed. This was followed by the demolition of 2, 3 and 4 St Margaret's Road. The Wolfson Building was then put up in their place.

1965   The Buttery (later called the Wordsworth Room) was completed.

1967   Nos. 11 and 12 Canterbury Road came into College use. The ground floor of 12 became the Middle Common Room.

1971   No. 74 Woodstock Road was refurbished, and then let out as flats.

1980   No. 76 Woodstock Road was refurbished, and then let out as flats.

1981   No. 10 Canterbury Road came into College use.

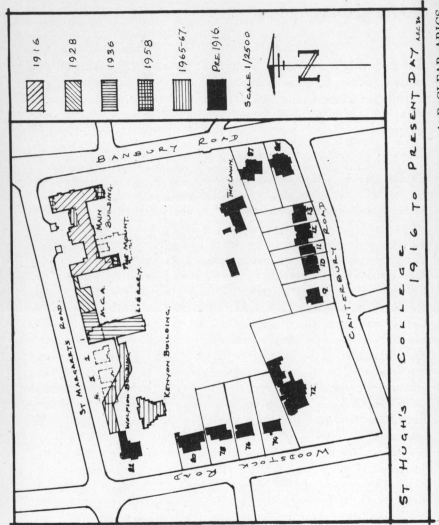

A. E. CLEAR, ARICS

St Hugh's College 1916 to Present Day

Appendix III: St Hugh's Garden

The following is a historical account of the early days of St Hugh's garden, written by Miss Procter, in 1952. Miss Procter was *Custos Hortulorum* from 1952 to 1962. The office had remained in abeyance from the time of Miss Roger's death until Miss Procter was appointed.

ST HUGH'S COLLEGE GARDEN

St Hugh's College Garden has never been planned as a whole; it is made up of a number of distinct units, laid out at different times, in different styles and acquired piecemeal by the College over a period of thirty-five years. In some case dividing walls, fences or hedges have been removed, in others they have been retained; extensions to the College buildings have necessitated some alterations and more have been brought about by the erection of temporary buildings when the College was requisitioned during the last war. The three largest units which have gone to the formation of the garden are the former 'Mount' garden at the junction of the Banbury Road and St Margaret's Road, the 'Lawn' garden next to it and an undeveloped area in the centre of the island site; besides these there are the smaller gardens of the College houses fronting on St Margaret's Road and on Woodstock Road, and part of the garden of the 'Shrubbery' – in all about ten acres.

The lease of the 'Mount' was acquired by St Hugh's College from University College in 1913; the freehold was not purchased until 1927. The garden of the 'Mount' extended to about $4\frac{1}{2}$ acres; the house faced the Banbury Road but stood well back from it, and was approached by a long drive between conifers, some of which still survive on the main lawn. The western boundary of the garden was marked by a line of fine beeches which probably once formed part of a hedge. The yews to the south, alongside the boundary of the 'Lawn' garden, stand so close together that they almost certainly grew from a hedge. Besides these two rows of trees to the west and south, the 'Mount' garden was notable for its profusion of timber trees which

305

formed a wooded belt between it and the garden of the 'Lawn'. These trees, most of which still survive, included beeches, hornbeams, elms, horse chestnuts, acacias, scotch firs and a fine specimen of silver cedar; underneath them evergreens and hazel bushes helped to form a wild garden which was much more wood-like than it is now. The southern portion of the present main lawn was then a paddock of rough grass, divided from the garden by a wire fence; some iron staples to which the fence was attached are still embedded in the trunk of a large pear-tree. To the south-west of the house a winding path bordered by flower beds led down to a dell, or depression – originally in all probability a shallow gravel pit – which a former tenant, the Reverend Robert Hartley, Vicar of St Margaret's from 1896 to 1906, had turned into a fernery. Beyond this dell was an old orchard, and around the dell, screening it from the orchard and the paddock, a ring of cypresses, conifers and ornamental trees and shrubs, including a clump of *Berberis vulgaris*, had been planted. The old house was pulled down and the much larger college building was sited nearer to St Margaret's Road, and so that it faced north and south, instead of east and west. This necessitated considerable alterations in the garden. Much of the kitchen garden, which lay to the north of the old house, was destroyed; most of the drive was rendered useless and was taken up; the paddock was levelled and turned into tennis courts. A number of the chief features of the present garden, however – the great trees to the south and west, the wild garden, the winding paths and shrubberies, and the elaborately laid out ornamental garden in the dell – were all inherited from the 'Mount' garden. The head gardener at the 'Mount', John Ball, was also taken into the service of the College.

In 1916 St Hugh's moved into its new buildings, and from the beginning of its occupation the oversight of the garden was assumed by Miss Annie Rogers, one of the chief protagonists of women's education in Oxford. Her control was nominally shared by a garden committee, whose secretary she was and whose meetings she convened. The earliest minutes of the committee reflect wartime exhortations to grow more food; there are references to the growing of rhubarb and potatoes, and to the planting of currant and gooseberry bushes, and of plum- and apple-trees. In 1918 the College was keeping both bees and pigs, but by the next year the bees had all died and had not been replaced. The College did not repeat its experiment in bee-keeping, but pigs were kept until 1933, when they were given up because Ball, by then an old man close on retirement, no longer felt able to look after them. The pig-sty was in the south-west corner of the garden, against the wall of the 'Lawn' coach house, and was hidden from the path by evergreens. The meetings of the first garden committee soon became intermittent, and after December 1923 they ceased; no reports were presented to the Council in 1925 and 1926. This lack of records makes it difficult to reconstruct the history of the garden during these years. After the incorporation of the College by Royal Charter the garden committee reappeared and in 1927 became one of the standing committees of the Council; at the same time the office of *Custos Hortulorum* was created for Miss Rogers, an office which she held until her death in October 1937. The new committee met once a year in the Michaelmas Term, when it approved for transmission to the Council the report on the previous year drawn up by the *Custos*, and gave general sanction to her plans for work during the succeeding year. Matters which arose between the annual meetings were dealt with by the *Custos* on her own authority, and only in exceptional circumstances, as when extra land was acquired, were special meetings of the committee held.

There is no doubt that the garden benefited greatly from the enlightened despotism of Miss Rogers. She devoted to it endless time and thought and, as she gave up one by one her other interests and activities, her devotion to St Hugh's garden increased and its care became an ever more absorbing interest. Day by day she could be seen in the garden, superintending the work of the gardeners or showing the rarer trees and plants to appreciative friends. Her greatest interest was in the acquisition of flowering trees and shrubs and for this purpose the garden is well suited. The long south front of the building gives ample space for wall shrubs and climbers; in the terrace front, sheltered by its shallow wings from wind and frost, such tender plants as passion flower, myrtle, loquat and pomegranate can survive unprotected through the winter. The spacious lawns, shrubberies and borders also give plenty of scope for the growing ornamental trees. A wide border was made alongside the Banbury Road and planted with varieties of cratægus, syringa, berberis, spirea and other shrubs. Flowering trees were also planted on the lawn and in the wild garden where the undergrowth was considerably thinned out. By the time of Miss Roger's death the garden had acquired a representative collection of ornamental trees and shrubs which by their flowers, foliage or fruits add to the beauty of the garden and certainly constitute its chief interest. This collection has since been kept up and enlarged. Nearly all these trees and shrubs were obtained by gift or exchange. The *Magnolia soulangiana* on the main lawn, for example, was given by the students to celebrate the armistice of 1918. Miss Rogers instituted the custom by which each new member of the Council presented a tree to the garden. This custom has been continued, and each new Fellow now presents one. Unfortunately there is no complete list of the ornamental trees and shrubs growing in the garden, but it is hoped that by degrees one may be compiled; nor are all the specimens as yet labelled, although an appreciable number of them are.

The chief new feature added to the garden when the College was built was the terrace, although it was not completely paved until some time after the building was occupied, and the design of the paving has since been altered. The paving as first laid out was not satisfactory. Most of the rough paving alongside the low containing wall and in the two rectangular areas surrounded by the flagged paths was laid on the soil instead of on concrete; when weeds became rampant the edges of the stones were cemented together in an attempt to check the weeds, thus making it impossible to move the stones to eradicate unwanted vegetation. The gardeners never had sufficient time to attend to the terrace, and the amateur labour of members of both the Senior and the Junior Common Rooms failed to make much impression. In spite of additional labour and expenditure in 1923, the condition of the terrace continued to deteriorate, and by 1926 it was a mass of weeds among which a few rock plants struggled for survival. In 1927 the Council voted up to £200 to put the terrace in order, and the paving was relaid according to a design prepared by the present Principal. This design aimed at drastically reducing the area on which plants could grow and at making the weeding of this area easy. The rough pavement in the two rectangular areas was taken up and most of it relaid on concrete and cemented. Each of the areas of permanent pavement was surrounded by four 'beds' for plants. These 'beds' were raised slightly above the level of the pavement and were lightly surfaced with stones which can be easily moved to facilitate weeding. Most of the border alongside the terrace wall was treated in the same way as the 'beds'. The work was carried out in the Long Vacation of 1927, partly by a contractor and partly by the gardeners, under the supervision of Miss Rogers who also supervised the planting of the 'beds'. The terrace is not a rock garden and, although there are some interesting plants on it, it is not intended as a collection of rare specimens. The effect aimed at is colour, and this is obtained by massing together helianthemums, alpine phloxes, saxifrages, campanulas, veronicas and other low-growing plants. Throughout Trinity Term the terrace is a mosaic of colours which blend together in ever changing patterns. It is at its best at the end of May and early June when the helianthemums are in full bloom, and at that season it is the principal attraction of the garden.

At different times between 1919 and 1932 the College bought first the leases and later the freeholds of the 'Lawn', and 3 and 4 St Margaret's Road, and 80 and 82 Woodstock Road and used the houses for the accommodation of undergraduates. All these houses have gardens; the largest being those of the 'Lawn' and 82 Woodstock Road. The 'Lawn' garden was only divided from the College garden by a fence and, when the freehold of the 'Lawn' was purchased from Lincoln College in 1928, this fence was removed and the two gardens thrown into one. The 'Lawn' garden with its shrubberies, timber trees and heart-shaped lawn between the road and the house harmonises well with the College garden. It is, indeed, probable that these two gardens were laid out at much the same time, for both reflect gardening fashion of the mid-nineteenth century. At this time the nurseries and seed-beds which had been located in the south-west corner of the College garden were removed to the 'Lawn' garden behind the house and their former site, which was partly enclosed by a hedge, was converted into a lawn on which some flowering trees were planted. The gardens of the other four College houses were surrounded by brick walls which were retained; these gardens thus remain distinct from the College garden.

In the spring of 1932 the College bought from St John's College the freehold of an undeveloped piece of land of rather over two acres in extent which occupies the centre of the island site. The westernmost and larger portion of this land was held by Lady Whitehead on a tenancy which terminated at Michaelmas 1932. It was used as a kitchen garden and was well stocked with fruit-trees. A broad gravel walk running north and south, with an herbaceous border on either side divided it into halves. Most of the plants from this border were removed by Lady Whitehead to the 'Shrubbery' garden and some of the rest were later used to restock the College borders. The College made comparatively little use of the 'Whitehead piece', and most of it was let out in small allotments. It had been bought to prevent possible development by St John's College and not because St Hugh's had any immediate use for it. The easternmost portion of this undeveloped area was held by Alderman Ansell, whose tenancy did not expire until 1934. It was divided into two distinct parts. Nearest the 'Lawn' was a small apple orchard enclosed by a hedge; this became a Fellows' garden. The remaining strip of ground was used by Alderman Ansell as an allotment, and access to it was by a rough cart track between the College garden and 1 St Margaret's Road. During the winter of 1934–5 the 'Ansell piece' was cleared, levelled and sown to form a lawn, and the fence dividing it from the College garden was removed. It was on this new lawn that the marquee was pitched for the Jubilee dinner on 27 June 1936. By that time the house at 1 St Margaret's Road had been demolished and the new Library built on its garden. One practical convenience accrued from the acquisition of the 'Whitehead' and 'Ansell' pieces – direct access was provided through the garden from the College to the College houses.

After Miss Roger's death in 1937 the Gardens Committee was enlarged and took over more control of the gardens; the office of *Custos Hortulorum* remained in abeyance until 1952, when the Principal was appointed *Custos*. Up to the outbreak of war the committee was occupied with two projects: the replanning of the area between the west wing of the main building and the new Library, and the provision of a memorial to Miss Rogers. The erection of the first part of the Mary Gray Allen Wing in 1927 had not necessitated any radical alterations in the garden but only some adaptation of the existing lawn, path and herbaceous border to the south. The second extension in 1936 created a new problem. The Mary Gray Allen Wing was extended on to the site of 1 St Margaret's Road and was then continued at right angles so that part of the residential block and the Library lie to the west of the former boundary of the 'Mount' garden. A conservative treatment, carried out according to a plan prepared by Professor Myres, was adopted. Although the trees marking the old boundary were left, the area enclosed by the west wing of the main building, the Mary Gray Allen Wing and the Library, was treated as a whole. The northern end of the path under the trees, together with a neglected rockery, were removed and the lawn was extended to the Library. The herbaceous border was also extended but was completely replanned; instead of a side border with an irregular line of fruit-trees down the centre, two borders were made divided by a grass path with half standard apple-trees on one side and varieties of thorns and crab apples on the other. These trees were the gift of Professor Myres. Although the western end of the southern border is under the shade of the largest beech, it has proved possible by careful planting to ensure a good show of summer and autumn flowers throughout the length of the border. The alterations in this part of the garden were begun in the autumn of 1938 and finished by the following spring. The memorial to Miss Rogers was put up just before the College was requisitioned in October 1939. It consists of a sundial erected at the entrance to the terrace. The brass dial by Richard Glynn, the carved stone pedestal, and the plinth of two steps all date from about 1700 and came from Grove House, South Woodford, Essex. The College obtained them through Percy Webster, Antiquarian Horologist of Mayfair. On the upper step of the plinth is inscribed:

(north side)   Annie Mary Anne Henley Rogers
       Custos Hortulorum
       MCMXXVII – MCMXXXVII
(south side)   Floribus Anna tuis faveat sol
        luce perenni

The inscription was composed by Professor Myres.

The College and houses, except the 'Lawn' and 82 Woodstock Road, were requisitioned for use as a Military Hospital in October 1939. In the summer of 1940 six wards, grouped in pairs, were erected in the garden. Two wards running east and west were built on the main lawn where the tennis courts had been, two running north and south and reaching to within twelve feet of the Library were built on the 'Ansell piece' and two, also running north and south, on the northern half of the 'Whitehead piece'. They were substantial, one-storied buildings of brick and concrete and connected to each other by brick corridors. A similar corridor across the lawn and the terrace connected the wards in the main garden with the College. This corridor engulfed the memorial sundial which was encased in brick for protection. Extensions were later added to the wards in the 'Whitehead piece' and two detached stores were put up in the Fellows' orchard. Other buildings and sheds were erected along the north front of the College. The War Office gave an undertaking to respect the trees and shrubs in the main garden; this undertaking was kept and plans were on more than one occasion modified to meet objections raised by the Bursar (Miss Thorneycroft) on behalf of the College, but a large number of fruit-trees in the orchard, the 'Whitehead piece' and to the north of the College were destroyed. George Harris, who had succeeded Ball as Head Gardener in 1934, was taken into the service of the Hospital and was able to see that the essential work to the shrubs, terrace and herbaceous borders was carried out. Thus the garden suffered less than it might have done. In

October 1945 the College reoccupied its own premises, and during the following winter the buildings to the north of the College and the corridor across the terrace and lawn were demolished. The rest of the buildings, however, remained and were let to the University as office accommodation from September 1946 to March 1952. The demolition finally took place in the spring and summer of 1952.

Early during the war the College acquired the 'Shrubbery' which was, however, requisitioned from 1943 to 1946 and used as an American Army Club. When it was derequisitioned the house, as it was unsuitable for College use, was let to the *Maison Française*, but part of the garden was retained by the College and is now used as a Fellows' garden in place of the orchard. The new Fellows' garden is bounded on three sides by brick walls and on the fourth by a clipped yew hedge. It was elaborately laid out by Sir George Whitehead when he lived at the 'Shrubbery', and it includes two features which the College garden has hitherto lacked – a sunk rose garden and some lily ponds. There are also some good flowering trees including a tulip-tree, two catalpas and a *Magnolia soulangiana*; the College has, however, other specimens of all these. Old plans show that at one time there were three rows of glasshouses of which only the middle one now remains. The lily ponds seem to have been formed from the tanks of one of these vanished greenhouses which had been built as an orchid house, and a winding path, planted with irises on either side, occupies the site of the third house.

It is now possible to see the changes caused by the erection of the Hospital buildings. In the main garden – that is the former 'Mount' garden – the layout has not been much altered, except that the hedge which partly surrounded the small lawn made in 1928 was so broken about that it has had to be removed, and once the newly sown grass has become turf this part of the garden will look much as it did before the war. On the other hand, the changes in the undeveloped land acquired in 1932–4 are profound. The orchard has lost many of its trees and its hedge to the east and north and is no longer a separate enclosure. The hedge between the 'Ansell' and 'Whitehead' pieces has also gone, so have most of the fruit-trees which were in the 'Whitehead piece' and the greater part of the path which bisected it. All this central portion of ground is now much more open than it used to be and much more part of the main garden. Most of it has been sown with grass to form one large lawn. In replanning this part of the garden the layout has had to be kept as simple as possible for two reasons. Firstly, the College cannot afford more labour, even if it could get it, and wide lawns and straight paths are comparatively easily kept in order. Secondly, the College will eventually have to increase its buildings and it would be wasteful to adopt an elaborate plan for what may be a building site. The whole effect is, however, at present rather too open and some judicious planting of the smaller varieties of flowering trees would be an improvement. Thus the garden is now much less a series of separate closes than it once was, although it still retains evidence of its diverse origin. It is the variety resulting from this diversity of origin which constitutes the great charm of the garden – the spacious lawns surrounded by tall trees; the borders of ornamental shrubs; the terrace and the herbaceous borders which act as foils to the buildings; the informal treatment of the dell and the formal rose beds in the Fellows' garden all afford examples of different styles of gardening, and provide interest and colour at every season of the year. The St Hugh's College garden can rightly claim to be one of the most beautiful of Oxford College gardens and deserves to be more widely known than it is.

AN INTERVIEW WITH GEORGE HARRIS, GARDENER AT ST HUGH'S, 1927–72

Priscilla West

George Harris came to St Hugh's in 1927, having served his apprenticeship at the big house in Headington, now the headquarters of the Pergamon Press. There he was initiated into greenhouse work, the care of a kitchen garden and flower garden and, as he ruefully recounts – digging.

On joining St Hugh's as an under-gardener to Mr Ball, then an elderly man, he found the garden undeveloped – there were 'only the bigger trees', and, of course, Miss Rogers. 'Miss Rogers knew what she was talking about trees and shrubs', but wasn't as knowledgeable 'about ordinary things . . . Soon she was asking "Do we think this can be done? That can be done?" to which I replied, "Yes, if there is the money and the labour" . . . When I first started working the College kept pigs, at the end of what was the stables of "The Lawn". There was a brick wall that backed on to the College gardens at "The Lawn" end. The arrangement was Mr Ball would have them, the College would feed them, and Mr Ball would have one for himself . . . Mr Ball [originally head gardener at The Mount] used to be a coachman and lived in the lodge. I used to miss him about the same time every day, and was eventually told that he was in the pub. He spent his money on fags and drink, and did no work during the couple of years I was supposed to be under him.'

At that time, the garden consisted of 'the big lawn right through in front of the College, and three grass tennis courts, and the Hollow as we call it, down in the lower part of the garden, where we put in iron rose arches, and three or four different kinds of climbing rose, a rose-bed on the West side. The path was always called the "squiggly path", because it came from the main path into the Hollow, turned round and up to the terrace and College, and the other bit wriggles round and met the other path again.' There was a croquet lawn. 'The family that had lived there had a grown up family who'd developed the lawn for croquet.' To improve the garden, Mr Harris 'planted two herbaceous borders, two rows of mixed standard apple trees with a wide grass path in between'. When he was digging 'the Banbury border', he discovered 'the old well in the garden of "The Mount" on the Banbury Road. I covered it again, and I'm probably the only person who still knows it's there.'

There was no terrace.

There was cat's tongue scattered about with weeds growing through. One morning, I saw Miss Rogers looking at it, and she said, 'Do you know, Harris, I think we'll have to do something about this mess.' So I said, 'Well, it's up to the College. If I can get the staff we'll do it.' Little did I know what I'd let myself in for! Anyway, between whiles, she found that St John's College had a lot of flat pieces of stone, and she persuaded them to let her have them, and paid for the carting and so on. We cleared the whole of the terrace, but the stone wall which is at the edge of the terrace now, that was there then, so we incorporated it.

Miss Rogers was known as 'The Garden Master', and was 'old-fashioned in her ideas'. She was 'not keen on fertiliser', and was very reluctant 'to sanction the purchase of a motor mower'. Mr Harris finally persuaded her that it would be very helpful, and as a result, 'the grass was mown in a day rather than a week'. Miss Rogers was 'very nice when you got to know her, but she was not liked by everyone. I once overhead somebody say at a meeting in the Library, "Here the old bitch comes!" She spoke Latin, and always referred to plants by their Latin names, and insisted I did too.'

Miss Rogers died in 1937, and previously Miss Thorneycroft [Bursar of St Hugh's] had confided to Mr Harris, '"If she carries on riding her bicycle, that's how she'll end, sure as anything!" She was eventually knocked off her bike. She was dangerous. She didn't recognise signals. She used to ride an upright bike.'

Shortly afterwards, in 1939, war came, and Mr Harris was called up. He went for a medical, and discovered he was deaf in one ear. The Medical Corps took over the College buildings and 'College moved to Holywell Manor'. 'I looked after the garden there until they had a chap good enough to get on with it himself.' Harris moved back to St Hugh's, to care for the garden, or rather what was left of it, after the Medical Corps had built

> two long wards on the tennis courts, crossed the path with a corridor, and built two more [wards] on the grass beyond. When after the war, they came to remove the buildings, I asked them to leave the Medical Officer's office. I wanted to turn it into a fruit room. It was quite a large building. They made a very good job of clearing up afterwards. The contractor was a very nice chappie, and followed my instructions to leave no foundations (which have never shown since, even in the worst dry summers), and replace topsoil, etc. . . .

In 1946, 'The Shrubbery' (now the Principal's Lodging, acquired in 1943, but requisitioned until 1946) came back to St Hugh's. Although the house was let to the *Maison Française*, part of the garden was retained.

The Principal's Residence used to belong to Sir George White-head, and his garden included great long greenhouses [by 1946 only one remained] full of nectarines. These died in due course, and I planted tomatoes all the length of the greenhouse to supply the College – and incidentally, some of the undergraduates! There was also a lily pond, and a large lawn. There were red and pink water lilies in one pond and white and yellow in the other.

At this time, Miss Procter was Principal, and gave Mr Harris 'the impression of being very straitlaced. "Why have you come to see me?" she would say. She were very severe.' Not so Miss Kenyon! When she was Principal, 'the mowing machine died. We were all in despair. We'd checked everything, changed parts, done everything.

Miss Kenyon came to see why all work seemed to have stopped. When we told her, she said, "Give it a bloody good kick!" We did, and of course, it started at once!' When Princess Alexandra came [to open the Wolfson Building], Miss Kenyon wanted Mr Harris to be in a photograph with Princess Alexandra. '"You stand there, Harris, I'll stand in the middle, and Princess Alexandra there," and Princess Alexandra obligingly obeyed.'

Mr and Mrs Harris went to stay with Miss Kenyon and her companion Miss Catlow in a cottage outside High Wycombe.

In 1972, Mr Harris retired, having worked for St Hugh's for forty-five years. On his retirement, someone said to him, 'Harris, the garden will never be the same without you.'

'You can't expect it to be', he replied.

Appendix IV: Extracts from the letters of Molly McNeill (1916–17)

[The spelling and punctuation have not been altered, except in a few places, in order to make her meaning clearer. Editor]

SUNDAY, 5 MARCH 1916: THE AIR RAID

... I've got a piece of thrilling news for you now. You may have seen in the papers that there was another air raid last night, though it only says over the North East coast. Well to begin with I'll tell you that nothing happened to us or to Oxford, so you can now enjoy the experience I'm going to tell you with a quiet mind. Last night I got into bed somewhere between 10.30 and 10.45. And as usual went to sleep. Soon however I began to hear bugles but it didn't waken me, I only thought I was dreaming. These bugles went on and on and there was what seemed to be an incessant tramping of soldiers' feet, you see we are quite near a place where a great many soldiers are billeted. Still I thought I was dreaming, but the next thing was a bell ringing very peculiarly. I heard that too and it woke me a little more but still I wasn't anything like really awake. Just then however there was a knock at my door and someone said 'Are you woken Molly. You had better get up and bring a coat.' With that I positively leapt out of bed and I began to realize it must be a raid. We couldn't put on the light. I pulled open the wardrobe and took out the first thing which came to my hand and got to the door and went out into the landing. Everywhere was pitch dark but I saw or heard two other people going down stairs and I followed them. By the way I got into my bedroom slippers as well. Going downstairs I put on the article of clothing which I had taken from the wardrobe, and which turned out to be a grey jacket, *most unsuitable*, but I couldn't go back for the checked coat. The other two girls that I was with had a match box and occasionally they struck a match. We had to go all downstairs and through the underground passage place (we cannot get from one side of the building to the other yet as the men haven't finished that part, and we have to go through what we call the tube), and into the Junior

Common Room. I can't quite explain how I felt, I was certainly rather cold in my nightdress and the skimpy jacket. We were in the Common Room one of the first and I immediately spotted Miss Richards and I went and sat on the floor by her and she wrapped part of her dressing gown round me. In the Common Room which is very large we had one candle. People came pouring in and nobody knew exactly what had happened. On the way down I thought I heard falling glass, but it must have been somebody breaking their electric lamp or else imagination. Well when the Common Room was fairly full the roll was called by Miss Holland who is the fire captain. It was found out that all the people on the ground floor evidently hadn't been wakened as none of them answered so they had to be brought. Then we had the roll again and everyone answered. By this time we had ascertained that it was about a quarter to one. Miss Jourdain was very calm and composed. I think she quite fancied herself at the work. There was no panic or anything like that at all, except one of the maids, but she was only nervous for about a minute. Really it was the most peculiar sight you ever saw to see by the light of one candle (hidden behind the coal scuttle) about 70 people all huddled together on the floor. Soon the order was given that all the ground floor and first floor west wing people were to go to another room so Miss Richards had to leave me. After about half an hour Miss Jourdain produced some biscuits, we were all famishing. I got the share of half a coat for my legs and so was quite warm. Well we all sat there getting sleepier and sleepier but hardly anyone went to sleep. Of course all the electric light and gas was turned off from the town, but besides we couldn't have shown any light at all. All the time we never heard a sound. At last at 3.30 the lights came back, we had turned the switches on so that we would get the light as soon as possible, and we all got back to bed again after sitting up for over 2 hours and a half. I was into bed at 20 to 4 and slept soundly till wakened at 7. Miss Wood never got to sleep until 6.30. Now I'll try and tell you how the alarm was first given. I've tried to find out as much about it as possible but no one seems to know very much. They say that the soldiers we[re] wakened at 11.30 for the girls whose rooms look on to the road heard them getting orders since then and the bugles that I heard in my sleep wakened them properly. The real signal we knew for an approaching raid was a hooter to be blown from the Gt. Western and then the lights to go out. Well some of the girls heard the hooter and some didn't. I didn't, it went about 12. One girl then went and wakened the fire captain Miss Holland, and the bells began in the different corridors. Another girl immediately she got up and dressed and consequently she appeared down in the common room fully dressed. The system of fire alarm, which is used for air raids in college, is like this. There is a fire captain Miss Holland and then besides in each corridor there is a fire sergeant who is responsible for the corridor, that is that all the people are wakened and down stairs and they have to ring the bells. Miss Holland was magnificent. She didn't hear the hooter, so she immediately got up when she was wakened and began ringing the bells and getting the different sergeants up. Then she called the roll, and she also with Miss Jourdain saw that all the outside doors were opened in case we'd have to go out. She did everything so quietly and calmly and they never even had a practice in the new building.

We are very anxious to hear where the Zepps really were. I think they must have been somewhere nearer than the North east coast. The paper says there will be further news later . . . So I've really had an experience of an air alarm and now I can think of it as quite amusing. At the time most of us were too sleepy to think of anything. Everyone behaved very well. I think it was extremely good of the girl to come and waken me, she lives next door but she wasn't our fire sergeant, however she had been woken by the hooter I think. I really wasn't at all frightened when I got going down with someone. It was very hard lines on one girl who wasn't well she had been in bed all day, and imagine what you'd feel like getting up and sitting in a cold room for $2\frac{1}{2}$ [hours] if you weren't well. Someone brought an eiderdown for her, and got her fixed up on a sofa . . . I do hope this doesn't make you the least nervous because really Oxford would never be touched only the[y] warn every town in the direction in which they think the Zepps are going . . .

4 NOVEMBER 1916: THE FANCY DRESS PARTY

. . . Now I must tell you about the dress. This is what the cape was like. It was black with a border of yellow and the cat and stars and things were yellow. The hat was black with a lovely yellow tassel at the end and yellow cat and stars. Then I had a black bag with a yellow bow and star and a long yellow chain to hold it by. On my slippers I had two large yellow rosettes. Then I pinned about half a dozen yellow stars on to my skirt. Altogether it was really very effective, and took very little time to make. A whole lot of people thought it was a proper dress I had had for the cape looked quite to belong to the skirt. They were very surprised when I told them what it was. It was the only dress that had been made up. I mean all the other girls had just borrowed somebody elses things, but not that for me. I had my hair down, and altogether I think it was very successful. I feel quite sorry to have to destroy it. At a quarter to 9 we all went to the Junior Common Room, and all the College and maids were there to inspect us. Miss Ady said I looked *very* well. Hilda Wood was a nurse and one of the other girls had got her father's volunteer uniform and went with her as a wounded Tommy. They were very good as far as the clothes went but it wasn't frightfully original. Then 4 girls went as North, South, East and West. South was dressed as a nigger in a red blanket and she had blackened all her arms, face and neck. I thought it looked just horrid. Then there was a French priest. She had had her things for the French charades the night before. Another girl went as an Indian Squaw, and another as an Oxford Don. She had borrowed a gown and mortar board. Then there were several peasants, and one really good couple went as a Shepherd and Shepherdess. The Shepherd had a most glorious old smock lent by Joan Evans. I tried to inspect it as well as I could and it was the most beautiful work you could imagine. It was the first real smock I had ever seen, the collar and cuffs were exquisitely embroidered. Another girl went as an early Victorian person. She had borrowed another person's best evening dress I think it is a disgusting trick. It was the same one as asked me for my tweed last term. I only had to lend my big black shoes to the French priest, and I really didn't mind because she is a quite nice girl. Then there were some characters out of Dickens. Madame Defarge from 'A Tale of Two Cities'. Some of the dresses were really very good indeed. After the inspection we started dancing and then about 9.30 we had lemonade and cakes and after the Sir Roger and Auld Lang Syne. It was really a very enjoyable evening, far far better than I expected. Everyone was quite nice and friendly. There were about 2 dozen of us. I can't remember any more dresses. Two girls went as children and there was a sandwich man and a chef. I was glad that I was the only thing in the nature of a witch . . .

[UNDATED] MICHAELMAS TERM, 1916: MISS ADY TO TEA

. . . I must tell you how the tea-party got on yesterday. It was a great success. I did my shopping in the morning. I got 1 doz. 1d cakes very nice ones, and $\frac{1}{2}$ doz. sort of biscuit things. Then I got a seed cake for 1/3d and 3d worth of $\frac{1}{2}$d scones. Hilda Wood got the butter for me in the afternoon. I had meant to get some flowers after lunch but found the shop was closed. Thursday is early closing here. About 2.30 I started my preparations feeling all the time as if I'd never be ready. I got the fire lit first of all, then I changed my dress. I put on the red tartan and it looked lovely, I thought I should try and appear as decent as possible for Miss Ady. After that I started getting the food ready, buttered the scones and laid the table. Then I tidied up my room. Put my suitcase under the bed, it usually stays out for convenience sake, dusted my chest of drawers and altogether got the room to look very nice. I was all ready, kettle boiling and everything, by about 25 minutes to 4, and Miss Ady arrived quite punctually at a quarter to. As soon as she came I infused the tea and in a few minutes we started. She thoroughly enjoyed her tea. She had one scone, one bit of seed cake, 2 penny cakes and a piece of my birthday cake, which was excellent, and three cups of tea. It was most delightful to see that she appreciated it. Everything did look quite nice and appetising. We also got on magnificently in the way of conversation. I was rather dreading that. We talked about everything. She had just got a letter from Miss Mills to say that she was going away for a week-end till next Thursday, so would miss her coaching. Miss Ady thought she might just as well say a week and be honest. However we are both quite glad for we'll have our coaching by ourselves tomorrow morning. I think Miss Ady thinks she isn't taking her work seriously enough. She really does expect you to be in earnest about whatever you do. That's why it is so frightfully nice to be praised by her because you feel she really means it. She was also very interested to hear I had been to the meetings in the Sheldonian, she had intended going last Sunday but was prevented. Then we got on to Mr. Lusk, and Miss Ady has a great opinion of him. She went to a class at Dr. Carlyle's and both Mr. and Mrs. Lusk attended it and she said he read an extremely good paper on Calvin, and she was very taken with them both. She really is a perfect angel, and the cleverness of her is wonderful. I was so glad to hear her speaking so nicely of the Lusks. She went away about 4.30 and said she had had a delicious tea and was most refreshed, wasn't that sweet of her. She had been feeling rather tired all day . . .

17 FEBRUARY 1917: TEA AT MRS MAUNSEL'S

I've quite a lot to tell you about Mrs. Maunsel's. To begin with the bus I was in broke down so I had to walk a good part of the way. I never saw anything like these buses. Well! when I got there I found another Irish girl so there was no foreign element in the party at all. This girl is at Somerville. She only came up last Summer. Her name is Starky [Starkie?]. I think her father is a professor or something at Trinity. She told me he used to be president of Queen's College, Galway. She was really very nice indeed. It was rather funny she asked me if I knew an undergraduate called Kyle. I of course I suddenly thought of Sibyll McConnell and I think it must be the same person. At any rate Miss Starkey says he comes not from Belfast but the North of Ireland. She doesn't know him but he is the greatest friend of her brothers. He got on frightfully well at Trinity and could have got anything he liked at Oxford only he didn't want to go into a big college. When I came back I looked up the register and find there is a Kyle, the only one in Oxford, at Lincoln, and that is one of the very smallest colleges. Miss Starkey also knows one of the Kyle girls of Wellington Park, the one that was up at Trinity. By the way she said that most of the brilliant Trinity men come from the North of Ireland. She had a terrible time during the rebellion there was fighting all round her house. I think I would like to have her to tea some day. She is very nice and very clever. She got a scholarship into Somerville. She comes to one set of my lectures the ones on French history. She is doing French.

Mrs. Maunsel is great value, excuse the language but it just suits her. I told you she was one of the Townshends and she has various relatives in Oxford, they are a most astounding connection both for numbers and cleverness. One of them is a professor of electricity in Oxford, the first one them [they] have ever had here. Miss Starkey knew some of them in Dublin. Mrs. Maunsel is the sort of person that has travelled a great deal and is most interesting, and thoroughly Irish, and her likeness to Miss Somerville isn't imagination at all and I can't get over the strangeness of it that I should have even met her and sort of know who she was. I am beginning to find out that there are quite a number of Irish people in Oxford after all. Mrs. Maunsel knows quite a lot and they are all very clever. Professor Adam's wife comes from Dublin the Starkey girl knows her, and there is an Irish don from Dublin at Somerville called O'Halleron.

I enjoyed my time immensely. Mrs. Maunsel is a widow. I don't know if she's got any children . . . Mrs. Maunsel had little hot scones made partly with yellow indian meal and they were really very good indeed. She was giving great reports of the preparations for the big push. She says that they are making miles and miles of railway lines at the front and that they have to tear up some of the lines in England and take them over to France, for the French gauge is narrower than ours and so won't fit our trains and they have not time or place to make them over there. She also says that they have brought over thousands of Chinese navvies to do the work, for of course all the French men are fighting. It does seem terrible. I am to go out and see her sometime again. She really is most kind, and I did enjoy myself . . . I forgot to tell you that Mrs. Maunsel knows someone in Oxford who used to work in a settlement somewhere on the Crumlin Road, I think it is. I never knew there was such a place, but this person was there for 9 years I think. She is English, and Mrs. M. is going to ask her to call on me.

27 MAY 1917: DEGREE GIVING

. . . Then in the morning I had heard that there was going to be a conferring of degrees at 2.30 so of course I took Aunt Ina there. It was held in Convocation House, perhaps Father will remember it. Tell him it is part of the Bodleian Library. I had never seen one before and it was thrillingly interesting. Anybody is allowed in free. I'll just draw you a plan of this too, to let you know what I am talking about. The V. Chancellor who is also the Dean of Christchurch was all robed in bright scarlet – a doctor's gown. The two proctors were in black with white fur capes, they sat on either side of the Vice Chancellor. When he came in followed by the proctors everyone stood up. The people who were to get their various degrees were all sitting together in the corner seats at the end of the hall. The whole proceedings were in Latin. First of all the Dean read out a whole oration in Latin, to open the proceedings. Then there was a sort of a clerk person who was sitting at a desk I've marked with a cross. He had to call the people up. The first man to come was a minister who was becoming a Dr. of Divinity. To begin with he had a black gown with a white hood on. He came forward and with a lot of bowing and all the rest of it, knelt down before the Vice Chancellor, while he read out some more Latin. Then he had to change his hood in the middle of all and get a black one put on, and he had to do some swearing that he believed in the

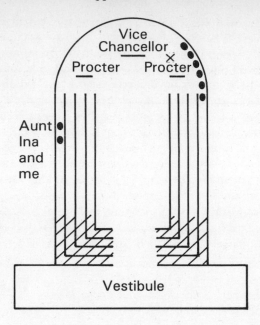

Creed, 39 Articles and other things, and listen to some more Latin. Then he went out into the vestibule place and changed gown, hood, everything for a bright scarlet one, came back again and after some more bowing and Latin went up and sat down in one of the little ink dots, reserved for doctors.

Then after that a whole batch of young clergy came up, not altogether though. The officious clerk (sitting on the cross) would call out:– the Dean of Magdalen, and up jumped the Dean (who was sitting with other college dignitaries in the 2 low front rows on either side of the aisle). In the meantime a youth would come out of the crowd of undergrads and taking the Dean of Magdalen by the hand went up and was presented to the Vice Chancellor, in a long Latin oration. I'm telling you all wrong, the ecclesiastics weren't done like this at all, these are the secular ones as I'll just go on and finish them. When they had all been presented by their various heads, they went altogether out to the vestibule, here their respective scouts were waiting to take off their short little undergrad gowns and robe them in their full-fledged graduate long black with white fur collars, and they all came trooping back again (there were about 40 of them) and they knelt in fours before the V. Chancellor, who read a Latin oration telling I expect their various degrees, and touched each one on the head with a book wh. I presume was a Bible. Then they went back to their places. The clerics were done rather differently, they were already M.A. and had their black gowns with white fur on. They all came up in a body and then went out and got on entirely black gowns and came back and were 'capped' just like the other men. The whole proceedings took about an hour and was most entertaining. I was so glad to have seen it, for of course except perhaps in Cambridge it is done no where else at any rate in England in such a style . . .

10 JUNE 1917: A WALK TO WYTHAM

. . . We started about 2 oclock. We went to a place called Wytham. It is a little old village about 3 miles I suppose away. We walked along the river most of the way and it was very pretty, then we turned into a country road with fields on either side which were just full of buttercups and lovely marguerites, it just looked like a lovely picture. When we got to Wytham we had tea at the Inn. They gave us very nice bread, butter and jam and plain cakes for a shilling each. We had it out in a little garden place. There are only half a dozen houses or so in the village. It is very tiny and thoroughly English. I don't think, you'd ever see anything like it in Ireland. There is a very sweet old church which we went into. I took some photos and bought three postcards of the village at the post office so you'll see what it's like when I get home. We just came back the way we came and we picked some daisies and buttercups which I now have in my room . . . It was lovely country, and it all seemed so utterly remote from war; except for an aeroplane now and again you wouldn't think there was any fighting at all. On the way we passed a small camp of the flying corps. It was on the river bank, the officers were on one side and the men on the other. We were very very close to the mess part, for they came up close to the path and we could see them having their tea in one tent, while others were tidying up their sleeping tents and putting all their belongings in little neat bundles. They had an open air kitchen where some of the men were cooking. One man I saw trying to wash his head and arms in a bucket. Everything was marvellously tidy. We saw into the recreation tent and all their magazines were neatly laid out on tables and they had pictures on the walls of the tent and on the tables. The officers' place was not so big, but as it was on the other side of the river we couldn't see anything particularly of it. That sort of life would be all very well for a fine day now and again, but I think you'd get pretty tired of it for always. The men looked more like Italians, they were so burnt.

When we were just going out of Oxford we went passed [past] the aerodrome. It was just on the opposite side of the river but you could see the great huge things on the grass perfectly plainly. We saw several going up and coming down. I was thinking the boys would have been so interested to see them. They were just on the opposite bank so we were really quite close. On our side of the river in one of the fields there had evidently been an accident. A tree was all battered about and most of the remains of an aeroplane in a similar state of destruction. It just looked as frail as match-wood. I do hope nobody had been injured. We saw men just taking away what was left of the machine. We got back to college about 6 o'clock. I was very glad I had gone the walk for it does do you good to get out of Oxford even for an afternoon, and the country was lovely . . .

Index

Compiled by Brenda Hall (née Henderson), MA (1945–8), registered indexer of the Society of Indexers, past council member of Society of Indexers.

The index contains references to both text and footnotes. For reasons of space it has been necessary to limit references derived from Chapter 4 (Reminiscences); these are in general given only for people, places and themes already referred to. Mention of the personalities of the various decades not members of St Hugh's College may be traced through the topics with which they are associated, e.g. Lectures, Oxford University Dramatic Society.